Alternate Ways of Organizing the Contents of this Book

PROCESS AND THOUGHT
IN COMPOSITION

WITH HANDBOOK

PROCESS AND THOUGHT IN COMPOSITION

WITH HANDBOOK

THIRD EDITION

Frank J. D'Angelo
ARIZONA STATE UNIVERSITY

LITTLE, BROWN AND COMPANY
BOSTON   TORONTO

Library of Congress Cataloging in
Publication Data

D'Angelo, Frank J.
   Process and thought in composition.

   Includes index.
   1. English language—Rhetoric. 2. English
language—Grammar—1950–   . I. Title.
PE1408.D15   1984   808'.042   84-21793
ISBN 0-316-16987-0

Library of Congress Catalog Card
Number 84-21793

ISBN 0-316-16987-0

9 8 7 6 5 4 3 2 1

BP

Published simultaneously in Canada by
Little, Brown & Company (Canada) Limited

Printed in the United States of America

Acknowledgments

"Mollusks" from *The Animal Kingdom*,
published by Bantam Books, by arrangement
with Grosset & Dunlap, Inc., July 1971. Reprinted by permission of Grosset & Dunlap,
Inc.
   AP Newsfeatures, "7000 Stolen Books
Found in New York." Reprinted by permission of AP Newsfeatures.

   Isaac Asimov, "UFOs, Are They Visitors
from Space—or Unreliable False Observations?" from *TV Guide®* Magazine, December 14, 1974. Copyright © 1974 by Triangle
Publications, Inc., Radnor, Pennsylvania.
   "Making Pasta by Hand," from *Attenzione*, February 1981. Reprinted by permission of Attenzione Magazine/Adam Publications.
   James Baldwin, excerpt from "The
Seventh Day" in *Go Tell It On the Mountain*. Copyright 1952, 1953 by James Baldwin. Reprinted by permission of Doubleday
& Company, Inc.
   Ray Allen Billington, "The Frontier Disappears," in *The American Story*, edited by
Earl S. Miers. Copyright © 1956 by Broad-
cast Music, Inc. Reprinted by permission.
Paragraph from *Westward Expansion: A History of the American Frontier*, Third Edition,
is reprinted by permission of Macmillan
Publishing Company.
   Ray Bradbury, "A Sound of Thunder,"
from *The Golden Apples of the Sun*. Copyright © 1952, renewed 1980 by Ray Bradbury. Reprinted by permission of Don Cong-
don Associates, Inc.
   Charles Brooks, "On the Difference Between Wit and Humor," from *On the Difference Between Wit and Humor* in Chimney
Pot Papers (1919). Reprinted by permission
of Yale University Press.
   Willa Cather, "The Garden" and "The
Men Who Fed the Bride to the Wolves,"
from *My Antonia*. Copyright 1918, 1926,
1946 by Willa Sibert Cather. Copyright 1954
by Edith Lewis. Copyright © renewed 1977
by Walter Havighurst. Reprinted by permission of Houghton Mifflin Company.
   Stuart Chase, "Mexico: A Study of Two
Americas." From *Mexico: A Study of Two
Americas* by Stuart Chase in collaboration
with Marian Tyler Chase. Copyright 1931,
renewed 1959 by Stuart Chase. Reprinted by
permission of Macmillan Publishing Company.
   Marchette Chute, "Shakespeare of London" from *Shakespeare of London*. Copyright 1949 by E. P. Dutton, Inc., and reprinted with their permission.

(continued on page 597)

Preface

In the first edition of *Process and Thought in Composition*, I maintained that all composition textbooks leak. In the second edition, I tried to repair some of the leaks by packing the seams to make the book watertight and repairing masts, sails, and rigging. I would like to believe that these changes kept the book stable, reliable, and sound. Five years have passed since the second edition was launched, and in preparing the third edition, I found that I needed to make more substantial changes—in the keel and the hull, as well as the masts, sails, and rigging. These changes have taken the following form.

I have completely reorganized Chapter 1, added new material, and given it a new title ("Contexts for Invention"), in keeping with my renewed emphasis on the rhetorical situation, the writer's intention, and the audience.

I have rewritten Chapter 2 ("Invention: Probing the Subject") in order to put more emphasis on the categories of invention as they relate not only to the subject, but also to the writer's intention and to the audience. I have expanded the concept of invention so that the topics provide a method for constructing thesis sentences as well as for reasoning about the subject. I have also added material on finding a thesis, analyzing it, and adjusting it to fit the writer's beliefs and values.

I have completely rewritten Chapter 3 ("Arrangement: The Whole Theme"), making more explicit the implicit connection between invention and arrangement in previous editions. More specifically, I demonstrate how the same categories of invention that were used to explore the subject in Chapter 2 and to construct thesis sentences can be used to construct the sentence form of the underlying pattern of arrangement that I call a paradigm. I also suggest ways in which the student can use the logical form of the paradigm for ethical and emotional appeals. Finally, I make an explicit connection between the concept of paradigms as logical forms (akin to the enthymeme in classical rhetoric) and the concept of paradigms as cognitive maps and psychological schemata.

In the middle chapters (Chapters 4 through 7)—those dealing with specific topics of invention and patterns of development—I have added a section on constructing paradigms similar to the one in Chapter 3. In these chapters, I show the student how to construct specific kinds of paradigms using the topics of invention, how to include ethical and emotional appeals, and how to analyze the completed paradigms.

Aside from some editing, I have made few substantial changes in Chapters 8, 9, and 10. I have, however, completely rewritten Chapter 11 ("Style: The Sentence") and divided it into two parts: modes of developing sentences and rhetorical sentence types. The section on sentence modes is new to any text. It consists of showing the close relationship between the topics of invention and sentence modes (that is, analysis sentences, classification sentences, and cause-and-effect sentences). The section on rhetorical sentence types draws heavily on classical rhetoric in enumerating and exemplifying rhetorical sentence types.

For Chapter 12 ("Style: Word Choice"), I intended to devote the entire chapter to tropes, but settled instead for an expanded discussion of figurative language. In Chapter 13, I have made editing changes only.

Chapter 14 ("Revising and Editing") remains substantially the same, but I have revised the first section to make it reflect the new attitude toward revision as part of the composing process. This is not merely a superficial change, however, because I prepare the way in Chapter 3 by illustrating how revision takes place as one is composing.

Thanks to Celest Martin, I am able to present the student with completely new material on the research paper in Chapter 15.

Finally, I have made relatively few changes, primarily editing changes, in the handbook section of the text.

These, then, are the major structural changes I have made in the hull and keel in the third edition of this text. But I have also considerably modified the masts, sails, and rigging. I have, for example, completely rewritten many of the original exercises and added new exercises in Chapters 1 through 7 and 11 through 15. I have replaced many professional and student essays with new ones. In both the essays and the exercises, I have paid much attention to the rhetorical situation, to the writer's intention, and to the audience. In many instances, I have deliberately chosen topics that are value-laden and that relate to the writer's and the reader's beliefs.

In sum, I have included these features in the third edition:

1. New material on the rhetorical situation, the writer, and the audience.
2. An expanded conception of invention, in which the categories of invention are applied at three stages in the composing process: to probe a subject, to formulate thesis sentences, and to construct sentence paradigms.
3. A conception of revision as part of the composing process.
4. A heuristic for examining the writer's and the reader's beliefs and values.
5. An expanded conception of the paradigm as a logical, structural form that incorporates ethical and emotional appeals.
6. The concept of paradigms as schemata or cognitive maps (not made fully explicit in the second edition).
7. A new chapter on sentence modes and rhetorical sentence types.
8. New material on figures of speech.
9. A new chapter on the research paper.
10. New student and professional essays and new and rewritten exercises.

In making these changes, I have retained the original emphasis on writing as a thinking process, on the concept of paradigms as global structures that mediate between invention and arrangement and between arrangement and style, and on the constant interweaving of matters pertaining to the rhetorical situation, audience, and purpose with matters of invention, arrangement, and style. Finally, I have kept my own audience in mind at all times—by adopting a conversational tone and by attempting to lead the student systematically and incrementally through all the stages in the composing process.

In making these changes, I hope that I have provided both students and teachers with a craft that will continue to be stable, reliable, and seaworthy. So, "Come, my friends, / 'Tis not too late to seek a newer world, / Push off, and sitting well in order smite / The sounding furrows; for my purpose holds / To sail beyond the sunset, and the baths / Of all the western stars. . . ."

For the making of this edition, I am indebted to many people. I begin with Paul O'Connell, now with Bobbs-Merrill, who was responsible for the first two editions and who encouraged me to begin this edition. Paul continues to be a good friend and a thoughtful editor.

To Carolyn Potts, who helped me make the transition from Winthrop Publishers to Little, Brown, I thank for her support and her helpful advice. I also wish to thank Virginia Pye, Julia Winston, Jane Aaron, and Adrienne Weiss for their help in the preparation of this book.

Thomas Farrell of Cobb/Dunlop Publisher Services has been an excellent production editor, and I am indebted to him for his help and patience.

For typing the manuscript and for assisting me in numerous ways to complete this manuscript, I thank Florence Livengood, Martha Hoffman, Janice Hampton, Lael Weston, and Ruth Bardrick.

To a host of scholars and colleagues, I extend my gratitude for their friendly criticism and helpful suggestions: Tommy Boley, University of Texas at El Paso; John Brereton, Wayne State University; Ruth Foreman, South Dakota State University; William Lutz, Rutgers University; Celest Martin, University of Rhode Island; Richard Meyer, Western Oregon State University; John Schafer, Humbolt State University; Judith Stanford, Merrimac College; Gary Tate, Texas Christian University; and Sam Watson, University of North Carolina at Charlotte.

Finally, to Sylvia, I extend my love and gratitude: "She excels each mortal thing / Upon the dull earth dwelling."

Contents

A REFERENCE HANDBOOK

THE WRITING PROCESS

CHAPTER 1

Contexts for Invention

The Importance of Literacy

Consider the activities of a single day. You get up in the morning and pick up the newspaper. As you eat your breakfast, you glance at the writing on the front of the cereal box or read the label on a jar of grape jelly. After you finish breakfast, you make a grocery list to remind you to pick up a few things after your late afternoon class. On your way to your early morning class, you put a letter in the mailbox, a letter that you wrote the previous evening. In your classes that day, you respond to a question from the instructor, participate in a classroom discussion, take a written exam, pass a note to your friend, hand in a finished report or a research paper—all the while taking copious notes.

Throughout the day, you express yourself in various ways: by a shrug of your shoulders, a nod of your head, a quick movement of your hands, a raised eyebrow, a grimace. But you will not get very far by gestures alone. You must use words, spoken or written, to let people know what you want, what you think, how you feel. Despite the claims of some critics that there is little need for people to learn how to read and write in an electronic age, there is still an insistent and persistent call for effective writing.

We are all becoming weary of brainlessness in public language: of public officials who cannot express themselves clearly in writing, of business people who cannot write letters that are accurate and concise, of writers of legal contracts who cannot explain coverage in everyday language, of politicians who deceive with language, of doctors and lawyers who use language to impress or befuddle, of friends and acquaintances who can't say what they mean.

Even in an electronic age, you can scarcely hope to succeed unless you can express yourself in writing with some degree of effectiveness.

Television announcers work from a script. Movies and TV depend in large part upon writing. People in various occupations and walks of life write memos, reports, business letters, personal letters, letters of complaint, sympathy notes, invitations, letters of congratulation, articles, essays, theses, examinations, ads, brochures, manuals, catalogs, captions for posters and photographs, minutes of meetings, accident reports—the list is endless. Writing is more pervasive and more important than you sometimes think.

But even if writing were not as important for many public uses as it was in the past, it would still be a valuable part of your education because it facilitates thought. Writing can help you to think critically. It can enable you to make connections, see relationships, deepen perception, solve problems, and give order to your experience. It can help you to clarify your thoughts. Often you discover what you really think and feel about people, ideas, issues, and events only in the actual process of writing.

The studies of cultural psychologists support the conclusion that literacy, especially writing, promotes intellectual development. More specifically, they have discovered that literacy transforms a person's mental processes by replacing practical, situation-bound thinking with abstract, theoretical thinking. Whatever may be the value of concrete, situation-bound thinking in nonliterate cultures, in a technological society a person who cannot think abstractly is at a disadvantage. To learn to write, then, is to learn to think in a certain way.

The Principles of Writing

Writing is a form of thinking, but it is thinking for a particular audience and for a particular occasion. One of your most important tasks as a writer is to master the principles of writing and thinking that will help you to achieve your goals. The most important of these principles are those of invention, arrangement, and style.

Invention is *the process of discovering ideas for speaking or writing.* Although for many writers the process is intuitive, you can learn to guide the process deliberately by using formal procedures for analyzing and searching.

Arrangement is *the process of discovering ordering principles so that you can organize your ideas in such a way as to make them understandable and believable to your readers.*

Style is *the process of making choices about sentence structure and diction while in the act of writing.* You can also make these choices consciously and deliberately when you review what you have written.

To divide the writing process into invention, arrangement, and style is merely a convenience. Invention, arrangement, and style may occur or recur at every step of the writing process.

The Rhetorical Situation

As a writer, one of your tasks is to find something to say. But writing does not occur in a vacuum. It always occurs in some kind of context. In other words, a piece of writing comes into existence to perform some task, to fulfill some need. It comes into existence *in response to a situation* that often demands immediate attention.

Let me illustrate this point with an example. You are away from home, attending a state university. The end of the semester is drawing near, and you discover you are broke. You had enough money to last the entire semester, but recently you bought some record albums, a few paperback books, and some clothing—things you could have done without, but they gave you satisfaction and pleasure. What to do? You decide to swallow your pride and to write to your parents, to a relative, or to a friend and ask for money. Your writing situation consists of the complex interrelations of persons, events, and objects which as a writer you must take into account in order to bring about a change in your financial state.

A writing situation must take into account a **need** (an urgency brought about by particular circumstances, a necessity, an exigency), the **occasion** (the time at which a particular event occurs, the place, the opportunity), the **writer,** the writer's **purpose** (the change you want to bring about in your reader), the **reader** or **audience,** and the **subject.**

Exercises

1. Describe a recent writing situation in which you were involved as a writer. Did you have to write or was it just something you wanted to do? What was the occasion? Who was your audience? What was your purpose in writing?

2. Name at least three writing situations that might serve as the basis of a writing assignment.

3. Analyze the following writing situations. Would any of them be suitable for a writing task? Why or why not?

   a. inadequate parking facilities on the campus

   b. widespread cheating

   c. under-the-table payoffs to clinch a business deal

   d. peacetime draft registration

The Subject

Ideally, most of the subjects you write about will be called into existence by the writing situation. Sometimes, however, your instructor will assign you a specific topic or a choice of two or three topics. If the subject is assigned to the class as a whole, it can provide an opportunity for class discussion and for an exchange of ideas. If the subject is assigned to you alone, it can provide a challenge in reasoning and thinking about the material.

When your instructor assigns you a subject, he or she has put you into a writing situation. Whether you confront an issue of your own choosing or one that has been chosen for you, your subject, your purpose, and your audience are implicit in the situation. The discovery of ideas and the development of lines of reasoning about your subject begin when you confront a subject or an issue in a particular situation.

Exercises

1. For what audiences would the following subjects be appropriate? What kinds of situations or occasions might call forth any of these subjects? Where might an article based on one of these subjects be published? (Think of a particular magazine, newspaper, or other publication.)

   a. Real men do clean house

   b. The pleasures of record collecting

c. Owning a new home

d. How to cope with inflation

e. Should we live together before marriage?

f. Family life in America

g. The Latinization of America

h. The future for working women

i. Caring for the elderly

j. Retire before fifty

2. What subjects or issues concern you? Pick a subject or an issue that is of interest and importance to you and your classmates and take sides. Your audience will be the other members of the class, and the situation will be the context you provide for your subject.

3. List three situations or occasions which called forth a particular kind of writing (letter, essay, invitation, note, memo, list, directions, etc.) and a particular subject, and be prepared to discuss them in class.

4. Analyze the following situations. What subjects and what kinds of writing might result from these situations?

a. You have just been given a traffic ticket you feel you don't deserve.

b. You have recently been mugged in a residential area.

c. A friend has been arrested for possession of marijuana and needs your help.

d. You or a friend have been accused of plagiarism (or some other form of cheating). You have to defend yourself against these charges.

e. You have been cheated by a dishonest auto repair shop. (Either the work wasn't done properly or not at all, or you were overcharged or charged for work it didn't do.)

5. Construct a situation, similar to one of the above, that has meaning for you. Then have someone collect these, type them, Xerox copies, and distribute them to members of the class. (You should have 25 or 30 situations.) Pick *one* of the best and analyze it in class. Consider the subject implicit in the situation, the audience, and your purpose in writing a paper called for by the situation.

The Audience

As a writer, you must not only take into account the writing situation, but you must also consider the part that your audience plays in helping you to shape your writing.

Adapt your writing to your readers. A piece of writing that may be appropriate for one kind of reader may be inappropriate for another. An article that might make interesting reading in *Psychology Today* might bore the readers of *The Reader's Digest.* An explanation that might be perfectly clear to readers of *Scientific American* might not be so clear to readers of *Popular Science.*

Naturally, in adapting your writing to your readers, you should know as much about your readers as possible. Some of your writing will be directed toward well-defined readers. For example, when you write an informal letter to a friend, or a personal letter to a loved one, you know with some degree of certainty the characteristics of these readers. When you write a paper for your instructor, you have some notion of what that instructor is like, some idea of what he or she is looking for.

Some of your writing, however, will be directed toward a less well-defined group of readers. For instance, suppose you decide to write a letter to the editor of a local newspaper. Even though you may know something about the editorial policies of the paper, you probably don't know the editor. On the other hand, you may know the editor of your college newspaper a little bit better. There are *degrees of definiteness* with respect to how well you know your audience. If you were to write an article for a city newspaper or for a national magazine, your audience would be much wider and more general.

Given the task of adapting your writing to your audience, how do you proceed? *You can analyze your readers* or *you can construct a picture of them in your imagination.*

You can determine the characteristics of your audience in a systematic way by asking certain basic questions:

What is the age of your readers?

What is their sex?

What is their race?

What is their nationality?

Where do they live?

What kind of education do they have?

What kinds of jobs do they hold? Are they professionals? White-collar workers? Blue-collar workers?

What are their political beliefs? To what political organizations do they belong?

What are their religious beliefs? Do they belong to any organized religions?

To what organizations do they belong?

What kinds of leisure activities are they interested in? Movies? Sports? Jogging? Reading? Going to plays?

Is there anything not typical about this particular audience?

To these questions can be added questions of a slightly different kind:

1. How much information do my readers have about my subject?

2. What will be their likely intellectual response? Emotional response? Ethical response?

3. Are my readers likely to be interested in my subject? Indifferent? Biased?

4. What will my readers expect from me as a writer?

The result of asking these questions is that you will come up with a more complete picture of your audience.

In addition to analyzing your readers, you can also construct pictures of them in your imagination. Actually, since you were a very small child, you have been building up *mental representations* or schemes of people and events in your imagination through play, games, personal experiences, reading, and so forth. For example, as a very young child, you imaginatively constructed the *actions* of others in your *play. You took the role* of a parent, a teacher, a nurse, a doctor, a dancer, a firefighter, a storekeeper, a heroine, a hero, a villain, and so on. As you grew older you played *games* in which *you mentally had to anticipate the intentions of some other person.* In playing a card game, for instance, you had to figure out what your opponent's next move might be. If you were in a baseball game with a player on first base, you had to anticipate whether that player would try to steal second base. As a young adult, there were occasions when you had to go mentally beyond your *self (I)* and a particular person *(you)* to considerations of a *group (he, she, they)* and even to some more abstract sense of *society.*

As a child, your primary audience was your *self.* Your idea of what other people were like was largely subjective. Then, in terms of increasing differentiation, you communicated your needs to your *parents,* then your *brothers* and *sisters,* your *relatives, adults, employers, fellow workers,* and so forth. Some of these people you knew very well; others you knew less well. With some, you were intimate; with others, familiar; with others, friendly; with some, cordial; with still others, private or detached. Some had a specialized knowledge of a subject, while others were non-experts. In brief, over a period of years you have internalized images of people in varying degrees of depth, complexity, and generality, and you can draw upon these images in your thinking to imaginatively construct your readers for a particular writing task.

One way of depicting these readers in relation to you as a writer would be as follows:

Writer → Self
Writer → Parents/Relatives
Writer → Teacher/Classmates
Writer → Peer Group
Writer → Friends
Writer → Acquaintances
Writer → Co-workers
Writer → Other Adults

To each of these individuals or groups, you stand in a particular personal relationship:

Known/Unknown
Particular/General
Intimate/Non-intimate

And each has varying degrees of knowledge about your subject:

Expert/Non-expert

To apply these concepts of audience to your own writing, in some writing situations you analyze your audience and then apply the results of that analysis in adapting your writing to your readers. In other situations, you role-play. You take the perspective of a particular individual or group of individuals and try to write from that perspective. Or you actually try to imagine a typical person that you might be writing to, and write to that person.

Exercises

1. Using the questions listed for determining the characteristics of an audience, analyze an audience for whom you are planning to write.

2. This question and the next two ask you to engage in role-playing. You have been appointed fashion editor of a major magazine. As editor, your job is to write articles on some aspect of fashion or the clothing industry. What subjects might you come up with if your readers were:

   a. women of limited income?   f. motorcycle riders?

   b. single men?   g. corporate executives?

   c. single women?   h. dry cleaners?

   d. weight watchers?   i. dog owners?

   e. travelers?

3. You have decided to write an essay about punk rock. How will your strategies change for each of the following readers?

   a. a music professor

   b. a group of college students

   c. Christian fundamentalists

   d. a group of white suburban rock fans

   e. a group of senior citizens

4. You have decided to write a letter to the editor of a local newspaper protesting the proposed building of a prison near your home. Your purpose is to encourage readers of the paper to join you in fighting the proposed building site. What arguments might you use to appeal to:

a. concerned parents?

b. people who live near the site?

c. politicians?

d. students?

e. taxpayers?

5. Bring to class a letter to the editor published in the local newspaper or in a magazine. Be prepared to discuss the following questions:

a. Who is the intended audience?

b. Is there more than one potential audience?

c. What is the purpose of the letter?

d. How does the writer adapt his or her writing to the intended audience?

The Writer

You always put something of yourself into a piece of writing. Even in so-called objective or impersonal writing, you appear as a certain kind of person, in a certain kind of role. As you have discovered, there is nothing negative about assuming a role; you have been doing it since you were a child. The doctor has a bedside manner, the lawyer a business manner, the salesperson a friendly manner, the judge sometimes appears stern. Like these people, you too assume certain roles. When you are with your friends, you act one way; when you are with your parents, you act another way; at a job interview, you try to appear as a certain kind of person; when you tell a joke, you assume another role.

In your writing, you want to gain acceptance from your particular readers. And gaining your readers' trust and respect is based on a combination of factors. First, you must show that you are a person of *good moral character.* You can do this by making ethical statements that indicate to your readers your attitude about those things in your subject that are morally desirable and those that are morally reprehensible. Second, you must convey the impression that you are *sincere.* A sincere writer is one who is totally committed to what he or she is doing in a piece of writing, one who is *honest* and who shows *genuine feeling.* Third, you must demonstrate that you are *intelligent.* You can do this by showing that you have a firm grasp of your subject and that you can reason correctly. Fourth, you must treat your subject with the proper *seriousness*, when it is appropriate to do so. This does not mean that you should take yourself too seriously or that you should be grim. It simply means that you should show your readers that you are in earnest when dealing with important matters. There are times, however, when you will want to use *humor* to make a telling point. Finally, there may be occasions, when to gain your reader's trust and respect, you will want to appear *moderate*. You can do this by avoiding extremes, by using understatement rather than overstatement, and by being reasonable.

Exercises

1. Bring to class a magazine ad in which someone is speaking for a product. Is the person sincere? How do you know? Is he or she telling the truth? Is the speaker serious? Is the speaker a competent judge of the product?

2. Bring to class an ad written in the third person, seemingly detached and impersonal. How is the writer's character rendered? Through the picture? The language? The tone? Is there anything in the ad that resembles a real voice?

3. Bring to class an article in which public officials are discussing sensitive issues. Do you believe them? Why or why not? What is there in the tone or in the language that makes you respond in a certain way?

Purpose and Aim

Every kind of writing has some purpose, but these purposes are so numerous that for the less experienced writer it would be helpful if they could be reduced to a few categories:

To inform or instruct   (car owner's manual)

To convince or persuade   (advertisement)

To entertain or please by calling
attention to language and form   (story, joke)

To express strong feelings
and emotions   (diary, love letter)

These categories, which are broad and general, I shall call the **aims** of writing, to distinguish them from the numerous specific intentions that you as a writer might have. The writer's **intention** is *the response that he or she expects to get from the reader.* Over the years, writers have developed terms to refer to these categories, so that writing that informs or instructs is said to have an **informative aim.** Writing that convinces or persuades has a **persuasive aim.** Writing that entertains or pleases has a **literary** or **aesthetic aim.** And writing that expresses strong feelings and emotions has a **self-expressive aim.** Clearly, these aims overlap, and you might be able to add some aims that are not included in the above list. But in most kinds of writing, a single aim is dominant. Because most of the writing you do in college and in the world of work will be informative and persuasive, in this text the emphasis will be on these two aims.

It ought to be obvious that as a writer you must know your purpose before you can go about achieving it. Lawyers must develop strategies to achieve their aims if they expect to be successful in the courtroom. Contractors must know the purpose of the buildings that they are going to construct. If you formulate your purpose in terms of reader response, your writing will more likely be appropriate for your intended audience. The following scheme shows how your purpose can be related to the desired response in your reader:

Writer's Purpose	*Reader's Purpose*
To inform or instruct	Understanding
To convince or persuade	Belief or action
To entertain or please	Aesthetic pleasure
To express strong feelings and emotions	Conduct or thought governed by emotion

Despite your good intentions, at times you might have difficulty keeping your dominant purpose in mind. One good strategy is to formulate a **purpose sentence.** This is a sentence that *explicitly sets forth your purpose in relation to your subject and to your audience.* Suppose, for example, you want to convince the director of Freshman English that Freshman English ought to be an elective. You might begin with an outline of the elements that will go into your purpose sentence:

> Subject: Freshman English ought to be an elective.
> Purpose: To persuade
> Audience: The director of Freshman English

Then you can easily combine the parts into a coherent whole:

> *Purpose sentence:* My purpose is to convince the director of Freshman English that Freshman English ought to be an elective.

The purpose sentence is not to be confused with your **thesis sentence**— one that *explicitly sets forth the main idea of your essay,* although it could easily be made into a thesis sentence:

> Freshman English ought to be an elective.

The purpose sentence is designed to help you to keep before you the response you expect to get from your reader. It can also be useful in helping you to plan your writing strategies.

Exercises

1. Using the following outline as a guide, fill in the content that might go into three purpose sentences for three separate subjects:

   Subject: (fill in the subject)
   Purpose: (fill in your purpose)
   Audience: (specify the audience)

2. Select a magazine ad and study it carefully. On a separate sheet of paper, answer the following questions:

   a. What is the purpose of the ad?

   b. Is there more than one purpose?

   c. Are some purposes immediate? Long-term? Hidden?

   d. Who is the audience?

   e. In what way is the ad's purpose and subject adapted to the audience?

f. Within the general readership of the magazine from which the ad was taken, how does the ad writer select out a more specific audience? By organizational strategies? By word choice? By subject matter? The illustration?

3. Some writers would not agree that the writer's dominant purpose ought to be clearly indicated in a piece of writing. To some writers, writing is a process of discovering one's intention as one writes. Do you agree with this point of view? Are there certain kinds of writing, perhaps, that might lend themselves to one or another of these views?

4. What is the dominant aim in the following kinds of written and spoken expression?

   a. a class lecture on regional dialects

   b. a sermon

   c. an informal conversation with a friend

   d. a debate about nuclear power

   e. a patriotic speech on a national holiday

   f. an oral interpretation of a poem

Forms of Discourse

Corresponding to the aims of discourse are the forms of discourse: *informative discourse, persuasive discourse, literary discourse,* and *self-expressive discourse.* The **forms of discourse** are *categories that represent the grouping of various kinds of writing based on the writer's aim.* For example, if your aim is to inform or instruct, you might write a cookbook, a driver's manual, an encyclopedia article, a news article, or a textbook. If your aim is to persuade, you might write a letter to the editor, a political speech, or an advertisement. If your aim is to entertain or please (i.e., if your aim is aesthetic or literary), you might tell a joke, or write a poem, a short narrative, a song, or a rock lyric. Finally, if your aim is expressive, you might choose some form of personal writing, perhaps journal or diary writing or a slogan.

   The following scheme depicts the relationship between the aims of discourse and the forms of discourse:

Aims of Discourse	*Forms of Discourse*
Informative	Informative discourse
Persuasive	Persuasive discourse
Literary	Literary discourse
Expressive	Self-expressive discourse

You should think of these four broad categories not as specific kinds of writing, but as **ways of classifying** the numerous kinds of writing or speaking that you will do:

Informative Discourse	*Literary Discourse*
cookbook	lyric poem
driver's manual	popular song
encyclopedia article	short story
news article	limerick
textbook	joke

Persuasive Discourse	*Self-expressive Discourse*
letter of protest	journal
political speech	diary
advertisement	prayer
editorial	slogan
sermon	

Modes of Discourse

A **mode** is *a way or manner of developing ideas.* You might call modes the "strategies" or "techniques" of discourse. You can use them to analyze ideas, to organize entire essays, or to develop paragraphs. These modes have familiar names such as analysis, description, classification, definition, comparison, contrast, exemplification, narration, process, and cause and effect.

Some writers use different terms to refer to these categories. As ways of exploring a subject, they are sometimes called **topics of invention.** As ways of developing paragraphs, they are referred to as **methods of development.** In the following chapters, I will be using all three terms to refer to these categories. The context will determine how I will be using them.

Your choice of modes will necessarily be determined by your aim, your audience, the form of writing you use, and the writing situation. For example, imagine that you are a copywriter for an advertising firm and that your task is to write a food ad for the readers of *Better Homes and Gardens*. Your aim would be to persuade. Your audience would be the readers of *Better Homes and Gardens*, and the form of discourse would be persuasion, or more specifically, a magazine ad. You might decide, based on this information, that description would be the most appropriate mode. Your strategy, therefore, would be to describe the product as concretely as possible, appealing to as many of the reader's senses as possible. In most writing, the modes are mixed, so that in your ad you might also use comparison and contrast or exemplification. But in much writing, there is a dominant mode, so that there may be considerable value in isolating the modes and seeing them as simple.

Exercises

1. Discuss in class. If you were writing advertising copy, what mode or modes might you choose to develop the following products? Why?

   a. candy, gum, cookies, pastries

   b. drinks, staple foods, desserts

   c. perfumes, cosmetics, toilet articles

   d. men's suits, hats, stockings, dresses, shirts

   e. jewelery, silverware, watches

   f. moving pictures, novels, magazine subscriptions

   g. cars, tires, batteries, motor oil

   h. stereos, TV sets, radios, tape recorders

2. For what *readers* would you select any of the above-mentioned products? Think of a typical magazine or newspaper where the ad might appear.

3. It is often assumed in this age of computers and television that writing is not as important as it used to be. Is this true? How could you verify this statement?

4. Interview the following people about the kinds of writing they do in their jobs: your mother or father; an uncle, aunt, cousin, brother, or sister; a friend; a celebrity. Then make a list and bring this list to class for discussion. Do not overlook even the seemingly most unimportant kinds of writing: a grocery list, a note, letters of various kinds, reports, memos, invitations, and so forth. In compiling this information, use the following questions: Who is doing the writing? What kind of writing is being done? For what purpose? When is it being done? Where? What are the rewards?

At the beginning of the semester, you might find it useful to attach a cover sheet to your essays on which you list in outline form all of the elements you must take into account in writing your essays. A typical outline for an assignment would look something like this:

General subject: Automobiles
Purpose: To convince readers to buy a luxury car
Audience: Readers of *Esquire* magazine
Kind of discourse: Magazine ad
Mode or modes: Description/comparison

CHAPTER 2

Invention:
Probing the Subject

Once you have decided upon a subject and determined your attitude toward it, your purpose, and your audience, you are ready to explore your subject more fully.

To do this, you need a plan, a way to reach somehow into the recesses of your mind. You'll need to spin out of yourself, as a spider spins out a filament, a thread of thought that will develop into an orderly web. For invention is a thinking process. In its broadest sense, **invention** is *any mental activity that will bring to conscious awareness something previously unknown.*

Thinking and Inventing: An Overview

The process of thinking about a subject is a gradual one. Thoughts take shape just as formless, irregular shapes in a blurred landscape after a hard snow grow in clarity and distinctness as you approach them. As you think about a subject, your thoughts develop by successive differentiations into well-defined and distinct elements rich in detail. There is a movement from a vague, indistinct, amorphous shape to a clear-cut, well-defined, complex unity.

The process begins with a kind of creative tension which, though it may be discomforting to you, seems necessary for the resolution of conflicts. In the beginning stage of invention, there is often a kind of indeterminacy, an inchoateness, a lack of clarity or precision. Actually there is an order of sorts, a potentiality waiting to be realized as you surrender to an inner necessity. Meanings are *felt*, rather than understood. There is something almost physical about the process at this early stage. The process is dynamic. Words and images jostle one another. Some of the images are visual. Some are acoustic. Some are "muscular."

At some stage in the process, you must exert some conscious effort on the task at hand. This takes the form of thinking about the subject, dividing it into parts, describing it, defining it, classifying it, comparing or contrasting it to something else, or seeking out its causes and effects. As you apply these approaches to the subject at hand, the original, amorphous, felt experience will progressively differentiate itself. You can then shape the experience more clearly for communication to others. As the process continues, the verbal aspects of your thinking become more and more detached from the images and the physical aspects.

Often this period of self-conscious activity is followed by a period in which you must while away the time or think about something else. Even in these moments of escape from the task at hand, your mind continues to work, making connections, sorting out ideas. Gradually, the original felt meanings, which are becoming more and more distinct and better articulated and organized, are put into appropriate linguistic forms for communication to others.

Exercises

1. How do you invent? Write a description of how you go about preparing for a writing assignment and how you actually think about your subject.

2. Daydream! Deliberately put yourself into a situation that is pleasant and let your thoughts wander freely about the subject.

3. Think of a childhood memory, joyful or painful, happy or sad. Let the order of memory determine the process of invention.

4. Sit down in a room or outside under a tree. Write down freely what you see, hear, smell, touch, perceive. Try to explore your mental activities as you perceive the world around you, as you think, and as you write.

The Categories of Invention

Although no two people would develop a general subject in exactly the same way, each of us follows certain lines of development in our thinking because of the principles on which the mind is organized. It recognizes temporal, spatial, logical, and psychological principles and relationships in the world around us.

Principles of composition such as analysis, classification, comparison and contrast, and cause and effect are *ways of thinking.* For example, not a day goes by that you don't analyze, classify, compare and contrast, or discover cause-and-effect relationships in the world around you. You see a tree and note the shape of its branches, the size of its trunk, or the color of its leaves. You classify it by naming it. You compare it to other trees. You observe it changing in time, notice that insects are causing it to decay or that it has been struck by lightning. When the tree is not in the immediate range of your vision, you substitute images or words to call it to mind, and these words or images facilitate your thinking about the tree. Every time you analyze, classify, exemplify, enumerate, compare, contrast, or discern cause-and-effect relationships, you are inventing ideas.

Compositional categories such as analysis, classification, and comparison and contrast, besides being principles of thought, are categories that can be used to explore ideas for writing. These categories are sometimes called **topics,** a word that originally meant "places." The topics were conceived of literally as places in the mind or in books where ideas were stored, where one could go to get ideas. The term "topic" today is more frequently used to refer to the subject matter of a discussion or conversation. But I would like to use the term to refer to *categories that can be used to direct the search for ideas or the arrangement of these ideas into some orderly pattern.*

I propose that in exploring a subject to get ideas for writing, you use these "topics" or "modes" in a systematic way. To help you to do this, I have put these categories into a scheme to enable you to use them more efficiently:

Topics of Invention
A.   Static modes
    1. Analysis
    2. Enumeration
    3. Description
    4. Classification
    5. Exemplification
    6. Definition
    7. Comparison
    8. Contrast
B.   Progressive modes
    1. Narration
    2. Process
    3. Cause and effect

The mental processes that underlie all of these categories probably work together in the composing process. You can't classify without perceiving similarities or divide something into parts without noticing differences. But for practical purposes, you can separate them and see them as distinct.

In order to use the topics to explore a subject, you move from one topic to another, applying each to the subject at hand. You can start with any category you like. Thus, you might begin by describing or defining your subject, dividing it into parts, classifying it, looking for significant examples, or comparing it to something else. Then you move on to the other topics, all the while obtaining a clearer idea of your subject as you apply each topic in turn. Once you have gone through the topics, you can repeat the procedure as often as you wish. As the result of applying each of these topics to your subject, you should have something to say and ways of saying it, or at least you will be aware of the gaps in your knowledge and can go on from there.

You might find that the topics may best be applied by putting them into the form of statements and applying these directly to the subject you are exploring. The following are just a few of the many statements suggested by these topics:

Identify the subject.
Describe it.
Divide it into parts.
Define it.
Classify it.
Give some examples of it.
Point out its similarities to or differences from something else.
Tell what happened, when it happened, and where.
Tell how it happened or how it is changing over time.
State its causes or effects.
Give reasons to support your opinion of it.

Another plan is to put the topics into the form of questions and apply these to the subject you are exploring.

Identification
Who or what is it?
Who or what is doing it or did it?
Who or what caused it to happen?
To whom did it happen?

Analysis

What are its pieces, parts, or sections?

How may they logically be divided?

Enumeration

What is the logical order?

What is the exact number?

Description

What are its constituent parts?

What are its features or physical characteristics?

How is it organized in space?

Classification

What are its types?

What are its basic categories?

Exemplification

What are some representative examples or illustrations?

Definition

What does it mean?

What is its genus?

What is its species?

What is its etymology?

Comparison and Contrast

What is it like?

How is it similar to other things?

How does it differ from other things?

Narration

What is happening?

What did happen or will happen?

When did it happen?

Where did it happen?

Process

How did it happen?

How does it work?

How do you make it or do it?

What are its stages or phases?

Cause and Effect
What is its purpose?
Why did it happen?
What are its causes?
What are its effects?
How is it related causally to something else?

Applying the Topics

To illustrate how the process might work with an actual subject, let us assume you find it necessary to evaluate the competing claims of rival products. You probably couldn't care less about which toothpaste gives you a brighter smile. But if you've ever bought a car that was a lemon or a product that didn't deliver what it promised, you could become irritated with ads that make exaggerated or misleading claims.

Imagine, then, that over the course of a year you had to shop for a car, low-cost air fares, a portable fan for your home or apartment, a coffee maker, or a home computer. Which car will give you the comfort, convenience, and economy you need? Which has the best repair record? The worst? If you're shopping for low-cost air fares, should you use an airline ticket service or a travel agent? What is the difference between a super-saver fare and an off-peak discount fare? These are not idle questions, as a look at almost any issue of *Consumer Reports* will reveal.

As a result of getting stuck with a defective product, you decide to write a letter to the manufacturer or to a consumer advocate. Or you decide to write an article to a general audience for a popular magazine such as *Good Housekeeping, Better Homes and Gardens, McCall's, Redbook,* or *Harper's*. Your subject is "the regulation of comparison advertising that presents exaggerated, misleading, or unsupported claims." Your immediate task is to examine your subject in a systematic way.

The process of systematically examining your subject might look something like this:

Identify the subject.
The regulation of comparison advertising that presents exaggerated, unsupported, or misleading claims.

Identify the key words and concepts.

Comparison advertising. Regulation. Exaggerated, unsupported, or misleading claims.

Define the key words and concepts.

Comparison advertising is that kind of advertising which states or implies that one product or service is better than another. In a sense, any advertising that claims to be "distinctive" is implicitly comparative.

The word *regulation* means "a principle, rule, or law designed to control or govern behavior." But its implications are that comparison advertising is susceptible to abuse.

Exaggerated, unsupported, or misleading claims are those that distort, overstate, fail to furnish evidence, or deceive.

Classify the key terms in the subject.

Kinds of exaggerated, unsupported, or misleading advertising. The so-called dangling, floating, or open comparison. The comparison that makes "exclusive" or "superlative claims." The comparison that names competitors, but can't always be substantiated. The comparison that does not name competitors directly. And the comparison that uses weasel words.

Give some representative examples.

Here are some examples of the "open" or "floating" comparison: "Face facts: Pine-Sol Cleans Grease Better." "Try Handle With Care on *your* summer washables. You'll say it really does more." "Whirlpool helps make your life easier." "Smooth some Balm Barr on your skin and see why it's better."

The following are some examples of "superlative" or "exclusivity" claims: "New Pace is the only toothpaste with the remarkable ICEN-3 system." "Only Tareyton has the *best* filter!" "No other toothpaste fights cavities better than Aim Regular or Aim Mint." "No other toothpaste fights cavities better than New Aquafresh." "True, the most enjoyable ultra low tar on Earth." "Nothing performs like a Saab." "Harvey's Bristol Cream. The best sherry in the world."

These are examples of comparisons that name competitors, but the claims are contradictory: "TYLENOL . . . safer than aspirin and just as effective when used as directed." "Tylenol was not found safer than Aspirin." *Bayer Aspirin Ad.* "Anacin can reduce inflammation that comes with most pain. Tylenol cannot." "Unlike Bayer or Anacin, Bufferin has special stomach protection." "Bufferin can reduce painful swelling and inflammation. Tylenol cannot." "Recent studies indicate: Datril is faster than Tylenol." "There's no question about it. *Now* is the *Ultra Lowest Tar brand.*" "U.S. Government laboratory tests confirm no cigarette lower in tar than Carlton." "Nationwide, more Coca-Cola drinkers prefer Pepsi than Coke!" "If you're a Pepsi drinker, Fresca has a surprise for you . . . one out of three Pepsi drinkers chose Fresca." "The Polo, Chevette, Renault 5, and Fiesta just don't compare with the new Mazda Hatchback." "Name one anti-perspirant that stops wetness better than Sure, Right Guard Silver, and Arrid Extra Dry sprays. Ban Roll-On."

The following comparisons are examples of advertising that do not name competitors: "Rise is thicker than the leading foam." "It's a fact. Concentrated Pine-Sol cleans grease better than any other liquid cleaner!" "Final Net over aerosols. Really, there's no comparison." "My pain reliever, Excedrin, worked better than your pain reliever in two medical studies." "Dial, the best selling deodorant soap, has twice the active ingredient as the #2 brand." "A popular polish gives you the blurs. Pledge gives you the beauty." "There are pens. Then there is Parker."

Here are a few examples of comparisons that use *weasel words:* "Cascade gets dishes *virtually* spotless." "Buc Wheats—*helps* you feel like a million bucks." "Bufferin's special ingredients *help* prevent the stomach upset plain aspirin can cause." "Reach toothbrush. Designed *like* a dental instrument." "*Like* a good neighbor, State Farm is there."

Analyze the key words and ideas.

Open comparisons such as "Pine-Sol Cleans Grease Better" and "Whirlpool helps make your life easier" provide little real information because they are incomplete. "Better" than what? "Easier" than what? The ads do not say. If an open comparison claims to be factual ("Face facts: Pine-Sol Cleans Grease Better") and implies a general comparison with similar products, the company should have the data to back up the comparison.

Superlative claims should be capable of being supported by evidence. Is it true that "Only Tareyton has the best filter" or that "Nothing performs like a Saab"? The key words in such exclusivity claims are words such as "no,," "no other," "nothing," "only," and "most," and "-est" words. Sometimes a company will put in a minor feature and give it a fancy name and then play up that feature as being exclusive in that particular product. For example, what is the "remarkable ICEN-3 system" in Pace toothpaste? It sounds impressive, and perhaps the company can verify the claim. But more often than not, the feature is incidental.

Not all superlative claims are deceptive. For example, some ads use the literary device of "hyperbole" to sell products. But in those instances, the reader or listener understands that the exaggeration is intentional.

Comparisons that name competitors seem safe from criticism. If a company claims that its product is better than a similar product, then it should be prepared to substantiate that claim. But often the claims of competing ads are contradictory. Is Tylenol safer than aspirin? Which pain reliever is faster? Do laboratory tests confirm that "no cigarette [is] lower in tar than Carlton"? The public has a right to be sceptical about contradictory claims.

Comparison ads that do not name competitors are easy to analyze. But since no names are used, in what sense are the ads comparative? As the Final Net ad ironically suggests, "Final Net over aerosols. Really, there's no comparison." On the other hand, if the ad implies a comparison with all other products ("It's a fact. Concentrated Pine-Sol cleans grease better than any other liquid cleaner!"), or if it refers to particular studies ("My pain reliever, Excedrin, worked better than your pain reliever in two medical studies"), then the manufacturer should be prepared to support its claim.

Finally, comparisons that use weasel words can be identified by their "weasels." For example, the word *virtually* in the statement "Cascade gets dishes *virtually* spotless" is a weasel word. It promises more than it can deliver. Upon reading this ad, the consumer is led to believe that Cascade will get dishes spotless. But "virtually spotless" dishes are not spotless dishes. The effect of the word *virtually* is to nullify the claim.

In the statement, "Bufferin's special ingredients *help* prevent the stomach upset plain aspirin can cause," the word *help* is another weasel word. This ad does not claim that Bufferin "prevents" stomach upset, although the reader is led to believe that this is what Bufferin does. Bufferin "helps" to prevent stomach upset. The word *helps* make the comparison with aspirin invalid.

Finally, the word *like,* when it is used in an analogy, can be a weasel word. For example, in the statement "Reach toothbrush. Designed *like* a dental instrument," the reader is given the impression that this toothbrush has the qualities attributed to a dental instrument. But Reach toothbrush is *not* a dental instrument. Therefore, the analogy is misleading.

Point out their similarities to or differences from something else.
Exaggerated and unsupported comparison advertising can easily be distinguished from advertising that uses factual comparisons. Factual comparisons are those that are based on recognizable features, qualities, characteristics, and other aspects of a product that can be measured, demonstrated, or substantiated in some way. Exaggerated or unsupported comparisons are those that are either incomplete or "hyperbolic." Some represent personal opinions or subjective opinions that cannot be substantiated.

Comparison advertising can be distinguished from non-comparative advertising by technique. Food ads, for example, tend to use descriptive copy, rather than comparisons, to sell their products. Many non-comparative ads use the testimonials of movie stars, athletes, and other famous people to sell their products. Other ads use narrative techniques, monologues, dialogues, examples, definitions, and cause and effect.

Point out the causes of unsupported or exaggerated comparison advertising.
Possible causes. Competitive rivalry may be one. One manufacturer may use unsupported or exaggerated comparison advertising to get a larger share of the market. Another manufacturer, a competitor, in order to hold on to his or her shares, may follow suit. Soon other manufacturers join the competition. Even if all the manufacturers manage to make a profit, they may take away the purchasing power from manufacturers in related industries. These other industries, in self-defense, then begin to use misleading comparison advertising.

Another possible cause. An advertiser may be so enthusiastic about a product that his or her enthusiasm leads to exaggeration. Exaggeration, in turn, may lead to deception.

Ultimately, advertisers that do use misleading comparison advertising do so because they want to make a profit. To make a profit, many feel that they've got to eliminate the competition.

Point out some of its effects.

One effect. The advertiser may fail to give consumers enough information to enable them to buy intelligently. Comparison advertising should give consumers enough facts about the product to form the basis for discriminating among the various brands.

Another effect. Consumers may become bewildered. If the claims of different products are contradictory, who is telling the truth? The consumer may conclude that all ads exaggerate or that all ads lie. The result is that consumers may become increasingly sceptical.

Misleading comparison advertising can also lead to unfair or false disparagement of the competition. As a result, consumers may come to distrust the manufacturer's competitors or to conclude that they offer inferior products.

Finally, exaggerated comparison advertising "puffs up" the product and increases its cost, when in fact it ought to sell for much less. These ads put an extra item of expense on the public without a compensating benefit. Ultimately, the cost of misleading advertising is passed on to the consumer.

Now that we have compiled a body of information about the thesis and the subject of comparison advertising, let's consider what we have done and where we go from here. We began systematically with some representative statements that the topics called to mind. We started by identifying the key terms and concepts and by defining them. We ended with cause and effect. Actually, we could have begun at any point. You will notice that we didn't use all of the categories. The ones we did use seemed to be the most appropriate for the subject. You will notice also that some categories generated a vast amount of material; others did not. This is to be expected. The amount of ideas generated by a particular topic will vary from subject to subject. Finally you may have noticed that some of the ideas derived from exploring the subject are not too coherent. Some are in sentence form. Some are not. This also is to be expected. When the ideas first come, you want to get them down on paper in any order, in sentences, fragments, catalog form, or whatever. Your primary purpose at this stage is to brainstorm for ideas. The process is a little like that of free association, in which you jot down anything that comes to mind about a particular subject. It differs, however, in that the categories of invention and the statements or questions they suggest give you a sense of direction often lacking in random associations.

Exercises

1. For class discussion: Assume that you have been asked to write an article for a magazine or a newspaper on one of the following subjects. Specify a particular magazine, consider the kinds of readers that might read the article, and then explore the subject in class, using the topics of invention in either statement or question form:

   a. How to talk to your parents.

   b. How some people handle conflict.

   c. Winning is everything.

   d. A guide to campus slang.

   e. Those unforgettable high school years.

   f. What we'll use instead of oil.

   g. Problems of growing up in the 80s.

   h. Life in the fast lane.

   i. How to get the lowest air fares.

   j. Lose weight and have fun too.

2. Consider a possible situation, purpose, and audience for one of the following subjects. Then probe the subject using the topics of invention:

   a. The meaning of a handshake.

   b. What it means to say no.

   c. How colors affect personality.

   d. Creating computer art.

   e. The value of video games.

   f. Women that men can't resist.

   g. Men that women can't resist.

   h. The fine art of dressing up.

   i. How to foil a car thief.

   j. Nobody lives in the real world.

   k. How to avoid reality.

   l. Fear of foreign languages.

m. Why students can't write.

n. What it's like to be alone.

o. What makes a tooth ache.

p. Can you cry your troubles away?

q. Why you need a home computer.

r. Why energy will cost more and more and . . . .

Finding a Thesis

Once you have explored your subject, you are ready to find a workable thesis. For a subject is not a thesis. A subject is the "matter" of a piece of writing, what it is about. A **thesis,** however, is *the working idea of a discourse*, an assertion so clear-cut that your reader has no doubts about what is to be discussed or proved. "Daytime television" is a subject, but "Daytime television is of very low quality" is a thesis.

Writers deduce their theses from the general subject in different ways. Should you formulate your thesis immediately after the determination of the general subject, or should you construct it after you accumulate a body of ideas and explore them thoroughly? There is no simple answer to this question. The thesis can either follow or precede the determination of the general subject or the exploration of ideas. Obviously, for many writers, there is considerable overlap in the process. When I write, more often than not, I begin with a title or a controlling idea and then, by reading and notetaking or by some kind of mental probing of my subject, I gather sufficient material to get my writing under way. I have on occasion formulated my thesis in the process of writing, but even then, I usually have more than a general idea about what I am going to say. If you decide, however, to formulate your thesis before you explore your subject thoroughly, your thesis could give you a more definite direction in which to proceed in inventing ideas.

Let us assume that you have probed your subject and that you are now ready to formulate your thesis:

1. State your thesis in a single declarative sentence. Take your subject ("comparison advertising") and then state something about it ("should be strictly regulated because it presents exaggerated or unsupported claims"). The completed thesis sentence will look like this:

Comparison advertising should be strictly regulated because it presents exaggerated or unsupported claims.

Since the thesis is to be used for your own aid, state it in such a way that it clearly and precisely expresses your central idea. Then you can frequently return to it to get your bearings at every step of your writing. Your thesis should constantly be in your mind as a point of reference. As the working idea of your writing, the thesis will also suggest the scope or limitations of your paper, and it can suggest ways of ordering your ideas.

2. Use the categories of invention to construct your thesis. Write your thesis so that it takes the form of an argument supported by reasons, a comparison, an enumeration, a cause-and-effect relationship, or a form suggested by one of the other categories of invention:

Advertising encourages people to buy products they don't need.

It's more important for a wife to have a career than to help her husband's career.

Strict, old-fashioned upbringing and discipline are still the best ways to raise children.

If you see someone cheating, you are honor-bound to report that person.

The wording of the first thesis statement ("Advertising encourages people to buy products they don't need") suggests that your paper will take the form of an argument supported by reasons. Thesis 2 ("It's more important for a wife to have a career than to help her husband's career") takes the form of a comparison. Thesis 3 ("Strict, old-fashioned upbringing and discipline are still the best ways to raise children") combines opinion with enumeration ("the best ways"). Thesis 4 ("If you see someone cheating, you are honor-bound to report that person") uses the categories of antecedent/consequent ("if" . . . "then") which are related to the topics of cause and effect.

In constructing thesis sentences based on the topics of invention, you can use certain words and phrases to provide meaningful clues so your reader can follow your thought. For example, in a thesis based on the topic of analysis, you can use key words such as "features," "aspects," "characteristics," "elements," "pieces," "parts," and "details," that suggest the mental process of dividing something into parts.

In a thesis based on the category of classification, you can use words and phrases such as "types," "kinds," "sorts," "classes," "categories," "main kinds of," "basic kinds of" to suggest the mental process of grouping items according to their similarities. Exemplification theses will use words and phrases such as "cite," "illustrate," "exemplify," "as follows," "for example," and the like. Theses based on definition use words like "define," "explain," "clarify," "in other words." A thesis in the form of comparison or contrast will use expressions such as "like," "as," "similar to," "in like manner," "resembles," "differ from," "unlike," "in contrast to." Theses based on the categories of cause and effect will have a characteristic vocabulary that will include words such as "thus," "consequently," "because," "for this reason," "cause," "effect," "if," "then," "it follows that."

Sometimes, however, the verbal cues used to construct theses based on the categories of invention may be more subtle. For instance, a thesis such as "To create the illusion of superiority, advertisers resort to the following techniques" suggests at least three categories of invention: enumeration, exemplification, and classification. Yet there are no specific words related to number ("two," "three," "four"), example ("exemplify," "illustrate"), or class ("kinds," "sorts," "types") in this thesis. The only verbal cues are the plural ending of the word "techniques" and the word "following."

3. Adjust your thesis to your beliefs. *A belief is any statement that you accept as true or that you bear witness to.* As a member of society, you hold certain beliefs and values. These may take the form of ethical precepts, legal obligations, political beliefs, or merely informal rules of social conduct. But whatever your beliefs, when you write you produce statements that contain these beliefs, and you hope that your reader will accept them. Even if your aim is to inform, instruct, or entertain, it is probable that, as your reader takes in the information or entertainment, changes will occur in his or her beliefs.

As you are writing your thesis, therefore, you can include words and phrases which will indicate to your readers what it is about your subject that you find morally admirable, desirable, or reprehensible. Your thesis may actually contain words such as *good* and *bad, moral,* or *immoral, right* or *wrong, shocking, shameful, justifiable, unjustifiable,* and the like. Or it may merely imply these terms and the ethical stance that they suggest. If, however, you find it difficult to include specific ethical terms in your thesis, as you are writing you can examine your thesis carefully in order to determine what your ethical assumptions and beliefs really are. Then you can rewrite your thesis to make it conform more accurately to your beliefs.

The following list of questions can act as a guide in clarifying your responses to your thesis:

1. Do I have something worth saying?

2. What values and beliefs are implicit in my thesis?

3. Are these values and beliefs really important to me?

4. Where did I get these values and beliefs?

5. How long have I held them?

6. Have I considered any alternatives?

7. What might be the consequences if my reader accepts the values and beliefs implicit in my thesis and acts on them?

4. Adjust your thesis to your readers. In Chapter 1 you considered ways of adapting your writing to your readers, so you may want to go back and examine the questions you used for analyzing audiences. You can use some of these same questions to analyze your thesis. To these questions, you might add the following: Does my thesis show evidence of *good will* toward my reader? Does it aim at some *good?* If my reader accepts my thesis, will the consequences of that acceptance contribute to my reader's *happiness* and *well-being?*

5. Finally, adapt your thesis to the rhetorical situation. This is, of course, much easier to do if your aim is persuasion. Propositions are often generated out of controversial situations which seem to call for some kind of response by an individual or group. In such situations, there is usually a point of disagreement between a writer and a reader. You might, for example, disagree with an editorial in a newspaper or on television, or you might want to respond to a letter to the editor on some burning issue of the day. That situation, and the issues involved, would be partly responsible for the stance you take in your thesis. On the other hand, you might examine a situation you think someone has overlooked and try to invest that situation with importance. In this case, you do not *discover* meaning and importance in a situation, but as a writer and a responsible citizen, you *create* meaning. It is in this latter sense that you can be said to adapt your thesis to the situation.

Exercises

1. Write a thesis sentence for five of the following subjects, assuming a particular purpose, audience, and occasion:

    a. Why I don't like cities.

    b. How to deal with a used car dealer.

    c. Can you love someone you don't like?

    d. The best junk food in the world.

    e. The value of ambition.

    f. How to listen to rock music.

    g. The decline of quality in the products we buy.

    h. Why the country needs a peacetime draft.

    i. On going to college.

    j. How to read a photograph.

    k. The advantages of jogging.

    l. Professions for women.

    m. Making friends.

    n. Movies and violence.

2. Discuss in class the topics of invention implicit in the following thesis sentences. What kind of support would you use to develop each? For what purpose? For what audiences?

    a. TV commercials insult women.

    b. People should have a voice in decisions that affect their jobs.

    c. The ideal woman is one who can manage a career as well as a home.

    d. If advertising can sell goods and services, it can also sell ideas.

    e. TV has a deep influence on our lives.

    f. Women who make more money than their husbands are less likely to love them.

    g. Frustration can be beneficial.

    h. My family background has influenced my life in a number of ways.

   i. Love needs to be expressed in words.

   j. Love should/shouldn't be the main reason for marrying someone.

3. Using the checklist on beliefs and values mentioned earlier in this chapter, analyze the thesis sentences in Exercise 2, above, and then discuss in class the values embedded in each. Do you agree with the opinions, values, and beliefs expressed in these sentences? If not, how would you rewrite these sentences to make them conform more closely to your beliefs?

Analyzing the Thesis

After you have constructed your thesis, you will want to analyze it carefully in order to determine if it accurately conveys your intended meaning and attitude toward your subject and if it will be acceptable to your readers. The questions that follow are intended to help you to examine your thesis:

For what readers is my thesis intended? For what purpose?

What values are implicit in my thesis?

Will my reader accept my thesis?

What kind of information will I need to support the thesis? Direct, factual information? Personal observation? Analyses and interpretations? Observations of others? Expert opinion?

Where will I get this information?

How general and inclusive is the thesis? How limited?

Are there alternative points of view?

What consequences will follow if my reader accepts my thesis?

If we apply these questions to the thesis that we formulated earlier about comparison advertising ("Comparison advertising should be strictly regulated because it presents exaggerated or unsupported claims"), we get the following information:

For what readers is my thesis intended? For what purpose?
A general audience of consumers. The aim is to persuade such readers that misleading, exaggerated comparison advertising should be strictly regulated.

What values are implicit in my thesis?
The word "should" in the thesis indicates a moral stance toward the subject. The words "exaggerated or unsupported claims" indicate that the writer values the plain, unadorned truth to exaggeration and statements not subject to verification.

Would your reader accept this thesis?
The statement of the thesis is both reasonable and ethical. Some readers would be naturally suspicious of all advertising. Others would have had personal experiences with misleading advertising. Some readers, however, would take a "so what?" attitude. Advertisers, they would contend, have always exaggerated, so people would not be taken in by these ads.

What kinds of information will you need to support the thesis?
Direct, factual evidence, in the form of specific ads that use comparison advertising. Personal observation, consisting of your own experience with ads. Your analyses and interpretations of these ads. The observations of others including your instructors, relatives, and friends. Expert opinion, consisting of evidence from critics of advertising, consumer advocates, etc. Evaluations of those opinions. Presumptions, based on past experience with advertising.

Where will you get this information?
You can obtain ads from newspapers and magazines. You can also videotape ads. You can find periodicals, such as *Consumer's Research Guide,* in the library. You can obtain large numbers of books supportive of and critical of advertising in the university library. To locate popular articles about advertising, consult the *Reader's Guide to Periodical Literature.* A subject such as this one, however, will not need extensive research. You could do an original paper based on primary sources, consisting of the ads themselves and your own observations, analyses, inferences, and interpretations of these ads.

How general and inclusive is the thesis? How limited is it?

While the thesis is limited to a specific kind of advertising ("comparison advertising"), the wording of the thesis suggests that all comparison advertising should be strictly regulated, not just misleading comparison advertising. It may be, of course, that you believe that comparison advertising lends itself to deceptive practices and that the thesis accurately conveys your intention. However, you may find that after rereading your thesis you will want to reword it so that it deals only with misleading advertising.

Are there alternative points of view?

One alternative is that comparison advertising should not be strictly regulated. Another is that only misleading comparison advertising should be strictly regulated. A third alternative is that the public knows that the claims of many ads are intentional exaggerations which represent personal, subjective, and emotional feelings about the worth of the manufacturer's product.

What consequences follow if your reader accepts your thesis?

Some readers will be intellectually convinced, but not take any action. Some will actually write to the manufacturers and ask them to substantiate the implied claim. Consumer advocates might write to a consumer agency and urge the banning of all comparison advertising. Others will retain a healthy scepticism when they buy advertised products. And there will always be those who won't believe that advertising can affect them.

There are undoubtedly other useful approaches to generating ideas for writing. This one is particularly interesting because of the close relationship of the categories of invention to mental processes. It must be discomforting to find yourself called upon to write something for a specific purpose, audience, or occasion, when you have only a vague notion of how to go about developing your ideas. The method discussed in this chapter is one useful way to discover ideas. Obviously, at least in the beginning stages, the process is somewhat artificial. The goal is to make the process habitual so that instead of having to probe every subject in a formal way, you so discipline your mind that it will automatically explore ideas logically and systematically, by analyzing, classifying, comparing, or contrasting.

Exercises

1. Provide a context for the following thesis sentences. In what situations might they conceivably be used? For what purposes? For what readers? Then analyze the key terms and concepts using the topics of invention.

   a. Advertising is ethical as long as it satisfies and benefits both parties.

   b. It is important for a child's development to have contact with the elderly.

   c. Children make marriage better.

   d. It is unethical for a sports figure or a celebrity to endorse a product he or she has never used.

   e. Sports metaphors abound in business talk, with interesting consequences.

   f. Military metaphors abound in business talk, with interesting consequences.

   g. People care more about economic survival these days than anything else.

   h. Duty should always come before pleasure.

   i. It is morally wrong to drive after having too many drinks.

   j. People in authority always know (do not always know) best.

2. Analyze the values implicit in each of the above sentences. Which ones do you agree with? Disagree with? Using the questions on pages 37–39 for analyzing the thesis, for class discussion analyze each of the above theses. Then pick one and write an essay, using it as a guide.

CHAPTER 3

Arrangement: The Whole Theme

In Chapter 2, you learned that invention is the process of discovering ideas for speaking and writing. Although for many writers the process is intuitive, you can learn to guide the process deliberately by using formal procedures for analyzing and searching. The method consists of applying the categories of invention to your subject, to your thesis, and to the ideas implicit in the terms of your thesis.

Now I would like to make a related point: The same categories you use to explore a subject you can also use to discover ordering principles to make your ideas understandable and believable to your readers. In other words, as you are probing a subject to get ideas, you are also putting these ideas into a pattern of arrangement. I call *the kind of pattern that results from applying the topics of invention* a **paradigm.**

Quite obviously, in planning a paper, you cannot keep in mind all of the specific details that will go into making the finished paper. But you can imagine a kind of general plan or structure that represents what you want to say and whom you want to say it to. In other words, you can construct a pattern that will represent your subject, your audience, and the reasoning you will use to inform or persuade your reader.

Paradigmatic Structure

A **paradigm** is *a pattern of organization based on the topics of invention.* It is a kind of model or design that is abstract and general. It is *an undetailed, general plan.* It is not to be confused with a traditional outline that is detailed and specific. Unlike a traditional outline, a paradigm is an *idealization,* a conception of a pattern in its absolute perfection. It represents the writer's *competence,* that is, the writer's *ability to use language.* But competence is always spilling over into performance, so that it is possible to use these formal patterns in your own writing. Because a traditional outline is so detailed, with its divisions and subdivisions, it can be used only for the specific piece of writing for which it is intended. A paradigm, however, represents *a global pattern* that recurs from one essay to another. In other words, you can use the same general plan and write completely different essays with it. This should not be surprising since a paradigm is *the organizational form that a specific topic of invention or mode of development takes.* Thus, it is possible to view a particular topic or mode (for example, comparison and contrast) as the principal method for organizing that discourse. A traditional outline is static. It represents a finished product. But a paradigm is dynamic. It represents *stages in thinking.*

A paradigm is *a form of reasoning* that leads the mind from one thing to another. But because thinking in composition is directed toward the reader as a whole person, a paradigm must engage not only the *intellect,* but also the *emotions* and the *innate moral sense* which serves as the basis of ethical decisions. In other words, a paradigm is *a structural form which incorporates appeals to the emotions and to the ethical sense, as well as to the reason.*

The following essay taken from Bertrand Russell's *Autobiography* is a good example of a professional essay that uses the paradigm as a principle of organization. As you read this essay, you will notice that although the underlying paradigmatic form is logical, the logical form also contains and organizes the emotional and ethical elements necessary to secure the reader's belief and conviction. Russell achieves this integration of form and meaning by including ethical and emotional words and phrases in the sentences that make up the paradigm, words and phrases such as *passions, the longing for love, the search for knowledge, unbearable pity for the suffering of mankind, ecstasy, loneliness, the hearts of men, children in famine, victims tortured by oppressors, helpless old people,* and *the whole world of loneliness, poverty, and pain.*

What I Have Lived For

Three passions, simple but overwhelmingly strong, have governed my life: the longing for love, the search for knowledge, and unbearable pity for the suffering of mankind. These passions, like great winds, have blown me hither and thither, in a wayward course, over a deep ocean of anguish, reaching to the very verge of despair.

I have sought love, first, because it brings ecstasy—ecstasy so great that I would often have sacrificed all the rest of life for a few hours of this joy. I have sought it, next, because it relieves loneliness—that terrible loneliness in which one shivering consciousness looks over the rim of the world into the cold unfathomable lifeless abyss. I have sought it, finally, because in the union of love I have seen, in a mystic miniature, the prefiguring vision of the heaven that saints and poets have imagined. This is what I sought, and though it might seem too good for human life, this is what—at last—I have found.

With equal passion I have sought knowledge. I have wished to understand the hearts of men. I have wished to know why the stars shine. And I have tried to apprehend the Pythagorean power by which number holds sway above the flux. A little of this, but not much, I have achieved.

Love and knowledge, so far as they were possible, led upward toward the heavens. But always pity brought me back to earth. Echoes of cries of pain reverberate in my heart. Children in famine, victims tortured by oppressors, helpless old people a hated burden to their sons, and the whole world of loneliness, poverty, and pain make a mockery of what human life should be. I long to alleviate the evil, but I cannot, and I too suffer.

This has been my life. I have found it worth living, and would gladly live it again if the chance were offered me.

—Bertrand Russell, *Autobiography*

A paradigm is based on the principle of repetition. In this essay, Bertrand Russell uses several methods of repetition. Sometimes he repeats words (three *passions* . . . these *passions* . . . with equal *passion*). Sometimes he uses synonyms *(three passions . . . love . . . knowledge . . . pity)*. And sometimes he repeats entire grammatical patterns. (I have sought love . . . because it brings ecstasy . . . I have sought it . . . because it relieves loneliness . . . I have sought it . . . because . . .)

Many essays are so regular in form that it is fairly easy to detect the underlying paradigm. The following is the structure of the Bertrand Russell essay:

1. Three passions . . . have governed my life: the longing for love, the search for knowledge, and unbearable pity for the suffering of mankind.

2. [I have sought love.]
   I have sought love . . . because it brings ecstasy . . .
   I have sought it . . . because it relieves loneliness . . .

> I have sought it . . . because . . . it contains a vision of the heavens that saints and poets have imagined.

3. I have sought knowledge.
   I have wished to understand the hearts of men.
   I have wished to know why the stars shine.
   I have tried to apprehend the Pythagorean power by which number holds sway above the flux.

4. [I have pitied.]
   [I have pitied] children in famine . . .
   [I have pitied] victims tortured by oppressors . . .
   [I have pitied] helpless old people . . .
   [I have pitied] the whole world of loneliness, poverty, and pain.

5. This has been my life.

In this essay, Russell wants to convince the reader that life is worth living. He does this by appealing to the reader's emotions, by evoking feelings of love, justice, and pity for the sufferings of humankind. The first sentence states the thesis. Russell is going to talk about the three passions that have governed his life. Each subsequent paragraph supports this thesis with concrete details. Paragraph 2 gives the reasons Russell has sought love. Paragraph 3 gives an explanation of the kinds of knowledge he sought. Paragraph 4 tells whom it is he pitied. Paragraph 5 returns to the beginning. The essay begins in sorrow and ends with affirmation and hope.

The dominant mode in the Bertrand Russell essay is *informal classification* (classifying kinds of passions), reinforced by *enumeration.* A subordinate mode is the use of reasons in the second paragraph.

Paradigms can be depicted in a number of ways. They can be represented by complete sentences:

Three passions have governed my life.
The first passion is the longing for love.
The second passion is the search for knowledge.
The third passion is pity for the suffering of mankind.
These are the passions that have governed my life.

Or they can be depicted by a more abstract scheme that emphasizes their relationship to the topics of invention and the modes of development. The following are some typical examples of paradigms in a more abbreviated form:

Analysis Paradigm

Introduction (states the thesis)
Characteristic 1
Characteristic 2
Characteristic 3
Characteristics 4, 5, 6 . . .
Conclusion (restates the thesis, summarizes, and so forth)

Classification Paradigm

Introduction (states the thesis)
Type 1
Type 2
Type 3
Types 4, 5, 6 . . .
Conclusion (restates the thesis, summarizes, and so forth)

Exemplification Paradigm

Introduction (states the thesis)
Example 1
Example 2
Example 3
Examples 4, 5, 6 . . .
Conclusion (restates the thesis, summarizes, and so forth)

Cause-to-Effect Paradigm

Introduction (states the thesis)
Cause 1
Cause 2
Causes 3, 4, 5 . . .
Effect
Conclusion (restate the thesis, summarizes, and so forth)

Effect-to-Cause Paradigm

Introduction (states the thesis)
Effect 1
Effect 2
Effects 3, 4, 5 . . .
Cause
Conclusion (restates the thesis, summarizes, and so forth)

The parts of the paradigm do not necessarily bear a one-to-one relationship to paragraph divisions. The divisions represent "chunks" or sections of the essay. You could, of course, write an essay consisting of five or six paragraphs if you were to follow each pattern exactly. But it should be obvious that each of these patterns can be shortened, lengthened, or modified to suit your own purpose. The following scheme is an expanded version of an analysis paradigm:

Paragraph 1 (Introduction)
Paragraph 2 (Statement of the Thesis)
Paragraph 3 (Characteristic 1)
Paragraph 4 (Qualification of Paragraph 3)
Paragraph 5 (Characteristic 2)
Paragraph 6 (Digression)
Paragraph 7 (Transitional Paragraph)
Paragraph 8 (Characteristic 3)
Paragraph 9 (Conclusion)

Exercises

1. Are you conscious of form in your own writing? In your sentences? In your paragraphs? In your essays? Discuss in class how you characteristically organize your ideas in writing.

2. Look up the words *pattern*, *paradigm*, *form*, *shape*, *structure*, *organization*, *arrangement*, *outline*, *contour*, *configuration*, and *design* in your dictionary. Then discuss their meanings in class. Is there a difference in their literal meanings? In suggested meanings?

3. Analyze an essay in your reader that uses a clear-cut organizational plan. What is the paradigm like? How is it used to convey the writer's intended meaning?

4. Construct a sentence paradigm in which you include a thesis sentence and supporting sentences in the manner of Bertrand Russell. Use a dominant mode (e.g., description, comparison, exemplification) as the basis for constructing the pattern.

Constructing Paradigms

To construct a sentence paradigm using the categories of invention, you begin with a thesis sentence:

America has lost its reputation for producing high-quality products.

Then you add sentences to the thesis in such a way that *the sentences that make up the paradigm* form a relational pattern *of exemplification, analysis, cause and effect, comparison and contrast, and so forth:*

New automobiles, *for example,* are in constant need of repair.

Appliances break as soon as their warranties expire.

Home furnishings and fixtures sag and crack shortly after they are purchased.

America has become a land plagued by defective and shoddy products.

In the above paradigm, **exemplification** is *the form of reasoning* that leads the reader's mind from one sentence to another. It also describes the *relationship* that exists among the sentences of the paradigm. The expression "for example" in the second sentence makes the relationship explicit, but even if there were no explicit signal words, the logical relationship between the first sentence and the middle sentences would still be that of a generalization followed by specific examples.

A paradigm constructed by means of a topic of invention, then, contains a specific form of reasoning. *But as a structural form, it also helps to organize the ethical and emotional material in a piece of writing.* To construct a paradigm using ethical and emotional appeals, *you include in your sentences ethical and emotional terms* that will indicate to your readers your attitude toward those things in your subject that are "morally desirable" or "obligatory" or "reprehensible" or "praiseworthy" or "one's moral duty" or "fearful" or "pitiful" or "spiteful" or "disgusting" or "pleasurable" and so forth. Not all paradigms, however, will contain explicit ethical or emotional words and phrases. A sentence in a paradigm will qualify as being an ethical or emotional statement *if it implies or suggests ethical values and emotional states.*

In the above paradigm, words and phrases such as *lost its reputation, plagued, defective,* and *shoddy* directly express the writer's attitude toward the subject and thus may move the reader. Reasoning can only take you so far in a piece of writing, for no matter how logical your reasoning or how compelling your evidence, you don't *feel* that you have made your point or won your argument until the person you are trying to convince or persuade agrees with you in feeling and motivation.

Notice that the thesis is written in such a way as to make the construction of the supporting sentences easier. The thesis presents a generalization in the form of an opinion. Each of the middle sentences presents an example of defective or shoddy products ("new automobiles," "appliances," "home furnishing and fixtures"). The last sentence restates the idea in the thesis sentence and acts as a "clincher."

The thesis should present an idea that will capture the attention of your reader. It contains that part of your argument or exposition that you want your reader to accept. The supporting sentences present the proof part of your paper. Each of the supporting sentences must be supported with facts, inferences, and expert and lay opinion.

The resultant paper may look nothing like the paradigm. In fact, the paradigm need not always be stated explicitly in the paper. However, underlying every piece of writing, there will be one or more paradigms that will control the structure of an entire discourse. The topics of invention will determine the kinds of relationships that can exist between the terms in your thesis sentence and among the sentences of your paradigm. *The topics are the elements out of which paradigms are constructed.*

Although paradigms can give you more conscious control of your writing, the mere construction of a paradigm will not guarantee that you will write a good paper. Therefore, after you have constructed your paradigm you will want to examine every sentence in it carefully to determine if you have anything worth saying, someone to say it to, and the means of saying it. In other words, you will want to adjust the ideas in your paradigm to your beliefs, to your intention, to your audience, and to the rhetorical situation. (You might want to go back to Chapters 1 and 2 to review these matters.)

Your first efforts at constructing paradigms may seem woefully inadequate. You may find that you will have to rewrite your thesis or your supporting sentences or perhaps the entire paradigm. You may discover that you have no clear idea of your audience or your purpose. You may discover that you can't find enough evidence to support your thesis. The process of applying the topics to your subject, of constructing thesis sentences and paradigms, of examining the ideas in the paradigm, of considering your purpose and your audience, and of writing and rewriting is only a part of what is meant by invention. However, at this point, you can begin to write your paper, remembering that in the process of writing you will continue to adjust your ideas to your purpose, your audience, and to the rhetorical situation.

After you have constructed your paradigm, your next step is to write your paper, using your paradigm as a guide. As you write your paper, you will need to provide a suitable introduction, appropriate supporting details, and an effective conclusion.

Here is another paradigm, this one based on the topic of **analysis:**

Strong families can be recognized by *a number of traits.*

They have *shared religious beliefs.*

They teach *a sense of right and wrong.*

They value *traditions and family rituals.*

They exhibit *a sense of play.*

Their members *affirm and support one another.*

These families often don't recognize *their good qualities,* but they have a kind of visible strength.

Notice that the thesis sentence uses analysis words *(a number of traits),* so that the reader has no doubt about the writer's intention. It also includes the subject to be analyzed *(strong families).* Each subsequent sentence takes up a specific feature of strong families *(shared religious beliefs, a sense of right and wrong, traditions and family rituals,* and so forth). The last sentence qualifies the ideas in the preceding sentences and returns to the beginning.

Notice also that the sentences in the paradigm contain ethical words and phrases such as *traits* ("distinguishing features of character") *shared religious beliefs, a sense of right and wrong, traditions, affirm and support, good qualities,* and *visible strength.* These terms constitute a set of moral principles or values which, the writer suggests, are the constituents of happiness. Families which exemplify these virtues deserve praise. Those which do not (it is implied) deserve blame.

After you have constructed your paradigm, you examine each sentence in the same manner as you did after constructing the exemplification paradigm. That is, you consider each sentence as it relates to your purpose, your audience, and the rhetorical situation. In examining the middle sentences, you try to determine the kind of evidence you need to support your thesis. Then, using your paradigm as a guide, you write your paper, providing an appropriate introduction, supporting details, and a conclusion.

Here is one more example, this one a paradigm constructed by means of the topic of **cause and effect**:

The *effects* of cigarette smoking on the individual are numerous and unsettling.

Cigarette smoking *causes* coronary heart disease.

Cigarette smoking *causes* deterioration of the lung tissue.

Cigarette smoking *causes* cancer of the mouth, larynx, esophagus, bladder, kidney, and pancreas.

The evidence that cigarette smoking *shortens* life is overwhelming.

The organizing sentence of this paradigm uses an explicit cause and effect word *(effects)*. Each of the middle sentences deals with one or several effects of cigarette smoking. The concluding sentence summarizes the ideas in the previous sentences.

This paradigm uses a combination of reason and emotion to convince the reader that cigarette smoking is harmful to the health. Embedded in the logical development of the cause-and-effect relationship is an emotional appeal to fear. This appeal is achieved by the use of emotion-laden words such as *unsettling* and *overwhelming* and by descriptive and evocative words and phrases such as *coronary heart disease, deterioration of the lung tissue,* and *cancer of the mouth.*

To write a paper based on this paradigm, you follow all of the steps previously outlined.

Not every paradigm or essay, of course, brings together the logical and psychological reasons that convey meaning to a reader. Each of the three appeals—logical, ethical, and emotional—can be used separately in a piece of writing as a way of winning belief or conviction. And in some kinds of writing, depending on the writer's subject, purpose, and audience, one appeal may dominate. But since every discourse directs itself to the whole person, the best approach is one that integrates the logical, ethical, and emotional appeals.

If my contention is true—that one or more paradigms underlie every piece of writing—then you can better learn to control your compositional processes by understanding how the paradigms that structure your thought actually function.

Exercises

1. Discuss the "topical" methods used to develop the following paradigms:

   a. Galaxies can be classified according to shape.
   Irregular galaxies have ill-defined shapes, with hints of spiral structure.
   Spiral galaxies have spiral arms and a big halo.
   Elliptical galaxies look like great, flattened, luminous beach balls.
   No galaxy is exactly alike in size and shape, but most can be reduced to this simple scheme.

   b. Over the past few decades, there have been some disturbing social developments in America.
   For example, violent crime is at an all-time high.
   Vandalism is widespread and unrestrained.
   Premarital and extramarital sex have become the norm.
   There are more divorces and broken families than ever before.
   These are signs that moral and spiritual values are at an all-time low.

   c. A field can change into a forest in a very short time.
   First, grass and weeds take hold.
   Then, shrubs and pines spring up, crowding out the grass and weeds.
   As the pines mature, deciduous saplings sprout in their shade.
   Finally, deciduous trees supersede the pines to form the forest.

   d. The U.S. must take a bold leap toward alternate sources of energy.
   One alternate source of energy is direct sun power.
   Another alternate source is wind power.
   A third alternate source is geothermal power.
   Each of these sources has limitations, but together they could reduce our dependence on oil.

   e. Jupiter and Saturn have features shared by no other planets.
   Both have dense, poisonous gaseous atmospheres.
   Both have frigid surface temperatures.
   Both have large numbers of satellites.
   Finally, both planets spin rapidly and have bulging waists and flattened poles.

   f. Women who are pursued by men have certain elusive qualities.
   They have an unshakable core of self-confidence.
   They always carry with them an element of surprise.
   They project an unusual aura of sensuality.
   Every generation has a name for these elusive qualities—charm, oomph, allure, sex appeal—that distinguish this kind of woman.

2. Examine each of the above paradigms carefully and discuss in class the following questions:

   a. What aim or aims is implicit in each?

   b. What kinds of readers might each appeal to?

   c. Out of what kind of writing situation might the need to write a paper based on a particular paradigm arise?

   d. Is there a dominant appeal in each paradigm? Logical? Emotional? Ethical? Or is there a combination of appeals?

   e. Do the subject matter, audience, and purpose have anything to do with the choice of appeals?

   f. Are the paradigms well-constructed? If not, can you think of better ways to construct them?

   g. What kinds of supporting evidence would you need to develop the ideas in the middle sentences of each?

3. Construct three paradigms of your own, and be prepared to discuss them in class. Base each paradigm on a dominant mode or topic of invention and, if possible, on a dominant appeal (logical, emotional, ethical). Be sure to consider your purpose, subject, audience, the writing situation, and the form (letter to the editor, essay, review, magazine ad) a paper based on each paradigm might take.

4. Write an essay based either on one of the model paradigms or on a paradigm you have constructed.

Paradigms as Cognitive Maps

The value of paradigms is that they enable you to move your thinking in an orderly manner from the beginning of an essay to its conclusion. In some respects, paradigms are like *maps*. Maps are *representations* of a part or a whole of a city or a geographical region. They enable you to get around in the environment. Paradigms are *mental representations* of some course of action. They are mental anticipations of a plan that you expect to carry out. They are maps in your head that help you to get around in your writing.

Imagine what happens when you try to find your way around a strange city. If you must go a good distance to your destination, you don't need to look at every detail on the map, but only at the main streets and avenues and at the major landmarks. As you drive down the street, you know in general where you are going, but you pick up more detailed information as you go along. As you go around the corner, you may see a landmark that the map helped you to anticipate. As you reach a wide avenue, you see new vistas, things that were previously hidden. Your map gives you information, and it creates information. The new information you pick up as you go on your way modifies your previous information. Subsequent trips enable you to build up internal representations of the world, and these mental representations will control to some extent your subsequent actions.

Another way to think of paradigms is to compare them to *sketches* or *rough drawings*. Like sketches, they are brief and incomplete, without much detail. Just as sketches for a painting depict only the prominent features of a painting, paradigms depict only the major parts of a piece of writing. Sketches are intended to serve as the basis of a more detailed picture. Paradigms are intended to serve as the basis of a more detailed piece of writing.

Paradigms are like *plans*. Like plans, they are worked out ahead of time to achieve a specific purpose. Like plans, they are schemes for doing something or organizing something. They "plot" the mental representation into the appropriate pattern of mental activity. Like plans, paradigms are tentative and flexible. Thus they can be altered in order to achieve a specific end.

Exercises

1. There is a relationship between cognitive maps (maps in your head) and games. Like maps, games help you to find your way around, to solve problems. Many games are based on spatial metaphors. Discuss in class the possible application of the following games to thinking, solving problems, and writing:

   a. jigsaw puzzles

   b. tic-tac-toe

   c. checkers

   d. Risk

   e. Diplomacy

   f. backgammon

   g. chess

   h. other games

2. For class discussion: Think of a place that you have previously visited. How much of what you remember consists of landmarks, major streets, and general images? How much consists of specific details?

Composing an Essay

What I have been suggesting is that in composing an essay, in the process of discovering and arranging your ideas, you use paradigms to facilitate the movement of your thought. How is this done?

As you begin to write, *you match what you are writing to a mental representation* that you carry in your head. That mental representation not only includes *your organizational plan*, but it also includes *your purpose* and *a generalized picture of your reader*. Your success in writing will depend to some degree on the extent to which you have previously built up internal representations and strategies to help you to achieve your goals.

As you write, you hear a kind of inner voice, and that inner voice (or *inner speech*, as it is sometimes called) is a part of the mental representation that you carry in your head. In addition to helping you to facilitate your thought, it also allows you to *audit* and *edit* what you are thinking.

After you have written a sentence or two, or perhaps after you have written an extended passage, you read what you have written to make sure that what you have written "feels" right. Your sense of its being right may be an almost physical sensation. If you are satisfied with what you have written, you begin again, using a word or idea from the passage that you have previously read as a means to get you going.

If you are not satisfied with what you have written, you may decide to begin all over again, recasting your ideas in a different form. Or you may decide to revise what you have written, discovering meaning as you are writing. Revising while writing may take several forms: *revising internally*, i.e., revising in your head as you are writing; *revising particular words and sentences on the page*; and even *recasting whole passages* in an attempt to match your meaning to your concern with your audience and your purpose. After you have finished writing, you look back at what you have done, editing, revising, and rewriting as is necessary.

To illustrate this process more concretely, let us write an essay, using one of the thesis sentences we formulated in the previous chapter as well as some of the ideas derived from the probe:

> Comparison advertising should be strictly regulated because it presents exaggerated, contradictory, and unsupported claims.

This is a thesis that a reasonable reader would accept as a promising thesis. The assumption is that any kind of advertising that presents exaggerated, contradictory, and unsupported claims should be strictly regulated. If comparison advertising does this (and this is what you have to prove to the satisfaction of your readers), then comparison advertising should be strictly regulated.

The wording of the thesis suggests that your thesis will be developed by reasons ("because it presents exaggerated, contradictory, and unsupported claims"). Because of the wording of the thesis, it is fairly easy to convert it into a paradigm:

> Comparison advertising should be strictly regulated because it presents *exaggerated, contradictory,* and *unsupported claims.*

> Comparison advertising presents *exaggerated claims.*

> Comparison advertising presents *contradictory claims.*

> Comparison advertising presents *unsupported claims.*

> *For these reasons,* comparison advertising should be strictly regulated.

Your next step is to plan your compositional strategies. Is there anything in the thesis that needs to be explained to your reader? What kind of evidence will you need in order to support each of the propositions in your paradigm? You may want to give specific examples of comparison advertising that presents exaggerated claims, contradictory claims, and unsupported claims. You may also want to analyze and comment on the examples. In the section on probing the subject and the thesis, you came up with dozens of examples of misleading comparison ads, and you analyzed them adequately. All you need to do as you are writing is to retrieve them from your memory (if you did the mental probing of the subject in your head) or from your notes. It may be that as you are writing you will come up with additional examples and ideas. This is to be expected, since invention continues throughout the composing process.

As you write, you might think of your overall compositional plan in terms of some kind of abstract pattern such as the following:

Introduction (includes thesis)
Reason 1 (plus supporting evidence)
Reason 2 (plus supporting evidence)
Reason 3 (plus supporting evidence)
Conclusion (restatement, summary, call to action)

Or you may use the actual sentence form of the paradigm, keeping it constantly in your mind, but remembering that these paradigms don't exist prior to, but are the results of your thinking. Using the sentence paradigm as the basis of your thinking, you begin by discussing the background of the situation:

> Advertising has always been an easy target for critics. But the attacks have become more widespread in recent years because of the economy and because the volume of advertising has increased so dramatically in recent years. Some critics estimate that in the U.S. alone, billions of dollars are spent each year for advertising.

Then you reread what you have written. As you read, you may decide that you don't like the repetition of the phrase "in recent years," so you scratch out one of the phrases. You also may not like the vagueness of the phrase "because of the economy." This phrase doesn't tell your reader much. So you try again.

> Advertising has always been an easy target for critics. But the attacks have become more widespread in recent years. One reason is that the volume of advertising has increased so dramatically. Some critics estimate that in the U.S. alone, billions of dollars are spent on advertising each year. Another related reason is that many critics don't feel that ~~that much~~ the money ~~should be~~ spent on advertising in bad economic times since, they contend, ~~that~~ people ~~can't afford to~~ can only afford to buy the necessities, and these don't need to be advertised. In addition, the cost of advertising is passed on to the consumer, ~~they say.~~

 can be justified

There is a bit more detail here, but there are a few passages that need reworking. You scratch out the poorly worded passages, insert what you think is better wording, and prepare to continue. Your task now is to find a bridge from the general comments on advertising to the idea of comparison advertising, and to your thesis:

consists

Even more frustrating, much of the advertising appearing in any given year ~~seems to be composed~~ of fiercely waged battles by manufacturers among competing brands. ~~Their claims conflict. They can't all be telling the truth.~~ These battles take the form of comparative campaigns designed to undermine the competition. Comparison advertising is not objectionable in itself. In fact, consumer information can become more meaningful through factual comparisons. Comparison advertising is objectionable only

the comparisons

~~if~~ when the public has no way of knowing to what extent ~~comparative~~ prices are literally true. No matter what its value, however, ~~when comparison advertising is used in a responsible manner,~~ many critics reject comparison advertising because it is often susceptible to abuse. They contend that *comparison advertising should be strictly regulated because it presents exaggerated, contradictory, and unsupported claims.*

Not a great introduction, but adequate to your purposes. You have introduced the general subject, narrowed down to a more specific subject in your second paragraph, and stated your thesis. You can always rewrite your introduction after you have finished your paper, but for now, you make a few editorial changes. Before you begin again, you reread the first two paragraphs to get your bearings, noting key words and scrutinizing your thesis sentence. As you continue to write, because you have a general organizational plan in mind in the form of a paradigm, you check your writing against this paradigm, which has been internalized as a mental representation:

those

Comparison advertising presents exaggerated claims. Exaggerated claims are ~~claims~~ that are used to place a certain product in a class of its own by using ~~the~~ extreme ~~degree of~~ comparison. The key words in such exclusivity claims are words such as "no," "no other," "nothing," "only," "most," and words ending in "-est." For example, True cigarettes advertises itself as "the most enjoyable ultra low-tar on Earth." Harvey's Bristol Cream makes the claim that it is "the best sherry in the world." Hyperbole? Poetic license? Perhaps, but the ubiquity of these claims suggests that they work. Here are a few more exaggerated claims: "Only Tareyton has the *best* filter!" "No other toothpaste fights cavities better than New Aquafresh." "Nothing performs like a Saab." Claims such as these are often tolerated under the assumption that nobody takes them seriously, but in some countries they cannot be used unless they are provable.

As you did with the first two paragraphs, you reread this paragraph before going on, looking at the overall shape of the argument and at the quality of the evidence.

Although the process is seldom strictly linear, there is a sequence of steps that you follow in writing a paper. But from time to time, you must backtrack to reread what you have written, to think about your ideas; to reconsider your organizational plan; to revise, if necessary, according to the needs of your purpose and audience; to recast entire sections of your paper; and even to start all over again should a different organizational plan occur to you. The advantage of using a paradigm as you write, however, is that it will help you to direct your thinking and enable you to avoid false starts.

After you reread this paragraph, you continue along the same lines as before, writing, reading, stopping to think about what you are doing and where you are heading, revising if you see the need to. As a result of following this process, you might end up with the rest of the paper looking like this:

Comparison advertising presents contradictory claims. Contradictory claims are those that express the direct opposite of other claims. Obviously, ~~contradictories~~ *contradictory claims* cannot both be true. For example, several years ago Tylenol ~~ran an ad claiming~~ *advertised* that it was "safer than aspirin and just as effective when used as directed." Shortly after, Bayer Aspirin countered with the claim that in their tests "Tylenol was not found safer than Aspirin." In a recent ad in *Time* magazine, Now cigarettes announced ~~that~~ the results of the latest U.S. government report on tar: "There's no question about it. *Now* is the *Ultra Lowest Tar brand.*" However, in the exact same month and year, ~~(July, 1982)~~ Carlton cigarettes, in the July 19, 1982 issue of *Time* magazine announced: "U.S. Government laboratory tests confirm no cigarette lower in tar than Carlton." What is the bewildered consumer supposed to believe? If a ~~company claims that~~ manufacturer claims that its product is better than a similar product then it should be prepared to substantiate that claim. Ban Roll-On, for instance, claims that it "stops wetness better than Sure, Right Guard Silver, and Arrid Extra Dry sprays." Two things are suspect in this ad. The first is that a roll-on is being compared to sprays. The second is that the claim ~~that Ban stops wetness better than the sprays~~ needs to be substantiated. But ~~how~~ *whom* is the consumer to believe when both Now and Carlton make contradictory claims based on U.S. government reports? Such claims can only be labeled misleading.

Comparison advertising presents unsupported claims. Unsupported claims take three forms: the open or floating comparison, the comparison that does not name competitors, and the comparison that uses weasel words. The open comparison is one that is incomplete because there is only one term in the comparison. For example, open comparisons such as "Pine-Sol Cleans Grease Better" and "Whirlpool helps make your life easier" are provide little real information because they are incomplete. "Better" than what? "Easier" than what? The ads do not say. If an open comparison claims to be factual and implies a general comparison with similar products, the company should have the data to back up the comparison.

The comparison that does not name competitors cannot be considered to be comparative in the strict sense. Yet the manufacturer which sponsors the ad should still be held accountable for ~~the~~ any unsupported claims. ~~For instance~~ Because the manufacturer does not name names, it is so easy for it to evade responsibility. For instance, in the ad "Rise is thicker than the leading foam," what is the leading foam? Palmolive? Colgate? What evidence is there to support this claim? In an ad for Pledge furniture polish, Johnson and Son claims: "A popular polish gives you the blurs. Pledge gives you the beauty." What is the name of this popular polish? Occasionally, an ad that does not name competitors implies a comparison with all other products. ("It's a fact. Concentrated Pine-Sol cleans grease better than any other liquid cleaner.") In ads such as these, the manufacturer should be prepared to support its claim.

The comparison that uses weasel words is an unsupported comparison because there is no way to pin down the exact meaning of the tricky word. For example, in the statement "Cascade gets dishes virtually spotless," what kind of claim is being made? What does the word "virtually" really mean? ~~How can the claim be supported.~~ Does Cascade get dishes spotless or doesn't it? Are there fewer spots on dishes that use Cascade? *For example,* Or to take ~~another example,~~ what does the statement "Reach Toothbrush. Designed like a dental instrument" really mean? In what way ~~can~~ it a toothbrush ~~be designed~~ like a dental instrument? Reach toothbrush is not a dental instrument. Therefore, the analogy is misleading.

The word "like" is another word to beware.

As long as competitors' names are mentioned, as long as the products identified are competitive with one another, as long as similar or related features are compared, as long as the claims can be verified, and as long as these claims are neither misleading nor unfair, comparison advertising can provide consumers with a useful service. But all too often comparison advertising presents exaggerated, contradictory, and unsupported claims. As a consequence, they seriously detract from the credibility of advertising as a whole. For these reasons, comparison advertising should be banned.

After you finish writing the paper, you reread the entire paper, making changes as you read, scratching out a word here or there, adding a new word, rephrasing an entire passage. At this point, you may even decide to rewrite considerable portions of the entire paper. If you are satisfied with what you have done, you retype your paper and put it in its finished form.

Advertising has always been an easy target for critics. But the attacks have become more widespread in recent years. One reason is that the volume of advertising has increased dramatically. Some critics estimate that in the U.S. alone billions of dollars are spent on advertising each year. Another related reason is that many critics don't feel that the money spent on advertising can be justified in bad economic times since, they contend, people can only afford to buy the necessities, and these don't need to be advertised. In addition, the cost of advertising is passed on to the consumer.

But even more frustrating, much of the advertising appearing in any given year seems to consist of fiercely waged battles by manufacturers among competing brands. These battles take the form of comparative campaigns to undermine the competition. Comparison advertising is not objectionable in itself. In fact, consumer information can become more meaningful through factual comparisons. Comparison advertising is objectionable only when the public has no way of knowing the extent to which the comparisons are literally true. No matter what its potential value, however, many critics reject comparison advertising because it is so often susceptible to abuse. They contend that *comparison advertising should be strictly regulated because it presents exaggerated, contradictory, and unsupported claims.*

Comparison advertising presents exaggerated claims. Exaggerated claims are those used to place a certain product in a class of its own by using extreme comparisons. The key words in such exclusivity claims are words such as *no, no other, nothing, only, most,* and words ending in *-est.* For example, True cigarettes advertises itself as "the most enjoyable ultra low tar on Earth." Harvey's Bristol Cream makes the claim that it is "the best sherry in the world." Hyperbole? Poetic license? Perhaps, but the ubiquity of these claims suggests that they work. Here are a few more exaggerated claims: "Only Tareyton has the *best* filter!" "No other toothpaste fights cavities better than New Aquafresh." "Nothing performs like a Saab." Claims such as these are often tolerated under the assumption that nobody takes them seriously but in some countries they cannot be used unless they are provable.

Comparison advertising presents contradictory claims. Contradictory claims are those that express the direct opposite of other claims. Obviously, two contradictory claims cannot both be true. For example, several years ago Tylenol advertised that it was "safer than aspirin and just as effective when used as directed." Shortly after, Bayer Aspirin countered with the claim that in their tests "Tylenol was not found safer than Aspirin." In a recent ad in *Time* magazine, Now cigarettes announced the results of the latest U.S. government report on tar: "There's no question about it. Now is the Ultra Lowest Tar Brand." However, in the exact same month and year, in *Time* magazine, Carlton cigarettes announced: "U.S.

Government laboratory tests confirm no cigarette lower in tar than Carlton." What is the bewildered consumer supposed to believe?

If a manufacturer claims that its product is better than a similar product, then it should be prepared to substantiate that claim. Ban Roll-On, for instance, claims that it "stops wetness better than Sure, Right Guard Silver, and Arrid Extra Dry sprays." Two things are suspect in this ad. The first is that a roll-on is being compared to a spray. The second is that the claim needs to be substantiated. But whom is the consumer to believe when both Now and Carlton make contradictory claims based on U.S. government reports? Such claims can only be labeled misleading.

Comparison advertising presents unsupported claims. Unsupported claims take three forms: the open or floating comparison, the comparison that does not name competitors, and the comparison that uses weasel words. The open comparison is one that is incomplete because there is only one term in the comparison. For example, open comparisons such as "Pine-Sol Cleans Grease Better" and "Whirlpool helps make your life easier" provide little real information because they are incomplete. "Better" than what? "Easier" than what? The ads do not say. If an open comparison claims to be factual and implies a general comparison with similar products, the company should have the data to back up the comparison.

The comparison that does not name competitors cannot be considered to be comparative in the strict sense. Yet the manufacturer which sponsors the ad should still be held accountable for any unsupported claims. Because the manufacturer does not name names, it is easy for it to evade responsibility. For instance, in the ad "Rise is thicker than the leading foam," what is the leading foam? Palmolive? Colgate? What evidence is there to support this claim? In an ad for Pledge furniture polish, Johnson and Son claims: "A popular polish gives you the blurs. Pledge gives you the beauty." What is the name of this popular polish? Occasionally, an ad that does not name competitors implies a comparison with all other products ("It's a fact. Concentrated Pine-Sol cleans grease better than any other liquid cleaner.") In ads such as these, the manufacturer should be prepared to support its claim.

The comparison that uses weasel words is an unsupported comparison because there is no way to pin down the exact meaning of the tricky word. For example, in the statement "Cascade gets dishes virtually spotless," what kind of claim is being made? What does the word *virtually* really mean? Does Cascade get dishes "spotless" or doesn't it? Are there fewer spots on dishes that use Cascade? The word *like* is another word to beware. For example, what does the statement "Reach toothbrush, designed like a dental instrument" mean? In what way is a toothbrush "like" a dental instrument? Reach toothbrush is not a dental instrument. Therefore, the analogy is misleading.

As long as competitors' names are mentioned, as long as the products identified are competitive with one another, as long as similar or related features are compared, as long as the claims are neither misleading nor unfair, comparison advertising can provide consumers with a useful service. But all too often *comparison advertising presents exaggerated, contradictory, and unsupported claims.* As a consequence, they seriously detract from the credibility of advertising as a whole. *For these reasons, comparison advertising should be strictly regulated.*

In using paradigms to organize your writing, you need not always follow the same kind of rigid order that was followed in the writing of this essay. Ultimately, it is more important that you understand the process of thinking that underlies these paradigms and that you make the process habitual in your own writing. Then, when you go to write, you will automatically begin to think in terms of reasons or examples, or stages, or progressions of some kind.

Exercises

1. Go back to Chapter 2. There is more than enough material derived from the probe on advertising for you to write an essay. Using this material, decide on the kind of essay you will write, your purpose, your audience, and your mode. Write a thesis, based on a particular mode or category of invention and develop a paradigm from it. Then write the essay.

2. For an in-class project, choose a particular subject, audience, purpose, and writing situation. Discuss the subject fully, and then construct a paradigm based on the foregoing considerations. Organize it around a dominant mode. Consider ways of including ethical and emotional appeals. Consider the kind of evidence you will need to support the middle sentences of the paradigm. Then rewrite the paradigm as often as is necessary in order to make it well-formed and suitable for presentation to your readers. Finally, write an essay based on this paradigm.

3. Choose an essay from your reader that uses the paradigm as a principle of construction. Analyze this essay in class, considering the writer's purpose and audience, the kinds of appeals, the dominant mode or modes, and so forth. Was the writer successful in achieving his or her purpose?

CHAPTER 4

Patterns of Thought: Analysis and Description

It would seem to be a valid statement that *for every process, there must be a corresponding system.* The topics of invention and the patterns of arrangement represent an unbroken line of development from process to system. Paradigms seem to mediate between the processes of discovering ideas and arranging these ideas into an orderly pattern. Thus, **paradigms** are on the one hand *patterns of thought* that give to your writing a determinate direction, and on the other hand *formal patterns* that help you to order your ideas.

To learn to compose, however, is not simply to memorize a set of paradigms. It is rather *to master the system of principles that will make it possible for you to understand and to produce discourse.* A paradigm is the result of paradigmatic thinking and should be considered as a means to an end, not an end in itself.

In the next chapters, you will be looking at a number of these compositional principles, in their paradigmatic form as well as in their larger patterns in the composition as a whole. The following are some of the most important of these compositional principles:

> Analysis/Description
> Classification/Exemplification/Definition
> Comparison/Contrast/Analogy
> Narration/Process/Cause and Effect

Analysis

Most of your day-to-day analyses are informal and intuitive. As you walk along the street, you may notice a tree, look at one of its branches, and discern its size or the texture of the bark or the shape and color of the leaves. After you see a movie, you may talk about the plot, isolate an exciting moment, or discuss a suspenseful scene. Every day, in almost everything you do, you analyze, dissect, differentiate, and trace things to their sources. Analysis is not only an important principle in your everyday thinking; it is also an important compositional principle.

Analysis is *the process of dividing anything complex into simple elements or components.* It is also the exact determination of those elements. It is the systematic separation of a whole into parts, pieces, or sections. Ideally, in the act of analyzing, you trace things back to their underlying principles.

Anything taken as a whole can be analyzed: a landscape, a seascape, a configuration of buildings in a city square, a painting, a picture, a poem, an argument, a philosophical system, a movie, a day in your life, an idea of any sort. In a *physical analysis*, you separate an object in space and break it into its components. In a *conceptual analysis*, you divide an idea into other ideas.

Purpose, Audience, Kinds of Discourse

Analysis can be found in almost any kind of writing, and it can be a means of achieving any of the broader aims of discourse: to inform or instruct, to convince or persuade, to entertain or please, and to express strong feelings and emotions. Your intention in analyzing is especially important because it will become the informing principle that shapes your perception of the whole. Unless you keep your intention constantly in view, your analyses will become mere classroom exercises.

To avoid making your analyses sterile exercises, you might ask yourself a number of questions about the purpose of your analysis in relation to your subject, your audience, and the kind of writing best suited to your needs:

1. What *subject* am I going to analyze? A physical object? A political issue? An institution? A current event? An idea? A work of art?
2. What *specific problems* might I encounter in analyzing this particular subject?
3. What is my *purpose* in making the analysis?
4. For what *audience* is the analysis intended? What features of my analysis might I include for one kind of reader but exclude for another?

5. How will my reader use the *results* of my analysis?
6. What is the most appropriate *kind of writing* in which to put my analysis? A scientific essay? A report? A printed brochure? A news story? A magazine article? An advertisement?

Invention and Analysis

What is the thought process like? In the process of analyzing anything, you begin with a general impression of the whole, keeping in mind the response you want to get from your reader. Then you have to abstract some feature or features from the whole to support your general impression, and focus your attention upon them. Next you have to hold these features in your mind as the object of your immediate thought in order to remember them later. After this, you have to attend to other features, noticing the connections among them and their relationship to other parts of the whole. Then, in order to understand the object of your analysis, you have to pull all of these features together, to see them as a whole. Finally, you have to come to some kind of conclusion about your analysis. Your conclusion will depend in part on your purpose and may be a comment on your analysis or a summary of your main points. All of this is a part of what I mean by **invention by analysis.**

If you decide to generalize from your experience and put the results of the process of analysis into the form of questions for subsequent invention, you will get something like the following questions: What are its pieces, parts, or sections? How may they logically be divided? What is the logical order? What is the relationship of the parts to the whole? You can then ask these questions of any new subject that you want to analyze.

Let me illustrate the process by analyzing with you the following familiar poem by E. A. Robinson:

Richard Cory

Whenever Richard Cory went down town,
We people on the pavement looked at him:
He was a gentleman from sole to crown,
Clean favored, and imperially slim.

And he was always quietly arrayed,
And he was always human when he talked;
But still he fluttered pulses when he said,
"Good morning," and he glittered when he walked.

And he was rich—yes, richer than a king—
And admirably schooled in every grace:
In fine, we thought that he was everything
To make us wish that we were in his place.

So on we worked, and waited for the light,
And went without the meat, and cursed the bread,
And Richard Cory, one calm summer night,
Went home and put a bullet through his head.

After several close readings of this poem, you begin to notice that there is an interesting pattern of imagery in the poem relating to royalty and another relating to bearing or upbringing, and you begin to isolate and to examine words and phrases that seem to make up these patterns.

You notice that there are patterns of words related to royalty, and you associate certain meanings with these:

Word	Associated Meanings
Richard Cory	Richard Coeur de Lion
crown	king's crown
imperially	like an emperor
arrayed	dressed like a king
glittered	gold and kingship
grace	an attribute of a good king

Then you notice that there is an overlapping pattern of words related to bearing or upbringing:

Word	Associated Meanings
gentleman	polite, gracious, and considerate
clean favored	complete, free from alterations
quietly arrayed	not showy, impressively orderly
always human	kind and courteous
admirably schooled in every grace	effortless charm and refinement

With additional readings and close analysis, you notice other features of the poem. Each of the first three stanzas is divided between a description of Richard Cory and the reaction of the people to him. The last stanza describes the people's attitude toward life and Richard Cory's denunciation of it.

The specific lines relating to the people's increasing degree of reaction to Cory can be abstracted from the poem and presented in a systematic way as follows:

Stanza 1: We people . . . *looked* at him
Stanza 2: he *fluttered* pulses
Stanza 3: we thought that he was *everything*
Stanza 4: our reaction (implicit in the stanza) when he shot him-
self was to be horrified

You will notice in the process so far that you have followed most of the steps needed to make a competent analysis: a careful reading of the lines, a critical examination of the parts, the separation of the parts from the whole.

Your final step is to try to determine the nature of the whole. You can do this by trying to abstract from the elements and from the poem as a whole what you take to be its theme or main idea. The theme unifies the whole and helps to order the parts.

Several statements of the theme are possible:

You can never judge a person's happiness from the outside.
Things are not always what they seem to be.
All that glitters is not gold.
Appearances are deceiving.

Putting the parts together, you arrive at a conclusion about the *meaning* of the poem, which goes something like this: Richard Cory was a man to whom people looked up. He seemed to have many excellent qualities. He was regal in bearing, well dressed, polite, gracious, and considerate. He had effortless charm and refinement. Less fortunate people, who seemed not to have his attainments and certainly not his money, envied him and cursed their own status in life. Yet evidently something in Cory was lacking. Perhaps he was more superficial than people thought. Perhaps the *glitter* was just that, a kind of surface glamour with no real depth of feeling. There is a hint of this in the phrase "admirably schooled in every grace." The word *schooled* suggests that Cory's gracious and charming manner was not natural. The theme suggested by all these details, then, seems to be that "appearances are deceiving; you cannot always judge people by their external appearance."

Exercises

1. Probe a subject using the questions related to the topic of analysis.
   (What are its pieces, parts, or sections? How may they logically be divided? What is the logical order? What is the relationship of the parts to the whole?)

2. Analyze one of the following general topics in class and list the subdivisions revealed by analysis:

a. a painting

b. a picture

c. a movie

d. a television show

e. a day in your life

f. a sentence

g. the layout of a supermarket

h. a magazine ad

i. an idea

j. a poem

Constructing Analysis Paradigms

As you are analyzing, your ideas will naturally fall into some kind of pattern. But the pattern may not always be well-formed or appropriate to your needs. Therefore, after you have made your analysis, your next step will be to construct a sentence paradigm.

To construct a paradigm using the mode of analysis, keeping in mind your purpose and audience, you begin with a thesis sentence and then you add sentences to the thesis in such a way that *the sentences that make up the paradigm form a relational pattern of analysis:*

Of all the *qualities* that an ideal *mate* should have, the following are the most important.

The first *quality* is affection.

The second *quality* is intelligence.

The third *quality* is integrity.

Good looks and a sense of humor are important, too, but affection, intelligence, and integrity rank high on my list.

Notice that the thesis sentence uses an analysis word (the word *qualities*), so that the reader has no doubt about your intention. (A quality is a *feature* or *aspect* of a subject or an idea.) It also includes the subject to be analyzed *(ideal mate)* and your attitude toward the subject (qualities that an ideal mate *should have, most important* qualities). Each subsequent sentence in the paradigm takes up a specific feature of the ideal mate (affection, intelligence, integrity). The last sentence qualifies the ideas in the preceding sentences and suggests alternatives that your reader might want to consider.

To construct a paradigm using ethical and emotional appeals, you include in the sentences of your paradigm ethical and emotional words and phrases as they relate to your purpose, your subject, and your audience. You can do this as you are constructing your paradigm, or you can go back and put these words in after you have finished. In the example given above, the terms are already there, so that all you need to do is to check each statement to make sure that it adequately fulfills your intention.

The key term in the thesis sentence is the word *qualities*, which suggests excellence or moral superiority. The words *intelligence* and *integrity* in the middle sentences suggest intellectual and moral attributes, and the words *affection* and *sense of humor*, because they signify emotional states as well as virtues, represent both an appeal to the emotions and an ethical appeal.

After you have finished constructing your paradigm, test it in order to obtain a clearer understanding of the kinds of appeals you are using. First, examine each sentence carefully to make sure each one accurately represents your beliefs, your attitude toward your subject and your reader, and your ethical and emotional stance. Second, study each sentence carefully to be certain that your reader can follow your reasoning. Does the thought move from a more general statement to a less general one, from a less general statement to a more general one, or from one statement to another within the same degree of generality? Since analysis (or "division into parts") is the "topical" method used to construct this paradigm, what is the relationship between the whole and the parts in the reasoning process? Third, consider the middle sentences of the paradigm. Are there any terms that need to be defined or explained? What kinds of evidence, facts, opinions, or proofs will you need to include as you are writing your paper to support these sentences? Finally, rewrite any sentence that needs rewriting.

If you are satisfied with your paradigm, your next step is to write your paper, using your paradigm as a guide. As you write your paper, you will need to provide a suitable introduction, appropriate supporting details, and an effective conclusion. As you write, you will continue to discover ideas and connections among ideas, revising as is necessary as you go along. The result will be a dynamic interplay between the discoveries you make before you write and the discoveries you make as you are writing.

The pattern of your overall paper, including the embedded paradigm, in its more abstract form will look like this:

Analysis Pattern 1
Introduction (includes thesis)
Characteristic 1 (plus supporting details)

Characteristic 2 (plus supporting details)
Characteristic 3, 4, 5 . . .
Conclusion (includes clincher sentence)

An alternative pattern may have a slightly different form:

Analysis Pattern 2
Introduction (includes thesis)
Cluster of features (related to one another)
Cluster of features (related to one another)
Cluster of features (related to one another)
Conclusion (includes clincher sentence)

Naturally, the features you include in your paradigm will be determined by your purpose, your subject, and your audience.

The following essay is a good example of a well-organized piece of history writing that uses an analysis paradigm. Its purpose is to inform.

The Frontier Disappears

1

Introduction The United States of today is the product of a variety of forces: its European origins, the continuing impact of ideas from abroad, the constant mingling of peoples, and the changes wrought by the Industrial Revolution. Yet none of these forces was more significant than the frontier in endowing the Americans with the traits that distinguish them from other peoples of the world. Down to the present time many of our basic attitudes toward society and the world around us reflect that pioneer background.

2

Thesis What are the characteristics that are traceable to this unique feature of our inheritance?

3

Characteristic 1 We are a mobile people, constantly on the move, and but lightly bound to home or community. If you were to ask any group of Americans today how many live in the homes where they were born, only a handful would reply in the affirmative. If you asked that same question of a group of Englishmen or Frenchmen or Italians, an opposite answer would be given. Like our frontier ancestors, who shifted about so regularly that mobility became a habit, we are always ready for any change that promises to better our lives.

4

*Character-
istic 2*
We are a wasteful people, unaccustomed to thrift or saving. The frontiersmen established that pattern, for nature's resources were so plentiful that
no one could envisage their exhaustion. Within a few years of the first Virginia settlement, for example, pioneers burned down their houses when
they were ready to move west; thus they were allowed to retrieve nails,
and none gave thought to the priceless hardwoods that went up in smoke.
As a people we still destroy much that others would save. I had this driven
home to me when, during a year's residence in England, I received a letter
from one of the nation's largest banks, enclosed in a second-hand envelope
that had been readdressed to me. Such saving would be unthinkable in the
United States, where even the most insignificant bank would never
address a client save on elaborately engraved stationery, usually with the
names of all twenty-eight vice presidents parading down one side of the
page.

5

*Character-
istic 3*
We are a practical, inventive people on whom the weight of tradition rests
but lightly. In many lands of the world, people confronted with an unpleasant situation will quietly adjust themselves; in the United States, a
man's first impulse is to change things for the better. This willingness to
experiment came naturally to the pioneers, who had no precedents on
which to build. It has remained a trait of the industrial pioneers, whose
ability to adapt and change has laid the basis for America's supremacy as a
manufacturing nation.

6

*Character-
istic 4*
We are individualistic people, deeply resentful of any intrusion into our
affairs by government or society, also a basic attitude among frontiersmen.
Aware that they were living in a land where resources were so abundant
that only their own energies were necessary for success, they wanted to be
left alone above all else. This trait persisted in American thought, even
though the passing of the frontier has forced the government to adopt a
more positive social role. Even today such activity is more resented in the
United States than elsewhere; and this resentment also helps explain the
almost fanatical American hatred of political systems such as fascism or
communism that are based on the subjugation of the individual.

7

*Character-
istic 5*
We are a democratic people. Our pioneering forefathers originated neither
the theory nor the practice of democracy; the western world was well on
its way to political equalitarianism when the continent was settled. But
conditions in frontier communities vastly stimulated the trend. There nature reduced men to equality by dimming the importance of wealth, or
hereditary privilege. There poverty served as a great leveler. There the de-

mand for self-rule was particularly strong, for frontiersmen knew that their problems were unique and must be solved locally. And so on the frontier the democratic tradition was strengthened, until it became a part of the American creed. The undying hatred of the United States for all forms of totalitarianism only mirrors the strength of this faith.

8

Conclu-sion   Thus has the frontier placed its stamp on America and its people. In the continuing rebirth of civilization during the three centuries required to settle the continent, nature modified the characteristics of its conquerors, even in the midst of their conquest. There emerged a new people, robust and strong, with an unwavering faith in the merits of the individual and an unswerving allegiance to the principles of democracy. The frontier is no more, but its heritage remains to give a strength as well as individuality to the civilization of the United States.

—Ray Allen Billington, "The Frontier Disappears"

Although the paradigm on which this essay is based is easy to pick out, I have abstracted it from the essay and reprinted it below to illustrate that when it is appropriate to their purposes, their audiences, and the kind of writing they select to use, even skilled writers will use paradigms to help them develop their ideas:

What are the characteristics that are traceable to this unique feature of our inheritance?
We are a mobile people, constantly on the move, and but lightly bound to home or community.
We are a wasteful people, unaccustomed to thrift or saving.
We are a practical, inventive people on whom the weight of tradition rests but lightly.
We are individualistic people, deeply resentful of any intrusion into our affairs by government or society, also a basic attitude among frontiersmen.
We are a democratic people.
Thus has the frontier placed its stamp on America and its people.

In an analysis essay, in addition to the characteristic paradigm, you come to expect words and phrases like the following:

characteristic	member	trait
feature	component	particular
aspect	constituent	division into parts
part	portion	subdivision

section	fraction	unit
sector	fragment	piece
segment	particle	detail
element	entity	ingredient

whole	analyze
totality	resolve
entirety	separate
collectiveness	dissect
unity	break up
embodiment	constitute
aggregate	compose
sum	embody
bulk	partition
mass	distinguish

These words and phrases provide meaningful clues that will enable your reader to follow the patterning of your ideas with less difficulty.

In your writing, it is more important for you to understand the principles of paradigmatic thinking and the principles of analysis than it is to follow these patterns exactly. At first, if you are having problems organizing your ideas, you might want to follow these patterns closely, until the kind of thinking that they represent becomes habitual. Later on, you will be able to use these patterns with a great deal of flexibility, as the following student paper illustrates:

A Diamond Is Forever

1

Rolling Stone magazine has never been a publication to concern itself with mushy, love-story-type themes. Most often, one finds articles on rock-and-roll music and the hazards of nuclear energy in the magazine. And yet, in the February 22, 1979, issue there is one full page of sentimental mush at its best (or worst). An advertisement for diamonds—specifically, what a diamond ring means to a young couple's budding romance—is nestled between an article on New Wave rock group Devo and a tongue-in-cheek ad suggesting a Valentine's Day gift of a Ted Nugent album. Has the diamond industry made a horrendous mistake? Probably. Not only is their ad laughably romantic and aimed at the wrong audience, but it is also poorly written.

2

A headline over the most prominent part of the diamond advertisement—a picture of a young couple enjoying a quiet moment together in a soda shop—starts the ad off in the wrong direction. It reads: "Our diamond means we now have the best of both worlds. Yours and mine." The phrase "yours and mine" takes up a separate line below the opening sentence and is centered between the tilted heads of the adoring couple in the picture. Now, *Rolling Stone* readers are *not* going to buy the premise of the opening sentence. A couple in love cannot miraculously attain a mixture of the best of their respective worlds simply by slipping a diamond ring onto a finger. What happens to the worst parts of their worlds when the ring goes on? Do his belching and her gum-cracking cease when the nineteen-hundred-dollar stone is purchased? *Rolling Stone* readers will, inevitably, ask these probing questions.

3

Next in line for rebuke is the centerpiece of the ad. The hairstyles and the clothing of the young couple in the picture seem to be right out of the late fifties or early sixties. The soft vignette of a young couple in an ice-cream parlor begs for criticism. A handsome male, not unlike Ryan O'Neal in appearance, leans over his dreamy-eyed, smiling gal to sip on an old-fashioned soda. The whipped topping of the soda appears about ready to topple onto the counter, and the moment is captured as if it were a candid snapshot. Sharing a soda with Sally went out with the Beach Boys. Injecting nostalgia into the ad is not going to sell diamond rings to readers of *Rolling Stone.*

4

The narrative form in which the ad is written continues below the ice-cream-parlor picture. The copy is written in the first person. The young woman, one would assume, does the narrating. "I still remember the day," she says, "you made this near-sighted musician see how exciting a game of football could be." She then goes on to reminisce about the time her boyfriend "sat through a concert without falling asleep." These recollections of times past are set apart in separate sentences so that the reader forms mental images of the events. Each mental image seems to pop into the frame occupied by the soda-fountain scene, so that the effect is like that of leafing through a photo album with the mind. This is a clever bit of psychology on the part of the advertisers, but it doesn't work for this audience. The reader that the diamond industry is reaching in *Rolling Stone* magazine is not one that is especially enthralled with football games and sitting through concerts. The type of concert implied in the ad is a classical concert. Just sitting through anything other than a rock concert would be almost unthinkable to most *Rolling Stone* readers.

5

A final point about the ad concerns the wording of the sentence "Being in love means we want to know what each other's all about." The wording here is awkward, if not grammatically incorrect. The phrase "each other's all about" in the sentence seems to be a shortening (decapitation might be a better word) of "each other's worlds are all about," but the omission of the two words leads the sentence, headed for sentimentality, into a brick wall of laughter and confusion. Because the reader must read the sentence again, this merely adds emphasis to the absurdity of the line.

6

The diamond industry would do better to include this kind of advertisement in a magazine whose readers are less apt to criticize and belittle established values. The ice-cream-parlor sweetness of this ad is laughable in almost any context, but buried within the pages of *Glamour* or *Seventeen* magazine, the absurdity would be less obvious.

—Ben

This is a well-written student essay. The student's purpose is to show how the magazine ad "A Diamond Is Forever" fails in relation to its intended audience. The features of the analysis are used as evidence to support his thesis. But these features are not presented without comment. The student writer sifts through the facts of the ad as he goes along, explaining and evaluating them and reaching conclusions about them.

In the professional essay entitled "The Frontier Disappears," the writer chooses to abstract the features of his analysis and present each one in a separate paragraph. In each paragraph, he expands on the particular characteristic by qualifying it, amplifying it, or commenting on it in some way.

In the student essay, the student writer, rather than devoting each supporting paragraph to a single characteristic of the ad, uses a cluster analysis as a way of presenting his ideas. In the first paragraph, he identifies his subject, provides the context for the reader's understanding of his discussion, and then states his thesis: "Not only is their ad laughably romantic and aimed at the wrong audience, but it is also poorly written." Then, in subsequent paragraphs, to support his thesis, he presents the results of his analysis in a cluster of features.

To achieve coherence, he organizes each cluster around a central idea. In paragraph 2, for example, he analyzes the headline and comments on its inadequacies. In paragraph 3, he criticizes the illustration.

In paragraph 4, he discusses the narrative form of the copy. In the next paragraph, he isolates a particular phrase and comments on it. Finally, he concludes with a comment about "the ice-cream-parlor sweetness" of the ad and its inappropriateness in a magazine such as *Rolling Stone.* His concluding paragraph actually is a restatement of his thesis, a kind of return to the beginning. This is a suitable ending for his essay because he has been evaluating aspects of the ad in the supporting paragraphs.

These two essays are excellent examples of how the mode of analysis can be used in different kinds of writing, for different aims. The professional essay is an example of historical exposition. The student paper is a good example of a critical essay, whose purpose is to inform or persuade.

Here is one last example, an example of scientific writing, which uses the mode of analysis to inform or instruct:

The Anatomy of a Mollusk

Mollusks have a solid, unsegmented body which can be divided into four main parts unless greatly modified.

First is the head, bearing tentacles, eyes, and other sense organs. The mouth opens close to the anterior end and is often armed with teeth. The brain, or cerebral ganglia, is internal and is highly developed in the cephalopods.

The visceral sac is the next distinct part and it houses the gut, heart, and reproductive organs.

The foot is a muscular structure used for locomotion and burrowing and is developed into tentacles in the cephalopods.

The mantle is the fourth region of the body and is a fold of skin which develops from the posterior part and folds over, enveloping the visceral mass and separating it from the shell, thus forming a cavity between the shell and the rest of the body. The anus and excretory ducts open into the mantle cavity inside which the gills develop. The shell is secreted by the edge of the mantle and consists of an outer horny layer, with an internal pearly or nacreous layer of calcium carbonate.

—Sali Money, *The Animal Kingdom*

This is a good example of scientific analysis. The opening paragraph identifies the subject ("mollusks") and sets up the division into "four main parts" ("head," "visceral sac," "foot," and "mantle"), then goes immediately into the analysis. The subsequent paragraphs each take up one of the divisions and extend the analysis initiated in the opening paragraph. The diction is Latinate and scientific ("anterior," "cerebral ganglia," "cephalopods," "visceral sac," "posterior," "nacreous," and "calcium carbonate") with some use of metaphorical language ("armed with teeth," "houses the gut, heart . . ."). Compared to the language of the student's critical essay which combines facts with evaluation, the language of this piece of writing is fairly objective.

Enumeration

Enumeration may be considered to be *a kind of informal analysis*, a subdivision of the topic of analysis. As a topic of invention, it answers such questions as: What is the exact number? What is the logical order? How is it constituted? Like analysis, enumeration considers aspects or features of things as separate units. The mental process of enumeration is concerned with *the sequential arrangement of successive things:* a group of objects, events, or ideas, generally following each other in the order of time in which they occurred. Number can be thought of as a kind of abstract order, but when it is tied to time, it is related to narration, process, and cause and effect.

As a pattern of arrangement, enumeration presents ideas in numerical order so that there is a distinct separation of the elements of a group. Each part of the series reveals a definite pattern of advance over the preceding part. The numerical order reveals a recurrent causal or logical pattern. However, sometimes you may want to use an enumeration pattern in an essay to hold together parts of a subject that do not ordinarily lend themselves to a logical form of organization. For example, if you are asked to give a speech, and you cannot think of a more logical way to present your ideas, at the very least you can announce to your audience that you are going to talk about three things or five things or some determinate number. This numbering will not only aid you in recalling the parts of your speech, but it will also give your audience a logical pattern to follow. There are times when you have some "things to say" about a subject, but the best you can do is to put them into some reasonable order. You could probably say more about the subject, but you limit yourself to a representative number, and this order at least serves your purpose.

Since enumeration is such a basic principle, it will often be found reinforcing other patterns such as partition, classification, process, and cause and effect. Whether you use it as a basic organizational pattern or in combination with other patterns, you will want to make clear to the reader your purpose and the basis of the enumeration.

Usually your thesis will indicate your purpose and your plan of development.

Because we will be looking at a number of essays that use enumeration as a major or subordinate pattern of development, I will not present any special examples of the type at this time. But it is quite obvious that the paradigm will contain number words like *first*, *second*, and *next*, as the following scheme illustrates:

Enumeration Pattern

Introduction (includes thesis)
First (the first, one) . . .
Second (the second, two) . . .
Third (the third, three) . . .
Fourth (the next, four) . . .
Fifth, sixth, seventh (another, five) . . .
Finally (the final, six) . . .
Conclusion (summary, return to beginning)

Enumeration themes, like analysis themes, have a characteristic vocabulary. The following are a few representative words and phrases that can be found in enumeration themes:

number	string	list	to count
order	chain	item	to catalog
series	set	catalog	to number
succession	sequel	tally	to enumerate
progression	sequence	analysis	to itemize

Enumeration is probably the simplest kind of organizational pattern. Its simplicity, however, should not deceive you about its relative importance. In chemistry, in physics, in mathematics, number is of fundamental importance. In your everyday activities, numbering is so basic that you may sometimes forget its importance. You compute your grocery bills, number the pages of your letters, call the roll, catalog, count, list, tally, add, score, calculate, and itemize. Like time and space, number is an important principle in the universe.

Exercises

1. For classroom discussion, analyze the paradigm on page 71. Do you agree that *affection, intelligence,* and *integrity* are the most important qualities of an ideal mate? If not, what would you substitute? How does the dictionary define these words? What kinds of facts, proofs, or opin-

ions would you use to support the middle sentences of the paradigm? Invent a writing situation and an audience for a paper based on this paradigm. Then write the paper, taking into account your purpose, audience, and writing situation.

2. Analyze one of the following subjects. Consider your purpose in doing so, a possible reader, and a writing situation. Then construct a paradigm based on the results of your analysis. If you think it appropriate for your purpose and your audience, include ethical and emotional appeals. Bring the paradigm to class for constructive criticism and discussion. After this, rewrite the paradigm if necessary, and write a paper using it as a guide.

a. pop music	f. a photograph
b. a rock lyric	g. a reproduction of a painting
c. a short poem	h. a life-style
d. a magazine ad	i. a fad or fashion
e. an editorial	j. a social or political issue

3. Bring to class copies of a magazine ad. Then analyze the illustration, the headline, and the written copy in the ad. Discuss these in relation to the ad's intended purpose and audience. Is the ad effective in achieving its purpose? What kinds of appeals does the ad use?

4. Analyze in class a movie or TV show the class has recently seen. If you were to write a review based on this show, where might you publish it? For what purpose? Audience?

5. You are called upon to give a talk about the values college students hold. Your audience is a group of senior citizens. (You can substitute another audience if you wish.) Consider your purpose in giving such a speech. Then write a speech in which you analyze these values and come to some kind of conclusion about them. (You can also use this topic for classroom discussion.)

6. Write a scientific or technical analysis of one of the following subjects or of a subject that interests you. Construct a paradigm based on your analysis, keeping in mind your subject, purpose, and audience.

a. the frame of a bicycle   f. a tool

b. a plant   g. a garden implement

c. a pocketknife   h. a design of some sort

d. a floor plan   i. an animal

e. a sea shell   j. a utensil

7. Select a newspaper article, a magazine article, or a short essay from your reader that deals with current issues or problems. Then do an analysis of the issues:

   a. Find out where the article first appeared.

   b. Identify the intended audience.

   c. Identify the writer's purpose in writing the article.

   d. Identify the issues with which the writer is concerned. Are they issues of fact, of opinion, of value, of policy, or some combination of these?

   e. Analyze the appeals: logical, ethical, emotional.

   f. Pick out all of the important general statements.

   g. Consider the supporting evidence for the general statements: examples, facts, opinions, statistics, details, descriptions.

   h. Identify the qualifying words: *all, many, most, some, several, a few, always, sometimes, usually, never, seldom, occasionally.*

   i. Look closely at the connections among ideas. Is the writer adding something new, exemplifying, qualifying, comparing, contrasting, defining, or evaluating?

   j. Identify the writer's conclusions.

Description

Description is a mental process, a way of perceiving objects in space and time. It is also a mode of analysis. Like analysis, it is a process of dividing anything complex into simple elements. Like analysis, it deals with its subject as a whole and in its parts. And like analysis, it is more than an enumeration of the parts or qualities of an object. Unlike analysis, however, it deals with its subject concretely. It relies heavily on sense impressions. Often, it depends for its effects on comparison and association. These are not absolute, but relative distinctions, of course. As it pertains to composition, **description** is *a way of picturing images verbally in speech or writing and of arranging those images in some kind of logical or associational pattern.*

Embedded in the word *description* are two words: *scribere,* meaning "to write," and *de,* meaning "down" or "about." There is a hint in the etymology of the word *description* that something is being traced or drawn, that in describing you will follow the outline of an object visually and then write it down or "draw" it in words. The word *draw* is not an accidental association. Many writers have likened the process of describing to that of painting.

Purpose, Audience, Kinds of Discourse

Description can be found in almost any kind of writing, but it is frequently found in books of travel, history books, guidebooks, geography books, scientific articles, magazine ads, brochures for art galleries, books on architecture, magazine articles, descriptive poems, character sketches, novels, and short stories. Although it may be found in almost pure form, as in some magazine advertisements, description is usually mixed with the other modes.

Perhaps your most important consideration before writing in describing a person, an object, or a scene is purpose, for your purpose will determine the nature of your description. For example, informative description will enable your reader accurately to identify the object you are describing. Persuasive description will enable you to appeal to the senses of your reader in such a way as to induce action. Evocative description will enable your reader to experience a mood or an emotion.

But to say that someone is describing something is immediately to give rise to the question To whom? The very act of describing implies an audience. Purpose and audience operate in the same fashion for description as they do for analysis.

Invention and Description

In getting ideas for writing a description, you might proceed exactly as a painter would. That is, whether you are looking at a landscape, a person, or an arrangement of fruit, you would ask yourself certain questions that would make the process of invention easier. What does the object or objects look like, or feel like, or smell like? How would you group them logically or artistically? Would you follow the natural lines of the object or scene to be described? Is the object linear, angular, or circular? In describing an object or a scene, would you begin from left to right, from right to left, from bottom to top, or from top to bottom? Is the object or scene near or far away? If far away, would you depict it in the same way as if it were near? What is your point of view? What is the dominant impression of the object or scene? Does the scene evoke a mood or stir your feelings? How best can you convey sense impressions? Notice how easily questions like these come to mind when you are dealing with a particular pattern of thought. In answering these questions, you are inventing.

But you are a painter using words, not pigments. Instead of putting down your impressions on canvas, you will be putting them down on paper. But your task is very similar to that of the painter: to put into some kind of formal pattern the results of your mental perceptions. Like the painter, you will be concerned with form, position, color, light, sound, taste, touch, odor. Like the painter, you will be dealing with the particular and the concrete, with individuals of a class, not with generalized classes. You are not just interested in dogs, but in hounds, pups, whelps, curs, mutts, Saint Bernards, German shepherds, and collies. You are not just interested in birds, but in larks, starlings, robins, sparrows, canaries, finches, nightingales, and mockingbirds.

In the process of writing, you must select particular details and group them. At that time, other questions come to mind. Do you stress contours or outlines, definite lines, colors, or shapes? Do you stress masses and volumes of things? Do you see planes or successions of planes parallel to the picture plane? Do the forms recede—in and out, forward and backward? Are the forms confined in closed space, or are the representations of space infinite? Is there unity, balance, rhythm? Is the order intellectually formal or biomorphic, that is, developing in a natural way? Are the forms fantastic, never seen or imagined before, or perhaps seen only in dreams, myths, hallucinations?

At the moment, I am simply putting into words many of the things you do intuitively. Your mind is constantly questioning, inventing, and probing, but I want you to make the process of invention and arrangement more self-conscious.

Exercises

1. Using questions such as those suggested (What is it? What are its constituent parts? How are the parts organized in space? What shape does the thing to be described have? What is its color, taste, feel, smell,

sound?), examine a subject as a landscape, a painting, a piece of fruit, or a person's face, for a possible writing assignment.

2. Study a natural landscape, a cluster of buildings, a city scene, or a marketplace. Observe the choice of details, the arrangement of space, the landscaping.

3. Study some paintings, reproductions, or artistic photographs of a landscape, a still life, or a person. What is the central feature of the picture? How are the objects or figures grouped? What choices of details has the painter or photographer made? What kind of balance is there in the picture? What is the dominant impression? The point of view?

4. Compare a cubist painting with a realistic painting. What is the difference in the handling of details, arrangement, point of view, and climax?

Constructing Description Paradigms

Because description is a mode of analysis, to construct a paradigm using the mode of description and keeping in mind your purpose and your intended reader, you follow the same steps you followed in constructing an analysis paradigm. You begin with a thesis sentence, and then you *add sentences* to the thesis in such a way as to *form a relational pattern of description*. If your subject lends itself to ethical and emotional appeals, as you are constructing the sentences of your paradigm, you include ethical and emotional words and phrases:

Visit *Idaho* because it has so many beautiful natural *features*.

It has *mountains* as majestic as the Alps.

It has sapphire *lakes* framed by green velvet mountains.

It has *canyons* deeper than the Grand Canyon.

Come discover the *unspoiled natural* beauty of Idaho.

Like the thesis sentence in the analysis paradigm, the thesis in this paradigm uses an analysis word *(features)*. It also includes the subject to be analyzed *(Idaho)*. Each subsequent sentence takes up a specific feature of Idaho *(mountains, lakes, canyons)*. Then each of these features is divided into particular aspects of color *(sapphire, green velvet)* and size *(deeper)*. There is also an appeal to the aesthetic emotions *(beautiful, majestic)* and to the moral sensibilities *(un-*

spoiled, natural). Even the words that appear to be purely descriptive, such as *sapphire, green velvet,* and *deeper,* support the ethical and emotional appeals.

After you have constructed your description paradigm, analyze it as you did the analysis paradigm. Examine your thesis to make sure it is one your readers will accept. Then carefully inspect the other sentences to be certain that they accurately represent your beliefs, your attitude toward your subject, and your ethical and emotional stance. Next, check the reasoning process, including the topical relationship that exists between the whole and the parts. After you do this, consider the kinds of evidence, facts, details, opinions, or proofs you will need to support your thesis and the middle sentences of your paradigm. Finally, revise the sentences of your paradigm if you think it necessary.

As you did in writing an analysis paper, to write a paper using a description paradigm you provide a suitable introduction, appropriate supporting details, and an effective conclusion, using your paradigm as a guide. As you write, you will continue to think about the development of your ideas and to revise whenever you think it necessary. In its more abstract form, the pattern of your overall paper will look very much like that of your analysis paper:

Description Pattern 1
Introduction (includes thesis)
Descriptive feature 1 (plus supporting details)
Descriptive feature 2 (plus supporting details)
Descriptive feature, 3, 4, 5 . . .
Conclusion (includes clincher sentence)

An alternative pattern will look somewhat like the alternative pattern based on the analysis paradigm:

Description Pattern 2
Introduction (includes thesis)
Cluster of descriptive details
Cluster of descriptive details
Cluster of descriptive details
Conclusion (includes clincher sentence)

Despite the similarity of description to analysis as a mode of developing ideas, description, unlike analysis, is seldom used as the sole method in a piece of writing. It is often mixed with other modes. Consequently, you may not always feel it necessary to follow a strict pattern in writing a paper based on the mode of description. There may be, however, other aspects of description that you will want to use in your writing.

Point of View and Order of Details

When you set out to describe a person, an object, or a scene, you have to decide at the outset your point of view, the choice of appropriate details, and the way you are going to arrange the details.

In description, **point of view** usually refers to *physical location*. But it may also refer to the *mental angle* from which you consider your subject. Occasionally, in describing, you may be able to *sense* your physical position in relation to the object. But it is usually better to determine your point of view in advance of your writing. In this way, your description will be more unified.

When moviemakers want to get several different views of a particular scene, they will move the camera from place to place. If they want to get a more general view of an object or scene, they will move the camera further away. If they want a more detailed view, they will move in close. Similarly, in describing, you may find it necessary to move from one point to another or from one scene to another.

Sometimes your point of view will determine your choice of details and the order of their arrangement. Sometimes the natural contours of the objects themselves will suggest a way of proceeding. But often you will have to impose some sort of order on your materials. The following selections illustrate a variety of patterns that you could follow:

Spatial Order: Depth

St. Mark's

And well may they fall back, for beyond those troops of ordered arches there rises a vision out of the earth, and all the great square seems to have opened from it in a kind of awe, that we may see it far away—a multitude of pillars and white domes, clustered into a long low pyramid of coloured light; a treasure-heap, it seems, partly of gold and partly of opal and mother-of-pearl, hollowed beneath into five great vaulted porches, ceiled with fair mosaic, and beset with sculpture of alabaster, clear as amber and delicate as ivory—sculpture fantastic and involved, of palm leaves and lilies, and grapes and pomegranates, and birds clinging and fluttering among the branches, all twined together into an endless network of buds and plumes; and, in the midst of it, the solemn forms of angels, sceptred, and robed to the feet, and leaning to each other across the gates, their figures indistinct among the gleaming of the golden ground through the leaves beside them, interrupted and dim, like the morning light as it faded back among the branches of Eden, when first its gates were angel-guarded long ago.

—John Ruskin, *The Stones of Venice*

Radiating Order: Moving Observer

A Tropical Landscape

On my right hand there were lines of fishing-stakes resembling a mysterious system of half-submerged bamboo fences, incomprehensible in its division of the domain of tropical fishes, and crazy of aspect as if abandoned forever by some nomad tribe of fishermen now gone to the other end of the ocean; for there was no sign of human habitation as far as the eye could reach. To the left a group of barren islets, suggesting ruins of stone walls, towers, and blockhouses, had its foundations set in a blue sea that itself looked solid, so still and stable did it lie below my feet; even the track of light from the westering sun shone smoothly, without that animated glitter which tells of an imperceptible ripple. And when I turned my head to take a parting glance at the tug which had just left us anchored outside the bar, I saw the straight line of the flat shore joined to the stable sea, edge to edge, with a perfect and unmarked closeness, in one leveled floor half-brown, half-blue under the enormous dome of the sky. Corresponding in their insignificance to the islets of the sea, two small clumps of trees, one on each side of the only fault in the impeccable joint, marked the mouth of the river Meinam we had just left on the preparatory stage of our homeward journey; and, far back on the inland level, a larger and loftier mass, the grove surrounding the great Paknam pagoda, was the only thing on which the eye could rest from the vain task of exploring the monotonous sweep of the horizon. Here and there gleams as of a few scattered pieces of silver marked the windings of the great river; and on the nearest of them, just within the bar, the tug steaming right into the land became lost to my sight, hull and funnel and masts, as though the impassive earth had swallowed her up without an effort, without a tremor. My eye followed the light cloud of her smoke, now here, now there, above the plain, according to the devious curves of the stream, but always fainter and farther away, till I lost it at last behind the miter-shaped hill of the great pagoda. And then I was left alone with my ship, anchored at the head of the Gulf of Siam.

—Joseph Conrad, *The Secret Sharer*

Dominant Image: Repetition

Fog

Fog everywhere. Fog up the river, where it flows among green aits and meadows; fog down the river, where it rolls defiled among the tiers of shipping, and the waterside pollutions of a great (and dirty) city. Fog on the Essex marshes, fog on the Kentish heights. Fog creeping into the cabooses of collier-brigs; fog lying out on the yards, and hovering in the rigging of great ships; fog drooping on the gunwales of barges and small boats. Fog in the eyes and throats of ancient Greenwich pensioners, wheezing by the firesides of their wards; fog in the stem and bowl of the afternoon pipe of the wrathful skipper, down in his close cabin; fog cruelly pinching the toes and fingers of his shivering little 'prentice boy on deck. Chance people on the bridges peeping over the parapets into a nether sky of fog, with fog all round them, as if they were up in a balloon, and hanging in the misty clouds.

—Charles Dickens, *Bleak House*

Order of Memory: Fantasy

Night Town

The Mabbot street entrance of nighttown, before which stretches an un-cobbled tramsiding set with skeleton tracks, red and green will-o'-the-wisps and danger signals. Rows of flimsy houses with gaping doors. Rare lamps with faint rainbow-fans. Round Rabaiotti's halted ice gondola stunted men and women squabble. They grab wafers which are wedged lumps of coal and copper snow. Sucking, they scatter slowly. Children. The swancomb of the gondola, highreared, forges on through the murk, white and blue under a lighthouse. Whistles call and answer.

—James Joyce, *Ulysses*

Order of Observation: Impressions

The Garden

I sat down in the middle of the garden, where snakes could scarcely approach unseen, and leaned my back against a warm yellow pumpkin. There were some ground-cherry bushes growing along the furrows, full of fruit. I turned back the papery sheaths that protected the berries and ate a few. All about me giant grasshoppers, twice as big as any I had ever seen, were doing acrobatic feats among the dried ground. There in the sheltered draw-bottom the wind did not blow very hard, but I could hear it singing its humming tune up on the level, and I could see the tall grasses wave. The earth was warm under me, and warm as I crumbled it through my fingers. Queer little red bugs came out and moved in slow squadrons around me. Their backs were polished vermilion, with black spots. I kept as still as I could. Nothing happened. I did not expect anything to happen. I was something that lay under the sun and felt it, like the pumpkins, and I did not want to be anything more. I was entirely happy. Perhaps we feel like that when we die and become part of something entire, whether it is sun and air, or goodness and knowledge. At any rate, this is happiness: to be dissolved into something complete and great. When it comes to one, it comes as naturally as sleep.

—Willa Cather, *My Antonia*

The first selection, by John Ruskin, displays an artistic grouping of details in space. The total effect is that of depth perception. In the Conrad selection, the observer first faces the sea and then turns completely around to face the shore. The effect is that of lines radiating from the observer to different parts of the picture. The Dickens selection uses a dominant image, the fog, as a way of organizing the description. The repetition of the word *fog* unifies the description and produces a dominant tone of dreariness. Quite obviously, not all descriptions are organized in space and time. The selection from *Ulysses* by James Joyce uses the order of memory, which is free from the confinements of space and time. It avoids logic. Memory, of course, is the voluntary calling to mind of past events. But this selection is further complicated by the fact that the mode of writing is a fantasy. The images therefore are bizarre, fanciful, hallucinatory, grotesque, whimsical, and unreal. In the absence of the objects of perception, the mind invents illusory images. Finally, the selection by Willa Cather uses no special order except that of reporting to the reader the random impressions received in the way in which they strike the observer.

The foregoing selections are specific examples of description, in all their concreteness.

The paradigmatic structure of spatial orders of description, however, may be illustrated as follows:

Paradigm 1: Vertical Order (bottom to top, top to bottom)
Paradigm 2: Horizontal Order (left to right, right to left)
Paradigm 3: Depth Order (inside, outside)
Paradigm 4: Circular Order (clockwise, counterclockwise)

A good example of horizontal order is this masterful description by James Joyce:

A fat brown goose lay at one end of the table and at the other end, on a bed of creased paper strewn with sprigs of parsley, lay a great ham, stripped of its outer skin and peppered over with crust crumbs, a neat paper frill round its shin and beside this was a round of spiced beef. Between these rival ends ran parallel lines of side-dishes: two little minsters of jelly, red and yellow, a shallow dish full of blocks of blancmange and red jam, a large green leaf-shaped dish with a stalk-shaped handle, on which lay bunches of purple raisins and peeled almonds, a companion dish on which lay a solid rectangle of Smyrna figs, a dish of custard topped with grated nutmeg, a small bowl of chocolates and sweets wrapped in gold and silver papers and a glass vase in which stood some tall celery stalks. In the centre of the table there stood, as sentries to a fruit-stand which upheld a pyramid of oranges and American apples, two squat old-fashioned decanters of cut glass, one containing port and the other dark sherry.

—James Joyce, "The Dead"

Joyce uses a frame device to organize the details of this description. The opening sentence presents an image of both ends of the table, with the goose at one end and the ham at the other. The rest of the description is organized from these points in space. Sentence 2 shows the progression of objects from the ends of the table to the center. Sentence 3 focuses on the objects in the middle of the table, laden with food. The reader can visualize the scene very vividly and grasp the relationships of the objects on the table to one another. Not only is there a spatial movement from the ends to the center, but there is also a movement from meat to drink.

Within this larger pattern, there are smaller patterns that help to make up the whole. The sentences are loose or cumulative sentences. (The main idea is stated first, followed by subordinate ideas.) Each sentence furthers the spatial description while at the same time giving the reader a catalog of the food in all its concreteness. Joyce puts the burden of the spatial patterning on the prepositional phrases:

at one end of the table
at the other end of the table
on a bed of creased paper
round its shin
beside this
between rival ends
on which lay bunches of purple raisins
on which lay a solid rectangle of Smyrna figs
in which stood some tall celery stalks
in the centre of the table

These phrases are phrases of location and direction.

The verb choices are primarily static verbs, the verb "to be" and verbs of rest *(lay, stood, was)*. These reinforce the spatial pattern and contribute to the effect the reader gets that he or she is looking at a static picture, a still life. The point of view is that of an observer who is close to the scene he is describing.

The word choice is specific and concrete. Joyce appeals to almost all the senses. He uses words and phrases pertaining to shape and size, color, texture, and taste:

Shape and Size

great	solid	blocks
little	round	leaf-shaped
full	shallow	stalk-shaped
large	fat	rectangle
small	bunches	pyramid
tall	squat	parallel

Color

brown	purple	peppered
red	gold	dark sherry
yellow	silver	chocolates
green	oranges	

Texture

creased	frill	glass
sprigs	peeled	cut
stripped	grated	
peppered over	crust	

Taste
Fat brown goose
peppered over with crust crumbs
a round of *spiced* beef
grated nutmeg
chocolates and *sweets*

Joyce also uses a number of figures of speech to lend concreteness to the description:

Figures of Speech
a large green *leaf-shaped* dish
a *stalk-shaped* handle

blocks of blancmange and red jam
a solid *rectangle* of Smyrna figs
two decanters of cut glass . . . as *sentries* to a fruit-stand
a *pyramid* of oranges and American apples

Principles of Description

In this very small compass, Joyce manages to touch upon almost all the aspects of description:

  I. Methods of development
      A. Spatial (linear—left to right, right to left, bottom to top, top to bottom, clockwise, counterclockwise, and so forth)
      B. Repetition (same image repeated)
      C. Cataloging (accumulation of details and images)
 II. Point of view
      A. Near or far
      B. Above or below
      C. Direct line
      D. Oblique
      E. Inside or outside
III. Imagery
      A. Literal
      B. Figurative
 IV. Sense Appeal
      A. Sight
          1. color (red, orange, lilac)
          2. form (spiral, star-shaped, tubular)
      B. Touch
          1. thermal (hot, cold, sunny)
          2. simple (soft, hard, featherlike)
          3. pressure (squeeze, whizz)
      C. Taste
          1. sweet
          2. salty
          3. sour
          4. bitter
          5. corrosive
          6. rough
          7. smooth
          8. soft

9. crisp
10. cool and warm
D. Sound
    1. high (shrill, piercing, screech)
    2. low (moan, groan)
E. Smell
    1. pungent (sharp, stinging, caustic)
    2. tart (sharp)
    3. sour (acid)

    4. rancid (rank)
    5. camphoraceous
    6. musky
    7. floral
    8. peppermintlike

Most of you will have little trouble with visual images. But you will find, as this list shows, that there are few terms to describe touch or taste or sound or smell. So you may have to have recourse to comparisons, to figures of speech.

On the surface, it would appear that there is nothing easier to do than to describe. But to describe is to do more than simply follow the natural contours of an object in space. It is also to be discriminating in selecting details and in grouping objects.

Imitation

One good way to learn to describe is to imitate. The following student paper is based on the Joyce model:

A Thanksgiving Table

A fat brown turkey lay at one end of the table and at the other end, on a silver platter covered with waxen paper, strewn with sprigs of parsley and bits of onions, lay a great duck, stripped of its feathers and outer skin and drenched in pools of cranberry sauce, encircled by thick clusters of dressing and beside this was a platter of spiced rolls. Between these rival ends were concave lines of side-dishes: two tiny cuplets of jelly, purple and red, a large silver bowl filled with billowy mounds of white potatoes, a small pear-shaped dish with a stem-shaped handle on which lay clusters of pitted grapes and crushed walnuts, a companion dish on which lay a quivering rectangle of fruit-laden salad, a dish of chocolate pudding dotted with whipped cream, a small bowl full of almonds and peanuts and a glass vase in which stood freshly cut stalks of garden onions and green celery. In the center of the table there stood, like majestic pillars, two graceful, ornate containers of spun glass, one containing pink wine and the other bubbly champagne, flanking a fruit bowl, upholding a pyramid of oranges and apples, mixed with freshly picked cherries and grapes.

—Jim

If you feel too constrained doing a strict imitation, you might try a loose one like the following:

A Wedding Table

In the center of the long lace-covered table towered a white cake, six layers high and decorated with delicate, sugary, pink roses set against light green leaves. Silver dishes containing creamy mints molded into roses and tinted in pink and green lay to the right of the cake. On the other side of the mints were two deep silver bowls filled with a mixture of salted nuts. To the left of the wedding cake were the forks, their prongs gleaming, arranged in three perfectly even rows. Beside the forks were the napkins, snowy white with fine silver engraving, placed in a diamondlike pattern on the tablecloth. Steaming urns of black coffee stood at one end of the table together with glass cups, delicately etched in silvery swirls. A small pitcher of cream, thick and golden, and a bowl of sugar that was perfectly molded into cubes were close by. At the opposite end of the table sat a large cut-glass punch bowl containing a sweet ruby-red juice and bulky chunks of glittering ice. The tall and slender candles, flaming on each side of the cake, created a soft glow over the entire table.

—Donna

Exercises

1. Analyze the paradigm on page 86. This paradigm would be appropriate in a magazine ad. In what kinds of magazines might such an ad appear? For what kinds of readers? What would be the purpose of such an ad? What kinds of supporting details would you use in order to write a paper based on this ad?

2. Assume that you have been asked to write the copy for a magazine ad that describes a place (city, town, country, scenic view, etc.) that you know well. After considering your purpose, subject, and audience, construct a paradigm based on the mode of analysis. Then write a paper, using your paradigm as a guide.

3. Using the still-life method, describe a holiday table laden with food, a bowl of fruit, a floral arrangement, or some other grouping. Use specific, concrete details and figures of speech.

4. Using one of the four spatial patterns outlined in this chapter, describe one of the following:

   a. a seascape   f. a graveyard

   b. a desert scene   g. an antique shop

   c. a mountain view   h. a junkyard

   d. a spring morning   i. a supermarket

   e. a street in the winter   j. a garden

5. Describe a painting or an artistic photograph and evaluate it. For what purpose might you create such a description? For what kinds of readers?

Scientific Description

Description is sometimes divided into two kinds: scientific description and literary or artistic description.

Scientific description is sometimes called *technical* or *objective description*. Objective description attempts to represent the object as accurately as possible. It adheres strictly to a part-by-part analysis, exact measurement, and enumeration of details. It is factual, detached, and impersonal, uninfluenced by emotion or personal involvement. It is usually written in the third person singular, with the agent of the action omitted. There is seldom any hint that a person is involved in describing. The focus is on the subject standing apart, known in and of itself.

The following is a good example of scientific description:

The Emerald Tree Boa

The Emerald Tree Boa *(Boa canina)* is found in tropical South America. As its name suggests, it is arboreal and it has an extremely prehensile tail. It feeds mainly on birds and squirrels and also on iguana lizards. It possesses front teeth that are highly developed, probably proportionately larger than those of any other nonvenomous snake. Tree boas grow to about six feet.

When adult, emerald tree boas are a bright emerald green with creamy or white spots. These boas rest in a characteristically coiled position on the top of branches, with the front of the body above and inside the outer rings, looking a little like a bunch of green bananas. The color, posture, and the light spots break up the outline of the snake's body, leaving them almost impossible to detect at rest in the trees. Although the adults are this uniform and striking color, the young specimens are more variable and differ from their parents. They are yellowish, or even pink, with white markings edged with dark purple or green. As they become mature, the markings change to the adult pattern. In captivity, emerald tree boas are usually quiet and can be handled without attempting to bite.

—John Stidworthy, *Snakes of the World*

This selection has most of the characteristics of a good scientific description: specific details, comparisons, and precise diction. The writer combines a description of the behavior of the boas ("It feeds mainly on birds and squirrels and also on iguana lizards," "In captivity, emerald tree boas are usually quiet . . .") with a concrete and specific description of its physical dimensions and characteristics. He describes the size of their teeth ("proportionately larger than those of any other nonvenomous snake"), by means of a literal comparison, and the size of their bodies ("about six feet"). He then describes the color, posture, and markings of the adults of the species ("a bright emerald green with creamy or white spots," "characteristically coiled position") and of the young specimens ("yellowish, or even pink, with white markings edged with dark purple or green"). In addition to color nouns and adjectives to describe the boas, the writer uses a metaphorical comparison ("looking a little like a bunch of green bananas") and a literal comparison (they are "more variable and differ from their parents"). Besides precise diction dealing with size, color, posture, and markings, the writer also uses formal and scientific diction for descriptive purposes ("arboreal," "prehensile tail," "*Boa canina*," "specimens"), yet the total description is not difficult to understand, written as it is for the general reader.

Literary Description

Literary description is *artistic description*. It is sometimes called **subjective** or **impressionistic description**. The *writer's aim* in this kind of description is not to give accurate, factual information, but to *create a* *mood, a feeling, or an impression by the use of imaginative language.* What is described is colored by the writer's subjective reactions to the object perceived. The style of literary description is characterized by colorful, suggestive, and vivid language and the artistic grouping of details. The selection from James Joyce's "The Dead" is a good example of literary description. Literary description is not confined to imaginative literature, however. Artistic description can be found in magazine ads where the aim is persuasion, in personal letters, in informal essays, and the like.

This selection from *The Red Badge of Courage,* by Stephen Crane, is an excellent example of literary description:

> The column that had butted stoutly at the obstacles in the roadway was barely out of the youth's sight before he saw dark waves of men come sweeping out of the woods and down through the fields. He knew at once that the steel fibers had been washed from their hearts. They were bursting from their coats and their equipments as from entanglements. They charged down upon him like terrified buffaloes.
>
> Behind them blue smoke curled and clouded above the treetops, and through the thickets he could sometimes see a distant pink glare. The voices of the cannon were clamoring in interminable chorus.
>
> The youth was horror stricken. He stared in agony and amazement. He forgot that he was engaged in combating the universe. He threw aside his mental pamphlets on the philosophy of the retreat and rules for the guidance of the damned.
>
> The fight was lost. The dragons were coming with invincible strides. The army, helpless in the matted thickets and blinded by the overhanging night, was going to be swallowed. War, the red animal, war, the blood-swollen god, would have bloated fill.
>
> —Stephen Crane, *The Red Badge of Courage*

This passage describes a young soldier's panic and that of his fellow soldiers as they retreat in his direction. The action is seen from the young man's point of view. His horror is expressed by an extensive use of figurative language.

In the first paragraph, the retreating soldiers are viewed impressionistically by the youth as "dark waves of men . . . sweeping out of the woods and down through the fields." The wave metaphor is then replaced by a simile that describes the horror-stricken men as charging on the youth "like terrified buffaloes." The cannon's roar is personified as sounding like a chorus of human voices "in interminable chorus." In the last paragraph, the enemy soldiers are described as "dragons . . .

coming with invincible strides." Finally, war itself is described as "the red animal" which would soon "have bloated fill." Crane's purpose in this passage is not to give a factual, objective picture of retreating soldiers, but to give us some insight into the young solder's feelings. The description is dominated by a single mood—horror.

Exercises

1. Write a technical description of one of the following subjects. Aim for precision of diction, accuracy, and objectivity.

   a. a stereo   f. a part of the body

   b. a solar invention   g. a kitchen utensil

   c. a new engine   h. a tool

   d. a plant   i. a mechanism

   e. a bird or an animal   j. a felt-tip pen

2. Cut a picture from a magazine. Describe the picture as accurately and as objectively as possible. Attach the picture to your description when you hand it in.

3. Describe a city scene, a marketplace, a landscape, or a similar subject from an objective point of view. Then write an impressionistic description of the same scene.

4. Describe some scene in fair weather. Then describe the same scene in fog, rain, or snow. Change the season, or time, or activity, or whatever.

5. Describe a strange or exotic landscape, perhaps on an unknown planet. Describe the plant life, the animal life, or the terrain.

6. One interesting kind of literary description is *expressionism*. Expressionism is the distortion of reality to communicate feelings and emotions. It is antirealistic, not being concerned with objective accuracy.
   Analyze the following excerpt from Edgar Allen Poe's "The Fall of the House of Usher." How does the language of description contribute to the ominous atmosphere? Consider the impressionistic diction, the surrealistic images, the sound devices, and the narrator's comments.

   > During the whole of a dull, dark, and soundless day in the autumn of
   > the year, when the clouds hung oppressively low in the heavens, I had

been passing alone, on horseback, through a singularly dreary track of country; and at length found myself, as the shades of the evening drew on, within view of the melancholy House of Usher. I know not how it was— but, with the first glimpse of the building, a sense of insufferable gloom pervaded my spirit. I say insufferable, for the feeling was unrelieved by any of that half pleasurable, because poetic, sentiment, with which the mind usually receives even the sternest natural images of the desolate or terrible. I looked upon the scene before me—upon the mere house, and the simple landscape features of the domain—upon the bleak walls—upon the vacant eye-like windows—upon a few rank sedges—and upon a few trunks of decayed trees—with an utter depression of soul which I can compare to no earthly sensation more properly than to the after dream of the reveler upon opium—the bitter lapse into everyday life—the hideous dropping off of the veil. There was an iciness, a sinking, a sickening of the heart—an unredeemed dreariness of thought which no goading of the imagination could torture into aught of the sublime. What was it—I paused to think—what was it that so unnerved me in the contemplation of the House of Usher?

—Edgar Allan Poe, *The Fall of the House of Usher*

CHAPTER 5

Patterns of Thought: Classification, Exemplification, Definition

Classification

Pick up the classified advertising section of your local newspaper and you will find broad categories such as the following: rentals, automotive, miscellaneous, livestock and produce, business and finance, business services, personals and services, educational, employment, and announcements. Then look at the subcategories of any of these broad categories and you will notice subdivisions such as these:

Automotive

Autos for Rent	Sports Cars
Autos for Sale	Trucks
Station Wagons	Autos
Convertibles	Imported Autos

Livestock and Produce

Dogs	Livestock
Cats	Poultry
Birds, Fish	Fruits
Pets	

Or go into a drugstore or a supermarket and look at the greeting cards. Some cards are classified according to commonly celebrated holidays:

American Holidays

Christmas	Father's Day
New Year's	Independence Day
Valentine's Day	Thanksgiving
Easter	Halloween
Mother's Day	

Others are classified under a miscellaneous category:

Miscellaneous

Formal	Birthday
Traditional	Death
Contemporary	Sickness
Humorous	Wedding
Floral	Anniversary
Cute	Sympathy

These are not very elegant ways of classifying things, but for special purposes it is sometimes convenient to group things together in a rough way, even though some of the categories may seem to be arbitrary. These examples illustrate that classifying is a familiar, everyday activity. Things may be classified; events may be classified; ideas may be classified.

Classifying is an important part of thinking. Yet the process as it develops in the child is a gradual one. In the first stage of concept formation, given an assortment of blocks or objects, a child will put them together at random, without any logical basis, because they appear together in time and space. But the objects have no intrinsic bonds according to the child's thinking. In the second phase of concept formation, the child puts objects together on the basis of bonds that actually exist between these objects. To be sure, the child's subjective impressions play some role in his or her thinking, but he or she no longer mistakes these impressions for connections between things. Instead, he or she groups objects on the basis of color, shape, or size. In the last phase of concept formation, the child is able to abstract and isolate elements and to view them apart from the concrete experience in which they are embedded.

Is classification merely the process of giving a common name to things, or is it the discovery of universal properties that things have in common? Anthropological linguists have noted that different cultures and languages categorize things differently. The Hopi Indians, for example, have one class word that includes everything that flies except birds. Thus airplane pilots, airplanes, and flying insects all belong to the same class. The Eskimos have numerous names for snow: *wind-driven snow, snow on the ground, slushy snow, icy snow, hard-packed snow, falling snow.* Color classification varies in different cultures. The Shona, a tribe in Zimbabwe, have three class names for colors. Other tribes have two. Botanists divide flower colors into blue (cyanic) and yellow (xanthic).

Purpose, Audience, Kind of Discourse

Classification is used constantly by people in hundreds of professions and occupations—by scientists, teachers, doctors, lawyers, historians, librarians, grocery clerks, and insurance agents. One of the simplest purposes to which classification can be put is the simple physical process of sorting. Consider the amount of sorting you do in your everyday life. You sort your clothes, your books, your record collection, stamps, coins, important papers of various kinds. In brief, one of your most important aims in classifying is to put experience in order.

Although classification can be found in many kinds of writing and used for a variety of purposes, one of the most important aims of classification is to inform or instruct. Therefore, you are more likely to find classification in expository than in persuasive or literary writing. Some typical examples of kinds of writing that use classification are articles and textbooks on botany, chemistry, biology, political science, anatomy, anthropology, psychology, sociology, and library classification; scientific essays, magazine articles, museum catalogs, and classified ads.

Naturally, your audience will be an important factor in making your classification. If your audience has a specialized knowledge of your subject, your classification will tend to be formal or scientific. If your audience has little or no knowledge of your subject, your classification will probably be informal. In scientific classification, your focus will be on the subject itself, and your classification will tend to be exhaustive. But informal classification is more audience-centered. In informal classification, you may classify the same subject in any number of ways, depending on your purpose and on your reader's knowledge, interests, level of understanding, and so forth.

Invention and Classification

Classifying is a basic mental activity. It is *the process of grouping similar ideas or objects, the systematic arrangement of things into classes on the basis of shared characteristics.* As a topic of invention, it is related to definition (to define is to put the thing to be defined into a class); analysis (to classify is to divide into parts or categories); enumeration (to classify is to enumerate members of a class); and comparison (to classify is to group similar things). The topic of classification suggests questions that you can ask of any subject, such as: How may an object or an idea be classified? What are its common attributes?

What are its basic categories? What is the basis of the classification? What is the purpose of the classification?

Any group of individuals or objects possessing something in common can be classified. But you should not confuse classification with analysis. When you analyze, you begin with one object or idea and divide it into parts on the basis of differences. When you classify, you begin with many things and group them according to similarities. The term in an analysis is always singular: *a painting, a movie, the human body, an apple, a poem, a sentence, a house.* The term in a classification is always plural: *cars, jobs, popular songs, drugs, blind dates, clothing styles.*

When you classify, you should first determine the basis of classification, the common feature or quality that unites all the elements of the group. If, for example, you are classifying apples, you can classify them by color.

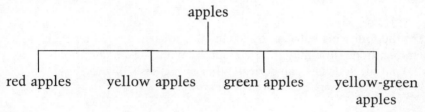

or you can classify them by taste:

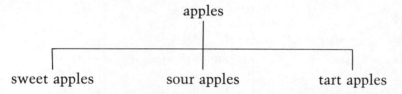

When you classify, always keep in mind the purpose of your classification. Your purpose should be clearly defined.

The principles of classification are similar in many respects to those of analysis:

> *There can be no classification unless the things to be classified are considered similar to each other in some respect.*

> *Only one principle of division may be applied at each level of classification.*

> *At each level, the classes must be mutually exclusive.*

> *In a scientific classification, the classes at each level must cover the whole field.*

To follow the principles of classification in your thinking is to participate in one of the most fundamental acts of the human mind.

Ludwig Wittgenstein gives some of the best practical advice about classifying for compositional purposes. He suggests that we look at those events or proceedings that we call games: "I mean board-games, card-games, ball-games, Olympic games, and so on. What is common to them all?—Don't say: 'There *must* be something common or they would not be called *games*'—but *look and see* whether there is anything common at all."

Exercises

1. Probe one of the following subjects by using questions suggested by the topic of classification (How may it be classified? What are its common attributes? What are its basic categories? What is the basis of the classification? What is the purpose of the classification?).

   a. movies   f. bad habits

   b. crimes   g. TV commercials

   c. drinks   h. junk foods

   d. useful things   i. compact cars

   e. sports fans   j. popular songs

2. Discuss in class the ways in which you are viewed (that is, classified) by different people.

3. The following items have been grouped together because they deal with the same subjects. Assume that you have been asked to write an article for a consumer magazine to evaluate these products for a general audience. How would you classify the items in each group? What would be your main divisions? Subdivisions? Would you have to exclude any items? What would be the *basis* of the kind of classification you would make?

   a. fountain pen, ballpoint pen, porous-point pen, rolling-ball pen

   b. regular colas, diet colas, caffeine-free regular colas, caffeine-free diet colas

c. regular coffee, drip, automatic drip, decaffeinated, whole-bean, flaked, instant, fine ground

d. flat paint, glass, eggshell, satin, enamel, semi-gloss, water-based, oil-based

Constructing Classification Paradigms

Unless you intend to present the results of your classification to your reader in an informal way, as you are classifying, or after you have made your classification, you will want to construct a classification paradigm.

To construct a paradigm using the mode of classification, keeping in mind your subject, your purpose, and your reader, you begin with a thesis sentence. Then, as you did in constructing other kinds of paradigms, you add sentences to the thesis in such a way that *the sentences form a relational pattern of classification.* In your thesis, and in the subsequent sentences of your paradigm, you include classification words, such as *kinds, sorts, types, classes,* or *varieties.* These words will enable your reader to grasp your meaning more readily. Finally, you put in ethical and emotional words and phrases if your purpose or your subject lends itself to ethical and emotional appeals:

Burns may be *classified* according to the depth and extent of the burn.

First-degree burns make the skin red and tender, but not blistered.

Second-degree burns make the skin blistered and swollen.

Third-degree burns destroy much of the underlying tissue.

A knowledge of how burns are classified can help determine the seriousness of burn injuries and may help burn victims to survive.

Notice that the thesis sentence uses a classification word *(classified).* It also includes the subject to be classified *(burns).* The middle sentences enumerate specific kinds of burns *(first-degree, second-degree, third-degree)* based on "the depth and extent of the burn." Although there are no explicit emotional words, there is an implicit emotional appeal in such descriptive phrases as *skin red and tender, skin blistered and swollen,* and the *destruction of the underlying tissues.* The basic appeal is to the reader's fear or anxiety. Similarly, although there are no explicit ethical terms, there is a moral appeal implicit in the purpose of the classification, which is to help burn victims survive. Words such as *knowledge, help, seriousness,* and *survive* also support the moral intention.

Once you have written your classification paradigm, examine each sentence to make certain that each accurately represents your intended meaning, your attitude toward your subject, and your ethical and emotional stance. Then check the reasoning process, including the topical relationship that exists between the class *(genus)* and members of the class *(species)*. Next consider the kinds of supporting evidence you will need. Finally, as you did after constructing the other kinds of paradigms, revise each sentence as necessary.

In order to write your paper, using your paradigm as a guide, you provide an appropriate introduction, supporting evidence or details, and a suitable conclusion. The pattern of your overall paper will look like this:

Classification Pattern
Introduction (included thesis)
Type 1 (or subclass 1)
Type 2 (or subclass 2)
Type 3, 4, 5 . . .
Conclusion (includes clincher sentence)

In addition to their basic paradigmatic structure, classification essays have a basic vocabulary that will enable your reader to follow the logical progression of your ideas:

kinds	categories	classify
sorts	sources	compile
types	orders	assemble
classes	clusters	string together
varieties	groups	collect

The essay that follows, taken from the March 1983 issue of *Consumer Reports,* is a good example of an informative essay that uses a classification paradigm:

A Guide to Grind-Your-Own Beans

1

People who grind their own beans hope to improve their brew through the use of fresher grounds or by locating a particular bean or blend of beans that best suits their taste. A & P stores have long offered shoppers three house brands of whole beans. Now whole beans are cropping up in many supermarkets, as mass merchandisers compete with specialty stores for the "gourmet" trade. If you want to get into coffee the way oenologists get into wine, you'll need a little bean lore to guide you.

2

Coffee trees grow best in hilly regions in the world's tropical areas. The beans they bring forth are usually one of two main species—*coffea arabica* and *coffea robusta*, each with a characteristic shape, size, color, flavor, and aroma. (The beans, by the way, are virtually all picked by hand; advertisements that boast of "hand picked" beans are meaningless.)

The robusta variety, grown mainly in Africa, India, and Indonesia, tends to have a harsh flavor. Robustas are used mainly in instant coffees and in blends such as those we tested for this report. They have about twice the caffeine content of arabicas. Many decaffeinated coffees are made from robusta beans, since the processing rids the bean of much of its natural harshness while providing a large harvest of caffeine for separate sale to makes of soft drinks, drug products, and other commercial users.

3

Most beans found in supermarkets and specialty stores are arabicas. There are two main kinds, brazils and milds.

4

Brazils. As you might expect, these comprise any Brazil-grown beans. There are dozens of varieties, but the main ones take their names from the ports of export. *Santos* beans have a sweet, clear flavor. *Rios* are pungent. Other important kinds are called *Victorias* and *Paranas.*

5

Milds are those arabica coffees not grown in Brazil. They come from Central and South America, the Caribbean, the Middle and Far East, and parts of Africa. Among the varieties:

6

Arabian. Only Arabian-grown coffees bear the designation *Mocha.* A fine mocha is heavy-bodied, with a smooth and delicious flavor and an unusual acid character.

7

Colombian. Experts consider these winy in body and fine in flavor and aroma. Colombian coffees you may encounter include *Supremo,* termed rich, mellow, full-bodied and mild in aroma; *Colombian Espresso,* a deep, dark roast like Italian espresso; and *Colombian Amaretto, Cinnamon,* and *Swiss Chocolate Almond,* varieties of flavored coffee.

8

Haitian. These coffees are described as mellow and rich, with a heavy body and fairly high acidity.

9

Hawaiian. The principal Hawaiian bean is *Kona,* a variety of excellent quality, with mild acidity, distinct sharpness and medium body.

10

Indonesian. Some robusta coffees are grown on the island of Java, but those sold in the U.S. as *Java* are traditionally arabicas. Another Indonesian, *Mandheling,* is grown in a district on Sumatra's west coast. Some experts term it one of the finest coffees in the world.

11

Tanzanian. Tanzania produces both arabicas and robustas. One popular arabica is *Tanzanian Kilimanjaro,* grown on the southern slopes of the Kilimanjaro range. The coffee is mild, aromatic, and rich, with a distinct sharpness.

12

In the store, you're likely to find blends of two types of beans, as well as one or more of the individual beans mentioned above. One of the most popular blends is *Mocha-Java*—the *Mocha* for flavor, the *Java* for body and aroma.

The first paragraph provides the background information necessary for the reader to understand the writer's purpose in writing this article. The second paragraph divides coffee beans into two main types: *coffea arabica* and *coffea robusta.* The third paragraph discusses the robusta variety. The fourth paragraph subdivides the arabica variety into two main kinds, brazils and milds. The fifth paragraph describes Brazil-grown beans. The sixth paragraph tells where mild arabica coffee beans come from and subdivides this class of beans into six varieties. The next six paragraphs take up each variety of milds in turn: Arabian, Colombian, Haitian, Hawaiian, Indonesian, and Tanzanian. The final paragraph tells readers that they are likely to find both the individual beans and blends of the two types in many stores.

The following classification essay, taken from the June 26, 1974, issue of *Time* magazine, uses a less formal means of classifying the kinds of audiences found at rock concerts in that decade:

Faces in the Crowd

1

*Introduc-
tion*
Who's playing at the local rock palace? One way to find out is to look at the marquee. Another, says California promoter Steve Wolf, is to watch the crowd strolling—or floating, in the case of heavy grass consumers—through the door. "Audiences resemble the groups they come to see," says Wolf. Those words are reckless understatements.

2

No one who has ever mixed with a San Francisco psychedelic-style concert crowd is likely to forget the experience. Going to see Boz Scaggs, Grace Slick, or Hot Tuna? Better take earmuffs and a flak jacket. Psychedelic rock crowds can be hostile collections of spacy Vietvets still suffering from post-Viet Nam syndrome, pimply feminists in granny glasses, and young high school dropouts. Bottles and firecrackers spin through the air. At a Grateful Dead concert, usually a four- or five-hour affair, the typical freak is a blend of drug hunger, male lonerism, and musical knowledgeability. He will attend somnolently to the music (probably after swilling a bottle of wine), sway ecstatically forward toward the performers. In contrast, the audience for balladeer James Taylor, or the country-rock group Poco, whose music has crisp pattern and infectious surfaces, has a well-scrubbed look and an enraptured response to the music.

3

Thesis   Of course, when hallowed groups like the Rolling Stones, the Who, or Bob Dylan make one of their infrequent appearances, categories crumble; everybody comes, just like the World Series. Still, it is possible to define five general types of audience on the basis of dress, manner, consumption, age, and music taste. The categories:

Type 1   *Heavy Metal.* So named because of the massive banks of amplifiers, drums, and loudspeakers employed by Grand Funk, Led Zeppelin, Black Sabbath, and Blue Oyster Cult. The music is pure buzz—heavy, simplistic blues played at maximum volume and wallowed in mostly by young teenagers, just experimenting with marijuana, the lingua franca of rock, and perhaps hard drugs too.

4

This audience can be trouble for concert-hall managers. Says Cleveland promoter Jules Belkin, "They are up on the seats boogieing and running around the hall." Dress ranges from scruffy jeans to $200 velveteen jackets. The girls may come in couples to ogle, say, at topless Mark Farner of Grand Funk. Then there are the brassy groupies with their stevedore vocabularies who haughtily flaunt their backstage passes. The boys come in gangs and do what gangs do—fling lighted matches, fight the bouncers, sometimes toss empty wine bottles. Vomiting from too much beer or wine is a status symbol. If these kids do not have tickets, they break in. A heavy security force, sometimes including local police, is *de rigueur* at most rock concerts.

5

Type 2   *The Listeners.* Performing groups that attract this crowd include the Moody Blues, Yes, Weather Report, and The Eleventh House. The music is predominantly classical or jazz rock. The Listeners tend to be Heavy Metal graduates—youths ranging in age into the early 20's, who know and care about musicianship. Sedated by grass, Seconals, and Quaaludes, they tend to applaud rather than scream their approval.

6

Type 3   *Squeaky Cleans.* A description used by singer Bette Midler to characterize fans of the soft, often poetic songs of such bards as Cat Stevens, James Taylor, Joni Mitchell, Melanie. This is an orderly dating crowd in its late teens and early 20's who are interested in love songs. Girls generally outnumber the boys by 2 to 1. Melanie's ethereal fans tend to invade the stage, only to sit quietly at her feet, perhaps lighting candles. Mitchell's following emulates her. "Since Joni started wearing gowns," says Wolf, "the girls have started wearing dresses and makeup."

7

Type 4   *Glitter Trippers.* Glitter stars do not seem so much to have created their fandom as to have been created by it. The fastest-growing audience in rock dotes on the finery of such brocade-, sequin-, mascara-, and rouge-wearing performers as Todd Rundgren, Suzi Quatro, Alice Cooper, and the New York Dolls. Occasionally a glitter singer like England's bisexual David Bowie is actually good. Mostly, though, admits the Dolls' David Johansen, "the whole glitter trip is just jive." A concert can also be simply an excuse for youngsters to come out for a reasonably harmless masquerade party. The kids go on parade to show off their white tuxedos and top hats, feather boas, and of course glitter, lavishly applied to face and body.

8

Type 5   *The Evening-Outers.* These are the young marrieds, who, says one New York promoter, "are dressed to the nines, and smoke where they're supposed to." As mellowed graduates of the 1960's rock revolution, they will naturally show up to hear the Stones or Dylan, but mostly they turn out for the Carpenters, or the Fifth Dimension. Promoters like the Evening-Outers because they spend money generously at the concession bars.

9

Conclu-
sion   Begun by the Beatles a decade ago, the rock revolution succeeded
beyond everyone's wildest dreams. Rock defined an emerging segment of
America, financed a counterculture, and spawned a $2 billion industry. Its
principal gift to those who were young in the 1960's was to provide a common means of expression—a common music, a common language, even a
kind of cathartic theater in which a Janis Joplin assumed almost mythic
dimensions as a tragic heroine and Dylan strolled the stage like an
Orpheus. It is no secret that rock's classic era is gone forever, along with
the social bonds that nurtured it. The current fragmentation of the rock
audience certifies that. In fairness, it mut be added that it also signifies a
diversity of personal taste and music style unknown previously in American pop music. If rock can be described as being in a somewhat self-
expressive romantic era, can its neoclassic period—or a pop Stravinsky—
be far behind?

The first two paragraphs introduce the essay. Paragraph 3 states
the thesis and helps to organize the classification pattern in the re-
mainder of the essay ("It is possible to define five general types of
audience on the basis of dress, manner, consumption, age, and music
taste"). The next six paragraphs define the types of audiences (Heavy
Metal, The Listeners, Squeaky Cleans, Glitter Trippers, and The Evening-Outers) and give specific examples of the types. And the final
paragraph concludes the essay.

I think that the preceding examples and discussion make abundantly clear that classification is the normal way in which our minds
perceive almost anything. But when you go to put the ideas received
from your classifying into patterns for writing, perhaps it is best to
follow some basic plan of organization, rather than to rely strictly on
the order of your impressions.

Exercises

1. For classroom discussion, analyze the paradigm on page 109. Is there a
   dominant appeal? Is it logical, ethical, or emotional? Or are the three
   appeals integrated throughout the sentences of the paradigm? Is there a
   moral stance implicit in every kind of writing? An emotional stance?
   What kinds of evidence would you need to support the sentences of the
   paradigm? What kind of paper might you write using this paradigm as a
   guide? For what kinds of readers? Can you imagine an occasion that
   might call for such a paper?

2. Construct a paradigm based on the mode of classification for a specific purpose and audience, using one of the following topics or one of your own:

   a. blind dates   f. plants or animals

   b. people   g. jobs

   c. clothing styles   h. people's voices

   d. television shows   i. vacations

   e. popular songs   j. dreamers

3. Write an essay in which you classify the audiences you have seen at a rock concert or at some other public affair. Assume a general audience, and specify your purpose and the occasion.

4. Movies are classified as *G, PG, PG-13, R, X,* and more recently on cable TV, *NC.* What is the basis of this classification? What kind of subject matter is involved? How do the subject matter and the rating relate to specific audiences?

5. Analyze an essay in your reader based on the mode of classification. Where did the article or essay first appear? When? For what readers? What is the author's purpose in writing the essay? What kinds of appeals does the writer use? What is his or her reasoning? What kinds of facts, opinions, proofs, or evidence does the essay use to support the generalization? Is the essay effective? Does it achieve its goal?

6. Classify the students on your campus. Consider carefully the basis of your classification (for instance, Jewish, Baptist, Catholic, Methodist, Buddist, hippie, jock, cowboy, punker, middle class, upper class, English, German, Spanish, French, freshman, sophomore, and so forth).

Exemplification

Exemplification is *the process of illustrating a general principle, statement, or law by citing specific examples.* It is the act of showing or illustrating by using examples.

Thinking by means of examples is one of the most important ways of making your ideas clear. Concrete ideas are almost always easier to understand than abstract ideas. How often in your own conversations have you paused after making a general statement and added, "for instance," "for example"? A significant and interesting example can lend much needed support and validity to your arguments.

Purpose, Audience, Kind of Discourse

Exemplification is generally found in those kinds of writing whose aim is to inform and persuade. Exemplification can be found in magazine articles; essays; critical reviews; legal writing, in which the example might serve as a precedent; scientific writing, in which examples serve as illustrations of laws or general principles; textbook writing, which uses the example to instruct; argumentative writing, where the example is used as proof; short narratives such as the fable and exemplum which point up a general truth; news articles; advertising; and manuals of various kinds.

By their very nature, examples are audience-centered. If you supply your readers with appropriate examples to support a general statement in an expository essay or the proposition in an argument, you will be helping them to grasp your ideas in a way that a page of abstract exposition will not. But a mere enumeration of examples is not enough. You want to give your readers examples close to their own experiences, and ensure their understanding of these examples by means of a short conclusion. In sum, examples can have both expository and persuasive force.

Invention and Exemplification

As a topic of invention, exemplification is closely related to classification (each example is a member of a group or class of persons or things); analysis (examples are parts of wholes); and definition (giving examples is one way of supporting definitions). Exemplification answers such questions as: What are some representative instances, examples, or illustrations? What is the supporting evidence?

Exemplification almost always accompanies generalization. **Generalization** is *the process of forming general concepts on the basis of observing particular instances or examples.* When you generalize, you extract the common element from a number of particular experiences. The process is often intuitive, but it is easy enough to test the validity of a generalization by reviewing a sufficiently large number of examples in your mind.

A generalization must contain at least one general term:

All men are created equal.
Some politicians are dishonest.
Many citizens are fed up with white-collar crime.
Political writing is generally bad writing.
Most humor is basically sadistic.

In formulating generalizations, you might want to keep a few points in mind. *First, a generalization is an inductive conclusion. Be certain, therefore, that you can support your generalizations with a reasonable number of examples. Second, the general terms in a general statement may be unnecessarily broad. Qualify your general terms when necessary. Suppose, for example, you make a statement that "politicians are dishonest." Do you mean that "all politicians are dishonest," "most politicians are dishonest," "some politicians are dishonest," or "a few politicians are dishonest"? Finally, general statements may be statements of fact, statements of opinion, or statements of inference. Be sure that you are clear in your own mind about the differences and that you convey these differences to your reader:*

The price of gasoline is rising. (statement of fact)
It is unfortunate that the price of gasoline is rising. (statement of opinion)
The price of gasoline will go up after the first of the year. (inference)

Exercises

1. Formulate a general statement and be prepared to probe it in class and support it with specific examples.

2. Give some examples of a successful person, a happy person. What makes a person happy or successful?

3. In class, give some examples of movies that present an optimistic view of life, a pessimistic view of life. Then discuss.

Constructing Exemplification Paradigms

To construct an exemplification paradigm, keeping in mind your subject, purpose, and intended reader, you begin with a generalization in the form of a single declarative sentence. Then, you *add sentences* that provide particular examples of your general statement in such a way as *to form a relational pattern of exemplification*. To enable your readers to follow the progression of your ideas more easily, you include logical tags such as "for example," "for instance," and so forth. Next, you include ethical and emotional words and phrases (unless these appeals are implicit in the wording of your sentences) to appeal to your reader's moral sensibilities and emotions:

Early American pioneers were unusually self-sufficient.

For example, they taught their children to read and write.

They produced their own food and clothing.

They did most of their own doctoring and nursing.

Unlike some modern American families, each family member shared the work.

After you construct your exemplification paradigm, you examine each sentence to see that it accurately represents your intended meaning, your purpose, your attitude toward your subject, and your ethical and emotional stance. Next, you check the reasoning process. Then you consider the kinds of evidence you will need to support the sentences of your paradigm. Finally, you revise the sentences of your paradigm.

To write a paper based on the completed exemplification paradigm, you provide a suitable introduction, using your paradigm as a guide. Then you add supporting details, arranging your examples in order of importance. At the end of your paper, you provide an appropriate conclusion. The following scheme represents the pattern of the entire essay:

Exemplification Pattern
Introduction (includes generalization)
Example 1 (or cluster of examples)
Example 2 (or cluster of examples)
Example 3, 4, 5 . . .
Conclusion (includes clincher sentence)

There can be several variations on the basic pattern. For example, you can use a single extended example rather than a series of examples. Or you can give several related examples in the same paragraph.

Like themes that use classification as a mode of developing ideas, essays that use exemplification to develop their ideas have a characteristic vocabulary:

for example	typical	generally
for instance	exemplary	on the whole
to illustrate	commonplace	for one thing
as proof	sample	cite
as a matter of course	specimen	quote
as follows	quotation	case

The following *New York Times* news story uses a wealth of examples to illustrate how "public sleepers steal the show":

Public Sleepers Steal the Show

1

The audience is enthralled. There's not a sound to be heard, other than the glorious music. But just a moment. Could it be? It could. It is.

2

The man in the fifth row is asleep, snoring, in fact. The woman beside him is jabbing her elbow into his ribs. Some of the neighbors are amused, others are irritated or horrified, but a surprising number of faces look sympathetic. Thank goodness, they seem to be saying, tonight at least, it's someone else.

3

Everyone knows someone who has fallen asleep in public, or continues to fall asleep in public, occasionally or frequently. Some sleepers are selective. They doze only at concerts, or at dinner parties, or at meetings, or in church. Others are indiscriminate. Any place is good enough, especially if it's a place they didn't want to be in the first place.

4

One of the most famous public sleepers is Teddy Kollek, the mayor of Jerusalem. Kollek has sat on many a dais with his eyes closed and his head falling to one side, or bobbing up or down. No one pokes him, and he is almost always forgiven, even by those on whom he is falling asleep, because it is well-known that he usually has a 20-hour workday. But the principal reason he is forgiven is that he is one of the briefest public speakers on record. If he gets to three or four minutes, it is practically considered a filibuster. Better a short-winded catnapper than a long-winded, wide-awake politician is obviously the gist of that message.

5

In her recent autobiography, Sophia Loren notes that her husband, Carlo Ponti, would get to certain film premieres, promptly "drop off," and "I must then nervously try to keep him awake! Carlo! Carlo!" Miss Loren added that she wasn't annoyed by the napping. It had been a fact of life for such a long time that it amused her.

6

Public sleepers are usually, but not always, men. The theory used to be that men were exhausted after a long day at the office, while women were at home eating chocolates and taking beauty naps. However, Margaret Thatcher and the late Golda Meir never were famous for chocolate consumption or beauty naps, and ever since Rosalynn Carter's staff outnumbered that of presidents of large corporations, the theory is advanced less often.

7

Jim Jensen a television news correspondent for WCBS-TV in New York, who has, on occasion fallen asleep in public, has two somewhat different theories. He thinks women may be more conscious of good manners, and that they may also be more concerned with the way they look to others. The idea of falling asleep with head lolling and mouth agape might, he believes, be enough subconsciously to keep them awake.

8

Jensen occasionally dozes at a meeting, and said, "I think I heard myself snoring in church once," but he admits that he, too, is conscious of a public image.

9

"My father would fall asleep any place he wanted to," he said admiringly. "That took a lot of courage."

10

George Abbott often falls asleep if someone shows home movies and, according to his wife, Janice, "snores enough to wake the dead."

11

Abbott, chairman of the board of Ithaca Textiles, admits to sleeping through the movies but denies the snores. He is, he said, a quiet sleeper.

12

"Once in a while, I kick or poke him," Mrs. Abbott said. "But I usually let him sleep because I feel sorry for him. I know he's tired." But she did give up their box at the opera because "he'd get in there and fall asleep."

13

When it comes to opera, the performance given by Robert Peltz some years ago probably remains unsurpassed. He had accompanied his mother to the old Metropolitan Opera house and was sitting in an aisle seat, dozing peacefully, when he was awakened in a spectacular fashion. He had fallen into the aisle with a thump so resounding, he said, that the whole house was in turmoil. The performance stopped, the house lights went on, and everyone looked to see who had fallen from what balcony.

14

Peltz, who is president of the Flagstaff Food Service Corp., was mortified, not only at the commotion he had caused but also because he hadn't even fallen from the balcony. He tried, with little success, to shrink himself into invisibility as he slithered back into his seat, only inches away.

15

Foxy Carter, a retired Foreign Service officer, occasionally finds himself having a quiet nap at a dinner table. It usually happens when he's tired and the hostess hasn't served dinner until 10 or 11 P.M.

16

"The kindest thing my date can do is give me a good swift kick in the shins," he said, and added thoughtfully, "I've had some very good dates, very helpful in that way."

17

Perhaps the most unusual case of nodding off in public was experienced by William L. Winter. Winter is executive director of Assistance Dogs International and is a frequent and popular lecturer. But one night:

18

"It was the weirdest feeling. I was lecturing, and I was putting myself to sleep. The audience was in good shape, and there I was, falling asleep."

The first two paragraphs provide a humorous introduction for the thesis ("Everyone knows someone who has fallen asleep in public, or continues to fall asleep in public, occasionally or selectively") that follows in paragraph 3. Paragraph 4 takes up the first of the famous public sleepers, Teddy Kollek, the mayor of Jerusalem. Paragraph 5 gives an example of how Carlo Ponti, Sophia Loren's husband, dozed off at film premieres. Paragraph 6 gives two examples of famous women who do not sleep in public—Margaret Thatcher and Golda Meir. The subsequent paragraphs give additional examples. Since this is a news story, the paragraphing is often unconventional, but the story does illustrate the pervasive use of examples in all kinds of writing.

The following student paper uses a simple exemplification pattern. The first paragraph states the thesis and qualifies it. The next four paragraphs give positive examples to support the thesis. The sixth paragraph gives a negative example. The next paragraph qualifies the idea in this one by analogy. And the final paragraph gives another negative example and concludes the essay.

Be a Touchable

Is American society full of untouchables? From my own experiences, I would say no. In fact, it never even occurred to me that some people might be repelled by a friendly pat on the shoulder. But after our discussion about this in class the other day, I did some visiting with several friends on the matter. My family and I seem to be somewhat in the minority.

For example, my family, while not being made up of the greatest cheek-kissers, has always been very generous with the hugs, hand squeezes, arm-in-arm walks, and comforting shoulder pats. All of this is spontaneous. Nobody has ever said to me, "Now, Linda, go kiss your Aunt Ada." It just so happened I thought enough of my Aunt Ada to *want* to kiss her now and then when she had been especially nice. When Dad introduces me to anyone, he always has that big protective arm right around my shoulders that tells me he is proud of me far better than his words could.

I wouldn't think of walking into Grandma's house without grabbing both of her hands in a tight squeeze and smiling into her eyes so that she can get a good look at her granddaughter.

My husband and I went bowling with my cousin and his wife the other night, and he often threw his arm around my shoulders or Virg's as we visited. I didn't think that was queer at all. In fact, I thought it was very sweet the way he has accepted Virg in the family.

How comforting it was to have my aunt's arm around me after my Grandpa's funeral! She knew how very close we were, and her words could never have been as warm and understanding as that arm was.

Several of the people I talked to about this had different thoughts. One lady I work with said she didn't like people "pawing" her. A girlfriend said she had no reservations about kissing her husband, but couldn't kiss her parents, although she wished she could.

My answer to that would be for heaven's sake TRY!!! Don't regret it later that you didn't. I was uneasy about going into a swimming pool for the first time, and even after that first step was taken, it was a long time before I felt comfortable in my role as a swimmer. Now I love to swim and I think what a loss it would have been if I had been afraid to try, then follow through. I think the analogy holds for life. If you *want* to be more affectionate with your loved ones, just try, and keep at it. Soon it may become so natural you will wonder what all the fuss was about.

Don't be like my cousin Jo, who loved her father dearly but just couldn't show it. When she was 18, she finally brought herself to kiss him, but it was too late; he was in his coffin, unable to feel the delightful sense of touch the living have to share, if we only will.

—Linda

The student paper reprinted below uses the same basic pattern, but is even simpler in form. The first paragraph states the thesis ("Professional athletes in a number of fields are making more money than ever before"). The next four paragraphs cite specific examples from different professional sports (golf, basketball, baseball, and football). And the final paragraph concludes the essay.

Playing for Pay

Recent years have been golden ones for professional athletes. Professional athletes in a number of fields are making more money than ever before.

For example, in golf there have been three professional golfers who topped the one-million-dollar mark in lifetime earnings.

In basketball, one player recently negotiated a contract providing him with an annual income of $200,000. And within the past year, several college All-Americans signed basketball contracts which made them millionaires overnight. Today the least amount that a pro basketball player can receive annually is in excess of $13,000.

Baseball's rosters contain a number of stars who receive $100,000 or more to play for a single season. Six-figure bonuses are commonplace.

The same is true in football. College stars sign contracts which guarantee them financial security before they have proven themselves on the field as professionals. Well-established players receive salaries comparable to the stars in the other sports.

All of the big names in the major sports profit handsomely from product endorsements, personal appearances, speaking engagements, and business opportunities made available to them. It all adds up to a highly lucrative business to those who possess the ability to participate.

—Bruce

Exercises

1. Analyze in class the paradigm on page 119 that begins: "Early American pioneers were unusually self-sufficient." What would be the purpose of a paper based on this paradigm? What is the reasoning process like? Is there an ethical or emotional appeal implicit in the sentences of the paradigm? What kind of evidence would you use to support the sentences of this paradigm? Where might a paper based on this paradigm be published? For what readers?

2. Keeping in mind your purpose, audience, and a possible writing situation, construct an exemplification paradigm based on one of the following general subjects or on a subject of your choice. Then write an essay based on your paradigm:

   a. local place-names

   b. peculiar personal names

   c. nicknames

   d. current fads

   e. slang

3. Construct five general statements that can be supported by examples. Then bring them to class and consider ways of expanding them into paradigms.

4. Discuss in class ways in which the following generalizations could be supported by examples:

   a. People are judged by their language.

   b. People are judged by their clothes.

   c. A person's early experiences with members of other races or nationalities may determine his or her prejudice or lack of it.

   d. People conform to what they think are the conventions of their own group.

   e. The best things in life are free.

   f. The best things in life cost money.

5. Can the following proverbs be supported by examples? Discuss in class the means you would use to write a paper based on any of these proverbs:

   a. We are all slaves of opinion.

   b. Love is blind.

   c. Everyone has his or her price.

   d. Truth is stranger than fiction.

   e. Discontent is the first step in progress.

Definition

Definition is closely related to classification. As such, it is *a way of thinking in classes*. But it is also *a way of thinking in differences*. Thus, definition is related to comparison and contrast. Definition and description are also closely related; definition is a kind of abstract description. Definition most resembles description when it restricts or sets boundaries to a thing, when it tries to tell exactly what a thing is. To **define,** then, is to *set bounds or limits to a thing, to state its essential nature.*

Purpose, Audience, Kind of Discourse

Definition has a number of purposes in your writing: to explain things to your readers, to make clear the key points in an argument, to make yourself understood in everyday affairs, to specify, particularize, itemize, individualize, and characterize.

Almost all expository or persuasive writing contains definitions. Definition often appears at the beginning of an expository or persuasive essay to explain unfamiliar terms or to make clear a specialized use of a word. It often combines with classification to limit class words. In analysis, it is used to characterize the parts that are separated from the whole.

Definition can be found in scientific essays, textbooks, dictionaries, books of reference, expository essays, magazine articles, encyclopedia articles, news stories, research reports, manuals, and government publications.

Invention and Definition

As a way of probing a subject, definition is closely related to both description and classification. It answers the questions: What is it? What are its limits or boundaries? What is its genus? What is its species? When someone asks you what something is, if it is a concrete object, you will most likely describe it; if it is an abstract entity, you will define it. Of course, concrete objects can be both described and defined. Defining is such a natural mental process that it is difficult to keep a person from defining. But although the process is intuitive, not everyone defines effectively, and some conscious attention to the process can be helpful.

The idea that the process is a natural one is constantly being reinforced by the conversations I hear every day. Some years ago, I was watching the "Good Night, America" program on television. Geraldo Rivera was interviewing one of the leaders of the Hell's Angels. Rivera commented that when he tried to take some unauthorized pictures of the Hell's Angels, he was almost "thumped." *Thumping*, he explained, is "beating someone to within an inch of their lives." Later, I was reading an interview between a local reviewer and a rock-music promoter. During the interview, the term *roadie* came up. "Roadies," the promoter was explaining, "are the male equivalent of groupies. They tag along with the band taking care of the equipment and doing odd jobs. They are attracted to the glamour surrounding the rock world. They only make $150 a week. They live on beer, chicks, and coke [cocaine]. Give them $150 a week and a motel room and they'll mutter, 'Hey, man, far out.' "

Although definition is a process that you use unconsciously almost every day of your life, in writing it has more formal uses. One use, quite obviously, is to clarify difficult or obscure terms in such a way that you will have no problem being understood.

Every discipline has its jargon. Linguists, for example, use terms such as *morpheme, phoneme, tagmeme, functional shift, clipping, blending*, and the like. Clearly, these terms need to be explained to a general audience. So if you are using a difficult or unfamiliar term in your writing, you should attempt to explain it before you go on to other ideas.

New terms also need to be defined. Within the past few years, you have absorbed, without any self-consciousness, hundreds of new words from newspapers, magazines, movies, and television, words such as *preppie, nerd, valley girl, break dance, rapping, freebase, yuppie, Walkman, veejay, word processing, VCR, PAC, gender gap, supply side, gelato, tofu, networking, wimp, veg out, Sunbelt, fast track, bicoastal.* Granted that you know in general what these words mean; you want to be precise in your writing, and precision often means definition.

Sometimes you may want to define a word whose meaning is so broad that it needs to be restricted. *Free world* is one of those terms. In the so-called *free world*, there are dictatorships such as those in some Central and South American countries, whereas beyond the *Iron Curtain* there are countries such as Yugoslavia and Bulgaria that have shown remarkable independence. What do you mean by the word *free* in your definition?

A final use of definition is to make fine distinctions between terms. For example, some people often use the words *love* and *sex* as synonyms. Do they in fact mean the same thing? What is the difference between love and sex? Love and affection? Love and devotion? Love and infatuation?

How to Form Logical Definitions

To define a word using **logical** or **formal definition,** *put the word to be defined into a class and then differentiate it from other members of the same class:*

Term	Class	Differentiation
A monorail	is a railway system	that uses cars that run on a single rail.
Flextime	is the work scheduling system	that allows employees to choose their own hours.
A wet lab	is a compartment in an undersea habitat	where aquanauts prepare for and return from missions.
To zap	is to destroy or kill	with a burst of gunfire, flame, or electric current.
A pollutant	is any gaseous, chemical, or organic waste	that contaminates air, soil, or water.

In putting a definition into a single sentence, use the same part of speech for the term to be defined as for the class term. Define a noun with a noun, an infinitive with an infinitive, and so forth. Keep the class word restricted. The larger the class, the more distinguishing characteristics you will have to add in order to separate the word from other members of the class.

Synonyms

To define a word using **synonyms,** simply *substitute for a word or phrase an equivalent word or phrase.* Although definition by synonym is not as exact as other methods of defining, it is a very common and useful method of defining words, because if you substitute a better known or less difficult word for one that is difficult or obscure, your reader will at least have a partial understanding of your intended meaning:

> *Uptight* means "tense or nervous."
> A *jock* is an "athlete."
> The word *ego* means "self."
> *To split* is "to go away" or "to leave."
> *Bellicose* is another word for "warlike."

Etymology

To define a word **etymologically,** *trace the origin and historical development of the word, including any change in its form or meaning.* For example, suppose you use the word *lucid* in a conversation and somebody says, "What does the word *lucid* mean?" You might reply: "The word *lucid* comes from the Latin word *lux, lucis,* which means 'light.' If you shed light on something, you make it clear. Hence the word *lucid* means 'clear.' "

These are the three main methods of defining. Some writers add definition by examples, by comparison, by description, or by repetition, but these latter seem more properly to be aids to definition rather than ways of defining.

Dictionary Definitions

A **dictionary definition** is not a special method of defining. It includes, rather, most of the methods that we have been discussing: logical or formal definitions, synonyms, and etymologies. Let us look at a typical dictionary entry:

> **suburb** (sub'ərb) n. abbr. *sub.* **1.** a usually residential area or community outlying a city. **2.** *Plural.* The perimeter of country around a major city; environs. Used with *the.* [Middle English, from Old French *suburbe,* from Latin *suburbum: sub=,* near + *urbs,* city (see **urban**).]

The entry contains the word itself, the pronunciation of the word, the part of speech, and either (or both) a formal definition or a definition by synonym, followed by the etymology of the word. In defining a word, you need not be bound by the dictionary definition of the word, but you will find it useful to take it into consideration.

Exercises

1. Write a one-sentence logical definition of five of the following words:

   a. dune buggy   f. fast food

   b. videotape   g. commute

   c. data bank   h. autocide

   d. condominium   i. sexism

   e. inner city   j. hardhat

2. Define one of the following terms in a single paragraph by tracing its etymology:

   a. nausea   f. zombie

   b. butcher   g. dandelion

   c. colossal   h. bunk

   d. cockroach   i. clinic

   e. steward   j. boycott

3. Write a one-sentence definition of five of the following slang terms:

   a. airhead   f. groupie

   b. tubular   g. flake

   c. cranking   h. dude

   d. edged   i. bad-mouth

   e. awesome   j. totally bummed

4. Coin a word, and then define it in as many ways as you can.

5. You are an advertiser with a new product. Invent a name for the product. Then define it in a single paragraph. Include the suggested meaning of the word as well as its literal meaning. Here are some product names to get you started: Cascade, Sealy Posturpedic mattress, Whirlpool, Crest toothpaste, Velveeta cheese spread, Kleenex Softique tissues, Brim.

6. For class discussion using any of the methods discussed in this chapter, define the following:

   a. the American Dream

   b. the perfect woman

   c. the perfect man

   d. the ideal gift

   e. the perfect date

   f. Middle America

   g. Black English

   h. Chicano

   i. the domino theory

   j. a good bargain

Patterns of Definition

How do you use definitions in your writing? Often at the beginning of an essay, you may need to explain key words necessary for understanding the meaning of what is to follow. Or you may want to explain a term that might be unfamiliar to the reader. In an argument, you would certainly want to make clear the terms of the argument. Definition is invaluable here.

Definition is seldom the length of an entire theme, although in some books or articles in which the author is trying to come to grips with the essence of a thing, it can be of essay length. More frequently, however, a definition goes on for a sentence or two or for the length of a paragraph. In the following selection from *The Theater of the Absurd*, Martin Esslin uses a variety of ways of defining:

> "Absurd" originally meant "out of harmony" in a musical context. Hence its dictionary definition: "out of harmony with reason or propriety: incongruous, unreasonable, illogical." In common usage in the English-speaking world, "absurd" may simply mean "ridiculous." But this is not the sense in which Camus uses the word, and in which it is used when we speak of the Theater of the Absurd. In an essay on Kafka, Ionesco defined his understanding of the term as follows: "Absurd is that which is devoid of purpose. . . . Cut off from his religious, metaphysical, and transcendental roots, man is lost; all his actions become senseless, absurd, useless."

The first sentence defines by etymology. The word there that gives the reader a clue is the word *originally*. The second sentence is the "dictionary definition." It gives a string of synonyms. The third sentence defines by giving another synonym. The next sentence merely states, but does not define, Camus's stipulative use of the word. The last sentence is a logical definition, which is also stipulative; that is, Ionesco specifies the way he is going to use the term in an essay on Kafka.

In the next selection, E. M. Forster distinguishes between a story and a plot by first defining each term logically, then adding examples, and finally, toward the end, defining by function:

> Let us define a plot. We have defined a story as a narrative of events arranged in their time-sequence. A plot is also a narrative of events, the emphasis falling on causality. "The king died and then the queen died" is a story. "The king died, and then the queen died of grief" is a plot. The time-sequence is preserved, but the sense of causality overshadows it. Or again: "The queen died, no one knew why, until it was discovered that it was through grief at the death of the king." This is a plot with a mystery in it, a form capable of high development. It suspends the time-sequence, it moves as far away from the story as its limitations will allow. Consider the death of the queen. If it is in a story we say, "and then?" If it is in a plot we ask, "why?" That is the fundamental difference between these two aspects of the novel. A plot cannot be told to a gaping audience of cavemen or to a tyrannical sultan or to their modern descendant the movie-public. They can only be kept wide awake by "and then—and then—." They can only supply curiosity. But a plot demands intelligence and memory also.

> —E. M. Forster, *Aspects of the Novel*

Constructing Definition Paradigms

Although a definition is seldom the length of an entire essay, there may be times when, depending on your audience and purpose, you will want to extend a definition. One way to extend a definition is to cite the different meanings of the term to be defined in different sections of your paper, rather than to define the term in a single sentence. To construct a definition paradigm based on this plan, you divide your definition into parts in your thesis sentence. You then add sentences to the thesis so that each successive sentence isolates and defines a part of the total meaning of the term. Each of the subsequent sentences will be in the form of a definition, and *the sentences* that make up the paradigm will *form a relational pattern of definition*. If your subject lends itself to ethical and emotional appeals, you include ethical and emotional words in the sentences of your paradigm.

The sentence paradigm below, adapted from an essay by Nelson Francis ("Three Meanings of Grammar") that follows in this chapter, is a good example of an extended definition paradigm:

People mean several things when they use the word *"grammar."*

The *first meaning* of *grammar* is "the set of formal patterns in which the words of a language are arranged in order to convey larger meanings."

The *second meaning* of *grammar* is "the branch of linguistic science which is concerned with the description, analysis, and formularization of formal language patterns."

The *third meaning* of *grammar* is "linguistic etiquette."

These, then, are the *three meanings* of *grammar:* a form of behavior; a field of study, of science; and a branch of etiquette.

As you have done with the other paradigms, after you construct your definition paradigm, you examine each sentence carefully, making certain that each accurately represents your intended meaning, your attitude toward your subject, and your ethical and emotional stance. Next, you review the reasoning process, and then you consider the kinds of supporting details you will need in the body of your paper. Finally, you revise the sentences of your paradigm.

To write a paper based on the mode of definition, using your paradigm as a guide, you provide a suitable introduction, appropriate supporting details, and a conclusion. The form of your overall paper will look like this:

Extended Definition Pattern 1
Introduction (includes thesis)
Meaning 1 (partial definition of key term)
Meaning 2 (partial definition of key term)
Meaning 3, 4, 5 . . .
Conclusion (includes clincher sentence)

Another way to write a paper based on the mode of definition is to begin with a logical definition in a single declarative sentence and then use that sentence as a thesis. Next you expand the *genus* or class word in the logical definition. Then you expand the attributes. The resultant pattern would have this form:

Extended Definition Pattern 2
Introduction (includes logical definition)
Expansion of the genus
Expansion of the differentia
Conclusion (includes clincher sentence)

A final way to write an extended definition paper paradigm is to begin with a sentence in the form of a logical definition and then add supporting details. This kind of pattern would look like this:

Extended Definition Pattern 3
Introduction (includes logical definition)
Supporting details
Supporting details
Supporting details
Conclusion (includes clincher sentence)

Like the other kinds of essay structures you have looked at, essays that use definition as a mode of developing ideas have a characteristic vocabulary that will help your readers to follow your thinking:

define	strictly speaking	interpretation
explain	particulars	literal
specify	in other words	synonym
limit	denotation	paraphrase
clarify	meaning	explanatory

The following essay by W. Nelson Francis follows the extended definition pattern that divides the definition of a term into parts:

Three Meanings of Grammar

1

A curious paradox exists in regard to grammar. On the one hand it is felt to be the dullest and driest of academic subjects, fit only for those in whose veins the red blood of life had long since turned to ink. On the other, it is a subject upon which people who would scorn to be professional grammarians hold very dogmatic opinions, which they will defend with considerable emotion. Much of this prejudice stems from the usual sources of prejudice—ignorance and confusion. Even highly educated people seldom have a clear idea of what grammarians do, and there is an unfortunate confusion about the meaning of the term "grammar" itself.

2

Hence it would be well to begin with definitions. What do people mean when they use the word "grammar"? Actually, the word is used to refer to three different things and much of the emotional thinking about matters grammatical arises from confusion about these three different meanings.

3

The first thing we mean by "grammar" is "the set of formal patterns in which the words of a language are arranged in order to convey larger meanings." It is not necessary that we be able to discuss these patterns self-consciously in order to be able to use them. In fact, all speakers of a language above the age of five or six know how to use its complex form of organization with considerable skill; in this sense of the word—call it "Grammar 1"—they are thoroughly familiar with its grammar.

4

The second meaning of "grammar"—call it "Grammar 2"—is "the branch of linguistic science which is concerned with the description, analysis, and formularization of formal language patterns." Just as gravity was in full operation before Newton's apple fell, so grammar in the first sense was in full operation before anyone formulated the first rule that began the history of grammar as a study.

5

The third sense in which people use the word "grammar" is "linguistic etiquette." This we may call "Grammar 3." The word in this sense is often coupled with a derogatory adjective: we say that the expression "he ain't here" is "bad grammar." What we mean is that such an expression is bad linguistic manners in certain circles. From the point of view of "Grammar 1" it is faultless; it conforms just as completely to the structural patterns of English as does "he isn't here." The trouble with it is like the trouble with Prince Hal in Shakespeare's play—it is "bad," not in itself, but in the company it keeps.

6

As has already been suggested, much confusion arises from mixing these meanings. One hears a good deal of criticism of teachers of English couched in such terms as "they don't teach grammar any more." Criticism of this sort is based on the wholly unproved assumption that teaching Grammar 2 will increase the student's proficiency in Grammar 1 or improve his manners in Grammar 3. Actually the form of Grammar 2 which is usually taught is a very inaccurate and misleading analysis of the facts of Grammar 1; and it is therefore of highly questionable value in improving a person's ability to handle the structural patterns of his language. It is hardly reasonable to expect that teaching a person some inaccurate grammatical analysis will either improve the effectiveness of his assertions or teach him what expressions are acceptable to use in a given context.

7

These, then are the three meanings of "grammar": Grammar 1, a form of behavior; Grammar 2, a field of study, or science; and Grammar 3, a branch of etiquette.

—W. Nelson Francis, "Revolution in Grammar"

The thesis sentence is the second sentence of the second paragraph: "What do people mean when they use the word 'grammar'?" The word *grammar* is the key word which is to be defined. The next sentence indicates the plan of development. ("The word is used to refer to three different things"). Then subsequent sentences and paragraphs enumerate a different meaning of the word *grammar* ("the first thing we mean . . .," "the second meaning of 'grammar' . . .," "the third sense in which people use the word 'grammar' . . .,").

The abstracted underlying pattern has the following structure:

The word *[grammar]* is used to *refer* to *three different things.* . . .

The *first [meaning of grammar]* is "the set of formal patterns in which the words of a language are arranged in order to convey larger meanings."

The *second meaning* of "grammar" . . . is "the branch of linguistic science which is concerned with the description, analysis, and formularization of formal language patterns."

The *third [meaning of grammar]* is "linguistic etiquette."

These, then, are the *three meanings* of "grammar". . . . a form of behavior, . . . a field of study, or science, and . . . a branch of etiquette.

In writing your own extended definitions, you may choose to follow a formal pattern very closely, as in the W. Nelson Francis essay, or you may want to use a less formal approach, as in the following student paper:

Environmentalist, Preservationist, Conservationist: What's the Difference?

The word *environmentalist* has been bandied about so much that a person can't be sure in a given instance whether the word is complimentary or pejorative, whether it applies to someone favoring an automobile noise-abatement program or someone wishing to close Yellowstone Park and convert it to a pristine wilderness. Once very modish, the word is now almost useless as a conveyor of precise meaning.

Until the 1960s, environmentalists were simply people who were concerned about the environment, about litter, polluted streams, and endangered wildlife. The word *environmentalist* was not a household word. But in the sixties, the term became identified with the youth protest movement and with causes as diverse as vegetarianism and antiwar demonstrations. Through the late sixties and into the seventies, the meaning of the word came to depend increasingly on the point of view of the user. Thus, land developers labeled Environmental Protection Agency officials as *progress-blocking environmentalists*. Concerned citizens who demanded that air- and water-polluting industries "clean up their act" proudly identified themselves as *concerned environmentalists*.

Probably the most serious consequence of the loose definition of the word has been the blurring of the distinction between *preservationist* and *conservationist*. Both are now indiscriminately referred to as *environmentalists*. A preservationist who advocates closing a wilderness area to all public use is termed an environmentalist, as is the conservationist who urges moderation that will permit public use of an area while preventing depletion of its natural resources. The term is more likely to be interpreted as the *radical preservationist*, with sometimes serious consequences.

If one can derive a moral from all of this, it might be as follows: There is a need for precision in the definition of words that one uses. Imprecise diction, whether deliberate or not, is potentially as dangerous as outright misrepresentation.

—Shirley

Exercises

1. Discuss the W. Nelson Francis essay in class. What is Francis's purpose in writing the essay? What is his attitude toward his subject? Does the essay include ethical or emotional appeals? What methods of definition does Francis use in this essay? How does he support the definitions?

2. Write an extended definition, in the manner of W. Nelson Francis, on one of the following terms or on one of your own choosing. Consider first your purpose, potential readers, and a writing situation. Then construct a paradigm, including ethical and emotional appeals if it suits your purpose; critique the paradigm; rewrite it if necessary; and write your paper:

a. success   f. leadership

b. happiness   g. patriotism

c. friendship   h. optimist

d. freedom   i. pessimist

e. loyalty   j. liberal education

3. Write an essay explaining to a friend the differences in meaning of these terms: liberal, conservative, radical, moderate. Include logical definitions and give specific examples.

4. Discuss in class, by defining the differences, the following terms:

   a. fair, open-minded, bigoted, prejudiced, narrow-minded

   b. clever, intelligent, wise, foolish, stupid, shallow

   c. love, affection, devotion, fondness, infatuation

   d. generosity, liberality, selfishness, meanness

   e. aggressive, assertive, timid, fearful, cowardly

5. Select one of the following words or phrases to define, analyze, and illustrate in context. Consider the following points: 1. denotation (literal meaning) and connotation (suggested meaning) of the word, 2. any technical or limited uses of the word, 3. your own reaction to the use of the word and your reasons, 4. a critical evaluation of the meaning and effectiveness of the word in general communication.

   a. academic freedom   e. sophistication

   b. open mind   f. adult

   c. progress   g. individualism

   d. modern   h. culture

6. According to chronological age, you probably can be described as a teenager, a youth, an adolescent, a juvenile, a young adult, a guy or a gal, a stud or a chick. Or you may be someone who can be described as an adult, a grownup, middle-aged, mature. . . . Write a short theme analyzing your personal responses to these words as they apply to you. Do you like them or dislike them? Why? What does each connote? Are there any other words that you prefer as self-description?

7. Examine your attitude toward abstractions such as honor, virtue, love, loyalty, brotherhood, and truth. Cite specific experiences of the use of these words, avoidance of them, and so forth.

CHAPTER 6

*Patterns of Thought:
Comparison, Contrast,
and Analogy*

Comparison and Contrast

Comparison and contrast are such familiar everyday activities that it may be difficult for you to think of them as important mental processes. Yet without the ability to perceive similarities, you could not classify, define, or generalize. And without the ability to perceive differences, you could not analyze, define, or describe.

Comparison is *the process of discovering similarities between two or more ideas, objects, or events.* **Contrast** is *the process of discovering differences between two or more ideas, objects, or events.* Both words conjure up all kinds of interesting images that reflect the widespread use of comparison and contrast in everyday thinking. The word *similarity* calls to mind words and expressions such as *twin, double, counterpart, pair, alter ego,* and *look-alikes.* The word contrast calls forth words and expressions such as *mismatched; a shade of difference; cast in a different mold;* and *this, that, or the other.*

Although comparison and contrast are closely related, they can be regarded as different mental processes. In examining any two things, you can mentally explore their similarities without necessarily exploring their differences, or you can mentally investigate their differences without investigating their similarities. In actuality, any relationship between two or more things will involve some degree of similarity as well as some degree of difference.

140

Purpose, Audience, Kind of Discourse

Of the rhetorical modes, comparison and contrast may well be the most important. Both words suggest choices from among alternatives. Seldom a day goes by that you don't have to make important choices. You have to choose between two careers, two or more products, two political candidates, two goals, two courses of action. In making your choices, you use comparisons for different aims and for different kinds of audiences.

Comparisons and contrasts underlie all of our intentions. Scientists use comparisons and contrasts in their experiments. Logicians use them to draw conclusions. Politicians use them to formulate policies. Judges use them to render decisions. Ministers and priests teach and admonish with comparisons and contrasts.

Comparisons and contrasts can be found in any kind of writing: magazine articles, advertising, essays, news articles, letters, editorials, textbooks, scientific writing, reports, political speeches, pamphlets, instruction manuals, poems, fables, and parables.

Invention and Comparison

The topics of similarity and difference, with their subtopics of literal and figurative similarity, difference in kind, and difference in degree, are perhaps the most fundamental topics in the inventive process. They give rise to such questions as: What is it like? How is it similar to other things? How does it differ from other things?

Literal similarity is based on perceiving likenesses between subjects that belong to the same class, as in these examples:

> This table is square. That table is square.
> Both trees have drooping branches.

Figurative similarity is based on perceiving likenesses between subjects that belong to different classes:

> The skin around his eyes is pulled tight, like the skin of an onion.
> We were as naked as stone.

Difference in kind is based upon perceiving differences in common *traits* or *aspects* of a thing:

> This flower has bright, colorful blossoms.

That flower has pale, faded blossoms.
Lincoln was largely self-educated; Ford was not.

Difference in degree is based upon perceiving the *extent* to which a thing is unlike something else:

Crest toothpaste is better than other toothpastes.
The influence of television is greater than that of newspapers.

In exploring a subject by using the topic of comparison, you would probably follow a sequence of steps that might be described as follows:

Choose subjects that are interesting enough to challenge your imagination.

Try, if you decide to compare two commonplace subjects, to look at them from a fresh point of view.

Consider your purpose and your angle of vision. What particular point of view, what particular insight can you give your readers to make them see what you see?

Be certain that there are enough aspects of the things to be compared to make a valid and interesting comparison. An aspect is a characteristic or feature considered from one point of view.

Choose only the most significant aspects of a subject to compare.

Exercises

1. For purposes of class discussion and as an exercise in invention, compare or contrast:

   a. two styles of clothing

   b. two movies

   c. two television shows

   d. two songs

   e. two talk-show hosts

   f. two ideas

   g. two kinds of music

   h. two dances

   i. two magazines

   j. two sports

2. Discuss, as an exercise in invention, some of the cultural differences that exist between any two nationalities, racial groups, special interest groups, or subcultural groups in the United States.

3. Write five sentences in which you point out the similarities between two things. Write five sentences in which you point out differences. Make five of the comparisons literal and five figurative. Then discuss these sentences in class.

4. Bring to class magazine ads that use comparisons to make a point, and discuss the effectiveness or lack of effectiveness of the comparisons.

Constructing Comparison and Contrast Paradigms

To construct paradigms based on the modes of comparison and contrast, you can choose from a number of possibilities, but the most basic patterns are the *half-and-half pattern* and the *characteristics pattern*.

To construct a paradigm based on the **half-and-half pattern,** you begin with a sentence that indicates the subjects you are going to compare. To that sentence, you add other sentences, arranging them so that you take up the points of comparison of the first subject in the first half of your paper, and the points of comparison of the second subject in the second part of your paper. As you are writing, you arrange the sentences in such a way that *they form a relational pattern of comparison and contrast*. To help your reader grasp your plan more easily, you include comparison words such as *similar to, different from, more than, less than, as, but, however*, and the like in the sentences of your paradigm. If your subject lends itself to ethical and emotional appeals, then as you are constructing your paradigm you include ethical and emotional words and phrases:

> Close, happy families have *more* in common *than* unhappy families.
>
> They know how to talk and how to listen.
>
> They have a sense of play or humor.
>
> They respect the privacy of its members.
>
> They teach a sense of right and wrong.
>
> Unhappy families, *however,* do not communicate their thoughts and feelings.
>
> They have little patience and are humorless.
>
> They fail to respect the privacy of their members.

They neglect to teach matters of right and wrong.

These are the signs that *differentiate* happy families *from* unhappy families and keep them close.

After you construct the sentences of your half-and-half pattern, analyze them as you did the sentences of the other paradigms. Scrutinize each sentence to make certain that each accurately represents your intended meaning, your purpose, your attitude toward your subject, considerations of audience, and your ethical and emotional stance. Next, consider the kinds of facts, statistics, opinions, proofs, or evidence you will need to support the sentences of your paradigm. Finally, revise the sentences of your paradigm.

To write a paper based on the half-and-half pattern, you provide an appropriate introduction, supporting details, and an effective conclusion, using your paradigm as a guide. The following pattern represents the plan of the entire essay:

The Half-and-Half Pattern
Introduction (includes thesis)
Subject 1
    Characteristic 1 (plus supporting details)
    Characteristic 2 (plus supporting details)
    Characteristic 3, 4, 5 . . .
Subject 2
    Characteristic 1 (plus supporting details)
    Characteristic 2 (plus supporting details)
    Characteristic 3, 4, 5 . . .
Conclusion (includes "clincher" sentence)

Like essays based on the other modes, comparison and contrast essays use a characteristic vocabulary to make explicit to the reader the logical progression of ideas:

similar to	differ from	otherwise
like	however	nevertheless
correspond to	in contrast to	less than
resemble	on the other hand	more than
as	on the contrary	unlike
in like manner	in opposition to	although

The following student paper is a good example of the *half-and-half pattern*:

Myrtle and Peterbone

Thesis   In the days of my younger youth, the days of popsicle addicts and hula-hoop freaks, I had two great friends I divided my time with. Myrtle and Peterbone were both my friends, but that is the closest they ever came to having anything in common.

Subject 1   Myrtle was my childhood Doris Day. Her hair was so blonde that it would turn green from swimming in public pools, and the sunkissed freckles on her nose and knees was all the tan she ever got. Her nose was pug and turned up, and she always seemed to have her front teeth missing. She invariably wore that no-teeth smile together with a pink sunsuit to offset her aquamarine twinkling-star eyes.

Myrtle's parents were sort of hicks. They wore cowboy clothes and boots and someone was always cleaning catfish in the sink. Myrtle's mother must have been kind of quiet because all I remember of her are the swooshing and squeaking her levis and cowboy boots made as she did her Saturday housecleaning on Sunday morning. Myrtle's father is just as vague to me, but I think he wore flowered cowboy shirts and talked in kind of a twang whenever he wasn't engrossed in a beer can and the TV wrestling match. So while Myrtle's parents swooshed and squeaked and twanged, we would go off to see what new activities we could create for amusement.

The best thing Myrtle and I did together, aside from normal girlhood play, was tying strings onto locusts' wings and flying them around our heads like motordriven model airplanes. We never seemed to hurt them, as cruel as it may seem. We only did it in the summer time when the locusts drove everyone crazy with their noisy symphonies. The rest of the year we conjured up new species of paper dolls, tortuously hard games of jacks, or different schemes for not getting caught playing in the nearby irrigation ditch. When I would get tired of girlish pastimes, I would go over to Peterbone's.

Subject 2   Peterbone was Myrtle's opposite. He was a coffee-with-cream colored Catholic Mexican, with charcoal-black crewcut hair and the deepest ebony eyes I'd ever seen. No swimming pool could turn his near-bald head green, and if Peterbone ever had freckles, they were all run together into a tawny bronze. Peterbone had one front tooth missing, but no natural occurrence was responsible—it had been knocked out by a mean older brother. A white shirt and old jeans were what he wore the most, along with scuffed black shoes (untied) and two different kinds of socks.

Peterbone's parents were Mexican, but they nearly always spoke English, except when a family fight began. Then a tidal wave of Spanish words would crash into the air and I would, if present, stare dumbfounded as the deluge of Latin curses deafened my ears.

Choo-chee was Peterbone's mother. She wore red bandana scarves on her raven hair and yellow zoris on her size ten feet. She was very kind to her naughty boys and laughed with them lots of times when they got into trouble. She never kept a really neat house because she liked daytime soap operas, but her smiles and hot tortillas kept you from noticing. Peterbone's dad was a fireman. He didn't have much of an accent, but he wore white shirts too and liked boxing matches on Friday nights.

When Peterbone's parents were busy, we liked to stomp on caps in the driveway or sail boats down the ditch. That was only if Peterbone was in a good mood. If he wasn't, he would hold back my arms and get his brother Bobby to sock me in the face or stomach. One day I retaliated and punched Peterbone right in the nose. It bled all down his white shirt and I played with Myrtle for a long time after; but Peterbone's mean streak was what I liked the most.

As a Kool-Aid wino, I had a childhood full of locusts and caps and two strange friends as different as jellybeans and brussel sprouts. Myrtle and Peterbone were as different as night and day. Or perchance they were more like two different novels, but both shelved under the title of friend in my faded rose scrapbook of people I know.

—Linda

This student paper is beautifully organized, interestingly written, and sensitively handled. The basic comparison between the two friends is set up in the opening paragraph ("Myrtle and Peterbone were both my friends, but that is the closest they ever came to having anything in common"). In the next three paragraphs, Myrtle, Myrtle's parents, and the activities of Linda and Myrtle are described. Then, in the following four paragraphs, Peterbone, Peterbone's parents, and the activities of Linda and Peterbone are described. Finally, the last paragraph returns to the beginning.

To construct a paradigm based on the **characteristics pattern,** you begin with a sentence that sets up the comparison. Then you add other sentences, arranging them so that you take up the first characteristic of both subject 1 and 2 in the first part of your paper, the second characteristic of both subjects in the second part of your paper, the third characteristic of both subjects in the third part of your paper, and so forth. In other words, in following this plan, you proceed by characteristics. As you did in constructing the half-and-half pattern, you arrange *the sentences* in such a way as to *form a relational pattern of comparison and contrast.* You also include ethical and emotional words and phrases, if you intend to appeal to your reader's moral sensibilities and emotions:

Close, happy families have *more* in common *than* unhappy families.

Happy families know how to talk and how to listen.

Unhappy families, *however*, do not know how to communicate their thoughts and feelings.

Happy families have a sense of play or humor.

Unhappy families have little patience and are humorless.

Happy families respect the privacy of their members.

Unhappy families fail to respect the privacy of their members.

Happy families teach a sense of right and wrong.

Unhappy families neglect to teach matters of right and wrong.

These are the signs that *differentiate* happy families *from* unhappy families and keep them close.

As you did in constructing paradigms based on the other modes, after you construct the sentences of your characteristics pattern, examine each one carefully to be sure that each accurately represents your intended meaning, your purpose, your attitude toward your subject, your audience, and your ethical and emotional stance. Then, consider the kind of evidence you will need to support the sentences of your paradigm. Finally, as you have done many times before, revise each sentence.

To write an essay based on the characteristics pattern, you provide a suitable introduction, supporting details for the body of the paper, and an effective conclusion. The pattern for the whole essay will have a shape like this:

The Characteristics Pattern
Introduction (includes thesis)
Characteristic 1 (plus supporting details)
   Subject 1
   Subject 2
Characteristic 2 (plus supporting details)
   Subject 1
   Subject 2
Characteristic 3, 4, 5 . . .
   Subject 1
   Subject 2
Conclusion (includes clincher sentence)

The following letter, taken from a *Dear Abby* column, uses a characteristics pattern, and suggests the ubiquity of patterns such as these even in informal writing:

It's a Man's World

Thesis	Anybody who thinks women have equal rights in this country is crazy.
Charac-teristic 1	If a man's trousers are too tight, he's just put on a little weight. (If a woman's skirt is too tight, she's trying to be sexy.)
Charac-teristic 2	If a man stands on a street corner, he's getting some fresh air. (If a woman stands on a corner, she's looking to be picked up.)
Charac-teristic 3	If a man has one drink too many, he's "feeling good." (If a woman has one drink too many, she's a lush.)
Charac-teristic 4	If a man has a night out with the boys, he's put in a hard day at work and needs to "relax." (If a woman has a night out with the girls, she's up to no good and should stay home with her family.)
Charac-teristic 5	If a man cheats on his wife, people say he's probably married to a cold fish and he's only human. (If a woman cheats, she's a tramp.)
Charac-teristic 6	If a kid turns out good, he's a chip off the old block. (If he turns out bad, his mother did the rotten job of raising him.)
Conclu-sion	It's still a man's world!

—Wants Equality

Dear Wants:

Only if he's single. If he's married, almost everything is in his wife's name.

—From *Dear Abby*, Abigail Van Buren (May 10, 1976)

The student paper that follows also uses the *characteristics pattern:*

Cézanne's *Orchard in Pontoise* and Pisarro's *Orchard with Flowering Fruit Trees, Springtime, Pontoise*

1

Thesis	When reading *The World of Cézanne* by Richard W. Murphy, I was surprised to learn that one of Paul Cézanne's paintings, called *Orchard in Pontoise,* is similar in some respects to a painting by Camille Pisarro. Both paintings are of a certain orchard in Pontoise, a village outside Paris; both were finished in 1877; both were painted by artists who were friends. Yet the two works are obviously different in a number of ways.

2

Charac-teristic 1 (subject matter)

Pisarro's painting, called *Orchard with Flowering Fruit Trees, Spring-time, Pontoise*, depicts several large houses on a hill. At the foot of the hill is an orchard of flowering trees. A small path, lined with bushes, is clearly visible through the tall trees. Cézanne's painting shows the same view of the orchard at a different time of the year when the trees were not flower-ing. The trees are fewer and shorter than those in Cézanne's painting, giv-ing a better view of the house on the hill. The path through the trees is hard to see, and it runs parallel to a long white wall not seen in the Pisarro painting.

3

Charac-teristic 2 (style)

Pisarro, who was an Impressionist painter, displayed several tech-niques characteristic of the Impressionists. He used short, delicate brush strokes to form images. There are no sharp outlines or contrasts in his painting. Instead, tiny patches of color are grouped to suggest buildings and trees. The houses seem to blend into the background, giving the work a soft, unfocused look. Like Pisarro, Cézanne used no sharp outlines or con-trasts, but he used slightly longer, more definite strokes on the buildings to make them sharper and more angular. Cézanne was obviously more in-terested in the linear contours and architectural structure of the buildings and walls than was Pisarro. His painting also has a soft unfocused look, but the shapes have more solidity and clarity than those in the Pisarro painting because the buildings stand out rather than blend in with the background.

4

Charac-teristic 3 (texture)

The short brush strokes and the build-up of paint give Pisarro's work a rough, bumpy texture. The sky in particular moves in quick, swirling licks of blue, yellow, and white. The leaves on the trees are simply dabs of color against a mottled background. Both areas reinforce the rough texture of the painting. Cézanne's painting has a smoother, glossier texture than Pisarro's, despite the similar brushwork. Cézanne used fewer layers of paint to achieve this texture. The sky is simplified. The leaves on the trees are represented by vague splotches of green that are less definite and less recognizable than Pisarro's.

5

Charac-teristic 4 (color)

Pisarro used mainly brown tones with blues and greens. However, he added bright spots of pure red pigment to give warmth and add interest. The background of the painting has a variety of dark earth tones and greens. Light green tones mixed with blues dominate the color scheme of Cézanne's painting. He used no reds or browns. Instead, he balanced the green with beige, white, and ivory. Overall, his painting is lighter in color and less realistic than the Pisarro painting.

6

Conclu-   Cézanne's *Orchard in Pontoise* and Pisarro's *Orchard with Flowering*
sion   *Fruit Trees, Springtime, Pontoise* demonstrate how two artists of similar backgrounds can interpret the same scene in very different ways.

—Michele

The last sentence of the first paragraph of this essay sets up the basic comparison. ("Yet the two works are obviously different in a number of ways.") The second paragraph takes up the first characteristic of the two paintings, subject matter. The third paragraph takes up the second characteristic, style or technique. The fourth paragraph takes up the third feature, texture. The fifth paragraph discusses the use of color. And the conclusion comments on the similarity of background of the two artists, but differences in interpretation.

Both the half-and-half pattern and the characteristics pattern are fairly easy to follow. The **point-by-point pattern** is a variation of the characteristics pattern, in which the features of the subjects to be compared are presented in single sentences, using words like *both*, *each*, *also*, and *too*. The following article, which appeared in the *New York Times* after John F. Kennedy's picture replaced that of Franklin on the half-dollar, uses a combination of the half-and-half pattern and the point-by-point pattern:

Kennedy and Franklin

Benjamin Franklin, symbol of American enlightenment in the Age of Reason, now steps aside for John Fitzgerald Kennedy, champion of reason in the Age of the Atom. Franklin, whose profile has graced the United States fifty-cent coin since 1948 is being replaced by the image of the thirty-fifth President. That Kennedy should occupy a place held by Franklin is appropriate, for there are many parallels in the lives, outlooks, and interests of the two American figures. Points of likeness range from the coincidental to the philosophical.

Both men were born in the Boston area: Franklin on Milk Street in the city proper and Kennedy in suburban Brookline. Both lived in England for a time, Franklin as an agent for the colonial Pennsylvania Assembly and Kennedy as the son of the American ambassador.

While in England, Franklin once considered establishing a swimming school. He was an excellent swimmer who one day covered the distance on the Thames from Chelsea to Blackfriars—about three miles. Kennedy's swimming ability saved his life when, as a young naval officer in World War II, he swam from his rammed PT boat to the safety of a lonely southwest Pacific islet. The distance was about three miles. At Harvard, he was a member of the swimming team.

Before entering public life both men were active journalists— Franklin was publisher of the *Pennsylvania Gazette* and, earlier, of his brother's *New England Courant;* Kennedy was a reporter for the International News Service in 1945. Both were authors of popular works in the field of biography: Franklin with his *Autobiography* and Kennedy with his Pulitzer-prize-winning *Profiles in Courage.*

Interests in culture and the intellectual life were common characteristics. Kennedy held his alma mater, Harvard University, in special esteem and served on its Board of Overseers. Franklin helped found the Academy of Philadelphia, which grew into the University of Pennsylvania.

Both were intensely concerned with science (Franklin was a scientist in his own right) and keenly aware of its value to mankind. In 1783 Franklin watched the first hydrogen balloon's ascension from Paris' Champ de Mars. To a sceptic who questioned the worth of the experiment Franklin replied: "What good is a newborn baby?" In February 1962 Kennedy was personally on hand at Cape Canaveral to honor Astronaut John H. Glenn on his return to the spaceport from America's first manned orbital flight. Kennedy devoted time and much effort to promote the nation's technological development.

—From the *New York Times*, Jan. 5, 1964

In using comparison patterns, you need not restrict yourself to these patterns exactly as outlined. Paradigms can be used with a great deal of skill and flexibility, as the following student paper illustrates:

Two Women

1

The Phoenix Art museum exhibits approximately fifteen sculptures on its grounds, all by twentieth-century artists, ranging from jagged iron abstractions to strictly representational bronze castings. The most commanding of these, at least in terms of sheer bulk, is Paolo Soleri's *Flying Woman.* One of the least commanding, or so it seems at first, is Francisco Zuniga's *Woman at Siesta.* Each is situated in the grassy mall area between the Phoenix Library and the museum, the Soleri rising from the lawn abruptly, the Zuniga sleeping peacefully beneath a Palo Verde.

2

Soleri's woman is constructed of welded plates of iron-ox, a sheet iron developed for commercial use, whose surface rusts evenly, creating a superficial shield against deeper rusting. The Zuniga is of cast bronze and has developed the light turquoise patina associated with that more traditional material. The rust-orange color of the Soleri heightens its distinctiveness from its grassy surroundings, while the greenish hue of the Zuniga causes it to blend even more unobtrusively with the grass and the blue-green leaves of the Palo Verde beneath which it rests.

3

The Soleri sculpture consists of two stacked cubes that rise to an overall height of fifteen feet. The lower, much smaller block has sides of five feet in length, with exactly centered circular openings in each of the vertical sides that are each three feet in diameter. The upper block duplicates this pattern on a larger scale: the sides are nine feet in length for the cube, with circular openings measuring almost seven feet in diameter. Through these circular openings the angular woman flies, parallel to the ground, one arm stretched in front of her, the other behind, in a sort of side-straddle swim stroke through the air and the cube. Her angular face is centered in the opening that faces the main entrance, her legs outstretched side by side behind her.

4

The Zuniga drapes over a folding chair, her head reclined against the topmost slat. From ground level to the top of her head measures four-and-one-half feet.

5

Each sculpture is an exaggeration. The Soleri is far too angular. The Zuniga is far too round. Soleri's woman owes more to geometry than to flesh-and-blood women; Zuniga's woman owes her rounded form to too many tortillas. The lines of the Zuniga woman are exaggerations taken from life—the high cheekbones and narrow nose are common features among native Mexican Indians. Soleri's woman seems, on the other hand, to be an exaggeration of an abstract idea. No woman I've ever heard of has eleven distinct planes in her left thigh. This is not an indictment. Artists are free to illustrate abstract ideas no less than to represent or exaggerate nature, certainly.

6

But this *is* an indictment. Soleri's woman, represented as flying, is actually supported beneath her rib cage by struts, which anchor her to the bottom inside of the upper cube. Her (angular) hair, as though duplicating the famous oversight of the *Boy Removing Thorn From Foot*, hangs straight down rather than streaming behind, as Newton's second law of motion insists that hair propelled through space at the speed necessary to keep such an enormous bulk aloft would do. Thus, the sculpture defies a law of craftsmanship—that the supporting elements be incorporated into the functional elements—and it also defies the laws of gravity and inertia we all must live with.

7

There is a worse flaw. The *Flying Woman* is two-dimensional. She was created to be seen from the front. Viewing her from any of the other three sides, one cannot discern exactly what the jumble of metal is—neither her function, her gender, nor her species is apparent, except from the front. Sculpture, by definition, presents a three-dimensional object.

8

By contrast, Zuniga's woman sleeps peacefully, not aspiring to much, perhaps—but still patiently complying with the laws of physics, the demands of careful craftsmanship, and the aims of sculpture. Approached from any angle, she is obviously a woman asleep, supported from the earth by a folding chair. Thus, her support is a functional part of the sculpture. She is three-dimensional, and she does not demand that the viewer temporarily discount physics.

9

The Soleri sculpture seems to me to represent a lofty idea that is attractive but not possible, or both attractive *and* possible—but in a form different from the expression. In either case, the sculpture fails. The Zuniga seems to take on a much smaller aim. This woman will never leap beyond the bounds of geometry. Instead, when she wakes, she is likely to eat again and perhaps call her children to her side. Except that she will not awaken. She is sleeping. We all sleep. We all at one time took for our domains of sleep the soft, inviting body of a mother. The Zuniga seems full of that invitation. It accomplishes what it seems to propose. It is a successful sculpture.

—Jim

In this paper, the student uses a comparison paradigm, but avoids the rigidity of a strict half-and-half pattern or point-by-point pattern. His purpose is aesthetic appreciation through evaluation and interpretation. His audience is the other members of the class, although one can imagine a similar kind of essay appearing in a newspaper or magazine. The kind of writing is a critical essay, and the mode is contrast. The comparison paradigms help the student to think through his subject and to illuminate the features of each piece of sculpture through contrast.

The opening paragraph provides the reader with the situation at the Phoenix Art Museum and sets up the comparison. The second paragraph uses a point-by-point comparison. It deals primarily with the materials from which the two pieces of sculpture are constructed. The next paragraph describes the physical appearance of the Soleri sculpture. Paragraph four describes the Zuniga sculpture. The juxtaposition of the two descriptive paragraphs provides the contrast. The next paragraph returns to a point-by-point comparison, on the sentence level of the exaggerated details of each sculpture. Sometimes the comparisons are made by juxtaposing sentences ("The Soleri is far too angular. The Zuniga is far too round"). Sometimes the comparisons are made within the same sentence ("Soleri's woman owes more to geometry than to flesh-and-blood women; Zuniga's woman owes her rounded form to too many tortillas"). Paragraphs 6 and 7, which point to the ostensible flaws in Soleri's conception, contrast with paragraph 8, which praises Zuniga's craftsmanship in relation to his aim. The last paragraph furthers the interpretation and concludes with an evaluation.

Exercises

1. Analyze the comparison and contrast paradigms, both the half-and-half pattern and the characteristics pattern. Where might an essay based on these patterns appear? For what kinds of readers? Are there any words in the sentences of these paradigms to suggest that there are ethical and emotional appeals? What kinds of supporting details would you use to expand the middle section of these paradigms? Do you agree or disagree about the traits of happy and unhappy families? Can you think of any traits that might be included?

2. After you have thoroughly discussed the ideas contained in the above-mentioned paradigms in class, write an essay based on one of these paradigms. Since you will all be using the same basic pattern, bring the completed papers to class for comparison and further study.

3. Keeping in mind your purpose, a possible reader, and a writing situation, construct a comparison and contrast paradigm based on one of the patterns discussed in this chapter. Use *one* of the following subjects or a subject of your choice. Then write an essay based on the paradigm:

   a. two paintings   d. two cities

   b. two art objects   e. two short poems

   c. two people   f. two current issues

g. values

h. two sports figures

i. two celebrities

j. two political parties

4. For classroom discussion or for a writing assign, construct a comparison and contrast paradigm together in class. Consider your purpose, audience, and writing situation. Use any of the above subjects, one of your choice, or any of the following:

a. lyrics of two rock songs

b. two TV commercials

c. two magazine ads

d. two places

e. two teams (in sports)

f. two places

5. Many interesting comparisons can be made of artworks in the same medium (two paintings, sculptures, artistic photographs) and artworks in different mediums (painting and poem, painting and sculpture, etc.). If you are acquainted with any of these, you can use them for class discussion or for a writing assignment. The pictures of artistically designed magazine ads can also be used. A few possibilities are:

a. The statues of David by Michelangelo, Donatello, and Verrocchio (get Xerox copies of reproductions in art books).

b. Botticelli's *Venus and Mars* and Veronese's *Mars and Venus United by Love.*

c. Henri Matisse's *The Red Studio* (painting) and W. D. Snodgrass's poem: "Matisse: *The Red Studio.*"

d. Van Gogh's picture *The Starry Night* and Anne Sexton's poem, "The Starry Night."

Analogy

An **analogy** is *an extended comparison.* It is a kind of logical inference based on the premise that if two things resemble each other in some respects, they will probably be alike in other respects. If you wish to explain a concept but believe that your readers may not be familiar with your subject or that your subject is difficult and complex, you can compare it point by point with something similar but more familiar and less complex. The etymology of the word, from the Latin word *analogia* and the Greek *analogos,* meaning "proportion" or "equality of ratios," supports this notion of a point-by-point comparison with something else. The Latin and Greek sources suggest equivalence, correspondence, and likeness of relations.

It is difficult to imagine thinking without analogies. The process of discovering ideas using analogies is very similar to that of discovering ideas using comparisons. You explore your subject by comparing it point by point with something similar. Thinking in analogies is so ubiquitous that it is hard to see how we could get along without it.

Constructing Analogy Paradigms

Patterns of analogy are similar in some respects to those of comparison and contrast. The point-by-point comparison pattern seems to be especially suitable for expressing ideas and analogically.

To construct a paradigm based on analogy, you begin with a sentence that announces the subjects you are going to compare. Then you add other sentences, arranging them so that you make a point-by-point comparison of both subjects as you go along. All of *the sentences will work together to form a relational pattern of analogy:*

Car-pooling might be the *best* gasoline-saving device ever invented.

If two people share a ride, it's *like* doubling their overall gasoline mileage.

If three people share a ride, it's *like* tripling their gasoline mileage.

If four people share a ride, it's *like* getting four times their gasoline mileage.

The *more* people in car pools, the *greater* will be the gasoline savings.

The organizing sentence in this paradigm uses the comparison word *best* to make the analogy explicit. It also includes the two subjects to be compared *(car-pooling* and *gasoline-saving).* Each successive sentence also uses a comparison word (the word *like),* and each sentence includes the subjects that are being compared *(two people car-pooling . . . two times the gas mileage, three people car-pooling . . . three times the gas mileage,* etc.). The final sentence puts the analogy in more general terms.

To write an essay based on this pattern, as you did in writing an essay based on the mode of comparison and contrast, you provide an introduction, supporting details, and a conclusion. This larger pattern will look like the following:

Point-by-Point Analogy Pattern

Introduction (sets up the analogy)

Subject 1 is similar to subject 2 in this respect

Subject 1 is similar to subject 2 in this respect

Subject 1 is similar to subject 2 in this respect

Subject 1 is similar to subject 2 in this respect

Conclusion (therefore, subject 1 is similar to subject 2 in some
 respect known of one, but not known of the other)

In the following selection the author uses a pattern of organization that might be described as a point-by-point analogy pattern. In this passage, the analogy of an airplane formation is used to point out that schizophrenia may be nothing more than a label that some people apply to others.

A revolution is currrently going on in relation to sanity and madness, both inside and outside psychiatry. The clinical point of view is giving way before a point of view that is both existential and social.

From an ideal vantage point on the ground, a formation of planes may be observed in the air. One plane may be out of formation. But the whole formation may be off course. The plane that is "out of formation" may be abnormal, bad or "mad," from the point of view of the formation. But the formation itself may be bad or mad from the point of view of the ideal observer. The plane that is out of formation may also be more or less off course than the formation itself is.

The "out of formation" criterion is the clinical positivist criterion.

The "off course' criterion is the ontological. One needs to make two judgments along these different parameters. In particular, it is of fundamental importance not to confuse the person who may be "out of formation" by telling him he is "off course" if he is not. It is of fundamental importance not to make the positivist mistake of assuming that, because a group are "in formation," this means they are necessarily "on course." This is the Gadarene swine fallacy. Nor is it necessarily the case that the person who is "out of formation" is more "on course" than the formation. There is no need to idealize someone just because he is labeled "out of formation." Nor is there any need to persuade the person who is "out of formation" that cure consists in getting back into formation. The person who is "out of formation" is often full of hatred toward the formation and of fears about being the odd man out.

If the formation is itself off course, then the man who is really to get "on course" must leave the formation. But it is possible to do so, if one desires, without screeches and screams, and without terrorizing the already terrified formation that one has to leave.

—R. D. Laing, *The Politics of Experience*

Laing's main point is that many people are labeled schizophrenic because they are "out of formation" with society. But being "out of formation," he contends, is not necessarily the same thing as being "off course." Quite often, it is society and society's values that are "off course." "The perfectly adjusted bomber pilot may be a greater threat to species survival than the hospitalized schizophrenic deluded that the Bomb is inside him," argues Laing elsewhere in *The Politics of Experience.*

The points of the comparison may be illustrated as follows:

society = formation of planes
people = planes
"abnormal" person = "out of formation" plane
"normal" person = "in formation plane
"abnormal" person = "off course" plane
"normal" person = "on course" plane

To many writers, an analogy is nothing more than an *extended metaphor* in which the comparison is put in terms of relationships. The following scientific analogy illustrates this process:

Observations indicate that the different clusters of galaxies are constantly moving apart from each other. To illustrate by a homely analogy, think of a raisin cake baking in an oven. Suppose the cake swells uniformly as it cooks, but the raisins themselves remain of the same size. Let each raisin represent a cluster of galaxies, and imagine yourself inside one of them. As the cake swells, you will observe that all the other raisins move away from you. Moreover, the farther away the raisin, the faster it will seem to move. When the cake has swollen to twice its initial dimensions, the distance between all the raisins will have doubled itself—two raisins that were a foot apart will have moved two feet apart. Since the entire action takes place within the same time interval, obviously the more distant raisins must move apart faster than those close at hand. So it happens with clusters of galaxies.

The analogy brings out another important point. No matter which raisin you happen to be inside, the others will always move away from you. Hence the fact that we observe all the other clusters of galaxies to be moving away from us *does not mean that we are situated at the center of the universe.* Indeed, it seems certain that the universe has no center. A cake may be said to have a center only because it has a boundary. We must imagine the cake to extend outward without any boundary, an infinite cake, so to speak, which means that however much cake we care to consider there is always more.

—Fred Hoyle, "When Time Began," *The Saturday Evening Post*

In this selection, the analogy is pretty straightforward. Hoyle wants to explain to the general reader a scientific concept: "the different clusters of galaxies are constantly moving apart from each other." The basic metaphor he uses is that of a raisin cake baking in an oven. The cake is the universe, constantly expanding. Each raisin represents a cluster of galaxies. The raisin is one of the clusters of galaxies, and the observer is inside.

Not every analogy is a scientific analogy or an explanation of a complex subject. The following magazine ad uses an analogy as a way of selling a product.

Judgment from the Bench

Those who sit in judgment of a piano come from many branches of musical achievement. But they all look for the same signs of truth to emerge. Responsiveness, for instance, is always called upon—especially when a new concerto is being tried.
Clarity must come forth—as in the case of enunciating vs. blurring the inner voices of Bach's fugues. Reliability, above all, will figure hard in the outcome of every rock concert.
To all these points, Yamaha pianos plead guilty as charged.
Judge one at your nearest Yamaha dealer. But whatever you do—don't sentence yourself to life without a piano. In fact, we'd rather you buy another piano than no piano at all.

—ad for *Yamaha* pianos

Exercises

1. Analyze the Yamaha ad in class. Set up an outline or equation showing the points of the comparison. Does the analogy break down at any point? Is the ad effective? This ad was taken from the *New Yorker*, October 7, 1972. Discuss the ad in relation to its intended audience.

2. Write an essay, using one of the following analogies:

   a. Thinking is like exploring.

   b. Courting is like playing a game.

   c. Life is a river (stream, tributary, eternal sea).

   d. Life is a journey (hourglass, book, plant).

   e. My moods are like the seasons.

   f. _____ is like falling leaves (a dying fire, a shooting star).

3. Select one of the following as the basis of an analogy and then write an essay using the analogy to illustrate an idea:

   a. a merry-go-round   d. a clock

   b. a bridge   e. a puzzle

   c. a broken mirror   f. a wasp's nest

4. Use one of the following proverbs as the basis of an analogy paper:

   a. Time is like an arrow.

   b. Words are like bees: They have honey and a sting.

   c. Marriage is a lottery.

   d. Lost credit is like a broken mirror.

   e. Courage is fire; bullying is smoke.

5. Write a scientific analogy to explain an idea.

6. Write a persuasive essay in the manner of the Yamaha ad, using an extended analogy.

CHAPTER 7

Patterns of Thought:
Narration, Process,
Cause and Effect

Narration

Seldom a day goes by without friends or acquaintances coming up to you and telling you a joke, an interesting story, an account of an incident that happened to them, or the plot of some movie or television show they have just seen. What happens to people in their work and in their leisure time constitutes the very pulse of life. Much of your conversation as well as much of your writing consists of narration.

Narration, as a pattern of thought, consists of *the act of following a sequence of actions or events in time.* It is *a recounting of the facts or particulars of some incident or experience.*

Purpose, Audience, Kind of Discourse

Narration can be used to inform or instruct, to convince or persuade, to entertain or please, or to express strong feelings and emotions. Narration as a process in and of itself does none of these. It all depends on the uses to which you put your narration. Tell a story in one context, and it will be entertaining. Tell the same story in another context, and it may be instructive or persuasive.

Narration can be found in numerous kinds of writing: the narration of personal experiences, biographies, autobiographies, journals, diaries, memoirs, reminiscences, logs, records, genealogies, newspaper stories, magazine ads, short stories, novels, ballads, folk songs, movie scripts, travel accounts, chronicles, histories, anecdotes, obituaries, and sermons.

Many of these forms have their own distinctive purposes, although the same narrative techniques and the same forms can be put to many different uses. Literary narratives such as the novel or short story usually have an aesthetic aim. Narration in sermons or magazine ads has a persuasive aim. Biography usually has an expository aim, which is to set forth a part or the whole of a person's life to explain his or her character, influence on others, or accomplishments. The aim of autobiography is similar to that of biography. Some obvious differences, of course, are that biography is an account of a person's life written by someone else, whereas autobiography is written by the person him- or herself. Biography is written in the third person; autobiography is written in the first person. Historical narratives, like biographies, have informative and instructive aims. In such writing, the author seeks to explain general trends, customs, worship, warfare, commerce, governments, and agriculture. Or the writer may seek to illuminate the characters of men and women, their wisdom or foolishness, intelligence or passions.

Whereas the autobiography puts its emphasis on introspection, journals and diaries are usually less introspective. They do, however, often give us personal impressions and fresh insights into experience. What they lack as connected narratives, they gain in vividness and immediacy. They are less structured than biographies and autobiographies and more anecdotal, containing brief observations, direct impressions of life, bits and pieces of information, personal reactions, and intimate thoughts.

Invention and Narration

As a method of invention, narration answers such questions as: What happened? What is happening? What will happen? When did it happen? Where did it happen?

Because of its concern with time, narration is related to process and cause and effect:

Narration	*What* happened?
Process	*How* did it happen?
Cause and effect	*Why* did it happen?

In narration, however, the emphasis is on the *what* (although the elements in a plot, for example, are related by cause and effect). In process, the emphasis is on the *how*. And in cause and effect, the emphasis is on the *why*. To recount the particulars of an occurrence in time and space is to invent.

It is interesting to note that time is usually conceived of in terms of space. Events are conceived in relation to one another:

event$_1$ event$_2$ event$_3$ event$_4$

Yet your awareness of time comes not from space, but from some inner sense of the passage of events. Number is sometimes associated with time, and this helps to give you some notion of what is meant by a "time sense." An important synonym for *narrate* is *recount*. But an equally strong synonym, *relate*, brings you back to the spatial relation. Whether you think of time as sequence or relation, your feeling for time helps you to penetrate deeply into the nature of reality.

I have said that narration is a recounting of particulars in a temporal sequence. The word *recounting* suggests a self-contained series: "This happened, and then this happened, and then this happened." The word *particulars* assumes that narration will be concerned with the individual and the concrete. The basis of narration, the *what*, is concerned with the simplest kind of progression in time, continuity. Particulars are related to each other because they occur in time. But in a plot or in a scientific process, they are also causally related.

To narrate is to invent. In the process of invention, you must come up with a succession of details, and shape and proportion each part. You must also keep in mind the end to be achieved. Each part must prepare for what is to follow.

Narration is a dynamic mode, for experience is dynamic and changing. The squirrel you looked at in the yard yesterday is no longer there. The tree you trimmed last summer has long since shed its leaves. You yourself are now probably taller, bigger, wider, or thinner than you were last year. When you go home for the Christmas holidays after a semester at school, you notice that everything seems strange or different. Your little brother or sister has grown an inch taller. Your father has another wrinkle. Your room seems different than you had imagined it; perhaps because your mother has moved the furniture around.

How do you express these changes in narration? By verbs, by prepositions, and by adverbs. "It started snowing on Saturday night," wrote one student, "the wind whipping about the house, moaning low and then shrieking high and shrill like a banshee, whirling gusts of snow around, blotting out the black of the night sky." Another wrote: "The raindrops fell against my window, tapping rhythmically against the glass, then spattering in all directions from the middle, slithering lazily down the smooth surface, and finally dripping from the corners of the sill."

In narratives, you normally think of the verb as carrying the burden of the action. Action verbs are much more vivid than verbs of being: *glide, slide, ramble, stroll, amble, plod, tramp, strut, stride, toddle, spurt, sprint, scamper, dash, crawl, loiter, waddle, slouch, hobble, limp, jostle, clash, crash, smack, whack, jab.* Prepositions and adverbs help to convey action: *now, then, afterwards, later, since, therefore, after, from that time on, hereafter, today, tomorrow, eventually, while, early, slow, fast, till, by, in, at, from, to.* Narration, like the other modes, has a characteristic vocabulary that gives the reader a sense of the passage of time:

now	first	previously
then	second	every day
before	third	a long time ago
after	once	one of these days
earlier	former	last year
later	latter	up to this time
soon	prior to	on that occasion

Exercises

1. Using the questions suggested by the topics of invention, probe a narrative subject.

2. As a classroom exercise, relate to other members of the class some simple experience that actually happened to you.

3. Tell the plot of a movie or television show that has a strong narrative interest.

4. Reinvent! Take a plot from an old story and bring it up to date with a new setting and new characters.

Constructing Narrative Paradigms

Most of the narratives you write will follow a simple chronological pattern. Therefore, you may feel no need to construct a sentence paradigm before you begin to write, relying instead on the order of memory. If you rely on memory, the abstract pattern of your overall narrative will look like this:

Narrative Pattern without Plot
Introduction (setting, character)
Event 1
Event 2
Event 3
Event 4, 5, 6 . . .
Conclusion

If, however, you decide to follow a more sophisticated narrative pattern, based on a plot, your narrative might take this shape:

Narrative Pattern with Plot
Introduction
Initial incident
Rising action
Suspense
    Foreshadowing
    Withholding information
    Surprise
Turning point
Falling action
Climax
Conclusion

The *introduction* sets the time and place of the action, introduces the characters, and shows their relationship to one another. The *initial incident* is the foundation of the plot. It brings the inciting force into action and moves the story forward. The *rising action* consists of a connected series of incidents or episodes which increase suspense. *Suspense* is that moment in the action that stirs excitement in the reader. It is an emotional appeal, making the reader fearful, or angry, or happy. *Foreshadowing* is a hint of something to come. *Withholding information* is one way of achieving suspense. Another way is to *surprise* the reader, to mislead deliberately. The *turning point* is that part of the narrative at which the conflicting forces of the story meet. The *falling action* is an intense series of events in which the writer begins "to tie the knot." The *climax* is the result of all of the elements of the story. It is the *resolution*, the point of highest intensity, and the place where the conflict rages fiercely. The *conclusion* is the logical ending of the story. It should be clear and satisfying and make sense. Not all of these elements will appear in a given narrative.

The *action* of a story may be *physical* or *mental*. Since a story involves people in action, there is usually some kind of *conflict* involved in the action. The main character is tested in some way and emerges victorious or defeated. Some familiar conflicts at the heart of most stories are the individual versus nature, the individual versus society, the individual versus God, the individual versus the supernatural, the individual versus other men or women, the individual versus himself or herself. When the conflict is internal or between an individual and another man or woman, the basis of the conflict is usually good or evil, virtues or vices: honesty/greed, hope/despair, courage/cowardice, generosity/selfishness, duty/lack of responsibility, forgiveness/revenge, chastity/lust, patience/impatience, compassion/lack of compassion, and so forth.

In many narratives, *character development* is more important than plot. The characters are the actors in a story. Characterization can be developed by *personal action*, by *speech*, by *introspection*, by what *other* characters tell us about a character, by the *author*, and by the *interests*, *tastes*, *possessions*, and *surroundings* of a character.

The *theme* of a story is its main point. It is an idea the writer wants to impress on his or her readers. It usually is expressed by means of character and incident.

In telling a story, a writer most often uses the *first person* or the *third person*. The first person is limited in that all of the events are seen through the eyes of one person. The third person allows the writer to portray the events from many angles.

Not all of the narratives that you write will have an extensive depiction of character or long, involved plots. Perhaps most will be merely a recounting of a series of events, as in personal narratives, reminiscences, and news stories. Autobiography and biography may or may not have consciously intended plots. Journals, diary entries, memoirs, and letters are usually too brief and too unconnected to allow for an extended treatment of plot.

The following narrative, taken from Willa Cather's *My Antonia*, is an excellent example of a literary narrative with an aesthetic aim. It follows very closely the pattern of a well-plotted narrative.

The Men Who Fed the Bride to the Wolves

When Pavel and Peter were young men, living at home in Russia, they were asked to be groomsmen for a friend who was to marry the belle of another village. It was in the dead of winter and the groom's party went over to the wedding in sledges. Peter and Pavel drove in the groom's sledge, and six sledges followed with all his relatives and friends.

After the ceremony at the church, the party went to a dinner given by the parents of the bride. The dinner lasted all afternoon; then it became a supper and continued far into the night. There was much dancing and drinking. At midnight the parents of the bride said goodbye to her and blessed her. The groom took her in his arms and carried her out to his sledge and tucked her under the blankets. He sprang in beside, and Pavel and Peter (our Pavel and Peter!) took the front seat. Pavel drove. The party set out with singing and the jingle of sleigh-bells, the groom's sledge going first. All the drivers were more or less the worse for merry-making, and the groom was absorbed in his bride.

The wolves were bad that winter, and everyone knew it, yet when they heard the first wolf-cry, the drivers were not much alarmed. They had too much good food and drink inside them. The first howls were taken up and echoed and with quickening repetitions. The wolves were coming together. There was no moon, but the starlight was clear on the snow. A black drove came up over the hill behind the wedding party. The wolves ran like streaks of shadow; they looked no bigger than dogs, but there were hundreds of them.

Something happened to the hindmost sledge; the driver lost control—he was probably very drunk—the horses left the road, the sledge was caught in a clump of trees, and overturned. The occupants rolled out over the snow, and the fleetest of the wolves sprang upon them. The shrieks that followed made everybody sober. The drivers stood up and lashed their horses. The groom had the best team and his sledge was lightest—all the others carried from six to a dozen people.

Another driver lost control. The screams of the horses were more terrible to hear than the cries of the men and women. Nothing seemed to check the wolves. It was hard to tell what was happening in the rear; the people who were falling behind shrieked as piteously as those who were already lost. The little bride hid her face on the groom's shoulder and sobbed. Pavel sat still and watched his horses. The road was clear and white, the the groom's three blacks went like the wind. It was only necessary to be calm and to guide them carefully.

At length, as they breasted a long hill, Peter rose cautiously and looked back. "There are only three sledges left," he whispered.

"And the wolves?" Pavel asked.

"Enough! Enough for all of us."

Pavel reached the brow of the hill, but only two sledges followed him down the other side. In that moment on the hilltop they saw the whirling black group on the snow. Presently the groom screamed. He saw his father's sledge overturned, with his mother and sisters. He sprang up as if he meant to jump, but the girl shrieked and held him back. It was even then too late. The black ground-shadows were already crowding over the heap in the road, and one horse ran out across the fields, his harness hanging to him, wolves at his heels. But the groom's movement had given Pavel an idea.

They were within a few miles of their village now. The only sledge left out of the six was not very far behind them, and Pavel's middle horse was failing. Beside a frozen pond something happened to the other sledge, Peter saw it plainly. Three big wolves got abreast of the horses, and the horses went crazy. They tried to jump over each other, got tangled up in the harness, and overturned the sledge.

When the shrieking behind them died away, Pavel realized that he was alone upon the familiar road. "They still come?" he asked Peter.

"Yes."

"How many?"

"Twenty, thirty—enough."

Now his middle horse was being almost dragged by the other two. Pavel gave Peter the reins and stepped carefully into the back of the sledge. He called to the groom that they must lighten—and pointed to the bride. The young man cursed him and held her tighter. Pavel tried to drag her away. In the struggle, the groom rose. Pavel knocked him over the side of the sledge and threw the girl after him. He said he never remembered exactly how he did it, or what happened afterward. Peter, crouching in the front seat, saw nothing. The first thing either of them noticed was a new sound that broke into the clear air, louder than they had ever heard it before—the bell of the monastery of their own village, ringing for early prayers.

Pavel and Peter drove into the village alone, and they have been alone ever since. They were run out of their village. Pavel's own mother would not look at him. They went away to strange towns, but when people learned where they came from, they were always asked if they knew the two men who had fed the bride to the wolves. Wherever they went, the story followed them. . . .

The first two paragraphs set the scene in time and place (a wedding in a small village in Russia in the middle of winter); introduce the characters (two brothers, Peter and Pavel, the bride and groom, the wedding guests); and set forth the initial incident (the wedding party, after much dancing and drinking, setting out at midnight for the groom's village). Subsequent paragraphs then take up each incident in turn.

The narrative progression might be depicted as follows:

The wedding party sets out in sledges at midnight for the groom's village.

The wolves come together to attack the sledges.

The hindmost sledge is lost.

Another driver loses control.

The sledge of the groom's father overturns.

The horses panic, and the second-to-last sledge overturns.

Pavel knocks the groom over the side to lighten the sledge, then throws the bride after him.

Finally, Pavel and Peter drive into the village alone, with the "bell of the monastery of their own village, ringing for early prayers."

Of the sixteen paragraphs in this selection, the shortest are those with dialogue. Most of these consist of a single phrase or sentence. The longest paragraph is paragraph 15, the second-to-last paragraph, which contains the largest number of words (135) and the largest number of sentences (10). The length seems natural when you consider that this is the most action-packed and suspenseful part of the narrative, that climactic moment when Pavel throws the bride and groom to the wolves.

Most of the sentences are short, or give the appearance of being short due to extensive use of coordination. Most of the short sentences come in the chase scenes, to convey rapid action and increase the excitement and tension. The longest sentences come at the beginning of the story (to set the scene in time and place), at the beginning of the chase scene, at the end of the chase scene (with Pavel and Peter riding into the village), and at the end of the narrative.

The sense of passing of time and the action is conveyed *by prepositional phrases:*

after the ceremony	across the fields
at midnight	at his heels
over the hill	behind them
behind the wedding party	beside the frozen pond
over the snow	abreast of the horses
at length	over each other
down the other side	into the village
in that moment	

adverbs and adverbial nouns:

over	too late
all afternoon	out
then	far
far	now
in	away
beside	alone
presently	ever since

and verbs:

sprang	breasted
drove	reached
set out	followed
were coming together	screamed
came up	overturned
ran	shrieked
left	ran
overturned	was failing
rolled out	got tangled up
sprang	overturned
stood up	must lighten
lashed	knocked
lost control	threw
were falling behind	drove
shrieked	run out
sobbed	went away
went	

In just sixteen paragraphs, Willa Cather is able to convey a wide range of human emotions: merriment, fear, tension, unspeakable horror, anger, and sadness. All the structural elements work together to produce a masterful narrative.

Whereas the previous narrative was written from the third person point of view, the following narrative is written in the first person. In this narrative, the writer recalls from his boyhood in South America his discovery of a strange kind of snake he had never seen before. The narrative movement is deceptively simple. The narrator focuses first on the *action* (the movement of the snake and the narrator's observations and description of it) and then on his *reaction* to the snake (he was "thrilled with terror," he did not dare "to make the slightest movement," the spot where the snake appeared was "frightfully danger-ous"). He flees from the spot, thinking that he will never return. But he does, again and again, each time failing to see the snake. Then, one day, he returns to the spot where he first saw the snake, and it reappears. The narrative pattern of *action* and *reaction* is then repeated.

The Snake

One hot day in December I had been standing perfectly still for a few min-utes among the dry weeds when a slight rustling sound came from near my feet, and glancing down I saw the head and neck of a large black ser-pent moving slowly past me. In a moment or two the flat head was lost to sight among the close-growing weeds, but the long body continued moving slowly by—so slowly that it hardly appeared to move, and as the creature must have been not less than six feet long, and probably more, it took a very long time, while I stood thrilled with terror, not daring to make the slightest movement, gazing down upon it. Although so long it was not a thick snake, and as it moved on over the white ground it had the appear-ance of a coal-black current flowing past me—a current not of water or other liquid but of some such element as quicksilver moving on in a rope-like stream. At last it vanished, and turning I fled from the ground, think-ing that never again would I venture into or near that frightfully dangerous spot in spite of its fascination.

Nevertheless I did venture. The image of that black mysterious ser-pent was always in my mind from the moment of waking in the morning until I fell asleep at night. Yet I never said a word about the snake to any one: it was my secret, and I knew it was a dangerous secret, but I did not want to be told not to visit that spot again. And I simply could not keep away from it; the desire to look again at that strange being was too strong. I began to visit the place again, day after day, and would hang about the borders of the barren weedy ground watching and listening, and still no black serpent appeared.

Then one day I ventured, though in fear and trembling, to go right in among the weeds, and still finding nothing began to advance step by step until I was right in the middle of the weedy ground and stood there a long time, waiting and watching. All I wanted was just to see it once more, and I had made up my mind that immediately on its appearance, if it did appear, I would take to my heels. It was when standing in this central spot that once again that slight rustling sound, like that of a few days before, reached my straining sense and sent an icy chill down my back. And there, within six inches of my toes, appeared the black head and neck, followed by the long, seemingly endless body. I dared not move, since to have attempted flight might have been fatal. The weeds were thinnest here, and the black head and slow-moving black coil could be followed by the eye for a little distance. About a yard from me there was a hole in the ground about the circumference of a breakfast-cup at the top, and into this hole the serpent put his head and slowly, slowly drew himself in, while I stood waiting until the whole body to the tip of the tail had vanished and all danger was over.

—W. H. Hudson, *Far Away and Long Ago*

Not all of your narratives will be this serious. The following is a humorous student narrative in which a college freshman looks back on an embarrassing high school experience.

Two Left Feet

When I was a sophomore in high school, the big thing was for all the girls to go to the dances together. Nobody really dated, mostly because none of the boys in our class were old enough to drive. The few girls who did date, dated older guys. It was the dream of every sophomore girl to be noticed by an older guy who could drive. I'll never forget the time I got the chance.

I'd gone to the dance with about five girls. None of us had seen much action, so at 10:30 we were thinking about calling somebody's father to come and pick us up. In the middle of our conversation, somebody noticed one of the older boys walking toward our group. He was one of the best football players in school and had lettered in both football and tennis. What a stud! And to make it even better, he was a senior, not a creepy sophomore or a junior, but a senior, a real man. Out of all the girls, he asked ME to dance. I couldn't believe it! Rotten, ugly, uncool me! My face felt hot, my hands got sweaty and I silently cursed myself for wearing Levis like everyone else. It took me about ten minutes to answer, but I finally squeaked out a weak "yes" and staggered my way to the floor.

I only looked at him once while we danced, but when I did, he smiled and I nearly fainted. We danced for a while and I began to feel a little calmer, even a little "cool" as my girlfriends watched me from the side of the room. I even went so far as to feel confident until he asked me if I wanted to go to King's restaurant. Again I turned hot and sweaty as I finally managed a squeaky "yes."

I acted like an idiot as he helped me with my coat. I couldn't find the armhole and tore the lining of my coat with my ring as I frantically searched for the opening. I ripped off a button with my shaking hands and being metal, it hit the cement floor with a most embarrassing clunk. At last we got outside, but my poise never showed itself. It had snowed that day and the sidewalks were very slippery as I aptly demonstrated by falling down on them. (I was glad that I had on Levis instead of a dress.)

After all this, I figured I couldn't do anything else wrong, but at this point, I couldn't even figure right. He had been to a birthday party for one of his buddies earlier and half of the cake was left over and in the front seat of his car. I daintily got into the car and flopped my fat behind right on a double layer chocolate cake. That was the move of the evening. Due to the condition of my pants and my pride, I told him I'd better not go to King's but maybe I ought to go right home. Somehow I sputtered out the location of my house and talked like a moron until we arrived there. I couldn't wait to go inside; already my eyes were filling with tears. I tried to console myself by thinking that if I were going to blow my chances, I might as well blow them good. He opened my door and I gracefully hit my head on the roof of the car as I got out. Jokingly, he told me to watch out for the ice and I somehow managed a watery laugh.

As he walked me to the door he asked if he could call me next week. I figured he was just trying to be nice, but you know, he did call. Things improved the next time I was with him; all I did was fall down the stairs at the theater.

—Ranene

Sometimes, in writing a story you may wish to make your theme explicit. The following student narrative follows an inductive pattern (from particular to general), with the narrative as a kind of extended example for the concluding generalization in the last paragraph.

The Promise That Grew

Some years ago, I was caught in a sudden, blinding snowstorm near Indiana, Pennsylvania. My car stalled at the edge of town. I floundered into town and into the nearest store. The proprietor phoned for help to get my car out of the snowdrift.

In a short time, a tall blond man showed up with a team of horses and pulled me out of the drift into town. I asked him how much I owed him for his trouble. He refused any pay, saying, "I will charge thee nothing but the promise that thee will help the next man thee finds in trouble." I thanked him and made the promise.

After he left, the storekeeper explained that my Good Samaritan was a Mennonite who considered it wrong to charge anyone for a service made necessary by an act of God.

Four years later, a friend and I were driving over flooded land south of St. Louis, Missouri. We crossed through water a foot deep without any trouble, but through my rearview mirror, I could see that the small car behind us stalled. I waded back while my companion reversed the car so I could hook up onto his bumper with tire chains.

We pulled the man out and waited until he got his engine started. Then he offered to pay me. I told him of my experience in Indiana, Pennsylvania, then repeated the Mennonite's words: "I will charge thee nothing but the promise that thee will help the next man thee finds in trouble." He promised, and we parted.

About one year later, my family and I were camping about one hundred miles from Aurora, Missouri, and we pitched our tents near the James River. We'd been told that it never flooded at that time of year, but the river evidently misread the calendar, for I awakened in the middle of the night with a very cold back from water deep enough to cover the canvas cot. We loaded our soggy equipment into our car, but we were unable to drive it to higher ground. I waded back to an inn some distance from our camping spot and asked the innkeeper if he could get help to pull us out.

In a short time, a farmer showed up with a tractor and a long rope and pulled us to safe ground. When I offered to pay him, he told me of a man who had helped him get his tractor out of the mud and then said: "I will charge thee nothing but the promise that thee will help the next man that thee finds in trouble." The quotation was identical to that of the man in Pennsylvania, although I know of no Mennonites or Quakers in that section of Missouri.

How far one man's act of kindness had traveled!

—Fred

In writing your own narratives, it is not necessary to develop long, involved plots. Unless you intend to become a novelist, most of your narratives will be of the kind found in the narration of personal experiences, anecdotes, autobiography, letters to friends, journals, diaries, and newspaper stories. Your stories may indeed have a built-in plot, but your main purpose will be to tell a compelling and interesting narrative based on personal experiences. Then the kind of concreteness that comes most easily in narrating firsthand experiences may carry into your more abstract writing.

Exercises

1. Analyze in class the narratives titled "The Snake," "Two Left Feet," and "The Promise That Grew." What narrative techniques does each writer use to achieve his or her effects? Use the checklist of traditional narrative techniques discussed earlier as a guide.

2. Using the selection titled "The Snake" as a guide, write about an exciting, thrilling, frightening, or disturbing experience you have had.

Like W. H. Hudson, first describe the action, then your reaction. Let the reader know how you felt about the experience. Use vivid and descriptive details.

3. In the manner of the student narrative "Two Left Feet," give a first-person account of an embarrassing experience you had as a child or as an adolescent.

4. Using "The Promise That Grew" as a model, write a first-person narrative about one of the following: an unselfish act, a brave act, a narrow escape, a practical joke, a foolish act.

5. Keeping in mind your purpose, your reader, and a possible writing situation, write a brief narrative based on one of the following general subjects:

   a. a date   f. a natural disaster

   b. a dream   g. a racial incident

   c. an accident   h. falling in love

   d. a job experience   i. a death or illness

   e. a college experience   j. a humorous experience

6. Write a newspaper-style account of a fire or some other incident. Assume that it will be published in the local newspaper.

7. Write a character sketch in the form of an obituary notice.

8. Write a biographical sketch of someone you know well.

9. Someone interested in employing a friend has asked you to give a frank summary of his or her character. Imagine the exact situation (i.e., kind of job, place of employment, etc.) and write the letter.

10. Expand one of the following into a full-length narrative:

    a. For one day, you will express all of your feelings about people truthfully, no matter whom you may hurt.

    b. You go to a party, only to discover that six people have on the same outfit you do.

    c. You have been drinking, and you hit an old man or woman at a crossing while you are driving.

    d. You arrive at the air terminal just as your plane is departing.

e. You are eating in a fancy restaurant, and when it is time to pay the bill, you discover you have left your wallet at home.

11. Bring to class magazine ads or newspaper articles that use the narrative mode for informative or persuasive purposes. Discuss the rhetorical situation (e.g., where did the ad or article appear? Was there a felt need?), the audience, the writer's intention, and so forth. How effective is the writer in achieving his or her intention?

12. Analyze in class a selection from your reader that uses the narrative mode. Where did that selection first appear? For what readers? What is the writer's aim? Is the aim explicit or implicit in the narrative? Is there a clear-cut narrative pattern? Is the use of the narrative mode effective? What are the sentences like? The word choice?

Process

A **process** is *a series of actions, changes, functions, steps, or operations that bring about a particular end or result.* Like narration, process suggests ongoing movement and continuous action. The emphasis in a process, however, is on the *how*, rather than the *what*. These are relative rather than absolute differences, since like narration, a process can be concerned with the *what*, and like cause and effect, it can be concerned with the *why*.

When you think of a process, you generally think of slow, gradual changes and of a series of interlocking steps whereby an end is achieved. Some synonyms for the word *process* are *change, alter, vary, modify, transform, convert,* and *transmute.* The word *change* is perhaps the most important synonym, suggesting as it does a transition from one state to another. A change alters the quality of a thing and modifies its form or appearance. Like the other topics and patterns with which you will be concerned, this one carries a train of rich images and expressions: *mutation, transformation, transfiguration, metamorphosis, transubstantiation, transmigration,* and *a kaleidoscope of colors.*

Purpose, Audience, Kind of Discourse

Process as a mode of developing a subject can be found in any kind of discourse that emphasizes a system of operations or steps in the production of something. It can also be found in discourse that shows a series of actions, changes, or phases that bring about an end or result. Although the primary aim of process exposition is to inform or instruct, it can also be used to persuade, as in certain magazine advertisements which outline the steps in the making of a product to convince the reader of the product's excellence.

Since process is by definition a sequence of actions, changes, or operations that brings about some desired end or result, as a writer you can best appeal to your audience by logically presenting the connected series of actions that lead to the desired end.

Process can be most profitably employed in the following kinds of writing, scientific essays, instruction manuals, booklets, research reports, cookbooks, directions for doing something, natural history, biology, chemistry, explanations of a mechanism, explanations of a social process or a historical process, explanations of a natural process, explanations of a creative process, advertising, and argumentation.

Invention and Process

As a topic of invention, process answers basic questions: How did it happen? How does it work? How do you make it or do it? What are the stages, phases, steps, or operations? To recount a series of changes, a sequence of steps, a particular method of doing something, an explanation of a scientific process, the steps in an argument, a course of action, a series of operations, a procedure, a function, or the alteration in the position, size, quantity, and quality of something is to invent.

Your awareness of process comes from a sense of some kind of change. You notice that the hands on your watch have changed position. You observe that the plants in your garden are changing in size and quantity. You change the quality of the water in your shower from hot to cold. You watch people, animals, and plants around you come into existence, mature, grow old, and die. You observe that the sky grows dark, it begins to rain, leaves fall from the trees, autumn comes, then winter, then spring, then summer. You notice the yellows in a sunset shade into the oranges, the oranges into the reds, and the reds into blues, purples, and greens. Life ebbs and flows, moves, pulsates, palpitates, throbs all around you.

Process analysis is a special form of exposition in which you present a step-by-step description of how some process takes place: a natural process, a scientific process, a mechanical process, a historical process, a social process, a creative process. Process exposition is concerned with *how* topics: how flowers changed the world, how the universe was formed, how the American Revolution began, how LSD was discovered, how liquor is made, how to operate a car, how the heart works, how to eat crabs, how to bake a cake.

Because process is a king of dynamic exposition, its characteristic vocabulary tends to emphasize change:

phase	state	inconstancy
occurrence	condition	inversion
step	conversion	permutation
change	displacement	modulation
alteration	transformation	qualification
mutation	fluctuation	metamorphosis

Some process terms are the same as those of narration: *now, then, next, afterwards, later, thereafter, from, to.* Others are the same as those of enumeration: *first, second, third, one, another, a third.* The verb tenses in a process may be present (if you are giving directions) or past (if you are explaining something that has already taken place). The voice may be active or passive (generally used in scientific descriptions). The person may be first (in an informal account), second (in giving directions), or third (in an objective description of a process).

Exercises

1. Using the questions suggested by the topics of invention, probe a process subject.

2. In class, for purposes of invention, analyze a natural process, a scientific process, a mechanical process, a historical process, a political process, a social process, or a creative process.

3. Explain in class how one of the following works:

   a. an eggbeater

   b. a bicycle

   c. a razor

   d. a rifle

   e. an engine

4. Play the game of "charades" in class. Choose sides and take turns acting out a process.

5. Explain to someone in class how to

a. swim

b. box

c. skate

d. lie

e. tell jokes

f. sell something

g. put down someone

h. make coffee

i. play a musical instrument

j. clean a rug

Constructing Process Paradigms

Like narrative paradigms, process paradigms follow the laws of chronological progression. To construct a process paradigm, keeping in mind your purpose and reader, you begin with a sentence that tells your reader your purpose in presenting the sequence of steps that will follow. Then, in subsequent sentences you divide your subject into steps, phases, or operations. To help your reader follow the logical progression of your ideas, you use process words, such as *step, phase,* or *direction* in your organizing sentence, and transitional words, such as *first, second, next, afterward,* and *then,* in the sentences that follow. As you have done in using the various modes to construct other paradigms, you arrange *the sentences* in such a way as to *form a relational pattern of process analysis.* Finally, if your purpose or subject lends itself to ethical and emotional appeals, you include ethical and emotional terms in the sentences of your paradigm:

Here's *what you can do* if someone is seriously burned.

First, put out the flames on the person.

Then, remove the burned clothing that does not stick to the burn.

Third, remove rings, bracelets, and other items before swelling begins.

Next, put the person in a reclining position with the feet slightly raised.

Fifth, keep the person warm with a clean sheet or blanket.

Finally, call a doctor or an emergency unit, or take the person immediately to the hospital.

Remember that burns are sometimes more serious than they appear, so prompt attention may save someone's life.

The organizing sentence in this paradigm does not use a process word such as *steps* or *directions*, but it does use the equivalent phrase *what you can do*. The middle sentences outline the steps the reader should follow, and the final sentence tells the reader the importance of prompt action. Although there are no explicit ethical and emotional words and phrases in this paradigm, there is an implicit ethical appeal in the concern for the welfare of burn victims and an implicit emotional appeal to fear.

After you have constructed your analysis paradigm, you will want to make sure that it accurately conveys your intended meaning, your attitude toward your subject, an understanding of your reader's needs, beliefs, and attitudes, and your ethical and emotional stance. Examine each sentence carefully for these features, and then consider the logical development of your ideas. Next, try to determine the kind of information you will use to support the sentences of your paradigm. Finally, revise the sentences of your paradigm or rewrite the paradigm completely.

To write a paper based on a process paradigm, you provide an introduction, supporting details, and a conclusion. If the process you want to explain involves giving directions or making something, your introduction should contain a description of the material and the tools or implements you will use. If it does not involve directions, as in the description of a natural process, your introduction may contain an explanation of the principles involved. The following is an example of what the larger patterning of your essay will look like:

Process Pattern
Introduction (organizing sentence, description of the material, principles, implements, etc.)
Step 1 (or phase 1)
Step 2 (or phase 2)
Step 3 (or phase 3)
Step 4 (or phase 4)
Steps 5, 6, 7 . . .
Conclusion (clincher sentence, summary, and so forth)

The following professional article, taken from the February 1981 issue of *Attenzione* magazine, is an excellent example of the directions-for-doing-something essay:

Making Pasta by Hand

Learning to make pasta from written instructions is almost as difficult as learning to make love from a book. By all means, if you have someone who can teach you, run, do not walk. You will catch on more quickly— and have a lot more fun, too.

If you'd like to try making pasta without the use of a machine, read the directions that follow several times so that you thoroughly understand them before you crack your first egg. If you have to sit down and pore over instructions, the dough will dry out.

1. Find a work surface where you have plenty of room. You can use a wooden board on a kitchen counter, but if you are planning to make pasta with three or more eggs, you will be much more comfortable moving around a table.

2. Pour the flour in a mound on one end of your work surface. If you have a very large, flat-bottomed wooden bowl (such as a salad bowl), pouring the flour into it may make cleaning up easier.

3. Make a hollow in the center of the mound, to form something resembling a volcano. This is known as the "well".

4. Put the eggs in the well with a pinch of salt, and beat them lightly with a fork. Use a circular motion to begin incorporating the flour from the inside wall of the well into the eggs. As the mixture thickens, put the fork aside and work the dough with your hands.

5. Add flour to the eggs until the mixture is no longer sticky. Although the ratio of ¾ cup of flour per large egg is a rule of thumb, proportions will change depending on the absorbency of the flour, the exact size of the eggs, and the day's temperature and barometer reading.

6. Now begin kneading. Use two hands, working the pasta between the fingers of one hand and the heel of the other, folding the dough over and over again until it is smooth and elastic. (It will take 8 to 10 minutes.) This step is crucial, because if the pasta is not elastic it will not roll out properly.

7. Flour the work surface lightly and set the dough down. (If you are making pasta with more than three eggs, try this with half the dough at a time until you have more experience. Cover the rest of the dough with a towel to prevent it from drying out while you are working.) Using a broom-handle-style rolling pin about two feet long, roll out the pasta as thin as you can, rotating the dough after each roll so that the sheet turns out roughly circular.

8. The dough should now be about one-eighth of an inch thick. Here's the trick to making it paper-thin; it sounds difficult at first, but once you get the hang of it you'll do it without a second thought. Roll about a third of the pasta from the far end of the sheet around your rolling pin. Now roll the pin back and forth quickly, while at the same time pressing the palms of your hands sideways so that the dough is stretched

in two directions at once. Repeat this movement on all of the dough, overlapping from segment to segment, working as quickly as you can so that the pasta does not get dried out.

   9. Dry the pasta on a dish towel for about fifteen minutes, until it looks like fine leather.

   10. To cut the pasta into noodles, roll up the sheet into a flattened jelly roll shape, and use a very sharp knife to cut it into slices. Unroll each slice and voilà, a noodle.

—*Attenzione Magazine*, Feb. 1981

   The following student essay takes a humorous view of its subject. It is a good example of an essay that mixes process with narration.

Lobe-Botomy

The first thing you need for a do-it-yourself-pierce-your-ears kit is a sadistic friend. Then you need lots of ice, a sharp sewing needle, and a good bottle of booze.

   Obtaining the sadistic friend was no problem for me. In fact, Linda had been "needling" me all semester to let her do the job. She had had her lobes gored since high school "and it looked so easy anybody could do it," she said, eager eyes fastened on my little lobes. My ears are tiny anyway and my earlobes are attached like a button-down shirt. This gave Linda momentary doubts because she remembered something about a nerve in the upper lobe that, if punctured, would paralyze that side of the body. This gave me more than momentary doubts, but she assured me that the story was just a rumor. Besides, the surgical tray and anesthesia were all ready.

   It was the night before my last final exam, first semester, freshman year. The next morning I was to take my seventh test. Since I had been gorging my head with knowledge for two solid weeks, I was so out of it I didn't even require the friendly Southern Comfort winking at me from the table.

   The lobe-botomy operation took place at Linda's apartment, which was abundantly stocked with ice cubes. There I sat limply in a cushiony old chair watching detachedly the frantic activity around me. First, Linda banged the ice tray against the sink, trying to chip a few hunks from the frozen mass in which she had forgotten to place the cube divider. Then, with a caldron of boiling water popping on the stove (you'd think I was having a baby), she scrounged through a drawer full of thread, paper clips, bottle openers, wire, plastic bags, thumbtacks, ashtrays, and Elmer's glue for a big-enough knitting needle.

   While Linda sterilized the needle, only slightly smaller than a whaling harpoon, I held a two-pound ice chunk in a washcloth to my right earlobe. After about fifteen minutes it was deadened enough so that I couldn't feel a pinch. Meanwhile much of the ice had trickled down my sleeve. After fifteen more minutes both patient and doctor were ready. I closed my eyes as Linda walked over to me, smiling, her hands behind her back. A few seconds later she plucked my ear away from my head and I felt the needle's searing jab. In the first place she had forgotten to let it cool, and secondly it hurt like hell. I yelped and at the same instant heard cartilage crushing inside my head. "My God! She missed," was my first thought, confirmed by blood trickling down my neck. But no, Linda had been only slightly off target due to my sudden jerk. But my scream and the blood had scared her, along with the difficulty she had getting the needle through my lobe. "I should have had a thimble," she berated herself. "Why not a hammer," I said tearfully.

That made her mad. "Ungrateful," she muttered. "You can just go around with a hole in one of your ears like a goddam pirate," she sniffed. I apologized and soothed and convinced Linda to take up the knife again because, no matter how much it hurt, I wasn't going to go around unbalanced. So this time I held the ice to my ear a whole hour and didn't feel the penetration nearly as much as before. But the blood—and especially the sound of popping cartilage—I'll never forget.

That was three and a half years ago. Since then my sadistic friend has kept her ears clean and abandoned the ear-bobbing business. And I've developed an allergy to gold and can't wear my much-suffered-for earrings.

—Carol

The pattern in "Lobe-Botomy" is less formal than that of the student essay that preceded it, but the puns, concrete description, and wit make it a delightful model to emulate.

Descriptions of processes in the natural sciences are very easy to come by. Although this example is taken from a book, it is not unlike the more popular kinds of scientific writing you might find in magazines. Its aim is to explain and inform.

How Snakes Shed Their Skins

When a snake has grown a new epidermis and is about to shed its skin, it secretes a thin layer of fluid between the old and new skin (which are no longer touching), giving the snake a clouded milky appearance. This can be seen especially at the eyes, for the milky fluid covers the pupils and make the snake almost, if not completely, blind. This condition may last for as much as a week; during this period, snakes normally remain in hiding.

A day or two after the cloudiness has cleared, the snake will shed its skin. This is accomplished by opening and stretching the mouth and rubbing it on surrounding objects until the old skin at the edges of the lips begins to split. Rubbing continually, the snake starts to wriggle out of its skin. This is usually sloughed off in one piece from head to tail, turned inside out in the process by the emerging snake. Sometimes the skin will break up, however, and come off in pieces, as during the shedding of lizards.

The sloughed-off skin is a perfect cast of the snake. The large belly scales, the pattern of scales on the back, the eye spectacle and even casts of facial pits can all be seen. It is completely devoid of color as the pigment cells remain in the dermis, which is never shed. The shed skin is transparent with a white tinge. After it has been detached from the snake for a while, it usually becomes brittle. The sloughed-off skin is not especially attractive, but the newly emerged snake is seen at its best. Most species show their best bright colors in the days immediately following molting; as the upper skin gets older, the colors do not show through as well.

—John Stidworthy, *Snakes of the World*

If you are asked to write a description of a scientific process, you may want to use the third person rather than the second, and make the tone more impersonal and objective.

Industrial Alcohol

Industrial alcohol is produced by a process known as fermentation. Fermentation is the process of producing alcohol and carbon dioxide from simple sugars such as glucose (a colorless, yellowish syrupy mixture) and fructose (a very sweet sugar that occurs in fruit and honey). The chemical change that occurs is brought about by the catalytic action of ferments (or enzymes).

The chief ingredient for the production of industrial alcohol is molasses, either cane-sugar molasses or beet-sugar molasses.

In the process of making industrial alcohol, the molasses is first diluted with water. It is then made slightly acid to promote the growth of yeast and to retard the growth of bacteria. Afterwards it is heated to 70 degrees Fahrenheit and to it is added a yeast culture. The yeast secretes an enzyme known as invertase which converts the sucrose in the molasses to glucose and fructose. The concentration of the alcohol can then be increased by distillation.

In addition to using cane-sugar or beet-sugar to produce alcohol, manufacturers use corn, potatoes, various kinds of grain, and other substances containing starch. When starch-containing substances are used, the starch is converted to sugar in the preliminary stages.

Although descriptions of scientific, mechanical, or natural processes tend to be impersonal and objective, you can make them less impersonal, if you wish, by basing them on personal experiences. The following student theme describes the process of canning pineapple with great accuracy, without sacrificing the personal element.

How to Can Pineapple

Two summers ago, our family flew to Hawaii. When we arrived at the hotel, the Royal Hawaiian proved how it had acquired its "royal" reputation. At five o'clock the evening of our arrival, a handsome, dark-skinned Hawaiian boy knocked on our door and presented us with a large, boat-shaped pineapple shell. It was filled with bright, juicy chunks of pineapple. This welcome became a daily ritual which we all looked forward to. The Dole Pineapple Cannery was on our list of places to visit. It proved educational as well as lots of fun!

The pineapple is a sweet, yellow fruit, especially thirst-quenching when eaten in the warm, humid climate of the Hawaiian Islands. It is grown on large plantations. The luscious fruit is produced in slices, chunks, tidbits, spears, and crushed form. How is this done? The process may be described as follows:

After the ripe pineapples arrive at the cannery in specially designed bins or trucks, and are unloaded mechanically for their long, rapid trip through the cannery, they are washed and sorted according to size. Then they enter the "ginaca" machine which removes the shell, cuts off both ends of the fruit, punches out the core, and leaves each fruit a golden cylinder. It even scrapes the shell, leaving the husk nearly dry, ready to be made into bran.

Next, the trimming tables receive the pineapple cylinders at the rate of fifty to one hundred a minute. Here women in white caps, aprons, and rubber gloves pick up each cylinder and trim away any eyes, bits of shells, or overripe portions left on the fruit.

The trimmer then puts the clean cylinder on a moving, stainless-steel conveyor which takes it through a cold-water spray to the slicer where guarded knives cut it into uniform slices. Then other white-capped workers select perfectly matched slices and place them in cans according to grades.

After the cans are filled with slices, chunks, or whatever size fruit is being processed, they move on to syrupers and through vacuum seamers where covers are attached and sealed. Still moving fast and steadily, they come to cookers, where they are sterilized and heated at 200 degrees Fahrenheit, for five to fifteen minutes, depending upon the size of the can and the kind of product.

The fruit, of course, is now very hot, so without pausing a second the cans move through water coolers. The cans of crushed fruit go through a cold-water spray device aptly called a "hula cooler" which shakes as it sprays, getting the contents cool in the center as well as on the outside.

The cans are then placed in cases, and the cases are stored in warehouses, where they leave the state as a finished product under many competitive brand names.

I'll always remember my first taste of fresh Hawaiian pineapple. I can still see the rows and rows of pineapples growing in the fields. I can hear the roar of the giant machines in the plant and the workers efficiently handling the fruit. I know now why Hawaii supplies 80% of the world's pineapple.

—Jackie

Like narration and the other temporal modes, process exposition is not simply the recounting of a sequence of actions or events. To be effective, a process theme must have a purpose. Here is a sequence of events, but what holds them together? A random sequence of events will make neither an interesting narrative nor a successful process theme. But if you keep in mind the question "What is it for?" you will be well on your way to writing a successful process theme.

Exercises

1. Discuss in class any of the essays in this chapter that depicts a process of some kind. What is the author's purpose? What logical, ethical, or emotional strategies does he or she use to achieve that purpose?

2. Discuss in class one of the following topics. How would you construct a paradigm for one of these subjects? Which ones would lend themselves to ethical and logical appeals? What kinds of information would you need to support the general statements of your paradigm? Where might you publish a paper based on this subject? For what readers?

   a. How to get through an interview

   b. How to become open to others

   c. How to cope with anxiety

   d. How to play the game _____

   e. How to cook the dish _____

   f. How to make the drink _____

   g. How to perform a particular physical operation

   h. How to control a crowd at a sporting event or a rock concert

3. Construct a sentence paradigm based on one of the following subjects, keeping in mind your purpose, audience, and a possible writing situation. Bring the paradigm to class for discussion. Then revise your paradigm, and write a paper, using your paradigm as a guide:

   a. How to meet people

   b. How to say "no"

   c. How to deal with loneliness

   d. How to deal with jealousy

   e. Coping with depression

   f. Coping with a broken relationship

   g. How to make _____

   h. How to prepare _____

   i. How to sell _____

   j. How to eat _____

   k. How to plan _____

   l. How to produce _____

4. Write a scientific essay in the manner of "How Snakes Shed Their Skins," or a humorous essay in the manner of "Lobe-Botomy."

5. Write analysis of a natural process such as the cycle of the seasons, the beat of a heart, the rhythm of your movements (or someone else's) as you dance or exercise; the composition of an essay, a painting, an artistic photograph, a song lyric, or a piece of music; a learning process of some kind; a thought process.

6. Discuss in class how you do one of the processes in exercise 5. Or if you have visited a factory or some other place where you observed a process, describe that process, the occasion, purpose, and so forth.

7. Analyze an essay in your reader, or bring to class a magazine ad that describes a process for a particular purpose. Use for class discussion.

Cause and Effect

Why does the wind blow? What causes it to rain? Why does the sun shine? Where does the rainbow come from? Why is the sky blue? Where do babies come from? How did the elephant get his trunk?

Almost all these questions a child would be likely to ask, but such questions should not be dismissed lightly for this reason. Scientists have written articles explaining why the sky is blue. Doctors have prepared manuals for parents and children explaining where babies come from. And Rudyard Kipling wrote a beautiful tale of causation in which he gave a fanciful explanation of how the elephant got his trunk. All these questions and their answers are related to the rhetorical process that we call cause and effect.

A **cause** is *a force or influence that produces an effect. It is an agency or operation responsible for bringing about an action, event, condition, or result.* The word calls to mind other words and expressions such as *origin, source, first principle, author, producer, agent, instrument, prime mover, foundation, support, influence, font, genesis, rationale, intention,* and *the straw that broke the camel's back.*

An **effect** is *anything that has been caused.* It is the *result* of a force or an action. Another meaning of the word **effect** is *something worked out, accomplished, or produced.* The word *effect* calls to mind such related words and expressions as *consequence, result, derivation, end, outcome, development, production, performance, offshoot, creation, handiwork, outgrowth, harvest,* and *issue.*

Cause and effect are correlative terms. The one always implies the other. If a tire on your car blows out and your car hits a lightpole, there is a correlation between the blowout and the accident. We say that one causes the other.

Cause-and-effect relationships are embedded in our language:

> February brings the rain
> Thaws the frozen lake again.
> March winds and April showers
> Bring forth May flowers.
> If in October you do marry,
> Love will come, but riches tarry.
> When December snows fall fast,
> Marry, and true love will last.

But in dealing with cause-and-effect relationships, you want to go beyond language, since language encodes relationships that are already operating in the universe.

What is it that you do when you discern cause-and-effect relationships? You notice that a particular cause or combination of causes is followed by a particular effect, or that a combination of effects follows from a particular cause or causes. A man lights a match near a leaking gas pipe. The man is subsequently killed by a gas explosion. The coroner concludes that the man's carlessness is the cause of his death, though the literal cause of death was the juxtaposition of the flame and the gas.

Another man is driving down the highway in the middle of the winter. It has been snowing, and the road is now covered with ice. The car hits a slick spot in the road, and the man swerves the car in such a way that the car skids and runs off the road, causing the car to overturn. Who or what caused the accident? Philosophers and scientists would say that any causal explanation should take into account not only the **immediate cause** of an effect, but also the **necessary conditions.** The immediate cause was the poor handling of the car by the driver. The necessary conditions were that it had snowed, the snow had turned to ice, and the ice had made the road slippery.

According to scientists, no effect is ever the product of a single cause. A cause is the sum total of all the conditions that help to bring about an effect. It is the combination that constitutes causality. Thus, in strict scientific terms, it would be inaccurate to say that "B is the cause of A" or "A is followed by B." It would be more accurate to state that events A, B, C, D, E in combination caused an event: X. But in everyday matters, it is usually sufficient to pick out one or two of the most conspicuous events and maintain that these produced a particular result. In such cases, you accept the necessary conditions as given.

A familiar old nursery rhyme illustrates this chain of causality beautifully:

> For want of a nail the shoe was lost,
> For want of a shoe the horse was lost,
> For want of a horse the rider was lost,
> For want of a rider the battle was lost,
> For want of a battle the kingdom was lost
> And all for the want of a horseshoe nail.

It is customary to compare causal events to the links in a chain. But causal events are not merely links in an observable chain. They are part of complex conceptual patterns. Causes *are* connected to effects, but they can be seen this way only if you tie them together through experience and reflection. Consider an accident in which one car goes through a red light and plows into another. According to the police, the driver of the first car caused the accident by negligence. The driver claims that his brakes did not hold, yet he just had new brake shoes put on the car. The automobile mechanic blames the failure on faulty construction by the maker of the brake shoes. The brake-shoe manufacturer blames the foreman, who in turn blames the workman, who in turn blames faulty equipment. When you discern cause-and-effect relationships, then, you bring to your understanding of causality certain assumptions and presuppositions. Otherwise you would not be able to explain anything. For compositional purposes, however, you would not be expected to take into account the total cause, including all the necessary conditions of an event. You are expected to be as careful as possible in your causal analyses.

Purpose, Audience, Kind of Discourse

Cause-and-effect thinking can be found in any kind of writing, for any purpose. Ordinarily, you may associate cause-and-effect thinking with scientific writing. But it can be found in everyday reasoning, formal arguments, reports, magazine articles, textbooks, historical explanations, scientific explanations, news articles, proposals, manuals, accident reports, political analyses. TV commentaries, and magazine ads.

Cause and effect can be used for any of the writer's purposes: to justify or condemn some action; to prove or disprove an idea, belief, or assertion; to explain; to give an account of something; to produce a feeling; to investigate; to draw conclusions.

Insofar as your readers are logical beings, they will be looking for reasons in your writing, especially when you want to inform them or ask them to accept or reject a course of action.

Invention and Cause and Effect

As a topic of invention, cause and effect answers such fundamental questions as: Why did it happen? What are its causes? What are its effects? What is its purpose? How is it related causally to something else? In inventing, you follow a sequence of events in time, notice the transference of a force or condition from one thing to another, and attempt to explain these relationships.

Cause and effect is related to narration and to process because all three are concerned with chronological progression. But in cause and effect, you are more interested in the *why* than in the *what* or the *how*.

Cause-and-effect exposition is special in that it presents a step-by-step description of *associated* sequences of events. Something more than just contiguity is involved in the process. Even though all that you observed may have been two or more events following each other in time, you reason from your knowledge of other kinds of causal connections that there is some kind of bond holding these events together, and you imagine what this connection might be. Experience teaches you that certain events are always followed by other events, and you ascribe to the sequence the idea of cause and effect.

The average person understands how to use the word *cause*. Ask her or him what a cause is, and the reply will probably be, "Something that makes something else happen." Cause-and-effect themes have a commonsense vocabulary to convey logical relationships that even the average person will have no trouble with:

cause	in	as a result of
effect	by	for this reason
bring about	of	therefore
produce	so	consequently
give reasons for	thus	accordingly
accomplish	since	on account of
originate	due to	owing to
follow from	because	by the agency of
make possible	if	by means of
result from	then	in effect

In addition to characteristic words and phrases, sentences that convey action imply cause-and-effect relationships:

The intruder was killed by a bullet.
Robert smashed the window with a rock.
The wind lifted the edge of the roof and sent it crashing to the ground.
Amy kicked George in the leg.
The leaves changed from a dark green to a bright orange.

In your sentences you usually attribute some cause to an agent (a person), an instrument, or some agency (a power or institution).

Exercises

1. Probe a cause-and-effect subject by using the questions in this chapter suggested by the topics of invention.

2. Write five thesis sentences for a causal analysis.

3. Discuss in class the cause of an accident which you witnessed or in which you were involved. Discuss the effects of the same accident.

4. Discuss in class your most embarrassing (happiest, saddest, angriest) moment. What caused this embarrassment? What were the effects?

5. Discuss the effects of:

   a. watching television late on a school night

   b. no breakfast before school

   c. no meal before heavy drinking

   d. staying outdoors on a freezing night

6. Discuss the causes of a solar eclipse, a rainbow, a flood, bird migration.

Constructing Cause-and-Effect Paradigms

Causal paradigms tend to fall into two basic types: those which move from cause to effect and those which move from effect to cause.

One way to construct a cause-and-effect paradigm is to begin with a sentence that states the cause of something or things that will follow in the paradigm. Then you add supporting sentences, each of which takes up a particular effect. In adding these sentences to your organizing sentence, you arrange them in such a way that *they form a relational pattern of cause and effect*. As you did for process paradigms, you make the logical progression of your ideas clear to your reader by using cause and effect words such as *cause, effect, result, reason,* and the like. To appeal to your reader's moral sensibilities and emotions, you include ethical and emotional words and phrases:

> Caffeine, as it is used in everyday life, is unquestionably a *potent* drug.
>
> It can *cause* loss of sleep.
>
> It can *cause* anxiety attacks.
>
> It can *cause* physical changes in the body.
>
> It can *create* a physical dependency.
>
> Caffeine can't be regulated because it is a natural food substance, but products containing it should require warning labels.

The organizing sentence of this paradigm does not use an explicit cause-and-effect word, but it does use the word *potent* in which the idea of cause is implicit. Although the middle sentences use the word *cause*, each of these sentences takes up one "effect" of using products with caffeine. There are no explicit ethical and emotional terms in the sentences of this paradigm, but there are implicit ethical and emotional appeals. The writer's intention is to warn the reader of the dangers of using caffeine.

As this paradigm suggests, you can use a number of stylistic alternatives in constructing cause-and-effect paradigms. For example, you can construct the middle sentences in such a way as to include an "effect" word. The following is another version of the above paradigm:

Caffeine, as it is used in everyday life, has potent *effects.*

One *effect* is loss of sleep.

Another *effect* is anxiety attacks.

A third *effect* is physical changes in the body.

A final *effect* is physical dependency.

Because it is a natural food substance, caffeine can't be regulated, but products containing it should require warning labels.

After you construct your paradigm, analyze it carefully to see if it accurately represents your intended meaning, your attitude toward your subject, your audience, your ethical and emotional stance, and your reasoning process. Then, consider the kinds of supporting details you will need. Finally, revise your paradigm.

To write a paper based on a cause-to-effect paradigm, as you have done in writing papers based on the other modes, you put this paradigm into a larger pattern that represents your entire paper. You provide a suitable introduction, appropriate supporting details, and a conclusion. Below are two possible ways of depicting cause-to-effect sequences:

Cause-to-Effect Pattern 1
Introduction (includes background material, thesis, etc.)
Cause (a single cause is mentioned)
Effect 1 (plus supporting details)
Effect 2 (plus supporting details)
Effect 3 (plus supporting details)
Effect 4, 5, 6 . . .
Conclusion (clincher sentence, etc.)

Cause-to-Effect Pattern 2
Introduction (includes background material)
Cause 1 (plus supporting details)

Cause 2 (plus supporting details)
Cause 3 (plus supporting details)
Cause 4, 5, 6 . . .
Effect (a single effect is mentioned)
Conclusion (clincher sentence, etc.)

The following student paper is a good example of an essay that moves from cause to effect:

The Metric Conversion Act

Introduction According to an article I read recently in the *National Geographic*, on December 23, 1975, Gerald Ford, who was at that time president of the United States, signed the Metric Conversion Act of 1975. This act calls for voluntary conversion to the metric system and establishes a Metric Board to coordinate the conversion.

Apparently, the United States has been dragging its feet when it comes to adopting the system. Great Britain switched to metrics in 1965. Australia followed in 1970, and Canada in 1971.

Many major countries had previously adopted the system. Since 1971, America has been standing alone, like a dinosaur in the twentieth century, clinging to its conventional standards of measure.

Thesis Changing to this new system will have far-ranging effects on the whole population. These changes will not be easy.

Effect 1 One effect, already in evidence, will be the dual labeling of grocery store items. For example, powdered sugar will be labeled in terms of ounces (16 oz.), pounds (1 lb.), and grams (454 grams). Triscuits will be labeled as follows: 9½ oz. (269 grams). Applesauce has this information on the label: net weight 16 oz. (454 grams). And everyone is already familiar with the liter sizes of Coca-Cola, Pepsi-Cola, 7-Up, and Dr. Pepper.

Effect 2 Another effect will be on the home. Housewives and househusbands may soon find themselves converting their favorite recipes from ounces to milliliters. A teaspoon, for example, in this new system, is five milliliters, and a tablespoon is fifteen. Change will come slowly, but recipes based on the metric system are already appearing in women's magazines.

Effect 3 A third effect will be on federal agencies. The Patent and Trademark Office now requires patent applications to include metric measurements. In addition, the Department of Agriculture uses metric tons to report crop yields and grain shipments.

Effect 4 A fourth effect will be on big business. The four major automobile manufacturing companies are spending millions to produce cars based on this system. A large number of other industrial and manufacturing companies in the United States are in the process of converting to the metric system.

Conclu-
sion To convert to the metric system will take a lot of time and energy. Some adults will find the system difficult to learn. Children, however, who learn the system in school, will find it a very natural system of measurement because they will know no other.

The United States is making some progress toward its goal. Some people believe that the system will be in effect within the next ten years. Until we convert to the metric system, we will be out of step with the rest of the world.

—Nicia

Here are two more sequences that move from effect to cause:

Effect-to-Cause Pattern 1
Introduction (includes thesis)
Effect (a single effect is mentioned)
Cause 1 (plus supporting details)
Cause 2 (plus supporting details)
Cause 3 (plus supporting details)
Cause 4, 5, 6 . . .
Conclusion (clincher sentence, etc.)

Effect-to-Cause Pattern 2
Introduction (includes thesis)
Effect 1 (plus supporting details)
Effect 2 (plus supporting details)
Effect 3 (plus supporting details)
Effect 4, 5, 6 . . .
Cause (a single cause is mentioned)
Conclusion (clincher sentence, etc.)

The student paper reprinted below moves from effect to cause.

No one familiar with the four televised Kennedy-Nixon debates during the presidential race in 1960 can deny the effect of television on American politics. The charisma of a candidate has become as important a factor as his political program, thanks to the mass exposure he gets through the medium of television. Richard Nixon, for example, could not compete with John F. Kennedy's charm, dry wit, and warm smile, as they debated on nationwide television in the autumn of Kennedy's presidential victory. Viewers responded to the style of the young Democrat—of the estimated 120,000 Americans who had seen at least one of the four debates, an opinion poll showed that seventy-five percent of those whose vote had been swayed by the television confrontation were influenced in favor of the charismatic senator from Massachusetts. Television had truly come into its own as a major factor in American politics as it exposed the public not only to the political facts but also to the political personalities in a way no other medium could.

Politics is not the only area of American life in which television has had a significant effect. Family life, too, has changed as a result of television. Conversation is a virtually nonexistent form of meaningful communication in many American households, for the family gathers only to eat and to cluster in front of the twenty-six-inch, full-color screen in what is called the living room. Often, even meals are eaten in front of a TV program that is too good to miss, and the evening dinner, traditionally a family gathering accompanied by a discussion of the day's events, is turned into an exercise in futility, as forks grope for nutritious food while eyes remain glued to the screen. Family games, outings, songfests, and reading are abandoned in favor of prime-time fare. Sometimes the only verbal communication two family members will have in a day is an argument over which TV program will reign on the evening's agenda, although the popularity of a second or even third television set is wiping out even this meager contact.

Social customs have also been affected by television. TV dates are common, eliminating the need for any involved verbal contact between those who date, and guests in a household are frequently invited to join the host in viewing a particular show, rather than in socializing by pleasant talk or by some more active form of entertainment such as a game. Indeed, much socializing has been eliminated by television, for it is much easier to sit at home and be amused than to force yourself to get up, make yourself attractive, and go out and amuse others.

Television has affected many varied and seemingly separate areas of American life, from politics to the dinner hour, from education to the crime rate. In 1938, E. B. White wrote, "I believe TV is going to be the test of our modern world. . . . We shall stand or fall by TV—of that I am quite sure." The boob tube, the living room babysitter, the electronic pacifier, whatever you call it, this twentieth century invention has affected the lives of virtually every modern American. It is now up to the American public to realize the significance of these effects and to channel them into more positive currents in American life.

—Sandra

Exercises

1. Discuss in class one of the following topics. Then construct a cause-and-effect paradigm based on one of the patterns in this chapter. Consider your purpose, audience, and a possible writing situation.

   a. causes of movie censorship

   b. effects (good or bad) of movie censorship

   c. likely effects of early marriages

   d. causes of the high divorce rate

   e. likely causes of widespread teenage drinking

   f. long-term effects of the energy crisis

   g. causes of your attitudes toward school, your parents, education, religion, sex, or politics

2. Describe in detail the effects of your first cigarette, drink, kiss, lie, or whatever.

3. You are a mad scientist. Describe the effects of a diabolical experiment on one of your enemies.

4. Keeping in mind your purpose, audience, ethical and emotional stance, and writing situation, construct a sentence paradigm based on one of the following subjects. Bring the paradigm to class for discussion. Then revise the paradigm and write an essay, using your paradigm as a guide:

   a. the causes of _____ (pick a subject)

   b. the effects of _____ (pick a subject)

   c. the causes of inflation in your personal life

   d. the effects of inflation on you personally

   e. the effects of taking some drug or hard liquor

   f. the effects of air, noise, or visual pollution in a place you know well

   g. the effects that certain television programs or movies might have on children

5. Select a brief cause-and-effect essay, magazine article, or newspaper article from your reader or other source. In class, discuss the place where the article first appeared, the intended audience, and the occasion. What is the writer's purpose? How does he or she go about achieving it? What reasoning is used? Is there a paradigm? If not, is there an implicit logical pattern that you can reconstruct? Are there ethical and emotional appeals? Is the article effective?

6. Analyze either the text or the picture of a magazine ad for cause-and-effect relationships. Can pictures and illustrations depict cause-and-effect relationships?

CHAPTER 8

Persuasion as an Aim: Induction and Deduction

In the preceding chapters, you have been asked to use a variety of modes in your writing and to consider a variety of aims: informative, persuasive, aesthetic, and expressive. Because persuasion is such an important aim, in this chapter and in the next I will focus on the kinds of thinking and compositional techniques appropriate to persuasion.

Actually, all of the compositional strategies you have learned can be used in the service of persuasion. Modes such as analysis, description, exemplification, narration, comparison, analogy, and cause and effect can be used for any of the writer's aims, for any audience, and for any kind of discourse. Traditionally, however, the kinds of logical thinking that go into the making of arguments have been given the names *induction* and *deduction*.

Every day you encounter numerous situations in which persuasion is used. Advertisers try to get you to buy their products. Politicians solicit your vote. Priests and ministers try to lead you on the path to salvation. Editorial writers attempt to convince you to vote for or against nuclear power plants. Friends and neighbors argue with you about anything and everything—religion, politics, nuclear energy, the oil crisis . . . . And you argue back—sometimes convincingly, sometimes ineffectively, usually unselfconsciously. In your writing, however, a self-conscious attention to the process can be helpful.

Public issues must necessarily be resolved by influencing the beliefs and actions of other people. Skill in argumentation and persuasion can be a means to help you get things done and to combat the evils of doublespeak and propaganda. You might think that all you have to do to get your point across is to be forceful and sincere, but to be persuasive, your arguments have to be presented effectively.

Argumentation is *the giving of reasons to support the truth or falsity of a proposition.* A **proposition** is *a statement upon which an argument is based or from which a conclusion is drawn.* It is a sentence phrased in such a way that it can be the basis of a discussion. It is the thesis of an argument. Think for a moment of what such a statement might contain: an opinion, an authoritative decision, a judgment, a sentiment, a conviction, an attitude, a belief, a criticism, an impression.

To write an argument, then, you begin with a proposition. Next you add other sentences to it, and other sentences to these sentences, and you depict the relationships among these sentences in such a way as to lead your readers to accept your conclusions and to act on them. Your proposition, in other words, must be supported by reasoning and evidence. Otherwise, it stands as an unsupported generalization. **Reasoning** is *thinking in a connected, logical manner by induction or deduction.* It is the drawing of conclusions from observations, facts, or hypotheses. **Evidence** is *the material used to prove your point—facts, ideas, statistics, examples, testimony,* and so forth.

Reasoning by Induction

When you reason inductively, you begin with particular bits and pieces of evidence and then draw a conclusion from this evidence. **Induction** is *reasoning from the particular to the general.* It is coming to a conclusion about all members of a class from examining only a few members of the class. Because the evidence is incomplete and the facts limited, you must leap from these facts to a general conclusion.

Induction tells you what to expect. If you reach into a basket of tomatoes and pick out six or seven that are rotten, you might conclude that the rest of the tomatoes are rotten, too. You might be right or you might be wrong. Your conclusion would be *probable,* but the only way you could be certain would be to examine every tomato.

Many of our conclusions are based on an *inductive leap.* We believe that aspirin cures headaches because we've taken aspirin in the past, and indeed aspirin did cure our headaches. Therefore, it is reasonable to believe that aspirin will cure our headaches in the future.

In its logical form, an inductive reasoning process looks like this:

Aspirin cured my headache a year ago.
Aspirin cured my headache six months ago.

Aspirin cured my headache last month.
Aspirin cured my headache two weeks ago.
Therefore, aspirin cures headaches.

Reasoning by Deduction

When you reason deductively, you begin with a general statement as a premise, apply it to a particular instance, and then draw a conclusion from it. **Deduction** is *reasoning from the general to the specific*. It proceeds through steps that comprise what is called a syllogism. A **syllogism** consists of three sentences or propositions. The first two sentences are called premises. The last sentence is called the conclusion. In its traditional form, the syllogism looks like this:

All women enjoy dancing.
Joan is a woman.
Therefore, Joan enjoys dancing.

The conclusion is valid because the reasoning is sound. But it may not necessarily be true. If the premises (sentences 1 and 2) are true, then the conclusion (sentence 3) is true. But a moment's thought will reveal that the major premise ("all women enjoy dancing") is not necessarily true. Therefore, the conclusion may be false.

Inductive reasoning generally takes the form of examples, testimony, analogy, and cause and effect. Deductive reasoning often takes the form of the syllogism and the enthymeme (a shortened form of the syllogism). However, even though you reason to a conclusion inductively, in your writing you can state your conclusion first and then supply reasons for supporting it.

Because of the close relationship that exists between induction and deduction, in this chapter we shall be moving back and forth between the two kinds of thinking. But we will also be looking at a wider range of categories than is ordinarily dealt with in discussions of argumentation. Besides the usual methods of reasoning by induction (examples, testimony, analogy, cause and effect), we will be examining categories such as analysis, description, narration, and comparison, usually associated with expository or literary writing. In the next chapter, we will be dealing almost exclusively with deduction as it relates to the syllogism and the enthymeme.

Arguing by Analysis

In Chapter 4, you learned that **analysis** is *the process of dividing anything complex into simple parts.* Besides being a thought process, analysis is a method of getting ideas and organizing those ideas. Although analysis can be used for any of the writer's aims and in any kind of writing, most of the analyses you have looked at thus far have been examples of informative writing. Yet analysis is also an important mode of developing arguments.

In writing an argument, you give features, characteristics, or details to amplify the central idea. In using analysis for persuasive purposes, you divide a whole into its component parts. But in writing expository essays, you proceed in much the same manner. Where does the difference lie? The most obvious difference is in the writer's intention. In persuasive writing, your purpose is to secure conviction or action. In expository writing, your purpose is to inform or instruct. In expository writing, all you have to do to achieve your purpose is to convince your readers of the soundness of your thinking. But in persuasive writing, you must also provide your readers with motives and reasons for believing your assertions. If you want your readers to do something, you've got to ask them to do it: to get out and vote, to fill in a questionnaire, to buy a particular product, to travel to a mountain resort, to fly to Hawaii.

How is this done? Not only by logical reasoning and evidence, but also by *direct command,* by *invitation,* and by *suggestion.* The most effective arguments extend the call for action throughout the text, embedded in the reasoning process, but many persuasive essays get action by calling for it near the end of the discourse. Here are some examples:

> *The Command*
> See and drive this great new car today.
> Vote for ————.
> Ban nuclear energy!
> Impeach ————.

And in a more humorous vein:

> Repeal inhibition.
> Fight air pollution—inhale.
> Be alert—the world needs more lerts.
> Get high on helium; it's a gas.

The Invitation
We invite you to join us at the Holiday Inn.
We hope you'll make your next cake with Swans Down Cake Mix.
Please try our coffee today.

The Suggestion
Why not give minorities job preferences?
Your girl will be impressed if you say it with flowers.
You will look so much better if you buy an Arrow shirt.

The direct command makes an urgent appeal to the reader. It uses exhortation to get action. The invitation employs polite and courteous language. It sometimes resembles a social invitation. The suggestion uses implication and inference. Like the invitation, it is courteous, but in addition it makes use of coaxing, flattery, and pleading.

In arguing by analysis, you can use both inductive and deductive thinking. In an inductive analysis, you proceed from the parts to the whole. In a deductive analysis, you go from broader to narrower elements.

The paradigmatic structure of analytic arguments is similar to that of expository essays, except that the thesis is a proposition to be argued:

Analysis Pattern 1
Introduction (includes proposition to be argued)
Feature 1 (or detail 1)
Feature 2 (or detail 2)
Feature 3 (or detail 3)
Feature 4 (or detail 4)
Feature 5, 6, 7 (or detail 5, 6, 7) . . .
Conclusion (includes call for action)

Analysis Pattern 2
Introduction (includes proposition to be argued)
Cluster of features (as evidence)
Cluster of features
Cluster of features
Cluster of features
Conclusion (includes call for action)

An inductive pattern is also possible. Here is an example of an inductive pattern in a less abstract form:

Analysis Pattern 3
This political candidate has this qualification.
This political candidate has this qualification.
This political candidate has this qualification.
This political candidate has this qualification.
This political candidate has outstanding qualifications.
Vote for him or her.

The following is a good example of a persuasive essay that uses inductive reasoning toward a conclusion:

> If you've never driven a car with front-wheel drive before, you're in for a new and rewarding experience. GM's new Chevrolet Citation, Pontiac, Phoenix, Oldsmobile Omega, and Buick Skylark are front-wheel-drive cars that will be GM's frontrunners for the '80s.
>
> They all have *transverse-mounted engines*. Because the engine sits sideways, overall length is reduced, yet each car has plenty of room for passengers and luggage. A 4-cylinder engine is standard, but a V-6 is also available.
>
> Each car has a *MacPherson Strut front suspension* that helps create a roomier passenger compartment.
>
> Each has *rack-and-pinion steering* for quick, easy response.
>
> All have *front disc brakes* with a new low-drag design with audible wear indicators.
>
> All have *radial tires* in a new design, with a special rubber compound to lower rolling resistance even more than conventional radials.
>
> Each has a maintenance-free *Delco Freedom battery* that never needs water.
>
> Each has a maintenance-free *wheel bearing assemblies,* completely sealed, preset for precise clearance, and lubed for life.
>
> These are just some of the *outstanding standard features* that you get on these exciting new front-wheel-drive cars. Drive one at your GM dealer's today and draw your own conclusions.
>
> —adapted from a General Motors ad

This essay uses an inductive chain of reasoning very much like that exemplified in analysis pattern 3. Each paragraph highlights a feature of the new GM front-wheel-drive cars. As the evidence mounts, paragraph by paragraph, the reader is led into *(induced)* the generalization in the final paragraph. The essay concludes with a call to action.

Advertisers make extensive use of the mode of analysis to convince their readers of the relative superiority of their products. In an inductive arrangement, the ad opens with attributes of the product, with features, facts, or other proof, and then shows how these selling points are beneficial to the reader. This inductive sequence gains conviction because it piles up facts about a product, explains its qualities, and then leads the reader to conclude that the product has benefits from which he or she can profit.

Arguing by Description

Description is *a mode of analysis*, and like analysis it can be found in any kind of writing, to achieve any of the writer's aims. In literary writing, where there may be long stretches of description, it tends to follow a spatial pattern. Often, however, it is subordinate to the mode of narration. But in persuasive writing, descriptive elements and details are arranged largely in the order of observation.

A good example of descriptive reasoning for persuasive purposes can be found in magazine advertising. As in magazine ads that use an abstract analysis of features to win conviction, magazine ads that use concrete sensory details present descriptive material in the form of product attributes or benefits. Advertisers present this material in such a way as to differentiate their brand from competitive brands and to convince their readers that the quality of their merchandise is consistent with the price.

In advertising, descriptive copy is often called human-interest copy because it appeals primarily to the senses and the emotions, and the reader's response to it is instinctive. Consequently, persuasive writing that uses description relies heavily on suggestion rather than deliberation. If all of our actions were based on deliberate choices, there would be little place in persuasive writing for description. But human beings are not always logical. They are also moved by instincts and by feelings of hunger, anger, fear, and desire.

Writers who use description for persuasive purposes often give conflicting advice about the techniques best suited to win conviction from their readers. According to some writers, vague, general words such as *beautiful*, *magnificent*, and *luxurious* have little human-interest value. They claim that the best descriptions individualize the person or object to be described. Therefore, the writer should fill his or her writing with concrete and vivid sensations of sight, smell, taste, and touch. Other writers claim that description need not always be concrete and specific to be good. Sometimes an object can be difficult to describe precisely. Other times, it seems better to give the observer's reactions to the perceived object than to give a precise description of the object. Whatever may be true in other kinds of writing, in persuasive writing a combination of sugestive and concrete description can be effective.

Here is an example of a magazine ad that uses a combination of concrete and suggestive description to achieve its purpose:

Caramel-Vanilla: A Golden Merger of Two of Nature's Richest Flavors

We've blended the taste of luscious vanilla with creamy caramel and now have a deliciously mellow cordial with a rich flavor that's more than equal to its parts. Sip it straight, blend it half-and-half with fresh cold milk, or be creative and experiment. It's delicious fun. And its name, Caramella, is as soft and mellow as its taste. Look for the distinctive white bottle from Arrow.

The headline serves the function of a thesis sentence: "Caramel-Vanilla [is] a golden merger of two of nature's richest flavors." This sentence organizes the descriptive details that follow by repeating the idea of the blending of ingredients in successive sentences. The term *caramel-vanilla* in the headline, which is a compound, introduces this idea, and then the idea is repeated in the words *merger, two, blended, Caramella, more than equal to its parts,* and *blend.*

Within this framework, the ad uses a combination of concrete and suggestive details to convince the reader to buy the product. The concrete details appeal directly to the senses: *mellow* ("soft, sweet, juicy, full-flavored"), *creamy* ("rich in cream"), *caramella* ("caramel and vanilla"). The suggestive details direct the reader to feel a certain way about the product: *delicious* ("pleasing, enjoyable"), *luscious* ("pleasant"), *rich* ("excessive proportion of pleasing ingredients"), *distinctive.* There is also an effective use of sound devices to reinforce the idea that Caramella is a pleasant experience: *creamy caramel,* de-*liciously mellow, Caramella,* soft and *mellow.* There is no direct call for action at the end of the ad. Instead, the act of description, with its appeal to the reader's sensations and feelings, makes an effective selling appeal.

Although magazine advertising may seem to be a specialized kind of persuasive writing, politicians, businessmen and -women, and religious organizations have borrowed techniques from copywriters to sell ideas, goods, and services. You can learn much from ad writers about how to use description for persuasive purposes.

Exercises

1. Bring to class a magazine ad that uses the mode of analysis to secure conviction (for example, a car ad, stereo ad, ad for soap). Discuss the chain of reasoning. Is it inductive or deductive? Is the argument convincing?

2. Bring to class for discussion a food ad, a perfume ad, a cosmetic ad, a clothing ad, or a jewelry ad that uses description for persuasive purposes. What is the method of organization: Inductive? Deductive? What is the order of impressions? What is the diction like? Is the selling appeal explicit or implicit?

3. Describe your home to make it appealing for someone who wants to swap homes for a summer vacation. The form of writing can be a letter or an ad.

4. You work for Japan Air Lines. Write an ad to get people to take a trip to the Orient.

5. Write an ad describing a Las Vegas holiday for two.

6. Describe the benefits of a pleasure cruise to South America or Europe.

7. Using the mode of description, write a persuasive essay to get your reader to do one of the following: see an exhibit; visit a special place; reevaluate a song, a painting, or another work of art; visit a place of historical interest; avoid a certain place.

Arguing from Example

Reasoning by example is *the typical inductive form of reasoning.* When using this method of developing ideas in persuasive writing, you cite a series of examples, all of which display a certain relationship to one another, and then draw a general conclusion from them.

The following ad for Coach Leatherware uses this process effectively. The illustration is simple. It consists of four pictures of leather bags or purses, arranged in a rectangular shape, two pictures at the top and two at the bottom. The text reads as follows:

Example 1: This is a Coach bag. You can get it at Goldwater's.
Example 2: This is a Coach bag. You can get it at Bonwit Teller.
Example 3: This is a Coach bag. You can get it at Dayton's Oval Room.
Example 4: This is a Coach bag. You can get it at Garfinckel's.
Conclusion: Coach bags are sold in the nicest stores.

Here is an ad for Aetna Life and Casualty that uses a similar chain of reasoning:

A truck without brake lights is hit from behind. For "psychic damages" to the driver, because his pride was hurt when his wife had to work, *a jury awards $480,000 above and beyond his medical bills and wage losses.*

A 67-year old factory worker loses an arm on the job. His lawyer argues that he should receive wages for all the remaining years of his life expectancy. He had been earning about $10,000 a year. The jury awards him a sum equal to almost $89,000 a year.

Then there's the one . . . but *you* can probably provide the next example. Most of us know hair-raising stories of windfall awards won in court. Justified claims should be compensated, of course. Aetna's point is that it is time to look hard at what windfall awards are costing.

What can we do? Several things:

We can stop assessing "liability" where there really *was* no fault—and express our sympathy for victims through other means.

We can ask juries to take into account a victim's *own* responsibility for his losses. And we can urge that awards realistically reflect the actual loss suffered—that they be a fair *compensation*, but not a reward.

Insurers, lawyers, judges—each of us shares some blame for this mess. But it is you, the public, who can best begin to clean it up. Don't underestimate your own influence. Use it, as we are trying to use ours.

Aetna wants insurance to be affordable.

Although reasoning by example is generally inductive, for purposes of writing persuasive essays you can present your conclusion in the beginning of your essay and then follow it up with representative examples to support your conclusions.

This ad for Texaco uses a single extended example to make its point:

Texaco is working to get more than oil out of the ground.

Texaco doesn't just look for new sources of oil, it also looks for new ways to conserve the oil we already have.

For example, Texaco has developed a way to produce one of the raw materials for making chemical fertilizer. This method, which is a coal gasification process, uses coal instead of natural gas or petroleum liquids.

Recently, Texaco's coal gasification process was selected by the Tennessee Valley Authority for use in its National Fertilizer Development Center in Alabama.

In the future, this process may be widely used and America will be able to save some of the natural gas and petroleum liquids which it so desperately needs.

This coal gasification process is just one example of how Texaco puts its resources to work for you.

In reasoning by example, try to avoid common weaknesses by keeping in mind the following advice:

1. *Cite a reasonable number of examples.* In arguments using examples, there is a danger of generalizing from too few examples. It is difficult, however, to determine how many examples are necessary to lend force to an argument. Sometimes a single long example can be effective.
2. *Cite typical examples.* If you select examples that are unusual or exceptional, the conclusions you draw from them might be misleading. Your examples should be representative.
3. *Account for negative examples.* In generalizing from examples, you might come across negative examples that do not support your conclusion. Nevertheless, you must account for these negative instances, perhaps by showing that they are not significant or that they are exceptions.

Hasty Generalization

A **hasty generalization** is *a generalization based on insufficient evidence.* The problem arises when the writer tries to extend his or her conclusion beyond the examples on which it is based. All arguments of this kind leap from the known to the unknown. But the difficulty lies in justifying this leap with too few examples, with a lack of typical examples, or with the failure to account for negative examples. Is it true, for instance, that "Americans are the most wasteful people on earth"?

Sweeping Generalization

A **sweeping generalization** is *one that needs to be qualified* by words and phrases such as *some, a few, many, most, usually,* and *sometimes.*

Advertisers use sweeping generalizations extensively to make claims of exclusivity (note my use of the sweeping word *extensively*), as in the following examples:

> No other product lets you bake so many things so quickly.
> Nothing performs like a Saab.
> Did you know that no leading oil tastes lighter than Mazola 100%
>   corn oil?

In your own writing, you will be more effective if your generalizations are less sweeping:

> All politicians are dishonest. (sweeping)
> *Most* politicians are dishonest. (still too sweeping)
> *Many* politicians are dishonest. (less sweeping)
> *A few* politicians are dishonest. (you're on safer ground)

Exercises

1. Analyze the Aetna ad. Besides the inductive use of examples, the ad uses other methods of development. What are they? Are they effective?

2. Write an inductive argument supported by examples.

3. Evaluate these generalizations:

    a. Children who read are not dropouts.

    b. The best American-made movies are the ones the major studios have absolutely no part in making.

    c. All Democrats are liberal.

    d. Most Republicans are conservative.

    e. Nothing can be perfectly safe. Should we ban automobiles, cigarettes, and bathtubs? The biggest danger of nuclear power is that we won't have enough.

    f. Most women are conceited.

    g. You mean you wear contact lenses, too? You're the fourth person with blue eyes I've met recently who wears contact lenses. Blue-eyed people must have weak eyes.

    h. Dan had his wallet stolen downtown. Carol lost her purse. If I go downtown, I'll be robbed.

i. I asked everyone in class if he or she smoked grass. Not one said yes.
    Marijuana is not used in this school.

j. This morning I got a flat tire. An hour later I got a speeding ticket.
    On the way home I got into an accident. Today sure was a lousy day.

Arguing by Narration

In **arguing by narration,** *you present your narrative in such a way that it serves as an inductive example to support your conclusion.* Narration as a mode of developing ideas has great human-interest appeal for readers. The narrative mode is intensely dramatic and dynamic. Because it is filled with action, it naturally lends itself to inducing action in others.

In using this mode of persuasion, you try to get your readers to identify with the characters in the narrative or with the situation being dramatized. This attempt to get your readers to identify with the characters or the situation is an important part of the persuasive appeal.

Narratives in argumentation can be of various kinds: factual narratives, fictional narratives, monologues, or dialogues. **Factual narratives** are *based on actual events,* and even when some liberty is taken with the names and places, the situation must be recognized as one that could take place in everyday life. **Fictional narratives** are *invented stories whose content is largely produced by the imagination.* However, a part of the content may be based on fact.

The following ad is a good example of a fictional narrative. The illustration depicts a man looking wistfully through a store window at a Steinway piano:

The Man Who Thought He Couldn't Own a Steinway

To him it had always been "the only piano."

Yet a little voice in the back of his head kept whispering, "You can't afford it."

Then one day he sharpened a pencil, quieted the voice in the back of his head, and did some serious figuring.

To his surprise, he discovered that the Steinway was not too much more expensive than the piano he'd been considering. Which didn't have the tone of a Steinway. Or the Steinway touch. It didn't have Steinway's Hexagrip Wrestplank. Or Steinway's Diaphramatic Soundboard. Or any of the exclusive features that makes a Steinway feel and sound like a Steinway.

"I'm being penny-wise but pound-foolish," he cried. So he bought the Steinway he's always wanted, which he and his wife and family are all enjoying.

He has only one regret. "I should have done it years ago," he says.

For more information, please write to John H. Steinway, 109 West 57th Street, New York 10019.

Monologues are *narratives in which the talk is by a single person.* The advantage of using a monologue instead of a fully developed story is that it allows a single character to act as a spokesperson for the writer. It is important in this kind of writing that the speaker talk with a believable voice.

The following ad for Timberland boots uses monologue copy very effectively. The illustration depicts an old man from the country sitting in the cab of his truck, with his feet extended from the cab. Naturally, he has on Timberland boots.

> "It was two of those fellers from the city come up the road in a big green car, asked me if I wanted some new boots. I didn't. Already had boots, had 'em for seven years: But they talked and we drank some and then we looked at the boots some, and I tried 'em on. Now, I have to say, they did seem to have my size. So I walked 'em about for maybe a week, and once I went over and stood in Orville Wade's creek, just to see if they were waterproof, which they were. When those boys came back from the city, this is what I said. One, I said thank you for the fine boots, which are warm and dry as a hen's bottom. Two, I'd like a pair of 13 wides for Cousin Luther, double wide on the left foot where the tractor run it over."
>
> TIMBERLAND.   A whole line of fine leather boots that cost plenty, and should.
>
> —Timberland Co.

Dialogues are *narratives that have at least two speakers.* In writing dialogues, use dialogue tags such as "said he" and "she said" sparingly to avoid monotony.

The dialogue reprinted below, taken from a Whirlpool ad, moves inductively from the telephone conversation to the conclusion and selling appeal at the end of the ad:

How One Family Got Their Laundry Done over the Phone (Based on an Actual Call)

(telephone rings)

Cool-Line Consultant: Whirlpool Cool-Line. May I help you?

Man: I certainly hope so. I rush home from work, gobble down dinner, pack the kids in the wagon, and head out to pick up our new Whirlpool washer. Then back home, hook it all up, and . . . nothing.

Consultant: Nothing?

Man: Absolutely zotz. Our four-year-old can make the door open and close, but that's all. So now, the store's closed, my wife's really steamed, and I'm not too thrilled myself. Now what are you gonna do about it?

Consultant: Our Cool-Line service is here to help get things working for you. Let's run through a quick checklist. First—now, don't get mad—did you plug it in?

Man: We're not that dense.

Consultant: Both water lines hooked up and the water turned on?

Man: Of course.

Consultant: And you set the dial to regular wash and pulled out the control knob?

Man: Look, the washer really doesn't work! Might take the repairman a whole day to fix it.

Consultant: Might take just a few minutes. You see, Whirlpool appliances are designed to make servicing as quick and easy as possible. But before you call for service, let me ask you one more question.

Man: Shoot.

Consultant: Why did you buy a new washer? What was wrong with the old one?

Man: It was really on the fritz. Blowing fuses and stuff. The service guy said it was hopeless.

Consultant: Is there any chance that old washer blew a fuse one last time without your knowing it? Will you check?

Man: Oh my aching. . . . hang on. *(minutes later)* This is embarrassing. All we needed was a new fuse. I'm sorry I hassled you.

Consultant: Sorry you had trouble. Glad we could help.

Man: Hey, thanks again.

This is the kind of two-way communication we've been having on our Whirlpool Cool-Line service for the past eleven years. It's just one example of the continuing concern we have for our customers who purchase Whirlpool appliances.

If you ever have a question or problem with your Whirlpool appliance, call our toll-free 24-hour Cool-Line service at 800–253–1301.

—Whirlpool Corporation

Appeal to Pity

The **appeal to pity** is *an emotional appeal*, often using the mode of narration combined with description, *in which the writer attempts to persuade his or her readers to accept a conclusion on the basis of pity or sympathy*. A good example of the appeal to pity is the ever-recurring situation in which a student asks a teacher to change a grade, saying that he or she will flunk out of school or lose a scholarship unless a higher grade is given.

An appeal to pity is not necessarily a logical fallacy. A relevant appeal is one that addresses an issue which *by its nature* arouses sympathy. If, for example, a charitable organization makes a plea for money in order to aid needy children and shows a picture of a starving, wretched child, this strategy is bound to evoke an emotional response in the reader. The child's wretched condition *is* the issue. Therefore, the emotional appeal is appropriate. If, however, the appeal to pity fails to touch on the issue, as in the case of the student who receives low grades because of poor performance, then the appeal is irrelevant.

Here is an appeal designed to get sponsors for needy children in India, Brazil, Taiwan (Formosa), Mexico, and the Philippines, that appeared in *Time* magazine several years ago:

She Needs Your Love

Little Mie-Wen in Formosa already knows many things . . . the gnawing of hunger . . . the shivering of fear . . . the misery of being unwanted.

But she has never known love. Her mother died when she was born. Her father was poor—and didn't want a girl child. So Mie-Wen has spent her baby years without the affection and security every child craves.

Your love can give Mie-Wen, and children just as needy, the privileges you would wish for your own child.

Through Christian Children's Fund you can sponsor one of these youngsters. We use the word *sponsor* to symbolize the bond of love that exists between you and the child.

The cost? Only $12 a month. Your love is demonstrated in a practical way because your money helps with nourishing meals . . . medical care . . . warm clothing . . . education . . . understanding housemothers. . . .

Little Mie-Wen and children like her need your love—won't you help? Today?

—Christian Children's Fund

Exercises

1. The Steinway piano ad appeared in *Harper's* in 1977. Discuss its relation to the intended audience. Is there a conflict in the story? Who are the characters? What is the diction like? How does the persuasive appeal work?

2. Does the voice of the speaker in the Timberland ad seem believable? Examine the ad closely. What is the language like? Pick out dialect features, words and phrases, or other stylistic devices that characterize the speaker. Is the ad convincing?

3. How would you characterize the customer in the Whirlpool ad? What is his language like? Does the language of the consultant seem as if it were part of the conversation of the actual telephone call? Is this ad persuasive?

4. Bring to class examples of writing that use narration for persuasive purposes. Try to find examples of each type: factual narratives, fictional narratives, monologues, and dialogues. Then discuss how the narrative mode is used in the service of persuasion.

5. Write an argument using the mode of narration.

6. Write an essay in which you use an appeal to pity as the basis of your argument.

Arguing from Authority

When you argue from **authority,** you include in your argument *statements from an expert in some particular field.* A mere assertion, such as "Everybody knows that . . . ," is not enough. You should name the authority, quote his or her exact words, or paraphrase them.

The statement of the authority may take the form of a letter of recommendation, a quotation, a testimonial, an opinion poll, a best-seller list, a critical statement about a book or a movie, or the testimony of a witness at a trial. The logical structure of an argument by authority consists simply of repeating the words of the expert. A more sophisticated form of argument by authority is that in which the statement of the expert becomes the premise of a deductive form of reasoning.

You must often rely on the opinions of others because you don't have firsthand evidence yourself, or because such evidence is difficult to obtain. You also draw on these opinions because the experts who offer them have special training and experience in a particular field and are thus more qualified to make judgments in that field than is the average person.

Authorities can be of various kinds. There is the *prestige author-ity*, whose fame is known to the audience. He or she may or may not be an expert. There is the *expert authority*, who has special knowledge and experience. There is the *nonexpert authority*, who has had no special training or experience. There is the *lay authority*, the common man or woman who is like the majority of people, whose opinion is solicited *because it is typical.*

The **testimonial** is *an effective form of arguing from authority in which a real person gives a sincere statement about a product or service.* The people are real in the sense that they are not fictitious, but they may be professional models rather than actual users of the pro-duct.

Here is a testimonial, in the form of a monologue, of a Head & Shoulders shampoo ad. The speaker is a young woman, seated in a chair, with a magazine opened before her and a bottle of Head & Shoulders shampoo prominently displayed in the foreground. The ad appeared in *Mademoiselle* magazine in March 1977.

> I never tried a dandruff shampoo. I just sort of ignored my occasional itches and flakes. After all, my hair had bounce and shine and was very delicate. And since I washed my hair an awful lot, I really wanted a mild shampoo.
>
> Then my best friend (who has gorgeous hair, by the way) told me about Head & Shoulders. She said I'd love the fresh smell, the thick, rich lather. And it would leave even my baby fine hair soft and shiny, while controlling dandruff at the same time. She told me Head & Shoulders was the only shampoo she used.
>
> I sure am glad I listened to her. Head & Shoulders is everything she said it was. You can see for yourself how wonderfully shiny my hair is. And not a worry about those itches and flakes. Now I wouldn't trust my hair to any shampoo but Head & Shoulders.
>
> —The Procter & Gamble Co.

It is difficult to determine the age of the young woman in the illustration. She could either be a high school student, perhaps a senior, or a college student. Not only is she young looking, but also she uses characteristic phrases such as *sort of, awful lot,* and *sure am glad* that a teenager might use.

It is also difficult to tell if the young woman in the ad is an actual user of the product or if she is a model. She is not identified by name, nor are her words included in quotations. Perhaps we would be justified in accepting this testimonial as a fictional narrative.

Many testimonials use *celebrities* to endorse products. People like to look at pictures of celebrities in magazine ads and to read about them. The extent to which testimonials from celebrities are effective is in direct proportion to the extent to which the reader believes the endorser actually has knowledge of the product he or she is credited with using.

The following testimonial by Carol Lawrence for General Foods International Coffees is a good example of the type.

Carol Lawrence Presents Orange Cappuccino

"I love Italy. I love oranges. I love coffee. I suppose that's why I love everything about Orange Cappuccino.

"Of all the countries I've visited, I've always had a special affection for Italy, land of good food, good art, and lots of my good relatives.

"So it wasn't surprising how much I enjoyed Orange Cappuccino. This flavor from General Foods International Coffees, inspired by Italian Cappuccino, is a delightful treat.

"It has a creamy brown color and a delicate aroma. Yet it's a wonderfully full-bodied coffee with an extra note of flavor: the enticing taste and bouquet of lively orange.

"Orange Cappuccino has such a satisfying flavor I drink it the way the Italians drink their own Cappuccino—in a relaxed and unhurried way. As you know, Rome wasn't built in a day."

—General Foods Corporation

Argument from authority frequently takes the form of *massed evidence* or *group authority*. **Massed evidence** is *a large collection of facts or quotations of the same kind, with little explanation or comment.* Massed evidence is used in magazine advertisements, on book jackets, and in movie ads. One ad for Woody Allen's film *Manhattan* consisted entirely of quotations such as these:

"*Manhattan* is inspired! One of Allen's most brilliant movies!"—Gene Shalit *(Today),* NBC-TV

"*Manhattan* deserves a stream of bravos! I can't urge you strongly enough to see *Manhattan.*"—Rona Barrett, ABC-TV

"A masterpiece! A perfect blend of style, substance, humor, and humanity!"—Richard Schickel, *Time*

While I was flying to Colorado on Frontier Airlines, I happened to run across these massed quotations in a Frontier Airlines magazine:

Frontier. For the Long Stretch

"You allow an amount of legroom that I thought had disappeared years ago."—B. W. McPherson, Huntsville
"I especially enjoyed the roominess offered in your seating arrangement."—J. W. Moeller, Wichita
"Thanks, Frontier, for your legroom, good food, and friendly service—don't change it."—C. Schuld, Ft. Collins
"We wish to compliment you on the roominess of the aircraft."—Mr. & Mrs. R. O. Zincke, St. Louis
"Frontier is definitely far superior to other airlines. Thank you for being you."—K. Bolles, Denver
FRONTIER AIRLINES: First-class comfort at coach prices.

—*Inflight*, Frontier Airlines, Inc.

Although there is a sense in which testimonials prove nothing, they have great psychological appeal. First, they present the point of view of the user of a product or service. Second, people tend to believe a statement if it comes from an authority. Third, people want to associate themselves with others whom they like or admire.

Fallacious Appeals to Authority

In the writing of arguments, the fallacious appeal to authority can take several forms: citing an authority in one field (for instance, Reggie Jackson in baseball) when deciding a question in a completely different field (automobiles); citing an all-inclusive or vague authority ("Experts agree," "Everyone knows"); citing authorities that may be outdated (such as an old science book); citing authorities who are biased; citing authorities who may have been paid for their testimony.

Here are some questions that you might ask to determine if the appeal to authority is valid:

1. *Is the argument you are preparing really a matter for authority?*
2. *Is the authority an expert on this subject (rather than on some other subject)?*

3. *Does the authority have knowledge and expertise? What positions does he or she hold? What kind of training and degrees does he or she have? Publications, awards, or grants?*
4. *Is the authority reliable?*
5. *Is the authority prejudiced? Is he or she influenced by self-interest? Does he or she represent a special interest group?*

Exercises

1. Over the past few years, cigarette advertisers have switched from the green-world archetype to which the Salem smoker takes his girl, to testimonials. Bring to class a group of ads for three different brands of cigarettes that use testimonials in their ads, and discuss the effectiveness or lack of effectiveness of the testimonials. Does the endorsement come from real people? How can you tell? Is the voice authentic? Compare the language of the various ads. Is the language similar?

2. Bring to class for discussion ads that use celebrities to sell a product.

3. In celebrity ads, there ought to be some kind of association between the celebrity and the product. Bring to class a celebrity ad for class discussion and analysis you wish to discuss. Are the ads convincing? Is the voice of the celebrity authentic? Is there a proper association between celebrity and product? Is any of the celebrities an authority for the product?

4. Bring to class some examples of massed evidence or group authority for discussion.

5. Bring to class examples of best-seller lists, lists of best popular albums, and so forth. Discuss their use as arguments from authority.

6. Proverbs, maxims, and wise sayings are a form of argument from authority. Discuss their uses to win arguments in everyday life. For example, did your parents ever use them on you? Have you ever heard politicians use them?

7. A friend is applying for a job and has given your name as a reference. Write a complimentary letter of recommendation for that friend. Now imagine that the friend has personal habits that would make you hesitate in writing a letter. Write the letter anyway, but qualify it in such a

way as to point out the friend's shortcomings, without jeopardizing the friend's chance for a job.

8. Write an argument, using some form of authority to support your argument. It can be in the form of an essay, a letter to the editor, or a magazine ad.

Arguing by Comparison

In **reasoning by comparison,** *you state a resemblance between two things and then draw a conclusion from that resemblance.* When you argue by comparison, you present two units of thought to your reader and then point out how one is different from, superior to, or more desirable than the other:

Spanish Olives: How to Tell the Original from the Reproduction

The olive on the left is a true-blue Spanish green olive. The olive on the right just looks like one.

The olive on the left was grown in Spain, where the dry climate and mineral-rich soil help an olive ripen to its tangiest best. There's no telling where the olive on the right was grown.

The olive on the left was treated with meticulous care. By people who learned long ago that a bruised olive hurts business. As for the olive on the right, you really can't be sure how it was treated.

How do you tell them apart? Simple. Just read the label.

The olive on the left comes in a jar with the Spanish Olive Man symbol on it. The olive on the right doesn't.

So now you can be sure of the green olive you're getting before you lay down your hard-earned green for it.

—The Spanish Olive Commission

This ad for Spanish olives was taken from *McCall's* magazine, October 1977. Because there are so many ads in magazines, a successful ad has to grab the reader's attention immediately and then attempt to gain conviction. The illustration is the means of getting attention in this ad. It consists of a picture of two green olives, contrasted with a background of dark blue shading into royal blue and then gray.

The writer of this ad uses a simple point-by-point comparison pattern. Never mind that this paradigm has been used repeatedly. It is effective *because* it is conventional. The very shape of the comparison pattern has persuasive force. I am convinced that when the reader finishes this ad, he or she is persuaded of the relative superiority of one product over the other on the basis of the reasoning process alone, for if you look carefully at the evidence within the process, you come away with the impression that there are very few facts on which to base a buying decision. Isolated from their context, the "facts" look like this:

The Olive on the Left	*The Olive on the Right*
true-blue Spanish green olive grown in Spain	looks like one
	no telling where the olive on the right was grown
treated with meticulous care	can't be sure how it was treated
comes in a jar with the Spanish Olive Man symbol on it	doesn't [come in a jar with the Spanish Olive Man symbol on it]

In using comparison as a mode in developing arguments, many writers find it natural to consider *both sides of a question.* Is the subject under discussion good or bad, desirable or undesirable? Use the pro-and-con method of comparison to present a balanced view of a subject. The process allows you to move from a narrow or one-sided view of a subject to a larger perspective. **The pro-and-con method of comparison** *begins by stating one side of the question, then contrasts this view with a counterstatement.* Using this method, you move back and forth until you come to a conclusion.

You can see the process at work in the following article by Isaac Asimov, taken from the *TV Guide* of December 14, 1974:

UFOs: Are They Visitors from Space— or Unreliable False Observations?

When most people think about flying saucers or, as they are more austerely called, "unidentified flying objects" (UFOs), they think of them as spaceships coming from outside Earth, and manned by intelligent beings.

Is there any chance of this? Do the "little green men" really exist? There are arguments pro and con.

Pro.   There is, according to the best astronomical thinking today, a strong chance that life is very common in the universe. Our own galaxy, containing over a hundred billion stars, is only one of perhaps a hundred billion galaxies.

Current theories about how stars are formed make it seem likely that planets are formed also, so that every star may have planets about it. Surely some of those planets would be like Earth in chemistry and temperature.

Current theories about how life got its start make it seem that any planet with something like Earth's chemistry and temperature would be sure to develop life. One reasonable estimate advanced by an astronomer was that there might be as many as 640,000,000 planets in our galaxy alone that are Earth-like and that bear life.

But on how many of these planets is there intelligent life? We can't say, but suppose that only one of a million life-bearing planets develops intelligent life forms and that only one out of 10 of these develops a technological civilization more advanced than our own. There might still be as many as 100 different advanced civilizations in our galaxy, and perhaps a hundred more in every other galaxy. Why shouldn't some of them have reached us?

Con. Assuming there are 100 advanced civilizations in our own galaxy and that they are evenly spread throughout the galaxy, the nearest one would be about 10,000 light-years away. Even assuming coverage of that distance at the fastest speed we know of—the speed of light—the trip would take at least 10,000 years. Why should anyone make such long journeys just to poke around curiously?

Pro. It is wrong to try to estimate the abilities of a far-advanced civilization, or their motives either. For one thing, the situation may not be average. The nearest advanced civilization may just happen to be only 100 light-years away, rather than 10,000.

Furthermore, because we know of no practical way of traveling faster than light doesn't mean an advanced civilization may not know of one. To an advanced civilization, a distance of 100 light-years or even 10,000 light-years may be very little. They may be delighted to explore over long distances just for the sake of exploring.

Con. But even if that were the case, it would make no sense to send so many spaceships so often (judging by the many UFO reports). Surely we are not that interesting. And if we are interesting, why not land and greet us? Or communicate without landing? They can't be afraid of us, since if they are so far advanced beyond us, they can surely defend themselves against any puny threats we can offer.

On the other hand, if they went to be merely observers, and not interfere with the development of our civilization in any way, they could surely so handle their observations that we would not be continually aware of them.

Pro. Again, we can't try to guess what the motives of these explorers might be. What might seem logical to us might not seem so logical to them. They may not care if we see them, and they also may not care to say hello. Besides, there are many reports of people who have seen the ships and have even been aboard. Surely some of these reports must have something to them.

Con.   Eyewitness reports of actual spaceships and actual extraterrestrials are, in themselves, totally unreliable. There have been innumerable eyewitness reports of almost everything that most rational people do not care to accept—of ghosts, angels, levitation, zombies, werewolves, and so on.

What we really want, in this case, is something material; some object or artifact that is clearly not of human manufacture or Earthly origin. These people who claim to have seen or entered a spaceship never end up with any button, rag, or other object that would substantiate their story.

Pro.   But how else can you account for all the UFO reports? Even after you exclude the mistaken, the gags and hoaxes—there remain many sightings that can't be explained by scientists within the present limits of knowledge. Aren't we forced to suppose these sightings are extraterrestrial spaceships?

Con.   No, because we don't know that the extraterrestrial spaceship is the only remaining explanation. If we can't think of any other, that may simply be a defect in our imagination. If any answer is unknown, then it is simply unknown. An Unidentified Flying Object is just that—unidentified.

The most serious and levelheaded investigator of UFOs I know is J. Allen Hynek, a logical astronomer who is convinced that some UFO reports are worth serious investigation. He doesn't think they represent extraterrestrial spaceships, but he does suggest that they represent phenomena that lie outside the present structure of science, and that understanding them will help us expand our knowledge and build a greatly enlarged structure of science.

The trouble is that whatever the UFO phenomenon is, it comes and goes unexpectedly. There is no way of examining it systematically. It appears suddenly and accidentally, is partially seen, and then is more or less inaccurately reported. We remain dependent on occasional anecdotal accounts.

Dr. Hynek, after a quarter of a century of devoted and honest research, so far ends with nothing. He not only has no solution, but he has no real idea of any possible solution. He has only his belief that when the solution comes, it will be important.

He may be right, but there are at least equal grounds for believing that the solution may never come, or that when it comes, it will be unimportant.

The organizational pattern of this article is very pronounced. Asimov sets up his thesis in the second paragraph ("Do the 'little green men' really exist?"), and then uses the last sentence in that paragraph to organize the essay ("There are arguments pro and con"). Then, in subsequent paragraphs, he takes up one point at a time, explores it thoroughly, and then considers a contrasting point of view. The resultant pattern is pro/con, pro/con, pro/con, pro/con, followed by a conclusion. The following scheme reveals the basic paradigm:

> Introduction (includes thesis)
> Pro (for)
> Con (against)
> Pro (for)
> Con (against)
> Pro (for)
> Con (against)
> Pro (for)
> Con (against)
> Conclusion

In this article, Asimov dispassionately analyzes the question of whether UFOs are visitors from other planets. He presents evidence and logical reasoning, refuting each argument point by point, but he does this within the framework of a comparison paradigm. He tries to convince his audience intellectually, by conviction, rather than by emotional appeal, and each step in the process is clearly formulated. Conviction is the logical part of argument that avoids the shaky emotional basis of some persuasive arguments.

Faulty Comparison

In reasoning by comparison, try to avoid the following errors in reasoning. These are most commonly found in advertising writing, but the principles are applicable to any kind of writing that uses the mode of comparison.

    Avoid the **floating comparison.** This is *a comparison in which one half of the comparison is missing, so that the comparison seems to be floating in the air.* One tire company claims to have a new tire that lasts "20 percent longer." Twenty percent longer than what? Last year's tire? A competitor's tire? A food manufacturer advertises an all-vegetable shortening that "is lighter, creamier, and more digestible." Lighter, creamier, and more digestible than what? Than it was before? Than all other brands? Than any brand of all-vegetable shortening?

Than any brand that sells for the same price? What is missing, of course, is reference to the other product. The comparison is made to things that don't even exist.

Avoid **excessive use of superlatives.** *Superlatives are exaggerated expressions of praise.* When every medicine ad promises the "fastest" relief, every soap powder gives the "whitest" wash, every toothpaste the "fewest" cavities, every cigarette the "mildest" smoke, then you've got to believe that these claims are idle boasts. The test is whether or not a superlative claim is *factually* true. Can the claim be verified by objective standards? Quite often, the language is not clear enough or believable enough to be meaningful.

Superlative claims can also be made by using such words as *the, only,* and *exclusive.* This strategy is often used when it is difficult to determine significant differences between products. It's "*the* car of the decade," one advertisement reads. "It's the *only* tire made with . . ." reads another.

Arguing by Analogy

An **analogy** is an *extended comparison.* It is *a process of reasoning based on similarity.* When you reason by analogy, you go from one particular case to another, basing your conclusion on similarities between two sets of circumstances. In arguing by analogy, you argue that if two things resemble one another in certain respects, they also resemble one another in other respects.

Analogies are often confused with metaphors. Both are based on similarity, but an analogy *argues from those similarities.*

An analogy may be literal or figurative. A **literal analogy** is *based on the same class of objects.* A **figurative analogy** is *based on different classes of objects.* Thus, if you compare a Buick with a Ford, that's a literal analogy. If you compare a Ford with a wild horse, that's a figurative analogy.

Here is an example of a figurative analogy from an ad that appeared in *The New Yorker* on October 7, 1972:

Do You Have an Unfaithful Watch?

At first you tell yourself, "What's a few minutes off?"

But when you catch your watch cheating on you time and time again, when you're forced to turn to the wrist of some stranger . . .

That's when you wish you had an Accutron watch. Accutron by Bulova. The true-blue tuning-fork watch.

Its tuning-fork movement is guaranteed to keep it faithful to within a minute a month.

It can't be led astray, like others can, by an unbalanced balance wheel.

And it's so loyal that even if you deserted it for months, it would do nothing but lie there and count the seconds until you returned.

—Bulova Watch Co., Inc.

Testing the Analogy

Test all arguments from analogy to determine if the reasoning is valid. Determine what the main issues are. Figure out precisely what is being compared. Determine if the similarities and differences are relevant. Extend the analogy. Attack half of the comparison. Attack the whole analogy.

Faulty Analogy

It has become a cliché to state that analogies never prove anything. Yet they do have persuasive force. An analogy is faulty if the points being compared *are not alike in all essential respects;* if there are *negative instances;* and if there is a *single comparison* on which to support the conclusion, rather than an extended series of comparisons.

Exercises

1. Evaluate the following comparisons and analogies:

   a. Try Handle With Care on *your* summer washables. You'll say it really does more.

   b. Smooth some Balm Barr [cocoa butter] on your skin and see why it's better.

   c. Nothing performs like a Saab.

   d. Reach toothbrush. Designed like a dental instrument.

   e. Rise is thicker than the leading foam.

   f. The Three Mile Island "event" will do for nuclear power what the Hindenburg did for zeppelins.

g. After the Three Mile Island accident, I intend to vote against any politicians who say "Maybe" to nuclear power, regardless of their opinions on all other matters. What good is a chicken in every pot if the broth is radioactive?

h. Strengthening the CIA is a step in the right direction. If we're so intent on being the world's babysitter, we need to know what the kids are doing.

i. Wake up to an ocean-fresh shave. Old Spice makes every shave smooth sailing.

j. Unless we are careful, the computer may soon warp our thinking abilities as a nation, just as the automobile has withered our walking ability.

2. Analyze and evaluate the Accutron watch ad.

3. Bring to class for discussion an ad that uses comparison or analogy for persuasive purposes.

4. Write a comparison paper in which you argue the superiority of one over the other of:

   a. two songs   f. two cars

   b. two political candidates   g. two sports commentators

   c. two similar movies   h. two magazines

   d. two talk-show hosts   i. two products

   e. two paintings   j. two TV shows

5. Discuss in class how the analogies in the following proverbs might be extended for a persuasive essay:

   a. Anger is a stone cast at a wasp's nest.

   b. Courage is fire; bullying is smoke.

   c. Confidence is a plant of slow growth.

   d. Lost credit is like a broken mirror.

   e. Gratitude is a heavy burden.

6. Write an argument, using a pro-and-con format, on one of the following topics:

   a. abolition of capital punishment

   b. motion-picture censorship

c. federal control of the oil industry

d. state or federal ownership of all utilities

e. strict wage and price controls on gasoline

f. nuclear power plants

g. keeping or doing away with the 55 MPH speed limit

7. You marry young. Your spouse is critically injured shortly after in an automobile accident. On his or her deathbed, your spouse asks you to promise not to remarry. Less than a year later, you fall in love again. Give arguments (reasons) for and against having to honor your promise.

Arguing from Cause and Effect

When you reason from **cause to effect** or from **effect to cause,** you note that certain actions produce certain effects and that certain effects are produced by certain causes. If, in writing an argument, you start off with causes and move to effects, you advance ideas deductively. The following public-service message that appeared in a local newspaper uses this method of development.

Shoplifting Is a Crime

Cause Shoplifting a 20¢ candy bar or a $1 lipstick doesn't sound like a serious crime. But if the shoplifter is caught, it will add up to more than $1.20. Storeowners are no longer giving a "second chance"—not even for a candy bar, and *an arrest for shoplifting can follow you the rest of your life.*

Effects Convicted shoplifters are denied admission into many colleges and are barred from holding government or bonded jobs. Professions that require special licensing, like law or insurance, are closed to them. They can't even get a mortgage, loan, or credit card. What can be even more tragic than the jail sentence or fine is the teenager delivered in a police car to his home or the business executive earning $25,000 a year who has to explain to his family why he shoplifted a couple of ties.

No matter how little the item costs, shoplifting is stealing.

S.T.E.M.—of Arizona

If you first describe certain effects, results, or consequences in writing an argument, and then move to the causes or agents that produced them, you advance ideas inductively. This ad by Caterpillar Tractor Company, which appeared in *Time* magazine on July 3, 1978, proceeds from effect to cause:

The Arizona Floods Cost Less Than the Copper Depression!

The March 1978 floods, dangerous and overwhelming as they were, caused a statewide property loss of 24 million dollars. But there is a copper industry depression in Arizona that caused far greater losses.

Effects   One effect of the copper industry depression is the loss of more than 46 million dollars in wages last year alone. Another is that Arizona businesses lost more than 39 million dollars in copper industry purchases. A third is that state and local governments lost more than 9 million dollars in taxes. A fourth effect is that one out of every four Arizona copper workers is unemployed. And there is no end in sight.

Causes   There are two main causes of the depression. The first is that foreign copper is cheaper than Arizona copper because of lower wages and lower environmental standards. American industry is buying copper from Chile, Peru, and other nations. An environmental tariff is one solution. A second cause is our own governmental policy. America should maintain a copper stockpile for defense purposes. It is not doing so. Yet its purchases would help.

Here's something you can do. Our statistics for Arizona's copper depression are verified. They are likely new to you. We suggest you send them to your state legislator. They may be new to him, too.

—Empire Machinery Co.

Faulty Causal Reasoning

Faulty causal reasoning, sometimes called by its Latin name, *post hoc, ergo propter hoc* ("after this, therefore because of this"), consists in *assuming that because one event comes before another in time, the first event is the cause of the other.* It is true that causes come before effects, but it does not follow that because one occurrence precedes another, there is necessarily a causal relation between them.

This form of reasoning is sometimes found in political arguments. It goes something like this: "After the Carter Administration came into power, the country suffered an energy shortage. Therefore, the policies of the Carter Administration are responsible for the energy crisis."

Superstitions are based on faulty causal reasoning.

> "Pretty soon," said Huckleberry Finn, "a spider went crawling up my shoulder, and I flipped it off and it lit in the candle; and before I could budge, it was all shriveled up. I didn't need anybody to tell me that that was an awful bad sign and would fetch me some bad luck, so I was scared and 'most shook the clothes off of me."
>
> —Mark Twain, *Huckleberry Finn*

Exercises

1. Evaluate these causal arguments:

   a. Smoking causes cancer. Don't smoke.

   b. You take away gasoline and you destroy the family.

   c. Anti-scientific and anti-intellectual activity is much more widespread than even a few years ago. There are ten times as many American college students enrolled in astrology courses as in astrophysics courses.

   d. If thousands of Catholics are turning to Pentecostalism, it is because they miss the ecstasy and mysticism of the old Mass.

   e. Last Saturday there were more people in line for confession than I have seen in years. Your story must have scared the hell out of them.

   f. We figure if we can make driving safe for these people, we'll be making driving safe for everybody.

   g. Like anyone who has been in party politics for a long time, our senator is tainted with ideological impurity.

   h. Your hair is a mess, and your face is as red as a beet. You must have gotten drunk last night.

   i. Listerine anti-enzyme toothpaste offers you continuous protection against tooth decay.

   j. Those students who type their themes get better grades than those who do not.

2. Bring to class several magazine ads that use cause-and-effect arguments for persuasive purposes, and discuss their effectiveness.

3. Write an essay, using cause-and-effect reasoning, in which you argue that television shows which depict physical violence cause violence in everyday life.

4. Imagine that because of an Arab boycott of oil in the Middle East or because of a dwindling supply of gasoline, Congress has voted to limit drastically the private ownership or use of cars to conserve energy. Write an argument in which you discuss the effects of such a policy.

5. Write an essay in which you argue against teenage marriages, citing harmful effects of early marriage.

6. Write a letter to your campus newspaper, in which you argue that doing away with final examinations will have beneficial (or harmful) effects.

7. Write a persuasive essay, using a topic of your own choice, in which you argue from cause to effect or from effect to cause.

CHAPTER 9

Persuasion as an Aim: The Syllogism and the Enthymeme

If a superstitious friend comes up to you and says, "I shall be unlucky today, because today is Friday the thirteenth," you might be amused at his superstitious beliefs, but you can't fault his logic. He has been engaged in a process called deductive thinking. The superstition is, of course, arrived at inductively. But the superstitious friend, by applying that superstition to a particular case, is reasoning deductively. **Deductive thinking** is *the process of reasoning from a general statement to a logical conclusion.* The syllogism is one form that deductive thinking takes.

The Categorical Syllogism

The **syllogism** is a *mode of thinking in which you reason from two statements, or propositions, called premises, to a third statement, or proposition, called the conclusion.* A **premise** is *a statement that serves as the basis of an argument.* An argument, in the form of a syllogism, looks like this:

> All people are basically honest.
> Joan is a person.
> Therefore, Joan is basically honest.

The first sentence is called the **major premise.** In an argument, the major premise is usually drawn from experience or assumed to be self-evident. The second sentence is called the **minor premise.** The minor premise states a new idea. It is a particular instance of the previously stated general idea. It needs to be supported with evidence. The third sentence is the **conclusion.** The conclusion follows logically from the two premises.

There are four kinds of statements that enter into a syllogism:

1. A *universal affirmative* statement (All people are basically honest. Everyone watches television.)

2. A *universal negative* statement (No person is basically honest. Not everyone watches television.)

3. A *particular affirmative* statement (Some people are basically honest. Some people watch television.)

4. A *particular negative* statement (Some people are not basically honest. Some people do not watch television.)

You can recognize a universal statement because it contains words such as *all, every, everyone,* and *everybody.* A particular statement will have words such as *some, many,* and *a few* in it. A negative statement uses words such as *no, not, not any, never,* and *nothing.* An affirmative statement is one in which the predicate asserts that something is true of the subject.

The simplest form of a statement that goes into a syllogism is the **categorical proposition.** (The *categorical syllogism* is so called because its major premise is a categorical proposition.) It consists of a subject, a copula (a form of the verb *to be*), and a predicate term. It has the following form:

Subject Term	Copula	Predicate Term
All women	are	beautiful.
No woman	is	beautiful.

Logicians use variations of this form, with the verb *to be,* because it is easy to spot the terms. The wording of the proposition below is found more in speech and writing. But because it contains no linking verb, it is harder to pick out the terms:

All Europeans appreciate jazz.

If you rewrite the sentence, however, to include a form of the verb *to be,* the terms are easier to pick out:

All Europeans   are   people who appreciate jazz.

In addition to having three sentences, a syllogism contains three terms: a major term, a middle term, and a minor term. In the following syllogism, the **major term** is *the predicate term in the major premise and in the conclusion (appreciate jazz).* The **middle term** is *the com-*

mon *term in each of the premises (all Europeans, European).* The **minor term** *(Marcello)* appears in the minor premise, and it *is the subject term* of the conclusion:

> All Europeans appreciate jazz.
> Marcello is a European.
> Therefore, Marcello appreciates jazz.

A syllogism is **valid** if the relationship among the terms is logical and if it follows certain set rules. In the above syllogism, there is a common term in each of the first two sentences *(all Europeans, European)* which allows us to connect the ideas in each sentence:

> All Europeans appreciate jazz.
> Marcello is a European.

This term drops out in the conclusion, and the remaining terms combine to form a sentence:

> Marcello appreciates jazz.

If the major premise had read *"Most* Europeans appreciate jazz," you would have had to qualify your conclusion with a word such as *probably:*

> Most Europeans appreciate jazz.
> Marcello is a European.
> Therefore, Marcello *probably* appreciates jazz.

Here is another valid syllogism, with a negative major premise:

> No Europeans appreciate jazz.
> Marcello is a European.
> Therefore, Marcello does not appreciate jazz.

Rules for a Valid Syllogism

1. You can have only *three terms* in a valid syllogism. The following syllogism is not valid because it contains four terms:

   > *All women* are *independent creatures.*
   > *No girls* are *servile.*
   > Therefore, no girls are independent creatures.

   Because there are four terms *(all women, independent creatures, no girls, servile),* there are no logical links to allow you to go from one sentence to another.

2. You must be sure to distribute the middle term at least once. A middle term is distributed if it refers to all or most of the individuals in a class *(all, every, most, no, not any)*. A middle term is undistributed if it refers to particular individuals in a class *(some, a few, many)*. The following syllogism is not valid because the middle term *(some women, woman)* is not distributed at least once. What is true of some women is not necessarily true of Joan:

> *Some women* are vain creatures.
> Joan is a *woman*.
> Therefore, Joan is a vain creature.

3. You cannot extend a term in the conclusion if it has not already been extended in the premise:

> All men are vain creatures.
> *Some Arizonans* are men.
> Therefore, *most Arizonans* are vain creatures.

In the above syllogism, the term *most Arizonans* in the conclusion is an extension of the term *some Arizonans* in the minor premise. Therefore, the syllogism is not valid.

4. You cannot draw a conclusion from two particular premises. The following syllogism is not valid because the major and minor premises are particular statements:

> *Some women* are vain.
> *Some Arizonans* are women.
> Therefore, some Arizonans are vain.

5. You cannot draw a conclusion from two negative premises. The syllogism that follows is not valid because the conclusion follows from two negative premises:

> *No men* are vain.
> *No Arizonans* are men.
> Therefore, no Arizonans are vain.

6. Finally, if one of your premises is negative, then your conclusion must be negative. The syllogism below is not valid because the major premise is negative, but the conclusion is affirmative:

> All women are *not* vain.
> Joan is a woman.
> Therefore, Joan is vain.

A syllogism is **valid,** then, if the form is such that you can logically deduce a conclusion from the premises. A syllogism is **true** if certain facts and evidence make the statements true.

In deducing conclusions, sometimes you can go immediately from one proposition to another, without a middle term. Common sense should help you in doing this: *What's true of the universal must be true of the particular.* If it is true that all people are basically honest, then it must be true that some people are basically honest. If it is true that no people are basically honest, then it must be true that some people are not basically honest.

Similarly, *contradictory statements cannot both be true.* If it is true that all people are basically honest, then the contradictory statements, some people are not basically honest, must be false. If it is true that no people are basically honest, then the contradictory statement, some people are basically honest, must be false.

Contrary statements cannot both be true. If it is true that all men are basically good, then it can't be true that no men are basically good. If it is true that some men are basically good, no deduction can be made about the statement that some men are not basically good.

The Hypothetical Syllogism

The **hypothetical syllogism** has a conditional proposition (a sentence containing an *if* clause) as its major premise. This premise expresses a hypothetical (*uncertain* or *conjectural*) relationship of causation or resemblance:

If the rain continues, the bridge will be lost.

In a conditional proposition, the *if* clause is called the **antecedent.** The second clause (the clause to which the "condition" is applied) is called the **consequent.**

The hypothetical syllogism, like the categorical syllogism, consists of three propositions: the major premise containing the *if* clause, the minor premise, and the conclusion:

If the rain continues, the bridge will be lost.
The rain will continue.
Therefore, the bridge will be lost.

Rules for the Hypothetical Syllogism

1. If you affirm the truth of the antecedent (the *if* clause) with the minor premise, then the consequent (stated in the main clause) necessarily follows, and your conclusion is valid:

> If you inject heroin, you will die.
> You inject heroin.
> Therefore, you will die.

2. If you affirm the truth of the consequent, it does not necessarily follow that the antecedent is true, and your conclusion is invalid:

> If you inject heroin, you will die.
> You will die.
> Therefore, you inject heroin.

3. If you deny the consequent, you may draw a valid conclusion. But be certain to make both the minor premise and the conclusion negative statements:

> If you inject heroin, you will die.
> You will not die.
> Therefore, you do not inject heroin.

4. If you deny the antecedent, then your conclusion is not valid:

> If you inject heroin, you will die.
> You do not inject heroin.
> Therefore, you will not die.

The Disjunctive Syllogism

The **disjunctive syllogism** has a disjunctive proposition (one that gives alternatives, such as *either... or...*) as its major premise. A disjunctive statement is one that sets forth alternative possibilities:

Either you are mortal, or you are immortal.

Like both the categorical syllogism and the hypothetical syllogism, the disjunctive syllogism contains three sentences: the major premise (which has the words *either, or*), the minor premise, and the conclusion:

Either you are mortal, or you are immortal.
You are not immortal.
Therefore, you are mortal.

In speech and in writing, the conclusion of a disjunctive syllogism is sometimes omitted:

Either you are coming, or you are not.
You are not coming?

Rules for the Disjunctive Syllogism

1. When formulating a disjunctive proposition, be careful to set up alternatives that are mutually exclusive and therefore contradictory. In the following example, the alternatives are not mutually exclusive:

   Either she is a singer or a dancer.
   She is not a singer.
   Therefore, she must be a dancer.

   Actually, she could be both a singer and a dancer, or she could be a musician or an actress. But if you recast the major premise to read

   Either she is a singer, or she is not a singer,
   then the alternatives are mutually exclusive.

2. Be sure to include all the possibilities in a disjunctive syllogism. Failure to do so destroys its validity, as in the following example:

   Either excessive heat or excessive moisture killed her roses.
   Excessive heat did not kill her roses.
   Therefore, it must have been excessive moisture.

   All that is needed to destroy this conclusion is to show that other causes, such as insects, heavy winds, frost, or hail, might have been responsible for killing the roses.

Exercises

1. Analyze the following syllogisms and comment on their validity or lack of validity:

a. Those who succeed in life work hard.
    Everyone is anxious to succeed in life.
    Everyone works hard.

b. All X is Y.
    Some Y is Z.
    Therefore, some Z is X.

c. No fish are mammals.
    No fish are birds.
    No birds are mammals.

d. Some soldiers get killed in battle.
    Some civilians get killed in battle.
    Some civilians are soldiers.

e. Some X is Y.
    All Y is Z.
    Some Z is X.

f. All lawyers are articulate people.
    Some doctors are not articulate people.
    Lawyers are not doctors.

g. Because some people are honest,
    and honest people want to avoid jail,
    some people want to avoid jail.

h. No sensible people are smokers.
    Some Americans are sensible people.
    Some Americans are smokers.

i. All left-wing liberals are radicals.
    All radicals are communist.
    Therefore, all left-wing liberals are communist.

j. Switzerland loves freedom.
    I love freedom.
    Therefore, I am Switzerland.

k. All Martians are green.
    Jeffrey is not green.
    Therefore, Jeffrey is not a Martian.

l. No Chinese are North Americans.
    All Americans are North Americans.
    All Americans are Chinese.

m. All drunken drivers are potentially dangerous.
    No thinking person is a drunken driver.
    No thinking person is potentially dangerous.

n. All price-fixing is immoral.
   Some immoral actions are illegal.
   Some price-fixing is illegal.

o. Since only lunatics want to go to the moon,
   this man cannot be a lunatic,
   because he wants to stay here on Earth.

p. If it rains, I will get wet.
   It rains,
   Therefore, I will get wet.

q. Unless you stop, I will get mad.
   You will not stop.
   Therefore, I will get mad.

r. Either Hitler is dead or he is hiding in Argentina.
   He is not hiding in Argentina.
   Therefore, he must be dead.

s. Either his shoes are Italian-made or they are British-made.
   They are Italian-made.
   Therefore, they are not British-made.

t. Obviously, whales have warm blood.
   They are mammals.

The Enthymeme

The **enthymeme** is *a shortened form of the syllogism in which one of the premises or the conclusion is implicit.* It is the form usually encountered in speech or writing.

Here is an enthymeme in which the major premise is missing:

The price of meat will go up
because of the poor corn crop.

The conclusion is stated in the main clause: "The price of meat will go up." The minor premise is stated in the *because* clause: "because of the poor corn crop." The major premise, which is missing, can easily be supplied:

The price of meat will go up whenever the corn crop is poor.
The corn crop is poor.
Therefore, the price of meat will go up.

Here is an enthymeme in which the conclusion is missing:

> Either Chris Evert Lloyd or Martina Navratilova will win the
> match.
> Chris Evert Lloyd's chances were lost when she sprained her
> ankle.

The conclusion of this enthymeme, like the major premise of the previous enthymeme, can easily be supplied:

> Therefore, Martina Navratilova will win the match.

In writing, enthymemes take various forms. They may take the form of a complex sentence with a *because* or *since* clause; a compound sentence joined by words such as *therefore, consequently, so,* and *for* ("The corn crop is poor; therefore, the price of meat will go up"); or two sentences placed together ("The corn crop is poor. The price of meat will go up.").

Enthymemes, like the syllogisms they replace, can be categorical, hypothetical, or disjunctive. A good example of a hypothetical enthymeme in an ad for Kent cigarettes depicts two cigarette packages with the following text:

> Come for the filter.
> You'll stay for the taste.

If you reword the sentences slightly, you get this conditional enthymeme:

> If you come for the filter,
> you'll stay for the taste.

Presumably, the reader will affirm the antecedent and be led to accept the inevitable conclusion.

An ad for the Texaco oil company uses a similar strategy. The illustration pictures an oil rig in the Gulf of Mexico with this caption:

> If we don't go into deep water,
> we'll all be in hot water.

Besides the argument embedded in the enthymeme, there is a larger argument implicit in the entire ad: Drilling in deep water costs money. We are in hot water because we're dependent on imported oil. We will be less dependent on imported oil if we explore more offshore sites. But leasing costs and expenses are higher for offshore wells than they are on land. Nevertheless, Texaco is continuing to drill deeper wells, literally getting into deep water. Of course, the ad doesn't say that the costs will be passed on to the consumer, but the argument is clearly designed to placate customers who are concerned over the increasing cost of gasoline and the high profits of the oil companies.

The disjunctive enthymeme, like the hypothetical enthymeme, can be found in many magazine ads, where it is used very effectively. Whatever one may think about the validity of the enthymeme in the following ad for True cigarettes, there is no doubt about its effectiveness. The picture depicts a man sitting on a log with his bare feet in the sand, holding a cigarette. The text reads as follows:

> After kicking around everything I'd heard about smoking,
> I decided to either quit or smoke True.
> I smoke True.

It's pretty obvious that the alternatives are not mutually exclusive. Yet the smoker seems to be given only two choices: quitting or smoking True. If he decides to smoke (what he has heard, of course, is that smoking is dangerous to his health), then he could smoke any kind of cigarette, not just True. But the alternatives are set up in such a way that if he decides to smoke, he must smoke True. The complete argument, reconstructed, goes something like this: "I've considered seriously everything I've heard about the dangers of smoking, but I enjoy smoking, so I've decided to continue. True cigarettes have a low tar and nicotine content. That's why I smoke True."

To test the validity of an enthymeme, simply rewrite it, putting it into the form of a syllogism. Then follow the same procedures you would follow to determine if a syllogism is valid.

One of the most important errors to guard against in using enthymemes is *hasty generalization in the major premise.* Ordinarily, in a syllogism, the major premise is there to be examined and evaluated. But in an enthymeme, the major premise must be assumed by the reader or listener.

The following is an example of a statement attributed to the Republican senator from California, S. I. Hayakawa, in the early summer of 1979, when long lines formed at the gas pumps and some members of Congress began to cry for decontrol of gas prices:

> "Let gas go to $1.50, even $2.00 per gallon.
> A lot of the poor don't need gas because they are not working."

Needless to say, Senator Hayakawa's remarks were greeted with public indignation. What is missing from this statement is the major premise:

Major Premise:
Minor Premise: They are not working.
   Conclusion: A lot of the poor don't need gas.

Reconstructed, the chain of reasoning goes something like this: "Anyone who is not working does not need gas. The poor are not working. Therefore, the poor don't need gas." The argument is valid, but not true because the assumed premise is faulty. The poor may need gas so they can obtain jobs. And, of course, all of us need gas for reasons other than to go to work: to go to the grocery, to visit friends, to run errands, perhaps to make an emergency trip to the hospital.

Exercises

1. Supply the missing proposition in each of the following enthymemes. Then determine if each is valid or not.

   a. If you're Spanish or Italian, you may as well resign yourself to being emotional.

   b. When we were in New Orleans, we went to the French Quarter. All of the architecture there is excellent.

   c. Most of Fellini's pictures are offbeat, so *Amarcord* is probably offbeat too.

   d. Smith must be crooked, all of those politicians are.

   e. These new clothes are really expensive, so I refuse to buy at Frederick's Department Store, because all their clothes are expensive.

   f. If you read about it in the local paper, don't believe it.

   g. There is no sense in paying high prices for coffee, since it is well known that coffee has no nutritional value.

   h. Because they are gas guzzlers, most large cars are not very economical.

2. Convert the following categorical syllogisms into enthymemes:

   a. All criminals ought to be prosecuted.
      Price fixers are criminals.
      Therefore, price fixers ought to be prosecuted.

b. All nutritional foods are healthy.
    Sugar is not a nutritional food.
    Sugar is not healthy.

c. All excellent movies are works of art.
    No Westerns are works of art.
    No Westerns are excellent movies.

d. Most hard drugs are habit-forming.
    Heroine is a hard drug.
    Heroine is habit-forming.

e. No man wants to be untruthful.
    Michael is a man.
    Michael wants to be truthful.

3. Bring to class magazine ads that use enthymemes, hypothetical syllogisms, or disjunctive syllogisms to sell a product or make a point. Then analyze the arguments in class.

Planning an Argument

You seldom state arguments in complete syllogisms, although I have come across an ad for Snowdrift shortening that uses the deductive sequence of a syllogism to make its selling point:

What Every Good Cook Knows

Just a little difference in ingredients makes a big difference in cooking results. Snowdrift is just a little lighter than ordinary shortening—and that can make the big difference in giving your family lighter, more digestible foods.

—Hunt-Wesson Foods

The major premise offers benefits that have a general appeal to the reader. ("Just a little difference in ingredients makes a big difference in cooking results.") The minor premise—the proof part—gives supporting details in the form of product attributes ("Snowdrift is just a little lighter than ordinary shortening"). The proof part is flexible. You can use it to enumerate several product attributes or, as in this ad, one or two. The conclusion applies directly to the reader ("and that can make the big difference in giving your family lighter, more digestible foods").

The advantage of the deductive sequence is that it enables the writer to analyze the proposition carefully and to pick out the facts that will be most effective with the reader. The deductive order gives the major premise or assertion first and then backs it up with evidence, explanations, and logical reasoning.

Most arguments, however, are based on the enthymeme rather than the syllogism. *The logical structure of an argument consists of a series of enthymemes that exhibit the framework of the chain of reasoning and the evidence upon which the argument is based.*

To write an argument based on the enthymeme, begin with the conclusion of the syllogism as your thesis. Then add the minor premise to it in the form of a *because* clause. The minor premise is the proof part of your argument. You must support it with the kinds of evidence considered in the previous chapter: facts, personal opinions, attributes, descriptive details, examples, statistics, testimony and other evidence from authority, narrative examples, comparisons, analogies, causes, and effects.

The following example, adapted from a public declaration by musicians and celebrities such as John Denver, Art Garfunkel, Mia Farrow, Israel Horovitz, John Simon, Stevie Wonder, and Howard Johnson, who oppose nuclear power plants, is a good example of a thesis in the form of an enthymeme:

> Nuclear power should be banned
> because it represents a grave threat to life on this planet.

In this thesis statement, the *main clause* states the conclusion of the enthymeme ("Nuclear power should be banned") and the *because* clause states the minor premise. Put into the form of an incomplete syllogism, the statement reads:

Major Premise:	
Minor Premise:	Nuclear power represents a grave threat to life on this planet.
Conclusion:	Nuclear power should be banned.

Taking the process one step further, you can easily supply a major premise so that the syllogism is complete:

Major Premise:	Any form of power that represents a grave threat to life on this planet should be banned.
Minor Premise:	Nuclear power represents a grave threat to life on this planet.
Conclusion:	Therefore, nuclear power should be banned.

Why not write an argument in the form of a syllogism, you might ask at this point? Well, you could write an argument in this way if you so desired. But in many arguments, you don't need to state the major premise, because the major premise usually contains assumptions that you already share with your reader. It is the common ground from which your argument starts. You don't need to prove the statement that "any form of power that represents a grave threat to life on this planet should be banned." Common sense and the law of self-preservation will tell you that none of us wants to endanger our lives. More important than explicitly stating the major premise in this argument is setting forth the conclusion that you want your readers to accept. And they will more readily accept your conclusion if your reasoning is sound and your evidence is substantial.

Stating your thesis in enthymeme form will spell out for your reader your specific intention. Second, it will help you as a writer to keep your intention clearly in mind. Third, it will help you to organize the sections of your essay more effectively.

You can expand the enthymeme which constitutes your thesis statement in a number of ways. One way is to state your proposition and its proof (the conclusion and the minor premise) in the form of a *because* clause and then add to your main reason *subordinate reasons* in the form of additional *because* clauses or phrases. These subordinate ideas will be the proof of the main idea, and each subordinate idea must be supported with evidence (facts, examples, testimony of witnesses, opinions of authorities, and so forth). The resulting paradigm for the proposition on nuclear power would look something like this:

Thesis:	Nuclear power should be banned
Main Reason:	because it represents a grave threat to life on this planet,
Sub. Reason:	because of the unresolved question of nuclear-waste storage,
Sub. Reason:	because of the failure of the emergency core-cooling system in tests,
Sub. Reason:	because of the danger of theft or accident during the transportation of nuclear materials, and
Sub. Reason:	because of the continuing rise in incidence of cancer, leukemia, and genetic disease, diseases that are known to be radiation-related.

This paradigm is in the shape of a single sentence, but for purposes of writing an argument, the thesis and the main reason could go together to form your thesis statement ("Nuclear power should be banned because it represents a grave threat to life on this planet"). Then each subordinate reason could be put into sentence form, each sentence marking a division of your essay. Naturally, each of the subordinate propositions has to be supported by evidence of some kind. So the thesis and the main reason (the enthymeme) constitute the proposition to be proved, and the supporting reasons constitute the proof of your argument. A more abstract version of the paradigm would look like this:

> Introduction (includes thesis and main reason)
> Reason 1 (plus supporting evidence)
> Reason 2 (plus supporting evidence)
> Reason 3 (plus supporting evidence)
> Reason 4 (plus supporting evidence)
> Reason 5, 6, 7 . . . (plus supporting evidence)
> Conclusion (application of above to reader)

Another way to expand an enthymeme for organizational purposes is to state your thesis in a single sentence. Then, instead of adding to it a single main reason, which has to be supported by subordinate reasons, you add a series of parallel reasons—all of which, presumably, are main reasons to support your assertion.

Here is an example of a thesis statement, taken from an article in *Esquire* magazine about an attempt to abolish the fraternity system at Dartmouth College. Incensed by what he believed to be immoral and uncivilized behavior on the part of some fraternity brothers, English professor James Epperson made a stirring speech to the Dartmouth faculty on November 6, 1978, in which he urged the college's board of trustees to ban fraternities from the campus. The outline of his argument goes something like this:

> Fraternities should be abolished
>> because they are racist,
>> because they encourage destructive behavior,
>> because they are anti-intellectual,
>> because they encourage drunkenness, and
>> because they are sexist.

What looks like a single enthymeme here is really a series of connected enthymemes, with the independent clause ("Fraternities should be abolished") serving as the conclusion of each enthymeme and each *because* clause serving as a minor premise:

Minor Premise: Fraternities are racist.
    Conclusion: Therefore, they should be abolished.
Minor Premise: Fraternities encourage destructive behavior.
    Conclusion: Therefore, they should be abolished.
Minor Premise: Fraternities are anti-intellectual.
    Conclusion: Therefore, they should be abolished.
Minor Premise: Fraternities encourage drunkenness.
    Conclusion: Therefore, they should be abolished.
Minor Premise: Fraternities are sexist.
    Conclusion: Therefore, they should be abolished.

If you put these enthymemes into an outline, you get the following paradigm:

    Thesis: Fraternities should be abolished.
    Reason: They are racist.
    Reason: They encourage destructive behavior.
    Reason: They are anti-intellectual.
    Reason: They encourage drunkenness.
    Reason: They are sexist.

In its more abstract form, the paradigm would look like this:

Introduction (includes the thesis or proposition to be proved)
Reason 1 (plus supporting evidence)
Reason 2 (plus supporting evidence)
Reason 3 (plus supporting evidence)
Reason 4 (plus supporting evidence)
Reason 5 (plus supporting evidence)
Conclusion (application of above to reader)

The paradigm can then be used as the basis of the essay:

Fraternities should be abolished because they are racist, they encourage destructive behavior, they are anti-intellectual, they encourage drunkenness, and they are sexist.

Fraternities are racist. They do not encourage blacks and other minorities to join.

Fraternities encourage destructive behavior. Their members are uncivilized. Theft and vandalism are frequent among their members.

Fraternities are anti-intellectual. Their members go to college to have a good time and to make social connections rather than to enrich their minds. Those who do study are scorned.

Fraternities encourage drunkenness. Heavy drinking is the norm.

Then, when fraternity brothers get drunk, their drunkenness is used to justify vandalism and other forms of offensive behavior.

Finally, fraternities are sexist. Almost all of them exclude women from being members. But even worse, they are actively and aggressively sexist. Women who walk along Fraternity Row at night must put up with obscene proposals. At fraternity parties, some women are scorned, ridiculed, and physically intimidated. Fraternity brothers who "make out" are frequently required to give detailed descriptions of what went on.

For these reasons, fraternities should be abolished.

This is not a complete argument, to be sure. The argument needs a more suitable introduction and a conclusion, and each of the reasons in the respective paragraphs needs more supporting details as proof of the argument. But the model does show how the enthymeme can be used to construct effective arguments.

In the beginning stages of learning to write deductive arguments, you might want to follow these paradigms closely. Ultimately, however, what is more important is that you make the process of deductive thinking habitual, so that in your written arguments the paradigms will be a direct result of your thought processes.

Here is another argument, this one developed more fully, which considers possible objections to the position advocated earlier in the paper:

Bottle Bills: Are They Worth the Cost?

In 1978, Michigan passed a law requiring a deposit on all beverage containers. Some time later, New York, Connecticut, Vermont, Massachusetts, Oregon, Maine, Iowa, and Delaware passed similar laws. Encouraged by the passage of laws in these states, advocates of a national deposit law are lobbying to get Congress to pass a national deposit law.

Is a national deposit law an idea whose time has come? Environmentalists and citizens who are fed up with the bottles and cans that litter our beaches, roadsides, and parks apparently think so. They would like to have a law adopted that would require a five or ten cent deposit on every beverage container. They argue that Congress should pass a national law because such a law would decrease the amount of litter, increase the number of containers recycled each year, reduce the cost of annual roadside cleanups, and create new jobs. The deposit would be refundable when the container is returned to a supermarket, a liquor store, or a recycling center. If deposits were required on beer and soft drink containers, they argue, few people would throw them away. And if they did, someone else would pick them up in order to get the refund. Let us look more closely at the advantages that proponents claim will accrue under a national deposit law.

A national bottle law would decrease the amount of litter on beaches, roadsides, parks, and rivers. The General Accounting Office estimates that a national deposit law would reduce litter by 80 percent. In Oregon, the Department of Environmental Quality reported that the first year a deposit law was in effect litter was down by 72 percent, and 80 percent the next year. A study in Michigan showed similar results. The number of cans was reduced by 79 percent the first year and the number of bottles by 76 percent. Evidently, a bottle law will make people think twice about throwing containers out their car windows.

A national bottle law would increase the number of bottles and cans recycled each year and therefore reduce the amount of trash that has to be hauled to public landfills. States with deposit laws report that 90 percent of cans sold are eventually recycled. States without deposit laws report that only 55 to 65 percent of the cans sold are recycled. The missing cans must be going some place—most likely a beach, a park, or a roadside.

A national bottle bill would reduce the cost of annual roadside cleanups. Oregon spent $589,000 a year to clean up its roadsides before a bottle bill was passed and $550,000 the first year the law was in effect. In Michigan, the annual costs stood at $2.1 million the year before a law was passed and $1.9 million the year after.

Finally, a national bottle bill would create new jobs. In Michigan, for example, 4,500 jobs were created as a result of the passage of a bottle bill. People were hired to collect, sort, and return bottles and cans. Others were hired to staff new aluminum recycling centers. In addition, existing centers expanded, hiring new people.

Opponents of a national deposit law, however, warn that consumers will pay higher prices for their beverages on top of the deposits mandated by law if a bottle bill is passed. Consumers will also be faced with the hassle of storing bottles and cans in their homes and hauling them to stores for their deposits. Retailers will need more space to accomodate the empty cans and bottles, and distributors will have to juggle their schedules so that drivers can collect the empties on their routes. Finally, unwashed bottles and cans will create problems with roaches, ants, and other insects.

Proponents of a national bottle bill believe that the advantages will far outweigh the disadvantages and that the time has come for action. In states that have passed anti-litter laws, fishermen, hunters, hikers, and motorists exclaim that for the first time in their memories lakes, rivers, roadsides, and parks are relatively free from bottles, cans, and other litter. They cry out with one voice that it's time to return to a beautiful America.

I said earlier that arguments are seldom stated in complete syllogisms because the major premise usually contains assumptions that you share with your reader, and therefore need not be stated explicitly. But what if your reader does not share the assumptions in your major premise? Then you might want to use the syllogism rather than the enthymeme to present your argument. In that case, you would want to present supporting evidence for both your major and your minor premise.

The following syllogism is one formulation of a traditional argument for the existence of God:

Major Premise: Anything that displays design, order, and harmony must have some intelligence directing it.

Minor Premise: The world displays design, order, and harmony.

Conclusion: Therefore, the world is the work of an intelligent being in the universe.

It can be embedded in the larger patterning of an essay to produce the following argument:

The Argument from Design

The idea that the universe exhibits an orderly design and that this design is proof of a purposeful intelligence in the universe is exemplified by the psalmist who sang, "The heavens declare the glory of God, and the firmament showeth his handiwork." Yet modern men and women, in an atmosphere of technical accomplishments and what might be called the new hedonism, often have doubts about the existence of God. To many modern thinkers, the existence of God has become the central religious problem of the twentieth century. In view of modern people's skepticism, is there any evidence that God exists? To many thinkers, proofs of God's existence have always been available, and many of these proofs are just as relevant today as they were in years gone by. One of the most popular of these proofs is the argument from design. The argument goes like this.

Anything that displays design, order, and harmony must have some intelligence directing it. Can there be a design without a designer? If you were asked to give an account of anything manmade, such as a car, a building, or a machine, you could not give a complete account if you omitted the maker. Similarly, if you were to try to give an account of the workings of the universe, of its organic regularities and its orderly structures and processes, you would have to conclude that the principle of order is an intelligence operating and directing it for some purpose toward some intelligible goal.

Order itself must have a cause. A work of art does not produce itself, but is the result of the intentions of an artist. Language is a formal creation in which a writer imposes form on his or her materials. A pool player striking a ball can be said to be operating with a purpose. Everything has a purpose. Why are there doors and windows at regular intervals in the walls of a house? Why are the streets of cities laid out in orderly designs? Why is the produce in supermarkets arranged in such an orderly fashion? What is the probability of an orderly structure in the universe coming into existence by chance? An intelligent order in the universe is the work of an intelligent being.

Everywhere, *the world displays design, order, and harmony.* The planets revolve around the sun in the same plane. The simplest molecules contain several thousand atoms, all intricately organized. The universe is an intricate and orderly balance of rhythms, forces, and processes. Numbers, scales, times, crystal forms, symbolic forms, sentences, and languages of all kinds reveal order and complexity. Order is a necessary condition for anything in the universe to function: the human body, plants, machines, athletic teams. The world's features repeat themselves over and over again: the patterns of leaves, the colors in sunsets, the symmetry of plants and flowers, the shapes of birds, the odor of roses, the rhythm of waves.

When things in the universe show orderly progression, design, and harmony, they cannot be said to do so of their own nature. It follows, therefore, that this order is a matter either of chance or of design. But as you have seen from numerous examples, whatever comes about in this world is not the result of accident. *Therefore, the world is the work of an intelligent being in the universe.*

Let us assume, now, that your readers do share the assumptions in your major premise. In that case, you turn your syllogism into an enthymeme:

The world must be the work of an intelligent being in the universe because it displays design, order, and harmony.

Then you use the enthymeme as the thesis in your argument and add the supporting evidence. But this time, let us consider possible objections to the argument and include them near the end of the essay:

The idea that the universe exhibits an orderly design and that this design is proof of a purposeful intelligence in the universe is exemplified by the psalmist who sang, "The heavens declare the glory of God, and the firmament showeth his handiwork." Yet modern man, in an atmosphere of technical accomplishments and what might be called the new hedonism, often has doubts about the existence of God. In view of modern people's skepticism, is there any evidence that God exists? To many thinkers, proofs of God's existence have always been available, and many of these proofs are just as relevant today as they were in years gone by. One of the most popular of these proofs is the argument from design, which states that *the world must be the work of an intelligent being in the universe because it displays design, order, and harmony.*

Everywhere, *the world displays signs of design, order, and harmony.* The planets revolve around the sun in the same plane. The simplest molecules contain several thousand atoms, all intricately organized. The universe is an intricate and orderly balance of rhythms, forces, and processes. Numbers, scales, times, crystal forms, groups, symbolic forms, sentences, and languages of all kinds reveal order and complexity. Order is a necessary condition for anything in the universe to function: the human body, plants, machines, athletic teams. The world's features repeat themselves over and over again: the patterns of leaves, the colors in sunsets, the symmetry of plants and flowers, the shapes of birds, the odor of roses, the rhythm of waves.

But some skeptics have serious objections to the argument from design. If the universe exhibits order and harmony, they say, it also exhibits an absence of order and harmony. Does not evil exist in the world? Are there not natural disasters and calamities such as floods, storms, tornadoes, cyclones, and earthquakes? The answer to these questions is that for order and harmony to exist in the universe, it is not necessary for them to be detectable in all parts of the universe. Besides, in order for us to experience disorder, we must first have had to experience some kind of order. If you were to go into a dormitory in which there were a hundred beds and see one unmade bed, would you necessarily conclude that the one unmade bed proves that disorder is characteristic of that dormitory? What is disorder, anyway? According to some scientists, disorder is the clash of uncoordinated orders, not the absence of order.

When things in the universe, then, show signs of orderly progression, design, and harmony, they cannot be said to do so of their own nature. It follows, therefore, that this order is a matter either of chance or of design, or the product of a designer who had a particular purpose in mind. But as we have seen from numerous examples and analogies, and as you know from personal experience, whatever comes about in this world is not the result of accident. *Therefore, God must be the designer of the universe.*

Exercises

1. Discuss the essay on fraternities. Do you agree with the charges made against fraternities? If not, give supporting evidence for the proposition that fraternities should *not* be abolished.

2. Analyze in class the essay, "Bottle Bills." What is the thesis? Where does it appear in the essay? What reasons are given to support the

thesis? How are these developed? Reconstruct the reasoning process underlying each enthymeme. What arguments would you use to refute the counter-argument of the opponents of a national deposit law?

3. Complete five of the following statements by adding at least three reasons in the form of *because* clauses. Then, for class discussion, consider a situation out of which these statements might come. Finally, think about a possible audience for a paper you could write based on the completed paradigm, your intention in writing the paper, and the evidence you might use to support each reason.

   a. Both sexes have the responsibility to care for small children.

   b. A creative life is better than financial well-being.

   c. It is important to be well-read and educated.

   d. The use of hard drugs is morally wrong.

   e. It's up to parents to educate teenagers about birth control.

   f. Duty to self is not a viable guide to conduct.

   g. The draft is a necessary evil.

   h. Husbands and wives should take separate vacations.

   i. Personality is more important to success than brains.

   j. Colleges should teach only salable skills.

4. Assume you believe smokers have a right to smoke in public places:

   a. Write a dialogue that might take place as you try to convince a non-smoker friend of your position.

   b. Write an ad a cigarette manufacturer might use to convince the general public that smoking should be allowed in restaurants.

   c. Write a letter to your parents (who won't let you smoke in their house) which persuades them to let you smoke when you go out with them in public.

5. For class discussion, take a position *for* or *against* one of the following propositions. Then, keeping in mind a rhetorical situation, your subject, purpose, and audience, write an article, a letter, or some other kind of discourse defending your position:

   a. People who do not have children are selfish.

   b. A woman should put her husband and children ahead of her career.

   c. If a husband plays around a little that's excusable, but a wife never should.

   d. Women who make more money than their husbands are less likely to love them.

   e. People should support their country whether it's right or wrong.

   f. It is morally wrong for couples to live together if they are not married.

   g. It is morally acceptable to be single and have children.

   h. Success, as it has been traditionally defined, is neither necessary nor sufficient to the good life.

   i. Abortion is not an acceptable alternative to an unwanted pregnancy.

   j. There is nothing worth dying for.

6. Write an essay on one of the following. Use either the enthymeme or the full syllogism as the basis of your argument. Include ethical and emotional appeals. You can take a position for or against the proposition. You can also reword the proposition so that it accurately reflects your intended meaning:

   a. If for financial or other reasons grown children want to move back in with their parents, they should be welcome for an unlimited amount of time with no reservations.

   b. Parents should stay together for the children's sake even if they are unhappy with each other.

   c. If a wife works outside the home, it means that the husband is incapable of providing for his family.

   d. If you lend a friend a large sum of money, you should spell out the terms of the loan, which should include a repayment schedule, interest, penalty for a late payment, and security.

   e. If a professional athlete has signed a long-term contract with a team, he is not justified in refusing to play for that team the next season unless he is given more money.

   f. American women are systematically and illegally underpaid for work that is different from, but just as demanding as that done by men.

   g. Equal pay should be required for jobs that are different in kind, but comparable in value.

h. Parents should be free to live their own lives even if it means spending less time with their children.

i. Children do not have an obligation to their parents regardless of what their parents have done for them.

j. Parents should spend what they've earned while they are alive even if it means leaving less to the children.

k. If elderly parents become incapable of living alone, they should move into their children's home.

l. If elderly parents become incapable of living alone, they should move into a nursing home.

7. To write an argument based on either a hypothetical syllogism or a disjunctive syllogism, you substitute a hypothetical or a disjunctive proposition for a categorical proposition. The following can be used for discussion or for a writing assignment:

a. If a law lacks support, it can't be enforced. The 55 MPH speed limit lacks public support. Therefore, it can't be enforced.

b. Either price controls will be imposed or there will be a recession.

c. If human beings were basically good, then laws would not be necessary.

d. If telling a certain kind of lie is not always wrong, then telling a lie can sometimes be ethically better than telling the truth.

e. If people begin to question rules, they won't know where to draw the line.

Errors in Reasoning

A **fallacy** is *an idea or opinion based on faulty logic.* It is an error in reasoning that may be deliberate or due to ignorance. The following fallacies are intended as a checklist to make you alert to possible errors in reasoning in your own arguments and in those of others. Ironically, as strategies of persuasion, they can be very effective. But as logical arguments, they are fallacious.

Begging the Question

This is a fallacy in which you assume the truth of the premise that you are supposed to prove in your argument. If you state, for example,

"Everybody knows that minorities commit most of the crimes in large cities," and then argue from that premise, you would be guilty of **begging the question.** Another form that begging the question takes is **arguing in a circle,** that is, assuming the truth of a premise, drawing a conclusion from this premise, and then using the conclusion to prove your initial premise. For example, if a salesperson says to you, "You should buy the new Chevrolet Impala because it's the best car on the market," and you ask why, and he or she answers, "Because it's made by Chevrolet," that's arguing in a circle. Still another form that begging the question takes is the use of prejudicial words in the proposition — for example, "Who wouldn't oppose this *idiotic* piece of legislation?"

Argumentum ad Hominem

If in an argument you attack or insult the person you are arguing against rather than deal with the issues, then you are guilty of **argumentum ad hominem** (arguing against the person). Opponents of John F. Kennedy, for example, argued that he was unfit for the presidency because he was a Catholic who would owe allegiance to the Pope. Opponents of Nelson Rockefeller criticized him because he had been divorced — as if his being divorced had anything to do with his qualifications for office. Other politicians have been accused of being socialistic or ultraconservative or too radical, the intent being to discredit the person rather than to address the argument.

Name-Calling

This fallacy is similar in some respects to that of the *argumentum ad hominem.* In arguing, you give bad names to a person, an issue, or an event, rather than examine the issues. Down through the years, people have been called heretics, fascists, communists, demagogues, and troublemakers by adversaries who appeal to hate and fear rather than to logical reasoning. Thus, if someone doesn't agree with an action taken by some group, they can avoid dealing with the action by calling it "communist-inspired," "radical," "left-wing," or "right-wing."

Argumentum ad Populum

Like the previous two fallacies, this is an emotional appeal in which you turn away from the real argument and appeal to the irrational fears and prejudices of your audience. You can do this by praising your audience extravagantly, praising the American way of life, resorting to appeals of God, country, home, and motherhood. In other words, you associate something good or bad with your argument. Writers who habitually include in their arguments stock appeals for or against "our free enterprise system," "bureaucracy and red tape," "government interference," and "big business" are guilty of appealing to the crowd.

Shifting Ground

This fallacy consists of ignoring the question by shifting from one question or proposition to another when you are cornered. This fallacy is also called **confusing the issue** and the **red herring.** You argue beside the point you are trying to prove. In other words, if you can't answer a question or meet your opponent's arguments straight on, you simply ignore the question and raise another one. Pat Brown, the former governor of California, was once asked, "Governor, what's your opinion of the rising crime rate in California?" He answered: "Rising crime is not the decisive factor. It is the increasing efficiency of crime reporting with the more accurate use of computer technology." Here is how his son, Jerry Brown, answered the same question: "Why don't you ask an intelligent question? You sound like you're giving me the Rorschach test, asking me what I think of the crime rate."

The Bandwagon

This is a technique used to get people to follow the crowd. Any time you call for an action or an opinion because it is popular, because "everybody's doing it," you are using the **bandwagon technique** of arguing. Because people are imitative, they like to do what everybody else does and to believe what other people believe. So this appeal has human-interest value. Advertisers use this appeal when they make claims about the popularity of an advertised product, based on the large number of people who buy the product or who remain faithful to a name brand: "Everybody loves delicious Wrigley's Spearmint Gum"; "Today, more people ask for Coke than for any other soft drink."

Slanting

In this technique you phrase a statement in such a way that you encourage your reader to take a favorable or unfavorable view of a subject. You can do this by selecting the facts and details of your subject that are favorable and omitting others that are unfavorable. Or you can distort the facts in such a way as to suggest things that are not completely true. **Slanting** can be achieved by using words connotatively, by ordering words in a certain way, by italicizing or underlining words you want to emphasize, by punctuating, and by using emotional or charged language. A humorous example of slanting is this conjugation of an irregular verb, attributed to Bertrand Russell: "I am firm; you are obstinate; he is pigheaded."

Either-Or Fallacy

This is a logical fallacy in which you oversimplify an issue by narrowing your reader's options to just two alternatives. The linguistic form of the **either-or** statement forces your reader to think in terms of black or white. If the options are genuine, there is no problem. But sometimes there may be an unnoticed third possibility hidden by the false dilemma. Thus, if someone argues that lifting price controls on gasoline will produce either more oil at cheaper prices or less oil at higher prices, what may go unnoticed is the possibility of producing the same amount of oil at higher or lower prices. The reader can escape the "horns of a dilemma" by going between them—that is, by not being caught by one or the other, but considering all of the alternatives.

The Complex Question

This is an error in reasoning in which you ask a question in such a way that it assumes an answer to another question, which has not even been asked. The fallacy is committed when a single answer is demanded of the question. "Why" or "how" questions are frequently of this type. Thus, the question "How long are we going to tolerate interference with our national interests by these large international corporations?" assumes that there has been such interference. The question "Why is it that girls are less interested in science than are boys?" contains the answer to the hidden question "Is it a fact that girls are less interested in science than boys?"

Hypothesis Contrary to Fact

If you begin an argument with a hypothesis that is not true or that is speculative and then draw conclusions from it, this is an error in reasoning called **hypothesis contrary to fact.** It takes this form: "What would the consequences have been *if* such and such had been true?" For example: "If the Shah of Iran were still ruler of that country, gasoline prices would be much lower in this country." There is, of course, evidence to show that the Shah encouraged higher prices when he was the ruler of Iran. Another example that keeps making the rounds is the statement "If Columbus hadn't discovered America, we wouldn't be living here today."

Argument from Ignorance

This fallacy is committed if you argue that a statement must be true because it has not been proven false, or that it must be false because it has not been proven true. In other words, if you try to justify a belief when there is no evidence for it, you are guilty of **arguing from ignorance.** For example: "There must be life on other planets, because no one can prove that there isn't." Or, "Psychic phenomena must exist, because eyewitnesses have given us reports of them for years, and nobody has ever disproved these reports."

Exercises

1. Identify the errors in reasoning in the following:

   a. Ever since we put men on the moon, we've been having unusual weather.

   b. When I get married, either I will run the house or my husband will.

   c. I cooked it. That's why it's good.

   d. I'd never vote for Carter. I don't like his Southern accent.

   e. The ranting of *Time* and the pseudo-Americans over the CIA disclosures would be comical were it not so childish and tragic. What the United States needs is a stronger CIA, and let the chips fall where they may.

   f. You accuse me of going over the 55 MPH speed limit, but everybody speeds on the highway.

   g. Everyone has a new car but me. Why can't I get a new car? After all, I'll be going to college next year.

   h. The West would have been won ten years sooner if the pioneers didn't have to stop and ride back forty times a day to pick up their hats.

i. My teacher is a hard grader. Three of my friends got an F on the midterm exam.

j. You are either a Republican or a Democrat.

k. The energy crisis could ultimately destroy our economy and bring down the world economy along with it. Such a collapse would precipitate world conflict and probably atomic war. We cannot escape the danger of the atom. But I would rather risk a mishap from a nuclear power plant once every twenty or thirty years than face one nuclear holocaust.

l. Everybody watches the NBC evening news. You ought to watch it, too.

m. The first chapter was so boring I concluded that it must be a lousy book.

2. Bring to class magazine ads that commit the fallacies cited in this and the previous chapter.

3. Bring to class for discussion examples of fallacies taken from letters to the editor in magazines such as *Time* or *Newsweek*, in your local newspaper, or in the campus newspaper.

4. Discuss the arguments and the errors in reasoning in the following letter to the editor:

> Dear Editor:
> The letter of Mrs. ——— is outstanding in that she links evolution with the proposed sex education in schools supported by tax money.
> We are in this fight against great odds and powers, "against spiritual wickedness in high places" (Ephesians, Chapter 6, especially Verse 12).
> With this thought in mind, we should make every effort to withdraw our children from such influence and place them in a Christian school where only dedicated teachers are employed.
> If we do not believe the account of Creation and the Flood, then we call God a liar. If we make God a liar, then we cannot believe any part of His word. This is the position of the supporters of evolution.
> God, the essence of life, is life itself, the source of life, plant and animal. This the evolutionist denies, and yet he goes to the swamp and steals from God's creation the smallest form of life, a microorganism, the physicochemical basis of living matter that forms the essential part of plant and animal life.
> The microscopic bit of life the evolutionist stole from God and placed into a never-never time resembling eternity, namely, billions upon billions of never-never years before time or matter were created. The amoeba is

that bit of protoplasm that the evolutionist has made to be his god, his idol, for he has claimed for it the power to evolve itself in billions of nev-er-never years into great animals such as lived before the Deluge.

There is no halfway point between evolution and the Creation, as some would have us believe. As Mrs. —— — says, "It is either evolution or God." The promoters of evolution despise and violate the moral law which contains the law of chastity. This law forbids the practice of the marriage act outside of marriage.

Adultery, fornication, rape, and what have you already have such a hold on our moral life, as a nation, that we do not need sex instruction by licentious teachers to foster a further drop in morality. Go-go girls, mini-skirts, Bikini suits: what next?

Remember, Rome and other great nations of the past have gone into oblivion by a similar route.

CHAPTER 10

Paragraphs and Paragraphing

The Paragraph as Part of a Longer Unit

There are several ways of looking at paragraphs. One way is to see the paragraph as a division of a longer piece of writing. Another is to think of the paragraph as a group of logically related sentences, composed of unified parts, based on a single idea. A third way is to view the paragraph as a kind of extended sentence.

Writers paragraph for a variety of reasons—for instance, to change tone, to shift rhythm, or to emphasize a point. One of the most important reasons for paragraphing, however, is for logical considerations. Understanding the logical basis of paragraphing is of primary importance in developing a consciousness of form in the writer.

Some writers claim that they are always conscious of paragraphing and of the logical basis of their paragraphing *when they write.* Others assert that they often go back *after they have completed their writing* and then make their paragraph divisions. These are not opposing points of view, in my opinion, but complementary ones. Writers who claim that they go back and paragraph after they have completed their writing usually end up paragraphing similarly to the way in which writers who use the opposite method do. Both kinds of writers know in general the end they want to achieve. Both have an intuitive grasp of the overall structure of their essays. But some writers are more self-conscious about the logical basis of their paragraphing *as they are writing.* Others are less so. Nevertheless, the latter necessarily have to group their ideas into thought units as they are writing, *whether they paragraph them as such or not.* I am not saying that writers cannot go back and paragraph their essays for reasons that have little to do with the logical progression of ideas. What I am saying is that the logical basis for dividing essays into paragraphs is there, if writers want to avail themselves of it. It is there because composition is an organic development that begins with an intuitive grasp of the whole. The writer knows in general the end he or she wants to achieve. **Paragraphing** is *the process of differentiating the parts within the whole to achieve the writer's purpose.*

The truth of this idea is easy to illustrate. Give an experienced writer a completed piece of writing, one that has been written without traditional paragraph divisions, and he or she can invariably divide that piece of writing into thought units that make sense. Although some writers may disagree slightly as to where some of the paragraph divisions should be, the extent to which they will agree is amazing.

Let's look at two kinds of writing: writing that is **over-differentiated,** in which there seem to be too many paragraph divisions and in which the basis of the paragraph divisions seems to be almost arbitrary, or at least nonlogical; and writing that is **under-differentiated,** in which there are few or no paragraph divisions.

Over-differentiated writing occurs in magazine ads and in newspaper writing, where considerations such as the educational level of the mass audience, the neat, orderly appearance that shorter paragraphs present, the readability of such paragraphs, and the balance achieved by making the paragraphs the same average length are of paramount importance. Under-differentiated writing occurs in encyclopedia articles, to give just one example.

Over-differentiated Paragraphing

Let us look at a few examples of over-differentiated writing, the first an ad for Kitchen Aid disposers:

Other Disposers Can't Compare to Kitchen Aid.

1

Kitchen Aid disposers have a cast iron drain chamber to fight corrosion.

2

Other disposers don't.

3

Kitchen Aid has a push-button Wham Jam Breaker to break up stubborn jams.

4

Other disposers don't.

5

Kitchen Aid has a powerful motor. Stronger start-up power than any other, to handle tough stuff like steak bones and corn husks.

6

Which some disposers can't.

7

In fact, when you make a point-by-point comparison, it turns out there really isn't much comparison.

8

And, perhaps, that's why so many people choose a new Kitchen Aid stainless steel disposer when it comes time to replace their worn-out disposers.

This ad appeared in the October 1978 issue of *Better Homes and Gardens*. The paragraphs are written in typical advertising-copy fashion. The copy is broken up into eight short paragraphs. Each contains a single sentence or a fragment punctuated as a sentence, with the exception of paragraph 5, which contains both a sentence and a fragment. Paragraph 1 has eleven words; paragraph 2, three words; paragraph 3, thirteen words; paragraph 4, three words; paragraph 5, twenty-two words; paragraph 6, four words; paragraph 7, eighteen words; paragraph 8, twenty-four words. The average paragraph length is twelve words.

The typical short paragraph in advertising copy is composed of three or four sentences. The paragraphing in this ad is even more extreme. If breaking up a block of printed matter into smaller units makes it easier to read and more inviting to the eye, then it follows that the more you break up the copy, the better it will be for advertising purposes.

In the typical short paragraph in an ad, there is little opportunity for extensive internal development. Yet most advertising copy has a logical progression of ideas through the various sections of the text. The section in advertising copy is often the equivalent of the paragraph in a longer essay. Naturally, the arrangement of logical units into paragraphs and sections will differ from advertisement to advertisement.

Are advertisers being perverse in writing such short paragraphs? Indeed not. They know a great deal about the psychology of their audiences. Ads with long paragraphs (as in some stereo ads) look like *hard reading* before readers even know what's in them. Short paragraphs look like *easy reading.* They are easy on the eyes. They are simple to follow. They aid emphasis. They get attention and hold it. This is especially important in magazines, where the ad has to compete with stories, feature articles, editorials, and reviews to make its selling point.

Yet despite the copywriter's grouping of the sentences into eight paragraphs, the logical basis for grouping these sentences into new paragraph units is there. A reorganization of the sentences based on logical considerations gives us four paragraphs that look like this:

Other Disposers Can't Compare to Kitchen Aid

1

Kitchen Aid disposers have a cast iron drain chamber to fight corrosion. Other disposers don't.

2

Kitchen Aid has a push-button Wham Jam Breaker to break up stubborn jams. Other disposers don't.

3

Kitchen Aid has a powerful motor, stronger start-up power than any other, to handle tough stuff like steak bones and corn husks, which some disposers can't.

4

In fact, when you make a point-by-point comparison, it turns out there really isn't much comparison. And perhaps that's why so many people choose a new Kitchen Aid stainless steel disposer when it comes time to replace their worn out disposers.

This rewritten version uses a point-by-point comparison paradigm. In the first two paragraphs, the first sentence in each lists a feature of Kitchen Aid disposers. The second sentence negates these features in the competitor's product. In the third paragraph, consisting of a single sentence, the first part of the sentence comments on Kitchen Aid's powerful motor and on what it is capable of doing. The second part denies this capability in the competitor's product. The last paragraph makes the point that there really isn't much of a comparison between Kitchen Aid and other products and concludes with an implicit appeal to the reader to buy Kitchen Aid disposers.

Here is a second example of over-differentiated paragraphing, this time a slightly more elaborated piece of writing, from a newspaper article:

7,000 Stolen Books Found in NY

NEW YORK—A middle-aged man with eclectic reading taste and sticky fingers brought public library officials to their knees Monday as they sorted through 7,000 volumes valued at $100,000 that were stashed in his apartment.

Inspectors from the New York and Queens public libraries picked their way delicately through wall-to-wall books stacked in the back bedroom of the Queens apartment abandoned three months ago by Caio A. D'Aurelio.

"It looks like they've all been stolen," said Cecil Greenidge, a Queens library inspector. Some of the books were stamped with library logos as distant as Florida State University in Tallahassee, but most were from libraries here.

"Now we can't be sure this guy stole these books. But somebody sure did," Greenidge said. Authorities at first thought the books had been checked out and never returned.

D'Aurelio rented the apartment for 10 years, said Armando Arias, the building superintendent. He stopped living in the apartment about two years ago, and he stopped paying his monthly $200 rent three months ago. No one has seen him since.

Arias and city marshals entered the apartment a week ago and found a riot of books—on the bed, the floor, even packed into the kitchen cabinets. They included books on Cicero, architecture and design, chemistry and archeology, flowers, Greek and Russian, and a guide to the rhythm method of birth control.

Some were dated as having been taken as long ago as 1952.

D'Aurelio was described by neighbors as an average-looking man in his 50's, with receding red hair and quiet demeanor. Arias said he once worked for the city as an architect, and apparently kept the Queens apartment as a place to work and study.

The street-level, one-bedroom apartment also had a litter of papers and magazines. Arias, once a military librarian in Ft. Polk, La., said he spent four days stacking most of the volumes in the bedroom because it would be easier for library officials to remove them through windows.

Arias said he used a shovel to plow through the strewn books and knee-high yellowed newspapers and magazines—some 11 years old—but it was two days before he could see the apartment's parquet floor.

At 10 cents a day, D'Aurelio's overdue charge in New York City for all 7,000 volumes would amount to $700 daily. Any book overdue since 1952 would have an accumulated fine of about $912. If all had been due back then, the bill would total more than $6.3 million.

—Associated Press

Like the paragraph structure of the Kitchen Aid ad, the paragraph structure of this news story is not completely logical. This does not mean that it is less effective, however. As I have previously pointed out, there are many reasons a writer would want to vary his or her paragraph structure: ease of reading, balance, emphasis, and the psychology of the audience being just a few. Like the paragraphs of the Kitchen Aid ad, the paragraphs in this news story contain few sentences. There is a total of eleven paragraphs in this article, ranging in length from one to three sentences.

Although the paragraph structuring is not strictly logical, the overall plan is logical. In typical journalistic fashion, the opening paragraph answers the questions who (public library officials), what (found 7,000 stolen or borrowed books), when (Monday), where (in the apartment of a middle-aged man with eclectic reading taste).

If you regroup the sentences from the original paragraphs and place them together in new paragraphs based on similar ideas, you get the following logical divisions:

7,000 Stolen Books Found in NY

1

NEW YORK—A middle-aged man with eclectic reading taste and sticky fingers brought public library officials to their knees Monday as they sorted through 7,000 volumes valued at $100,000 that were stashed in his apartment.

2

Inspectors from the New York and Queens public libraries picked their way delicately through wall-to-wall books stacked in the back bedroom of the Queens apartment abandoned three months ago by Caio A. D'Aurelio. "It looks like they've all be stolen," said Cecil Greenidge, a Queens library inspector. Some of the books were stamped with library logos as distant as Florida State University in Tallahassee, but most were from libraries here. "Now we can't be sure this guy stole these books. But somebody sure did," Greenidge said. Authorities at first thought the books had been checked out and never returned.

3

D'Aurelio rented the apartment for 10 years, said Armando Arias, the building superintendent. He stopped living in the apartment about two years ago, and he stopped paying his monthly $200 rent three months ago. No one has seen him since.

4

Arias and city marshals entered the apartment a week ago and found a riot of books—on the bed, the floor, even packed into the kitchen cabinets. They included books on Cicero, architecture and design, chemistry and archeology, flowers, Greek and Russian, and a guide to the rhythm method of birth control. Some were dated as having been taken as long ago as 1952.

5

D'Aurelio was described by neighbors as an average-looking man in his 50's, with receding red hair and quiet demeanor. Arias said he once worked for the city as an architect, and apparently kept the Queens apartment as a place to work and study.

6

The street-level, one-bedroom apartment also had a litter of papers and magazines. Arias, once a military librarian in Ft. Polk, La., said he spent four days stacking most of the volumes in the bedroom because it would be easier for library officials to remove them through windows. Arias said he used a shovel to plow through the strewn books and knee-high yellowed newspapers and magazines—some 11 years old—but it was two days before he could see the apartment's parquet floor.

7

At 10 cents a day, D'Aurelio's overdue charge in New York City for all 7,000 volumes would amount to $700 daily. Any book overdue since 1952 would have an accumulated fine of about $912. If all had been due back then, the bill would total more than $6.3 million.

—Associated Press

Paragraph 2 depicts inspectors from the New York and Queens public libraries picking their way through wall-to-wall books in D'Aurelio's bedroom in Queens and records their comments. Paragraph 3 discusses the length of time D'Aurelio stayed in the apartment and when he left. Paragraph 4 gives a catalog of D'Aurelio's eclectic reading tastes. Paragraph 5 describes D'Aurelio. Paragraph 6 emphasizes the litter of books, papers, and magazines. Paragraph 7 gives an account of the overdue charges.

Under-differentiated Paragraphing

If over-differentiated writing can be described as the kind of writing in which the writer, for whatever reasons, makes a large number of paragraph divisions, then under-differentiated writing is the type in which the writer makes few, if any, paragraph divisions. Nevertheless, there are units of thought within this kind of writing that can be separated into paragraphs.

A typical example of this kind of writing is the following article, taken from *The Columbia Encyclopedia:*

Lingua Franca

An auxiliary language, generally of a hybrid and partially developed nature, that is employed over an extensive area by people speaking different and mutually unintelligible tongues in order to communicate with one another. Such a language frequently is used primarily for commercial purposes. Examples are the several varieties of the hybrid pidgin English; Swahili, a native language of East Africa; Chinook jargon, a lingua franca formerly used in the American Northwest that was a mixture of Chinook, other American Indian languages, English, and French; and a variety of Malay (called *bazaar Malay*), which served as a compromise language in the area of British Malaya, the Dutch East Indies, and neighboring regions. The original lingua franca was a tongue actually called Lingua Franca (or sabir) that was employed for commerce in the Mediterranean area during the Middle Ages. Now extinct, it had Italian as its base with an admixture of words from Spanish, French, Greek, and Arabic. The designation "Lingua Franca" [Language of the Franks] came about because the Arabs in the medieval period used to refer to Western Europeans in general as "Franks." Occasionally the term *lingua franca* is applied to a fully established formal language; thus formerly it was said that French was the lingua franca of diplomacy.

—*The Columbia Encyclopedia*, 3rd ed.

The structure of this article is very much like that of many encyclopedia articles. The entire article consists of a single unit the size of a long paragraph. The opening statement is not a complete sentence, but it could be made into a complete sentence by the addition of a main verb. Despite the lack of paragraph divisions, however, this article has a logical progression of ideas that could be paragraphed like this:

Lingua Franca

1

[A *lingua franca* is] an auxiliary language, generally of a hybrid and partially developed nature, that is employed over an extensive area by people speaking different and mutually unintelligible tongues in order to communicate with one another. Such a language frequently is used primarily for commercial purposes.

2

Examples are the several varieties of the hybrid pidgin English; Swahili, a native language of East Africa; Chinook jargon, a lingua franca formerly used in the American Northwest that was a mixture of Chinook, other American Indian languages, English, and French; and a variety of Malay (called *bazaar Malay*), which served as a compromise language in the area of British Malaya, the Dutch East Indies, and neighboring regions.

3

The original lingua franca was a tongue actually called Lingua Franca (or sabir) that was employed for commerce in the Mediterranean area during the Middle Ages. Now extinct, it had Italian as its base with an admixture of words from Spanish, French, Greek, and Arabic. The designation "Lingua Franca" [Language of the Franks] came about because the Arabs in the medieval period used to refer to Western Europeans in general as "Franks."

4

Occasionally the term *lingua franca* is applied to a fully established formal language; thus formerly it was said that French was the lingua franca of diplomacy.

The logical basis for grouping these sentences into paragraphs is as follows. Paragraph 1 defines a *lingua franca*. Paragraph 2 gives examples of an auxiliary language. Paragraph 3 gives the origin of the word and traces the original language that was used as a *lingua franca*. Finally, paragraph 4 discusses another application of the term.

What, then, can you conclude about paragraphing from the study of over-differentiated writing and under-differentiated writing? That the structure of sentences, paragraphs, and sections of the whole essay interact. That paragrphing is the process of differentiating the parts within the whole, whether that differentiation comes as you are writing or after you have completed your first draft. And that paragraphing can be based on a number of considerations, depending on the writer's intention, although the logical basis of paragraphing may be the most important one.

Exercises

1. Rewrite the following news story, regrouping the sentences into new thought divisions:

Chair Commands High Spot in Human History

Is civilization possible without the chair?

Think about it. Plenty of animals make their own beds, but did you ever see even the sharpest rat sit in a chair?

The chair is no mere piece of furniture; it's a concept. It says something about human power. Long before the kings of Scotland were crowned on the Stone of Scone, the idea of a throne must have existed.

After all, if you could afford to sit down in the presence of strangers, that is, enemies, and not stand ready for combat, it must mean you didn't fear them very much. Where do you think the word chairman came from?

In our homes, this curiously ambiguous emblem of authority and relaxation is almost a member of the family.

My grandfather, an old soldier from the Gold Rush days, took up wood-carving in his last years and made a marvelous mahogany armchair with claws and scrolls.

It was always my father's chair in the dining room, and mine in my turn. My father also had his special armchair, by the fire in the library, deep, profoundly comfortable, with a high back and generous arms: it was a chair to take a nap in. Sometimes I would sit in this chair to read his paper, but never when he was around.

Something made me get up and offer it to him when he came in the room. Not that he was in the least threatening, or that I was in the least polite. It was something about the chair.

We still have that chair, all but reupholstered to death, and are about to retire it, but people still shy away from sitting in it unless I insist.

Even today, in an executive office, the chair has mojo. Try asking the boss for a raise when you're sitting in a chair lower than the one across the desk.

My mother also had her special chair: elegant, dowel-backed and efficient. It was the chair she sat in to write checks. If she wanted to relax, she would lie on the sofa.

Another one, a fine old wing chair, used to be stationed by a window in the living room overlooking the lawn and the valley beyond. It was in a nook, so you could sit perfectly still in it and someone looking for you to do a chore would walk right past.

I decided to make it my official reading chair. But it was too formal, too sternly straight-backed, so I never warmed to it. We still have that one too, in the attic, too valuable to throw away, not valuable enough to sell. It's as unaccommodating as ever.

Another disaster is the loveseat, which is good for nothing except arm wrestling.

You can tell a lot about a family by its chairs: whether it's socially ambitious, puritanical, lazy or whatever. Some living rooms contain all those springy-bottomed, stiff-backed antique chairs. You can't feel really welcome in such a place, and you wonder if even the people who live there do.

Doubtless those chairs were Louis XVI, Chippendale or some such. Which brings up the question: Why didn't the master chaircrafters make comfortable chairs? Was there some social prestige attached to sitting up straight? Is this the origin of "Don't slouch"?

The more you think about chairs, the stranger they get. The electric chair:

Why? Wouldn't it be much more practical to put the poor soul on a stretcher? Even in the gas chamber, the executee sits on a chair. Maybe it is a vestige of the homage paid to the sacrificial victim from times primeval.

—Michael Kernan, *The Washington Post*

2. Rewrite the following encyclopedia article, dividing it into paragraphs that make sense:

[A *pidgin* is] a LINGUA FRANCA that is not the mother tongue of anyone using it and that has a simplified grammar and a restricted, often polyglot vocabulary. Pidgins that have developed from English and other tongues have been employed in different regions since the 17th century. An example is the variety of pidgin English that resulted from contacts between English traders and the Chinese in Chinese ports. In fact, the word *pidgin* supposedly is a Chinese (Cantonese) corruption of the English word *business.* Another well-known form of pidgin English is the Beach-la-Mar (or *Beche-de-Mer*) of the South Seas. The different kinds of pidgin English have preserved the basic grammatical features of English, at the same time incorporating a number of non-English syntactical characteristics. The great majority of words in pidgin English are of English origin, but there are also Malay, Chinese, and Portuguese elements. As a result of bringing to the Caribbean area large numbers of Negro slaves from West Africa who spoke different languages, other pidgins evolved in that region that were based on English, Portuguese, French, and Spanish.

—*The Columbia Enclyclopedia*, 3rd ed.

The Paragraph as a Group of Logically Related Sentences

The paragraph as a group of logically related sentences represents, for the most part, the traditional approach to composition. In this view, the paragraph is a collection of sentences on a single subject. It expresses a single thought and it contains no idea that does not advance the main topic. The thought of such a paragraph can usually be expressed in a single, concise statement called the **topic sentence,** which is ordinarily stated at the beginning of the paragraph. The **topic sentence** is *the sentence that expresses the main idea of the paragraph.* In this position, all the subsequent ideas in the paragraph are developed from it:

1. Apart from teaching him Latin, *Stratford Grammar School* taught *Shakespeare* nothing at all.

2. *It* did not teach *him* mathematics or any of the natural sciences.

2. *It* did not teach *him* history, unless a few pieces of information about ancient events strayed in through Latin quotations.

2. *It* did not teach *him* geography, for the first (and most inadequate) textbook on geography did not appear until the end of the century, and maps and atlases were rare even in university circles.

2. *It* did not teach *him* modern languages, for when a second language was taught at grammar school it was invariably Greek.

—Marchette Chute, Shakespeare of London

In this paragraph the first sentence is the topic sentence and each of the next four sentences adds a supporting detail. The paragraph is unified because it deals with a single topic, the things that Stratford Grammar School did not teach Shakespeare.

In the traditional view of the paragraph, the relationship of every sentence to every other sentence and to the main idea is made clear and orderly through logical development and proper transitions:

1. Applied to language, the adjective *good* can have *two meanings:* "effective, adequate for the purpose to which it is put" and "acceptable, conforming to approved usage."

2. The *first* of *these* is truly a value judgment of the language itself.

  3. In this *sense* the language of Shakespeare, for example, is "good English" because it serves as a highly effective vehicle for his material.

  3. On the other hand, the language of a poorer writer, which does not meet adequately the demands put upon it, might be called "bad English."

2. The *second meaning* of *good* is not really a judgment of the language itself but a social appraisal of the persons who use it.

  3. An expression like *I ain't got no time for youse* may be most effective in the situation in which it is used, and hence "good English" in the first *sense*.

    4. But most people, including those who naturally speak this way, will call it "bad English" because grammatical features like *ain't, youse,* and the double negative construction belong to a variety of English commonly used by people with little education and low social and economic status.

—W. N. Francis, The English Language

This paragraph has the form of an extended definition. The opening sentence is the topic sentence. It introduces the term to be defined, *good language.* It also indicates the plan of development. The adjective *good*, the writer states, can have two meanings when it is applied to language: "effective" and "adequate for the purpose," or "acceptable" and "conforming to approved usage." Then he goes on to comment on the two meanings. He does this by dividing the remaining sentences into two groups. Sentence two and the two subordinate sentences related to it extend one part of the meaning of the term (the first meaning of *good*, followed by two examples). The language of Shakespeare is *good* because Shakespeare uses it effectively. The language of a poorer writer is bad, not because it is intrinsically bad, but because the poor writer does not use it effectively. Sentence five and its qualifying sentences take up the second meaning of the term, "a social appraisal of the persons who use it." Most people will label an expression *bad*, regardless of its effectiveness, if it has grammatical features that people of little education and low economic status use, the writer contends in the last two sentences.

In addition to the logical order of ideas, this paragraph uses a number of other methods to achieve unity and coherence:

Parallelism
the first of these is
the second meaning . . . is
in this sense
on the other hand
the language of Shakespeare
the language of a poorer writer

Repetition

the adjective *good*	highly effective
good English	most effective
the second meaning of *good*	language
bad English	the language of Shakespeare
good English in the first sense	the language of a poorer writer
bad English	the language itself
effective	

Synonyms
meanings
these
sense
meaning
sense

Transitional Expressions
in this sense
on the other hand
and hence
but

Exercises

1. Compose five topic sentences to be used in developing paragraphs.

2. Develop a paragraph from one of the following topic sentences:

   a. Education reduces prejudice.

   b. All people are motivated by self-interest.

   c. People should always be honest with each other.

   d. I was startled by what I saw when I entered the room.

   e. There are at least two good arguments to be made against pornography.

   f. Aside from its interest, _____ is an informative book (or television show, movie, and so forth).

Modes of Developing Paragraphs

Because writing is a unified process, the same principles which apply at the essay level also apply at the paragraph level. You have learned in earlier chapters that a **mode** is *a way or manner of developing ideas.* At times, I have used the term to refer both to the process of invention and to that of arrangement. But a mode is also a way of developing paragraphs.

Categories such as analysis, classification, comparison and contrast, and cause and effect, besides referring to mental processes and processes of invention and arrangement, also represent methods of developing paragraphs. They appear in paragraphs because our minds think along those lines.

Although it is true that in much writing the modes are mixed, it is useful at this point in your work on your writing for you to see them as simple. Just as in invention, the modes rarely appear in pure form (for instance, when you classify, you must also compare), in paragraphs, the modes are often mixed.

The following are typical examples of the modes as they appear in paragraphs. (You might want to go back and review the discussion of modes in the first chapter and in the chapters titled "Arrangement" and "Patterns of Thought.")

Analysis

Organize *analysis paragraphs* by dividing a complex subject into its component parts. In the following paragraph by Bertrand Russell, the topic sentence introduces the term *patriotism* (in the first sentence), and the following sentences break this term into its elements:

> Patriotism is a very complex feeling, built up out of primitive instincts and highly intellectual convictions. There is love of home and family and friends, making us peculiarly anxious to preserve our own country from invasion. There is the mild instinctive liking for compatriots as against foreigners. There is pride, which is bound up with the success of the community to which we feel that we belong. There is a belief, suggested by pride but reinforced by history, that one's own nation represents a great tradition and stands for ideals that are important to the human race. But besides all these, there is another element, at once nobler and more open to attack, an element of worship, of willing sacrifice, of joyful merging of the individual life in the life of the nation. This religious element in patriotism is essential to the strength of the State, since it enlists the best that is in most men on the side of national sacrifice.
>
> —Bertrand Russell, *Why Men Fight*

Description

Descriptive paragraphs consist basically of sentences representing objects arranged in space. In its simplest form, the principle of organization is based on the way you perceive objects in space—left to right, right to left, bottom to top, top to bottom, and so forth. In writing descriptive paragraphs, you can make the scene easier to follow if you use a particular principle of spatial arrangement:

> As you enter the forest, your eyes used to the glare of the sun, it seems dark and shadowy, and as cool as a butter dish. The light is filtered through a million leaves, and so has a curious green aquarium-like quality which makes everything seem unreal. The centuries of dead leaves that

have fluttered to the ground have provided a rich layer of mold, soft as any carpet, and giving off a pleasant earthy smell. On every side are the huge trees with their great curling buttress roots, their thick smooth trunks towering hundreds of feet above, their head foliage and branches merging indistinguishably into the endless green roof of the forest. Between these the floor of the forest is covered with the young trees, thin tender growths just shaken free of the cradle of leaf mold, long thin stalks with a handful of pale green leaves on top. They stand in the everlasting shade of their parents, ready for the great effort of shooting up to the life-giving sun. In between their thin trunks, rambling across the floor of the forest, one can see faint paths twisting and turning. These are the roads of the bush and are followed by all its inhabitants.

—Gerald Durrell, *The Overloaded Ark*

Classification

Classification deals with systems of classes. Begin classification paragraphs with a general statement and support this statement by an enumeration and explanation of the types or subtypes:

Meteorites are of three general classes: irons—composed 98 percent or more of nickel-iron; stony irons—composed roughly half and half of nickel-iron and of a kind of rock known as olivine; and, finally, stones. The stones are further subdivided, depending on whether they contain tiny bodies (or chondrules) of the minerals olivine and pyroxene. The stones that possess them—more than 90 percent of all known meteoritic stones—are called chondrites. The few stones that lack these minerals are known as achondrites. All these categories offer useful clues to those who try to reconstruct the history of the earth, for not only are meteorites fellow members of the solar system, but radioactive dating indicates that they are as old as the earth itself.

—Time-Life Books, *The Earth*

Exemplification

Exemplification paragraphs use supporting examples to illustrate a generalization. Begin exemplification paragraphs with a general statement and then support this statement by specific examples:

Almost no feature of the interior design of our current cars provides safeguards against injury in the event of collision. Doors that fly open on impact, inadequately secured seats, the sharp-edged rearview mirror, pointed knobs on instrument panels and doors, flying glass, the overhead structure—all illustrate the lethal potential of poor design. A sudden deceleration turns a collapsed steering wheel or a sharp-edged dashboard into a bone-and-chest-crushing agent. Penetration of the shatterproof windshield can chisel one's head into fractions. A flying seat cushion can cause a fatal injury. The apparently harmless glove-compartment door has been known to unlatch under impact and guillotine a child. Roof-supporting structure has deteriorated to a point where it provides scarcely more protection to the occupants, in common roll-over accidents, than an open convertible.

—Ralph Nader, "The Safe Car You Can't Buy,"
The Nation (April 11, 1957)

Definition

Definition paragraphs tell what a thing is. They also explain what words or phrases mean. One way of developing paragraphs of definition is to lead off with a general statement or with a logical definition. Then expand the general statement by other methods of defining:

"Desert" is an unfortunate word all around and most of its usual associations are inaccurate as well as unfavorable. In the first place the word doesn't even mean "dry," but simply uninhabited or deserted—like Robinson Crusoe's island. In that sense, the expanse about me is far from being a desert, for it is teeming with live things very glad indeed to be right there. Even in its secondary meaning, "desert" suggests to most people the rolling sand dunes of the Sahara. Something like that one may find in Death Valley; perhaps in parts of the Mojave; and especially, with an added weirdness, in the hundreds of square miles of New Mexico's White Sands, where the great dunes of glistening gypsum drift like the snowbanks one can hardly believe they are not. Most of my Lower Sonoran Desert, however, is not at all like that. The sandy soil is firm and hard-packed; it supports life, less crowded than in wetter regions but pleasantly flourishing. Nature does not frown here. She smiles invitingly.

—Joseph Wood Krutch, *The Desert Year*

Comparison and Contrast

Comparison and contrast paragraphs deal with similarities and differences. One way of organizing such paragraphs is as follows. In the first half of the paragraph, deal with one subject or aspect of a subject, and in the second half, take up the second subject or aspect of the subject to be compared:

The way of the desert and the way of the jungle represent the two opposite methods of reaching stability at two extremes of density. In the jungle there is plenty of everything life needs except more space, and it is not for the want of anything else that individuals die or that races have any limit set to their proliferation. Everything is on top of everything else; there is no cranny which is not both occupied and disputed. At every moment, war to the death rages fiercely. The place left vacant by any creature that dies is seized almost instantly by another, and life seems to suffer from nothing except too favorable an environment. In the desert, on the other hand, it is the environment itself which serves as the limiting factor. To some extent the struggle of creature against creature is mitigated, though it is of course not abolished even in the vegetable kingdom. For the plant which in the one place would be strangled to death by its neighbor dies a thirsty seedling in the desert because that same neighbor has drawn the scant moisture from the spot of earth out of which it was attempting to spring.

—Joseph Wood Krutch, *The Desert Year*

Narration

In *narrative paragraphs*, the emphasis is usually on the action, on the connected series of events that take place in chronological order. Of course, description is often included in narrative paragraphs in order to present the action in the most vivid terms. Organize narrative paragraphs chronologically. Since narrative paragraphs seldom use topic sentences, begin with a sentence that gets the action started. Then add sentences to advance the action:

Slowly the minutes ticked away toward the zero hour. Officers, their watches synchronized, waited with guns in the air, ready to fire the shots that signaled the opening. At last the revolvers barked, and along the line pandemonium broke loose. Men whipped up their horses, wagons careened wildly forward, horses freed from overturned vehicles galloped madly about—all was hurrah and excitement. The Santa Fe trains, streaming slowly forward at a regulated pace which would not give their passengers an undue advantage, disgorged riders along the route as men leaped from roofs or platforms and rushed about in search of a claim. Noise and confusion reigned as the shouts of successful "Boomers," the crash of hammers on stakes, the clatter of wagons, the crash of overturned vehicles, and the curses of disappointed homeseekers mingled to create a bedlam unique in the annals of the nation.

—Ray Allen Billington, *Westward Expansion*

Process

Organize *process paragraphs* chronologically, as you would narrative paragraphs. Place the emphasis, however, on *the steps* involved in the process:

> The process of précis writing is fivefold: (1) The student reads slowly the entire selection he intends to summarize, concentrating his attention on getting at the author's central idea. (2) He then rereads the selection, picking out the essential points or subdivisions; and, if the selection is long, jotting down the points made in successive paragraphs. (3) Either with or without reference to these notes, he next constructs sentences expressing the different points concisely but accurately, and groups these sentences into paragraphs representing sections or larger divisions of the whole. (4) He reads the selection a third time, comparing it with the summary he has prepared, and making sure that nothing important has been omitted, nothing unimportant included, and nothing at all unclearly expressed. (5) He finally revises and recopies or rewrites his summary. The précis which results from this process will generally be from one-quarter to one-third the length of the original.
>
> —Harry Robbins and Roscoe Parker, *Advanced Exposition*

Cause and Effect

Compose *cause-and-effect paragraphs* by moving from cause to effect or from effect to cause. The assumption is that a event takes place in time *because* an initial event caused it to occur or because it is part of a causal chain:

> The intellectual life of the nineteenth century was more complex than that of any previous age. This was due to several causes. First: The area concerned was larger than ever before; America and Russia made important contributions, and Europe became more aware than formerly of Indian philosophies, both ancient and modern. Second: Science, which had been a chief source of novelty since the seventeenth century, made new conquests, especially in geology, biology, and organic chemistry. Third: Machine production profoundly altered the social structure, and gave men a new conception of their powers in relation to the physical environment. Fourth: A profound revolt, both philosophical and political, against traditional systems in thought, in politics, and in economics, gave rise to attacks upon many beliefs and institutions that had hitherto been regarded as unassailable. This revolt had two very different forms, one romantic, the other rationalistic. (I am using these words in a liberal sense.) The

romantic revolt passes from Byron, Schopenhauer, and Nietzsche to Mussolini and Hitler; the rationalistic revolt begins with the French philosophers of the Revolution, passes on, somewhat softened, to the philosophical radicals in England, then acquires a deeper form in Marx and issues in Soviet Russia.

—Bertrand Russell, *A History of Western Philosophy*

Exercises

1. Analyze the paragraphs given as examples above. Usually the topic sentence is the first sentence of the paragraph. Is this true in these paragraphs? What are the specific sentences in each paragraph that relate to the respective modes of development?

2. Write an analysis paragraph, listing the characteristics, features, aspects, or parts revealed by your analysis, based on one of the following topics:

   a. a song lyric

   b. the human body

   c. a day in your life

   d. a landscape

   e. an album cover

   f. a part of your room

   g. some object or possession

   h. a poster

   i. a picture or painting

   j. a magazine ad

3. In a single paragraph, describe a person, an object, or a scene.

4. Write a classification paragraph based on one of the topics listed below:

   a. popular songs

   b. clothing styles

   c. graffiti

   d. people

   e. blind dates

5. Write a paragraph giving examples of:

   a. things that disturb you

   b. prejudiced people

   c. current fads

   d. doublespeak in language

   e. ads that use subliminal appeals

6. In a single paragraph, write an extended definition of one of the following terms: *myth, romance, love, beauty, truth, success.*

7. Coin a word and then write a paragraph defining it.

8. In a well-written paragraph, compare or contrast:

   a. two songs (rock lyrics)   d. two ads

   b. two people   e. two of anything

   c. two dances

9. Write a one-paragraph narrative on one of the following subjects: an embarrassing moment, a frightening experience, a college experience.

10. In a single paragraph, describe a process:

    a. how to cook something

    b. how to play a certain game

    c. how to eat a certain dish

    d. how to produce (sell, prepare, build, plan, solve, and so forth)

11. Write a cause-and-effect paragraph based on one of the following topics:

    a. the effect of inflation on my life

    b. the effects of taking some drug (or of drinking a certain liquor)

    c. the cause of an accident in which you or a friend were involved

    d. the effects of a love affair

    e. the cause of some natural occurrence

The Paragraph as an Extended Sentence

Another way of looking at paragraph structure is to think of a paragraph as an extended sentence. This approach to paragraph construction is based on the work of Francis Christensen, who sees a close relationship between a particular type of sentence that he calls the **cumulative sentence** and the paragraph. According to Christensen, the cumulative sentence begins with a sentence base. This base contains the main subject, the main verb, and any bound or restrictive modifiers:

    1. The boys ate warily,

To the base is added an accumulation (hence the designation *cumulative*) of details, in the form of free or sentence modifiers:

   1. The boys ate warily.
      2. trying not to be seen or heard,
         3. the cornbread sticking,
         3. the buttermilk gurgling,
            4. as it went down their gullets.

—Katherine Anne Porter

The base clause is often stated in general terms. The modifiers add specific details to the base so that there is a deductive movement from the general (level 1) to the particular (levels 2, 3, and 4). The sentence levels are numbered and indented to show the grammatical and logical progression of ideas.

If sentences tend to have a base, to which details in the form of modifiers are added, then paragraphs, according to Christensen, have a similar movement. The paragraph, in this view, is a kind of extended sentence. The top sentence of the paragraph is similar to the base clause of the cumulative sentence. The supporting sentences in the paragraph are similar to the sentence modifiers. The successive sentences in the paragraph are related to each other by coordination and subordination.

If it is possible to consider the paragraph as having the same kind of structure as the cumulative sentence, then clearly some sentences can be rewritten as paragraphs. Below is a rewritten version of the Katherine Anne Porter sentence (cited above) as a paragraph:

   1. The boys ate warily.
      2. They were trying not to be seen or heard.
         3. The cornbread was sticking.
         3. The buttermilk was gurgling.
            4. It went down their gullets.

Implicit in Christensen's approach to paragraph construction is the idea that an inductive study of the paragraph can be useful in learning to write paragraphs, that analyzing paragraphs will enable the writer to see what goes with what. Since all writers must necessarily use the same basic compositional principles, one can learn a great deal about these principles by studying the writing of others.

Composing Paragraphs

For the purposes of writing your own paragraphs, you could follow a sequence of steps very much like these:

> *Begin with a base sentence.*
> *Add a supporting sentence.*
> *Add a second supporting sentence.*
> *Add a third supporting sentence.*
> *Conclude with a final supporting sentence.*

Or you could use some variation on the basic pattern:

> *Write a base sentence.*
> *Qualify that base.*
> *Add a specific detail.*
> *Add another detail.*
> *Qualify that detail.*

Visually, the two basic movements of thought in such paragraphs can be depicted as follows:

The Two-Level Paragraph
1. _____
   2. _____
   2. _____
   2. _____
   2. _____

The Multi-Level Paragraph
1. _____
   2. _____
      3. _____
      3. _____
         4. _____

In the two-level paragraph, all the sentences in the paragraph follow from and "depend" upon the base sentence. In a multi-level paragraph, the sentences follow from and "depend" upon each other.

Exercises

1. Some sentences have a structure remarkably like the structure of paragraphs. Transform the sentences below into paragraphs, as in the following example:

Sentence

1. A host of laughing children bestrode the animals,
    2. bending forward like charging cavalrymen, and
    2. shaking reins and whooping in glee.

—Stephen Crane

Sentence into paragraph

1. A host of laughing children bestrode the animals.
    2. They bent forward like charging cavalrymen.
    2. They shook the reins and whooped in glee.

1. It was really a lovely day,
    2. the first dandelions making suns,
    2. the first daisies so white.

—D. H. Lawrence

1. The boys ate warily,
    2. trying not to be seen or heard,
        3. the cornbread sticking,
        3. the buttermilk gurgling,
            4. as it went down their gullets.

—Katherine Anne Porter

1. The dentist began his work,
    2. probing into sensitive cavities,
    2. swabbing the tender area with a dulling liquid,
    2. his fingers pressing the gumline,
        3. searching for the exact spot to insert his needle,
            4. still hidden from the patient's cringing eyes.

    2. NAs the snow melted on the roof,
1. streams of clear, cold water rippled over the slanted, brown-glazed shingles and slid off the edge,
    2. forming a waterfall which splashed on the grey cement walk below.

1. The old woman prayed alone in the huge cathedral,
    2. her head covered by a dark shawl,
        3. making her round face wide and Slavic,
    2. her elbows leaning heavily on the pew in front of her,
2. her thick hands cradling her chin and mouth,
3. the fingers clasped about a wooden rosary,
3. the large roughened knuckles bent away from the center,
    4. forming a basket with which to collect prayers before releasing them to heaven.

2. Using the kind of analyses illustrated in this section, analyze a few of the example paragraphs, numbering and indenting the levels. Be prepared to discuss the structure, ideas, and language of these paragraphs.

3. Select one or two paragraphs from your own reading and analyze them in the same manner, or bring them to class, put them on the board, and analyze and discuss them.

4. Write a few paragraphs of your own, beginning with narrative and descriptive paragraphs, and then move on to expository paragraphs. Try writing two-level as well as multi-level paragraphs.

Throughout this chapter, my assumption has been that one good way to learn to write effective paragraphs is to look carefully at the principles other writers use to achieve their purposes and then to use these principles in your own writing. When you write, you are carried along by the movement of the prose, by the flow of ideas, by the logical, spatial, or temporal progression. Often you may have an intuitive sense of paragraph structure, but this is not enough. Good writers usually have a developed consciousness of form, and often they can be self-conscious about their writing when there is a need to be. Good writing is planned in such a way as to exploit all the resources of language—the sentence structure, the word choice, and the paragraph structure. Learning to write is in part learning to recognize and to use the best available resources of the language.

Achieving Coherence

The best way of achieving coherence in your writing is to develop your powers of consecutive thinking so that your paragraphs unfold in a logical, step-by-step manner. Sometimes, however, it may be helpful to your reader if you use **transitional devices** to make the relationship among the parts of your essay clear. You can achieve coherence by breaking your writing into logical units, but sometimes you need *connecting words and phrases to make the flow of your thoughts smooth and effortless.*

Careful writers use transitional words and phrases to show connections in thought. These coherence devices link words within a sentence, sentences within a paragraph, and sentences between paragraphs. The following are some typical examples:

Addition

Use connectives to suggest simple addition to the thought in the preceding sentence: *and, too, also, again, and then, moreover, further, indeed, in addition to, plus, likewise, besides, together, jointly.*

> This is a wine to enjoy with your dinner. You will *also* enjoy its delicious flavor with fruit, cheese, and dessert after dinner is over.

> Ask to visit several classrooms. *Also* make the most of parent-teacher conferences.

Series

Use transitional devices to link items in a series: *first, second, third; next, again, last; primarily, secondarily; in the first place, in the second place; finally, additionally, first and foremost, the former, the latter.*

> *At first,* it may be Grand Prix's beautiful styling that captivates you the most. *The next time,* it may be Grand Prix's luxurious interior that charms you.

> *First* we let blueberry pie dry on a dessert dish overnight. *Then* we washed it with Electrasol.

Pronoun Reference

Use a pronoun to refer to a noun, another person, or a clause in the preceding sentence: *this, that, these, those, he, she, it, you, they, we, such, some, many, none.*

> Welcome to *Hawaii. It* is a place as unique and varied as *its* flowers.

> Some *people* dream of relaxing on a secluded island. *Others* dream of more lavish surroundings.

Repeated Word

Repeat a key word, or a word derived from the same root: *told/tell, arrived/arrival, rare/rarity, moisture/moistness/moisten/moist, depth/deep, mix/mixture/admixture/mixed.*

There are crippled *children* who want to walk so badly it hurts. *There are children* for whom even the simple act of moving a pencil becomes an agonizing test of determination. *There are children* whose courage in therapy would astonish you.

He *arrived* early. His *arrival* filled us with dread.

Synonyms

If the repetition of key words gets tiresome or if variety is needed, use a different word or phrase to refer to an element in the preceding sentence: *car/automobile, spectator/onlooker/observer/viewer, purchase/buy, join/unite/connect, exterior/outside, mere words/nonsense.*

One of the hottest topics in public education today is *"back to the basics."* PTA meetings resound with debates on the *subject.*

It was a rare *caper,* planned to the second and full of acrobatic derring-do: Thieves dropped in through the roof at San Francisco's De Young Memorial Museum and made off with several Dutch paintings, including Rembrandt's "The Rabbi," worth about a million dollars. Such elaborate *heists* are becoming increasingly common nowadays.

Whole-Part

Use a word or a phrase that names a whole in one sentence, and then use another word or a phrase that names a part of the whole: *television/picture tube, stereo/tuner, water/wave, flower/petal, book/chapter/section/paragraph, landscape/meadow.*

The roof on this house is made of a new kind of *non-wood shingle.* The *edges* are thick and irregular.

The creosote *bush* is a wispy shrub. It has scraggly *branches* two to five feet high.

Class-Members

Name a general class in one sentence and a member of that class in another: *vehicle/car, sound/noise, fluid/water, fuel/coal/gas, fragrance/perfume, span of time/decade, place of worship/cathedral.*

Supersoil is a superbly balanced *nutrient potting mix.* It contains rich *sphagnum peat, redwood, fir bark,* and *granite-based river sand.*

In speed, power, and appetite, the *shark* is a formidable ocean predator. The little we know of this dangerous, unpredictable *fish* has been learned at a high cost in human life.

Emphasis

Use connectives to reinforce the thought in a previous clause or to give emphasis to that thought: *obviously, certainly, perhaps, surely, naturally, really, to be sure, in truth, very likely, undoubtedly, assuredly, without fail.*

Add fresh taste and variety to your salad with country-fresh mushrooms. They're full of flavor and *surprisingly* low in calories.

Naturally, a teething baby or even a small child cannot be expected to brush its own teeth. But you can—and must.

Comparison

Use connectives that reveal to the reader significant likenesses in thought: *equally important, similarly, in the same way, also, comparably, corresponding, equally, like.*

Animal life on the desert is *like* life anywhere else. It is completely dependent upon plant life for sustenance.

The killer whale is one of the most dangerous marine animals. *Equally* dangerous is the moray eel.

Contrast

Connect sentences with linking devices that show contrast and that reveal to the reader signficant differences in thought: *but, yet, however, still, nevertheless, on the contrary, on the other hand, in spite of, conversely, although, unlike, be that as it may.*

Until now, all bran cereals were made from wheat. *But* many people think corn tastes better.

Taking care of wood is a constant job. *Unlike* wood, vinyl siding takes care of itself.

Result

Use transitional devices when you want to show result: *consequently, therefore, thus, as a result, for this reason, on this account, it follows that, accordingly, hence, so, necessarily.*

The color of the roof is soft and muted. *So* it blends in naturally with the architecture and the surroundings.

No matter how many trash cans you buy, it always seems that there isn't enough room for the trash. *That's why* a Kitchen Aid trash compactor is so worth having.

Example

Use transitional words and phrases to introduce illustrations or examples: *for instance, for example, namely, that is, thus.*

The new cars are quieter than last year's models. You will be surprised, *for example,* by the almost complete absence of road noise and body vibrations.

Nouns which consist of two or more root words are called compound nouns. Often they are written as one word, but they can be written as two words. "Ice cream," *for instance,* is just as much of a compound as is "blueberry."

Parallel Structure

Repeat in the second clause a grammatical structure similar to that in a previous clause: *in the morning/in the evening, some things will never change/some things will always be the same.*

Have you ever seen a killer whale or a live shark up close? Have your children ever touched a real dolphin?

Come and watch Kabuki, a Japanese drama. Visit gilded palaces in Bangkok. Admire ancient temples in Malaysia.

Place

Use linking devices that indicate place or change of place: *here, there, above, under, near by, beyond, on the other side, opposite, adjacent to, in.*

> Spend your vacation in *British Columbia.* Your American dollar's worth much more *there.*

> Odors used to be an everyday problem *in my house* until I started using Lysol Disinfectant Spray every day. *In the bathroom,* Lysol doesn't just cover up odors, it eliminates them fast.

Time

Use connectives that indicate time or a change of time: *not long after, then, soon, now, after a short while, meanwhile, immediately.*

> *During the day,* you can swim, sun, relax, and play. *At night,* you can watch a floor show.

> *When* your cab pulls up in front of the London Hilton, you can expect a most gracious welcome from our doormen. *When* they open your cab door, they'll tip their hats and usher you in with a friendly smile.

Exercises

1. Analyze the following paragraphs. What methods are used to achieve coherence? Mark each paragraph in detail to illustrate the use of transitional devices (for example, put one line under pronouns and their antecedents, two lines under connectives, circle appropriate words and phrases, draw arrows, use squiggly lines, etc.). Then be prepared to discuss these paragraphs in class.

   a. Italians are convinced that it is good to be alive, and they spend considerable time and energy proving themselves right. With gusto, they sail on warm seas and chill lakes, bowl in the nearest back yard, race about sunbaked soccer fields or argue among themselves at a sidewalk café. But nothing reflects their enjoyment more than their cookery, which is as diverse as the nation's regions, as imaginative as the Italian character. Whether the cook presides in a swank hotel or an ancient farmhouse, the meal is likely to be superb. For, to an Italian, to eat is to live.

—*Italy*, Life World Library

b. For no other art do the Italians have more natural talent than they have for dramatic vocal music. The most extroverted and demonstrative people of the Mediterranean, they have since Dante and Petrarch spoken a language that is the most melodious in the world. Furthermore, the Italians seem, peculiarly blessed with throats which naturally emit sweet, free-flowing sounds. Perhaps this is because they have been essentially a pastoral people free from many of the tensions of urban life—even when living in cities

—*Italy*, Life World Library

c. Another farsighted practice of the English was to bring along their women. This made for a more homogeneous society than that of the French and Spanish colonies, in which men took native wives. And it also meant the family unit was to provide a solid core for a racially well-knit people, who early indicated that they had come to stay. For the next 300 years, as the descendants of these early settlers pushed westward across the continent, building the nation, it was the presence of the women and of the unit that provided stability and permanence to the new communities. It was they who demanded schools, religion, and order. It was their presence that encouraged a cultural uplift and broke down some of the rough-house tendencies of the masculine frontier. While the Spanish and French ranged over vast stretches of land, unhampered by any family ties, except momentary domesticity with occasional native women, the English stayed close to home. The result was a family type of frontier, characterized by small farms, that remained much more compact, more easily defended, and permanent in nature.

—*The New World*, American Heritage

2. Select an article from your reader or from a magazine. Identify the words and phrases that are used as explicit transitions *from paragraph to paragraph.*

Introductory Paragraphs

Have formal introductions gone out of style? According to some writers, they have. Because of television and the mass media, readers are impatient with long and formal introductions. They want you to get right to the point.

But even if you decide to keep your beginning paragraphs brief and informal, you must not forget that in your opening paragraphs you make a commitment to your readers that you are expected to fulfill.

What should you do in your opening paragraph or paragraphs? At the very least, give your readers some idea of what you are going to write about, state your purpose, and indicate your plan of development. If your subject is a difficult one, you might also want to include a preliminary explanation.

Introductory paragraphs, then, should lead into the subject. But they should do more. They should also arouse the curiosity and interest of your readers and create the proper tone.

In considering strategies for your opening paragraphs, it might be helpful to ask yourself the following questions:

1. *Who are my readers?*
2. *Do they have any knowledge of my subject?*
3. *Do they have any interest in my subject?*
4. *How can I best gain their attention?*
5. *Is my purpose to present my readers with new ideas or information, to persuade them to take a certain course of action, or to entertain them?*
6. *How can I best convey to my readers my own interest in, and attitude toward, my subject?*

Experienced writers use a number of strategies in their opening paragraphs. Here are a few you may want to try.

Begin with Descriptive Details

Staring from the poster, they looked like a nightmare of what might be, that terrifying day when the street gangs take over the city, any city. Some of them wore leather vests over bare chests. Others had on Arab headdresses. A few, their faces painted harlequin colors, wore baseball uniforms and carried bats. Massed as far as the eye could see, all looked menacing, and the threat was underscored by the text above the picture: "These are the Armies of the Night. They are 100,000 strong. They outnumber the cops five to one. They could run New York City. Tonight they're all out to get the Warriors."

That Paramount ad was chillingly effective, bringing into 670 theaters around the country thousands of youths keen to see *The Warriors*—and eager for trouble. Since the film opened on Feb. 9, three young men have been killed by *Warrior*-inspired fights, and other brawls have broken out at moviehouses in several cities. More than a half a dozen theaters have dropped the film entirely; others are hiring some muscle of their own, which Paramount will pay for. In Washington, D.C., two full-time guards were on duty last week at the Town Downtown and will stay there until *The Warriors* finishes its run. Not since Stanley Kubrick's *A Clockwork Orange* opened in 1971 has a movie generated such anxiety about the seeming power of a film to engender gang violence in those who see it.

—"The Flick of Violence," *Time*

Begin with an Anecdote

Nearly five years ago I sat in the courtyard of a household in the village I call Tudu, Niger, haranguing the head of the household in an attempt to determine the year his first son was born. His replies were desultory as I sought to find out whether the son was older or younger than other men whose ages I knew fairly well. In the middle of this important but tedious part of demographic data collection, the man's daughter-in-law came out of her hut with an infant in her arms. She hurried over to me, and with tears running down her cheeks, her body shaking with sobs, she placed the baby in my lap and pleaded, "Ladi just stopped breathing in her sleep. Can you do anything?" Ladi—her stomach distended, the bones of her arms and legs like fragile spindles—was dead, and Ladi's mother, in spite of her question, knew that there was nothing I could do. At that moment my inability to get help in a tangible way, as well as the needlessness of Ladi's death, ignited my anger and frustration at the effects of the Sahelian drought.

The drought in West Africa south of the Sahara was due to four straight years of poor rainfall—from 1970 to 1973—each year worse than the one before. The drought was reported to the United States and Europe in terms of thousands of deaths, hundreds of thousands made homeless, the encroaching Sahara, and somber declarations of international relief aid for the region.

—Ralph H. Faulkingham, "Where the Lifeboat Ethic Breaks Down,"
Human Nature

Begin with a Quotation

"We cannot tolerate the Cubans to go swashbuckling unchecked in Africa, the Middle East and other areas, nor can we tolerate the Cubans of the Orient to go swashbuckling in Laos, Kampuchea or even in the Chinese border areas. Now some people in the world are afraid of offending them, even if they do something terrible. These people wouldn't dare take action against them."

So said China's Vice Premier Teng Hsiao-p'ing last week, puffing on a Panda cigarette as he aimed an unmistakable rebuke at what Peking considers the jelly-bellied Western response to adventurism by the Soviets and their clients. Teng also gave the fullest explanation yet of the motives behind China's two-week-old "punitive" invasion of its southern neighbor, Viet Nam. In an effort to placate international alarm, he repeated assurances that the operation "will be limited in degree and will not last a long time," perhaps no longer than China's four-week invasion of India in 1962. There were reports at week's end, in fact, that the Chinese were considering a ceasefire and might begin pulling back this week.

—"Suck Them In and Out-Flank Them," *Time*

Begin with the Thesis Statement

A revolution was spinning out of control. With nonviolent protests and uncommon discipline, the people of Iran had ended the tyranny of the Shah. Their reward was not freedom but chaos, as the forces united around Ayatollah Ruhollah Khomeini last week showed the first dread signs of schism. Suddenly, guns were everywhere, in every hand, as self-styled "freedom fighters" liberated weapons from police stations and army barracks. In Tehran, Tabriz and other cities, sporadic fighting raised the death toll for the week to an estimated 1,500. A bewildering motley of forces was involved: troops loyal to the Shah, ethnic separatists, *mojahedeen* (literally, crusaders) who backed the new government of Prime Minister Mehdi Bazargan, and, ominously, Marxist *fedayeen* (sacrificers) who felt that the revolution had not moved far enough to the left.

—"Guns, Death, and Chaos," *Time*

Begin with a Question

Is it possible that a cigar-shaped spaceship descended over the tiny town of Aurora, Texas (pop. 237), and crashed into Judge J. S. Proctor's windmill? And that a tiny spaceman was buried in the Aurora cemetery?

That was the tale sent to newspapers in nearby Dallas and Fort Worth one April day in 1897 by a local correspondent named S. E. Hayden. It was generally ridiculed at the time, and most citizens of Aurora still scoff. "Hayden wrote it as a joke and to bring interest to Aurora," says Etta Pegues, 86. "The railroad bypassed us, and the town was dying."

—"Close Encounters of a Kind," *Time*

Begin with a Figure of Speech

Like fast-approaching storm clouds, the consequences of the political turmoil that shut down Iran's oil fields became clearer last week, presaging a period of trouble and uncertainty for Western nations. Higher fuel prices and some scarcities are inevitable in the U.S. President Carter warned that though the situation created by the Iranian cutoff is "not critical" yet, it "certainly could get worse." He said that the difficulties might be manageable if Americans "honor the 55-mph speed limit, set thermostats no higher than 65° and limit discretionary driving." Otherwise, the President added, "more strenuous action" would be needed to curb fuel use.

—"The Price of Stormy Petrol," *Time*

Begin with a Cryptic Statement

Winnipeg is jumping. Airline reservations to the frostbitten Canadian city (pop. 560,000) have been booked for months. Hotels are full up too. The cause of this midwinter madness: the last solar eclipse over the continental U.S. until 2017. On Monday, Feb. 26, the moon will slip between the earth and sun, and progressively blot out the solar disc along a so-called path of totality that begins in the Pacific Ocean west of Washington State, cuts northeast over Canada, then darts off and away toward Greenland.

—"A Matter of Night and Day," *Time*

Begin with an Analogy

From Florida to Maine there is a war. Between man and man, fish and bird, wave and sand. The battle rages and storms over the coast. Yet the battlefield is strangely quiet. Grasses bend softly in the wind. Herons stalk silently through shallow waters. This war is being fought in the narrow green-and-tawny band of salt marsh that stretches along our eastern shore.

For millenniums there could be no final victory or defeat. Nature's contending forces stayed in balance. The rising sea stole from the marshland, and the marshland rebuilt its defenses. The marsh grass died and, decaying, nourished the animal life of the estuaries. Fish warred on fish and the birds on them, but all at last fell in the battle, and, in dissolution, fed the grass roots. The circle closed, and the battle was joined again.

Now, however, we humans can impose a final decision in this immemorial war of the wetlands along all our coasts. We even have it in our power to obliterate the battlefield. And if we do, will that be victory or defeat? Are we about to conquer nature, or about to conquer ourselves?

The salt marshes are disappearing before the onslaught of factories, dump and fill, homes with a seaward view. As chemicals and sewage pollute the wetlands, the encroachment of industrialists and developers is also the route of oyster dredgers, clammers, crabbers, sportsmen, and lovers of nature.

—Stephen W. Hitchcock, "Can We Save Our Salt Marshes?"
National Geographic

Concluding Paragraphs

The concluding paragraph should conclude. Nothing could be so obvious or so simple. Yet inexperienced writers often have a difficult time concluding their essays. When they run out of something to say, they just stop.

If your writing is to have any effect on your readers, it ought to have an appropriate ending. If your essay is relatively short, you might end it with the most important point. If your essay is relatively long, you might repeat the main points you made in the body of your paper. If your ideas are difficult, you might want to summarize in your concluding paragraph what you have said in the body of your paper. In brief, you want to leave your readers with the feeling that your essay is complete.

Here are some suggestions for concluding your essays:

1. *End with the most important point of your essay.*
2. *Repeat the main points of your essay.*
3. *Present your reader with a summary of your main ideas.*
4. *Conclude with a call for action.*
5. *End with a question.*
6. *Conclude with a prediction or forecast.*
7. *Give your reader an opinion, based on your previous discussion.*
8. *Discuss the broader implications of your subject.*
9. *End with an anecdote.*
10. *Conclude with a striking example.*

The following are a few examples of concluding paragraphs.

End with a Restatement of Your Main Points

The rules that govern the act of kissing, in short, are complex and varied. The human kiss has evolved a long way from its probable origins in the sniff of animal recognition and the warmth of human bonding. It can be a reflexive gesture of greeting or deference, or a carefully planned sign of personal feeling. The first deep kiss, a passionate kiss from one's beloved, the last kiss exchanged between close friends or relatives, the happy kisses for a newborn baby—all evoke powerful emotions that are remembered for life.The simple kiss carries complex meaning, which poets will continue to praise, scientists will continue to explain, and all of us will continue to practice.

> —Leonore Teifer, "The Kiss," *Human Nature*

End with a Generalization

Nothing in the universe has more grandeur than the infinity of the human mind. Even pea-sized computers capable of forecasting the movement of the galaxies are not more wondrous than the mysterious human creature that produced them. The ultimate frontier is not geographical or spatial but intellectual.

> —Norman Cousins, "The Conquest of Pain," *Saturday Review*

End with a Quotation

Sir Richard Livingstone, late vice-chancellor of Oxford, once wrote that "true education is the habitual vision of greatness"—the study of great individuals, great events, and great art and literature. Teachers of English should demand greatness in what their students read and aim for greatness in what their students write. To do less is to condemn the next generation to mumbling mediocrity.

> —Edward T. Hall, "Why Americans Can't Write," *Human Nature*

Exercises

1. Discuss the following introductory paragraphs in class. What method is used to begin each paragraph or set of paragraphs? Do they arouse your interest? Why or why not? How do they lead into the body of the paper?

   a. The China-Viet Nam War wilted like a frostbitten blossom last week. China's 100,000 or so infantry and armored troops arrested their languid advance 15 to 20 miles inside the Viet Nam border, wheeled, and began a gradual, piecemeal withdrawal. Vietnamese artillery and front-line units of the 70,000-man-strong border defense force put on a show of hot pursuit but coolly refrained from any real, obstructive attack. Judging from the ferocity of each side's victory claims, it seemed safe to conclude that neither side had won—or lost.

—"Windup of a No-Win War," *Time*

b. "Maps speak, and through the language of a map speaks the mind of a society," wrote Barbara Aziz (August 1978). Aziz skewered any lingering beliefs a citizen might have that maps are somehow independent of the people who create them. A 20th-century sophisticate, after all, is likely to regard a Rand-McNally atlas or an *Encyclopedia Britannica* geographical sketch as revealed truth.

But, as Aziz has demonstrated, geographic reality is culturally determined: "Maps, like language, select certain features and ignore others, and like language, maps are cultural expressions of elements significant to a society."

—"Maps and the Mind," *Human Nature*

c. Seething gases and liquids mask its rocky core. Its frigid atmosphere consists mostly of hydrogen and helium. Great cyclones and hurricanes swirl in its turbulent sky, with brilliant red and orange clouds constantly merging and breaking apart in ever changing patterns. Often the turbulence creates trails of sinuous white vapors thousands of miles long. The awesome, forbiddingly beautiful world is that of Jupiter, a planet so large it could swallow more than 1,300 earths.

—"Intimate Glimpses of a Giant," *Time*

d. Skimming down a steep, snow-covered road at Camp David in Maryland's lovely Catoctin Mountains, Jimmy Carter was enjoying the brisk air of an afternoon in the woods when the tip of one of his thin skis caught beneath a crust of rough ice. The President of the United States went down hard. The consequence of this tumble were clearly visible when he returned to snow-paralyzed Washington the next day: an ugly purple bruise the size of a silver dollar over his right eye, several bright red scratches on his cheek, a puffy lip and a slight limp. It took the deftest ministrations of his makeup woman to hide the wounds before public appearances.

The bruising of the President did not stop all week. Despite Carter's efforts to appear decisive and determined in his handling of the nation's affairs, he kept encountering hidden obstacles. And as his standing in U.S. public opinion polls once again sank, world events seemed conspiring to prove his frequently repeated assertion that "the United States cannot control events within other nations."

—"Carter: Black and Blue," *Time*

e. What if it were possible to cut heating costs to a fraction of the current rate? Wouldn't this be worthwhile—particularly if it could be done without spending billions for solar retrofits and insulation, and if the final result would be a healthier, more satisfying heat like that provided by a fireplace or an old-fashioned potbellied stove? I believe we could do it if we would remember that regardless of the problem that faces us, it makes no sense to ignore human nature. In this case, the problem under discussion is the transaction between human beings and a variety of heat sources.

There is an abundance of data on the thermal requirements of heating buildings and none on heating people. We heat buildings in order to heat people (and even that job is often done rather badly). We behave like the mythical primitive who burned down his house in order to cook his pig.

—Edward T. Hall, "Let's Heat People Instead of Houses,"
Human Nature

f. In ten summers of rewarding work at Aphrodisias, a great ruined city of the Greco-Roman age in Turkey's Anatolian uplands, I have learned that past and present often merge. For example, as we excavated the city's agora, or marketplace, we came upon some 300 fragments of inscribed stone panels. Fitted together like a giant jigsaw puzzle, they proved to be exactly what Americans find posted in neighborhood supermarkets today—a table of fixed prices.

In A.D. 301, runaway inflation had threatened to destroy the economy of the Roman Empire. To deal with this situation so closely paralleling that of our own era, the Emperor Diocletian froze all prices. It was his edict, and the prices he established, that we discovered in the agora of Aphrodisias. The roster of items is exhaustive, including commodities as varied as melons and marble, kerchiefs and cattle. Violations of the edict drew severe penalties, even death.

—Kenan T. Erim, "Aphrodisias: Awakened City of Ancient Art,"
National Geographic

g. A man in bright orange trousers asked me to close my eyes and hold his hand. I did as he said. In my other hand he put one end of a forked plastic rod. He held the other side. Then he told me to breathe deeply, clear my mind, and think only of water. The rod pointed into the sky, but as we walked slowly across the grass it was pulled down as if by a magnet. I opened my eyes and saw the rod pointing directly to the ground in front of the fire hydrant on the green in Danville, Vermont.

Dowsing, also called divining, witching, wishing, or striking, is the process of discovering hidden objects by means of a divining rod. Many dowsers claim that the practice goes back to Biblical times, citing the story in Numbers of Moses striking a rock with his rod and water spurting forth. Some say that the Chinese relied on it for the placement of their houses. The image of a man pacing the earth with a divining rod in hand is certainly part of American folklore, but it is an imported rather than native-born practice. The first clear-cut account of dowsing is a report on German mining by Georgius Agricola in *De Re Metallica*, published in 1556. From Germany it spread to the rest of Europe and finally to the United States.

—Nancy Hechinger, "Discovering Human Nature," *Human Nature*

2. Bring to class at least three closing paragraphs from current magazine articles. Be prepared to discuss the techniques used for concluding the respective articles.

3. Write three introductory paragraphs, using one of the methods previously discussed.

4. Write three different types of concluding paragraphs, making sure to leave your reader with a sense of completeness.

CHAPTER 11

Style: The Sentence

Style has been variously defined as the *manner* in which something is said or done, as distinguished from its *content;* as the sum total of *distinctive features* in a piece of writing; and as the *characteristic way* that a writer presents his or her ideas to a reader. Style is also a function of the writing as a whole.

Modes of Developing Sentences

In previous chapters, you used modes to develop ideas in paragraphs and in longer stretches of writing. You can also use modes to develop ideas in sentences. Actually, the modal sentences you construct *will be a function of your writing as a whole* and will be related to your purpose, your subject, and your audience.

If, for example, you are developing ideas in an essay and you are thinking along modal lines (that is, in terms of dividing something into parts, describing, defining, comparing, contrasting, and the like), *many of your individual sentences would develop stylistically along the same lines as the larger patterning of your ideas.* To give a typical example, if your dominant mode in developing an essay is comparison, then you would expect literal or figurative comparisons on the sentence level. What follows is a discussion of the sentence modes that are implicit in the larger patterning of the whole and of ways of constructing such sentences.

Analysis Sentences

Analysis is *the process of dividing a complex subject into its component parts.* To construct a sentence based on the mode of analysis, you begin with a subject thought of as a whole and then divide it into pieces, parts, features, or characteristics:

> The earth's crust consists of two layers: a top layer composed mostly of folded granite and a bottom layer of basalt.

> Running throughout the leaf of a tree is an intricate system of veins and veinlets.

> The word immovable can be divided into three parts—a stem or base (*mov-*), a prefix (*im-*), and a suffix (*-able*).

Description Sentences

Description is *a mode of analysis.* It differs from physical or conceptual analysis, however, in its emphasis on "picturing" its object, i.e., depicting it in concrete, sensory detail. To construct a sentence based on the mode of description, you begin with the subject you want to describe and then add concrete, specific details to it:

> The coral snake is known for its brilliant red and yellow bandings contrasted with black rings which encircle its body.

> His bared breast glistened soft and greasy as though he had sweated out his fat in his sleep.
>
> —Joseph Conrad

> The carpet was red; the table at the foot of the bed was covered with a crimson cloth; the walls were a soft fawn color, with a blush of pink in it; the wardrobe, the toilet-table, the chairs, were of darkly-polished old mahogany.
>
> —Charlotte Bronte

Classification Sentences

Classification is *the process of putting ideas and things into categories according to their common characteristics.* To compose a sentence based on the mode of classification, you divide your subject into categories and indicate the basis of the classification:

> Birds have a variety of ways of sending messages—by voice, by action, and by display of plumage or adornment.

Clouds were first classified in 1803 according to the Latin names for their shapes: *cirrus* for ringlet, *cumulus* for heap, and *stratus* for scattering.

Faucets are of two basic types: compression or washerless.

Exemplification Sentences

Exemplification is *the process of inferring a generalized conclusion from a number of particular cases.* To generate sentences based on the mode of exemplification, you begin with a general statement and then support that statement with representative examples, or you begin with examples and conclude with a generalization:

Animals bed down in every conceivable position: For example, birds sleep while sitting, horses sleep while standing, and silky anteaters curl up and use their bushy tails as blankets.

Tornadoes sweeping across the Great Plains, eddies produced by the stroke of an oar, whirlpools formed when water enters the drain of a tub or sink—all are examples of vortices, whirling cores of fluid that may occur in any liquid or gas.

In constructing sentences based on the modes of discourse, the important thing to remember is that *the modes deal with relationships.* You may not always be able to express all of these relationships in a single sentence. You might have to construct a sequence of sentences, as in the following example, taken from a letter to the editor:

Margaret Thatcher represents many of the virtues that have faded in our nation. She is hard-working, thrifty, self-reliant, and not afraid to believe in herself and her ideals.

The relationship expressed in these two sentences could also be expressed in a single sentence:

Margaret Thatcher represents many of the virtues that have faded in our nation: she is hard-working, thrifty, self-reliant, and not afraid to believe in herself and her ideals.

Definition Sentences

Definition is *the process of stating what a thing is or what a word means.* There are several methods of defining. The following are a few of the most important methods.

To define a word using a formal or logical definition, you indicate the class to which a word belongs and show how it differs from other members of its class:

Arachibutyrophobia is the fear of having peanut butter stick to your mouth.

To define a word using synonyms, you substitute an equivalent, but more familiar, word or phrase for the term to be defined:

The word *epoch* means age.

To define a word etymologically, you state its origin, its historical development, and any changes in its form or meaning:

The word *planet* comes from the Greek word *planetai*, which means "wanderers," and it refers to the erratic way in which the planets seem to drift among the fixed stars.

As you did in constructing sentences using the other modes, in writing sentences based on the mode of definition, you can present your definition in a single sentence or in a sequence of sentences, as indicated below:

The word *Hispanic* originally referred to those people who come from the Iberian peninsula of Spain and Portugal, which is the land of "Hispania." In the U.S., the term *Hispanic* has evolved to refer collectively to those people who speak Spanish or whose origins are in Spain or its former colonies.

Comparison Sentences

Comparison is *the process of examining two or more things in order to establish their similarities.* To generate a sentence based on the mode of comparison, you juxtapose the things you want to compare and use comparison words and phrases to make your comparison explicit:

A wart, like a weed, is annoying and unsightly.

That penguins can run as fast as people is truly remarkable since the length of their stride is but six inches.

Contrast Sentences

Contrast is *the process of examining two or more things in order to establish their differences.* To frame sentences based on the mode of contrast, you follow the same method you used in constructing comparison sentences, emphasizing differences instead of similarities:

> Few substances look less alike than coal and diamonds, yet both are fashioned from carbon.

> Most lizards can close their eyes, but a snake's eyes remain permanently open.

Analogy Sentences

An **analogy** is *an extended comparison based on the idea that if two things are alike in some respects, they must be alike in other respects.* Analogies can be either literal or figurative. To produce a sentence based on the mode of analogy, you compare two or more things, that are otherwise dissimilar:

> Anger is like a stone cast at a wasp's nest.

> Potholes are to cars what gopher holes are to horses.

Narration Sentences

Narration is *the process of recounting a series of actions or events in time.* To construct narrative sentences, you depict a subject in action and, usually, its setting:

> A silver-coated fox came up, sniffed, and padded away.

> The red flag flashes down, the green flag pops up, an air horn blasts—and the long outrigger canoes lunge from the starting line.

Because narration depends on a sequence of actions, narrative sentences seldom appear alone. However, it is possible to tell a complete story in two or three sentences, as the following news stories reveal:

> A three-day party in a suburb was noisy enough to wake the dead, but it didn't disturb one man sitting quietly in the corner. He died on the first day and none of his fellow guests noticed.

> A young man wrote 700 love letters to his girl over two years to get her to marry him. His persistence finally brought results. She

became engaged to the postman who faithfully delivered the letters.

Process Sentences

A **process** is *a series of operations, steps, phases, or changes that bring about a desired end or result.* To create a process sentence, you depict a systematic series of actions, involving a transition from one state or phase to another, leading toward some goal. The most common kinds of sentences based on the mode of process are scientific process sentences:

> The beetle undergoes a complete metamorphosis, progressing from worm to winged form.

> Millions of creatures eat algae and are in turn eaten, in a food chain culminating in the great fish and aquatic mammals.

and directions for doing something:

> To renew and freshen sponges, soak them overnight in salt or baking soda water, and then wash them in dishwater.

> If your car is hard to start on a cold morning, blow hot air on the carburetor with a hair dryer.

Like narrative sentences, process sentences can depict a series of operations, steps, or phases in a single sentence or in a sequence of sentences:

> To remove unsightly bulges from wall paper, slit the bulge with a razor blade. Next, using a knife, insert some paste under the paper. Finally, smooth with a wet sponge.

Cause-and-Effect Sentences

A **cause** is *a person, force, or other agent that brings about an effect.* An **effect** is *anything that has been caused.* To compose cause-and-effect sentences, you connect two or more events in time and show what makes one event lead to the next:

> Drinking any amount of alcohol can impair your ability to drive.

Most of the waves we know best are the result of wind driving against water.

The clothing industry maintains that imports from low-wage nations are causing social problems in the U.S.

Without rain, there can be no crops. Without crops, there is no food, no money, and ultimately no hope.

Exercises

1. Identify the dominant *mode* in each of the following sentences. Then discuss the following questions: In what kind of writing might it have appeared? For what purpose? For what kinds of readers? Does the choice of mode seem appropriate for the writer's purpose?

   a. To most people, the term "wave" denotes any vertical rise or swelling of the sea.

   b. Flaming pink flamingos gathered in thick groups and danced an ancient courtship ritual with necks upstretched.

   c. Venus is mostly carbon dioxide, containing perhaps a little water, but devoid of life-sustaining free oxygen.

   d. Just as a bird ruffles its feathers, a dog or wolf or fox can fluff out its fur to trap air and gain temporary warmth.

   e. Mitosis, or cell division, is the process by which one cell splits into identical twins.

   f. Thin spring ice, formed on a lake during the cold night, glows yellow in the morning sun.

   g. There are three principal categories of mountains: volcanic mountains, block mountains, and folded mountains.

   h. The word *desert* comes from a Latin word meaning "abandoned."

   i. To rid tired eyes of redness and puffiness, place cold cucumbers on your eyelids.

   j. Plain generic packaging started sweeping through U.S. grocery chains five years ago. The result was lower prices for many standard items, ranging from bathroom tissue to light bulbs.

2. Take any *five* of the above sentences or sentence units and *five* sentences from the section dealing with "Modes of Developing Sentences."

Rewrite each sentence or group of sentences. Combine several sentences into one. Divide a single sentence into two or more. Create a context and purpose for each rewrite.

3. Bring to class *ten* sentences, from books or magazines, each in a different mode. Distribute copies to other members of the class. Be prepared to discuss the context, purpose, audience, and kind of writing.

4. Compose *ten* sentences of your own, using a different mode to develop each sentence. Consider a possible context, purpose, and audience for each.

Rhetorical Sentence Types

In the previous section, you examined sentence types that are related to a dominant mode and that function in a larger stretch of writing to further the writer's purpose and attention to subject and audience. In this section, you will be looking at a variety of rhetorical sentence types that can function in any kind of discourse, for any of the writer's purposes, and for various audiences.

The Loose Sentence

The **loose sentence** is *one in which the most important thought* (expressed in the main clause) *comes at the beginning of the sentence, and the subordinate ideas* (in the form of modifying phrases and clauses) *come at the end.* The loose sentence can be brought to a close at almost any point after the main subject and predicate. The loose sentence is a less formal, more conversational sentence than other rhetorical types. To construct a loose sentence, you put your main idea at the beginning of your sentence and your subordinate ideas at the end:

> *They came from outer space,* thousands of them, clinging to the buildings and making people's skin crawl.

> *We came to the end of our journey at last,* feeling very tired after having to put up with bad roads and terrible weather.

> *She had left him, really,* packing up suddenly in a cold quiet fury, stabbing him with her elbows when he tried to get his arms

around her, now and again cutting him to the bone with a short sentence expelled through her clenched teeth.

—Katherine Anne Porter

The Periodic Sentence

The **periodic sentence** is *one in which the main idea is not completed until near the end of the sentence.* The main idea is delayed by qualifying phrases and clauses which come at the beginning of the sentence. The periodic sentence is characterized by length and complexity of structure. The advantage of placing the main idea at the end of the sentence is that it holds the reader's attention and focuses it on the most important part of the sentence. To compose a periodic sentence, you position the subordinate ideas at the beginning of your sentence and the main ideas at the end:

> Whipped together by a storm, traveling at different speeds, *waves may combine in superwaves* that can rise out of the driving, howling sea *to rake the biggest ship.*

> When a writer begins to be successful, when he begins to soar, outwardly but especially inwardly, then, to save him from infatuation, *he needs to be pelted with bitter apples.*

—Van Wyck Brooks

> Crossing a bare common, in snow puddles, at twilight, under a clouded sky, without having in my thoughts any occurrence of special good fortune, *I have enjoyed a perfect exhilaration.*

—Ralph Waldo Emerson

The Cumulative Sentence

The **cumulative sentence** combines elements of two traditional sentence types: the loose sentence and the periodic sentence. It consists of a *sentence base* and one or more *free* or *sentence modifiers.* The sentence base contains the main idea. The sentence modifiers add subordinate ideas to the base.

Grammatically, the base consists of the *main subject* and the *main verb,* together with any *bound modifiers* (articles, adjectives, adverbs, phrases, and clauses that can't be freely moved about in the sentence):

1 The cumulative *sentence* in unskillful hands is unsteady,

The sentence modifiers are words, phrases, and clauses that qualify or add details to the base and that can be freely moved about in the sentence:

    2 allowing a writer to ramble on,
      3 adding modifier after modifier,
        4 until the reader is almost overwhelmed,
          5 because the writer's central idea is lost.

To generate a cumulative sentence *in its loose form*, you begin with a base and then add to it one or more sentence modifiers:

1 The cumulative sentence in unskilled hands is unsteady,
  2 allowing a writer to ramble on,
    3 adding modifier after modifier,
      4 until the reader is almost overwhelmed,
        5 because the writer's central idea is lost.

To generate a cumulative sentence *in its periodic form*, you begin with the sentence modifiers and put the base clause at the end of the sentence:

  2 Allowing a writer to ramble on,
    3 adding modifier after modifier,
      4 until the reader is almost overwhelmed,
        5 because the writer's central idea is lost,
1 the cumulative sentence in unskillful hands is unsteady,

There is a third type of cumulative sentence that seems to fall between the loose and the periodic. To construct this kind of sentence, you put the sentence modifier in the middle of the sentence, between the subject and the verb:

The ostrich, that giant among living birds, attains a stature of eight feet.

Rewritten in a diagrammatic form to offset the modifier, the sentence looks like this:

  2 that giant among living birds
1 The ostrich, / , attains a stature of eight feet.

The style of the cumulative sentence in its loose form is much like that of spoken prose, in which the speaker makes a point, amplifies it, and then expands, limits, or illustrates it by successive phrases and clauses. In its periodic form, the cumulative sentence is more formal and emphatic.

The Parallel Sentence

The **parallel sentence** is *one in which two or more words, phrases, or clauses are joined together in a coordinate relationship using similar grammatical constructions.* To construct parallel sentences, you can join words, phrases, and clauses in parallel structure:

> You cannot serve God and
> Mammon.

> He had a broad head,
> a large nose, and
> an athletic body.

> The canals twist and turn without any plan,
> and
> the alleys follow the same disordered pattern.

The Balanced Sentence

The **balanced sentence** is *one that uses parallel structure, but arranges the parts in such a way that they are of approximately the same length.* Word is balanced against word, phrase against phrase, and clause against clause. Because both the parallel sentence and the balanced sentence depend upon similarity of structure, they can be used effectively with the mode of comparison. And like other rhetorical types, they can also be used with the other modes, in any kind of writing, for any of the writer's intentions.

To compose a balanced sentence, you join two or more sentences in parallel structure, making sure that the parts are of almost equal length:

> Some insects bite,
> some sting, and
> some simply stink.

> The good lawyer knows the law;
> the clever one knows the judge.

> First build your house, and
> then think of your furniture.

The Antithetical Sentence

The **antithetical sentence** is *a special type of parallel sentence in which contrasting ideas are juxtaposed in balanced or parallel structures.* Because the antithetical sentence is based on the principle of contrast, it can be used effectively with the mode of contrast. Antithetical sentences can help you to achieve emphasis, clarity, and force in your writing.

To produce antithetical sentences, you juxtapose contrasting ideas in parallel structure:

> Moths spin cocoons;
> butterflies do not.

> The sea can build
> as well as destroy.

> French cuisine in its classic forms is
> mostly verbs and modifiers;
> high Japanese cooking is by contrast
> all nouns.

The Repeated Word Sentence

The **repeated word sentence** is *one in which the same word or group of words is repeated in various positions in a sentence or in a sequence of sentences* for emphasis or rhythm. To compose a repeated word sentence, you repeat a word or a phrase at the beginning of successive sentences, at the end of a sequence of sentences, or in various positions within the sentence:

> *There are* crippled *children* who want to walk so bad it hurts. *There are children* for whom even the simple act of moving a pencil becomes an agonizing test of determination. *There are children* whose courage in therapy would astonish you.

> The Italians are wise before *the deed*, the Germans in *the deed*, and the French after *the deed*.

> *Rest* comes from *unrest* and *unrest* from *rest*.

> If a thing is *worth doing*, it's *worth doing* well.

The Inverted Sentence

The **inverted sentence** is *one in which the normal word order of the basic elements is reversed for purposes of emphasis.* To generate an inverted sentence, you reverse the position of the words or phrases:

> After a storm comes a calm.

> A more miserable time I never had.

> What people see on television they remember.

The Elliptical Sentence

The **elliptical sentence** is *one in which a part has deliberately been omitted, but can easily be supplied by the context.* An elliptical sentence can add conciseness and emphasis to your writing. To frame an elliptical sentence, you omit those parts of the sentence that can easily be inferred:

> None so deaf as those who will not hear.

> Easier said than done.

> In November, the days grow short, and the nights cold.

The Parenthetical Sentence

The **parenthetical sentence** is *one in which an explanatory, qualifying, or digressive word, phrase, or clause is inserted into the sentence in such a way that it does not have any grammatical connection with the rest of the sentence.* The parenthetical expression adds a bit of information to the main idea of the sentence, but it also interrupts the thought; the sentence would be grammatically complete without it. Nevertheless, the parenthetical sentence can be useful in your writing to give emphasis, to add qualifying information, to add interesting asides, and to enhance the rhythm of your sentences.

To form a parenthetical sentence, you enclose supplementary explanatory or qualifying material, setting it off by commas, dashes, or parentheses:

> It is, as far as I know, the truth.

There is really nothing—except, of course, the money—to keep me here.

Red (especially dark red) depicts violence or deep emotion.

Exercises

1. Identify the *rhetorical type* to which the following sentences belong. Some sentences may belong to more than one sentence type. Imagine a context for each sentence. Then, tell what you can about the writer's purpose, the kind of writing, and the audience for each.

   a. Welcome to Hawaii, a place as unique and varied as its flowers.

   b. The desert is a forbidding wasteland—sun-seared and wind-scoured, waterless and endless, empty of shelter and devoid of life.

   c. Generals pray for war and doctors for disease.

   d. To the west are the mountains.

   e. In the trunks of trees, in dead limbs, in weathered fence posts, and in the wooden structures that humans build, myriad insects dig, bore, and tunnel.

   f. Streams run; glaciers merely crawl.

   g. Unlike an orator who has a date with a microphone, the writer of a letter must address an audience of one. Unlike a politican pursuing an office, he has no aides in the background to turn to for help. Unlike a performer on a stage, his only applause is a thankful thoughtful letter written by someone in return.

      —1982 Magazine Publishers Association

   h. I don't agree, to be honest, with that statement.

   i. Stray dogs, alone or in packs, roam the streets of inner cities across the U.S.

   j. The sun appears highest in the summer, sinks until midwinter, and then rises again.

   k. You can't control the purity of your tap water, but you can control the purity of your drinking water.

   l. Love makes time pass away, and time makes love pass away.

   m. Pubs and palaces, London has plenty of both.

n. The Roman empire had many virtues and many vices.

2. Bring to class ten sentences from books or magazines, each of which exemplifies a particular rhetorical sentence type. If possible, choose sentences that fit several patterns. Distribute copies to other members of the class. Be prepared to discuss the context, purpose, audience, and kind of writing.

3. Compose one loose sentence, one periodic sentence, and one cumulative sentence for each of the following base clauses:

   a. The music began.

   b. The sky outside was changing.

   c. The door began to open slowly.

   d. The aroma was tantalizing.

   e. The dentist began his work.

4. Bring to class a single paragraph that uses a variety of rhetorical sentence types and discuss their use.

5. Pick out a passage from your reader that has a variety of rhetorical sentence types. Then discuss the function of each in relation to the kind of writing, the writer's purpose, the audience, and the subject.

6. Compose one sentence for each of the ten rhetorical types discussed in this chapter (loose, periodic, cumulative, parallel, balanced, antithetical, repeated word, inverted, elliptical, and parenthetical).

7. Identify both the sentence modes and the rhetorical sentence types in the following passages. The first three passages are from works of fiction. The last is from a speech. What effect does sentence style have on meaning? On tone? On the writer's audience?

   a. Soon afterwards they retired, Mama in her big oak bed on one side of the room, Emilio and Rosy in their boxes full of straw and sheepskins on the other side of the room.

   The moon went over the sky and the surf roared on the rocks. The roosters crowed the first call. The surf subsided to a whispering surge against the reef. The moon dropped toward the sea. The roosters crowed again.

   The moon was near down to the water when Pepe rode on a winged horse to his home flat. His dog bounced out and circled the horse yelping with pleasure. Pepe slid off the saddle to the ground. The weathered little shack was silver in the moonlight and the square shadow of it was black to the north and east. Against the east the piling mountains were misty with light, their tops melted into the sky.

—John Steinbeck, "Flight"

b. It came on great oiled, resilient, striding legs. It towered thirty feet above half of the trees, a great evil god, folding its delicate watchmaker's claws close to its oily reptilian chest. Each lower leg was a piston, a thousand pounds of white bone, sunk in thick ropes of muscle, sheathed over in a gleam of pebbled skin like the mail of a terrible warrior. Each thigh was a ton of meat, ivory, and steel mesh. And from the great breathing cage of the upper body those two delicate arms dangled out front, arms with hands which might pick up and examine men like toys, while the snake neck coiled. And the head itself, a ton of sculptured stone, lifted easily upon the sky. Its mouth gaped, exposing a fence of teeth like daggers. Its eyes rolled, ostrich eggs, empty of all expression save hunger. It closed its mouth in a death grin. It ran, its pelvic bones crushing aside trees and bushes, its taloned feet clawing damp earth, leaving prints six inches deep wherever it settled its weight. It ran with a gliding ballet step, far too poised and balanced for its ten tons. It moved into a sunlit area warily, its beautifully reptile hands feeling the air.

—Ray Bradbury, "A Sound of Thunder"

c. None of them knew the color of the sky. Their eyes glanced level, and were fastened upon the waves that swept toward them. These waves were of the hue of slate, save for the tops, which were of foaming white, and all of the men knew the colors of the sea. The horizon narrowed and widened, and dipped and rose, and at all times its edge was jagged with waves that seemed to thrust up in points like rocks. Many a man ought to have a bathtub larger than the boat which here rode upon the sea. These waves were most wrongfully and barbarously abrupt and tall, and each froth-top was a problem in small-boat navigation.

—Stephen Crane, "The Open Boat"

d. We observe today not a victory of party but a celebration of freedom— symbolizing an end as well as a beginning—signifying renewal as well as change. For I have sworn before you and Almighty God the same solemn oath our forebears prescribed nearly a century and three-quarters ago.

The world is very different now. For man holds in his mortal hands the power to abolish all forms of human poverty and all forms of human life. And yet the same revolutionary beliefs for which our for-bears fought are still at issue around the globe—the belief that the rights of man come not from the generosity of the state but from the hand of God.

We dare not forget today that we are the heirs of that first revolution. Let the word go forth from this time and place, to friend and foe alike, that the torch has been passed to a new generation of Americans—born in this century, tempered by war, disciplined by a hard and bitter peace, proud of our ancient heritage, and unwilling to witness or permit the slow undoing of those human rights to which this nation has always been committed, and to which we are committed today at home and around the world.

Let every nation know, whether it wishes us well or ill, that we shall pay any price, bear any burden, meet any hardship, support any friend, oppose any foe to assure the survival and the success of liberty.

—John F. Kennedy, inaugural address, 1961

CHAPTER 12

Style: Word Choice

Whether or not you write extensively, you are faced constantly with the problem of choosing between two or more words. Quite often you make your choices unconsciously, but the choice still has to be made. You may have an intuitive feeling for language, but the problem is using words effectively in writing. Communication of some kind can be carried on with a small or imprecise vocabulary, and such communication can at times be moderately effective. But to have a small number of words at your disposal is to limit your resources, and intelligent choices among words cannot be made unless you have a store of words from which to choose.

"But I don't know much about words," one student protested, and then proceeded to write an imaginative and original paper about diction:

No Experience

While I'm thinking to myself, "What dialect? I haven't had any experience with dialect!" a sudden but not uncommon wail is heard through the hall. "Ay-un, kin I borrrr-oww you-ur pi-unk le-o-tards?" (TRANSL: Ann, can I borrow your pink leotards?) "Whaaaaa?" is the extremely nasal and immediate reply. "Pi-unk le-o-tards, do ye-u hay-ave iny I kin way-er?" Ignoring another "Whaaaaa?" the Voice goes on to implore, "Tha-ey hay-ave te-u be pi-unk, I cay-n't way-er bu-lack ones. I'ull wash they-um ou-oot ay-und ever-y-th-yang. Pu-lease?" The resultant reply from down the hall is very long and very unintelligible, but it doesn't daunt the seeker-of-leotards. "Way-ell, tha-ey cay-un be ao-paque whe-ite wuns. Way-ell?" Then, just as suddenly as it began, it is over. How can I concentrate on dialects with such interruptions?

Dialect, dialect, it's driving me bananas! A friend wanders in, momentarily halting my leap from the window.

"Hi. Yeah, well . . . watcha doin'?"

"Uh. Nothin' . . . Inglish . . ."

"Uh . . ."

"Well, I can't write anything, ya know?"

"Um . . . yeah . . . I know . . ."

"Um . . ."

"Ya know what I mean?"

"Um . . ."

After another half-hour or so of mutual commiseration, the friend wanders out and once again I am left without an idea in my head.

Before I can really get into some deep thinking on the subject, my mother calls. And while "discussing" money matters with her I hear another conversation in the background. "Oh, you sweet wittle baby-kins," my sister croons to the dog. "You is such a good wittle doggie-poo. Yes, um is de sweetest . . ." etc., etc. After hanging up, still nothing— except homesickness for my doggie-poo. I try thinking of something other than dialect, such as jargon, slang, idioms. Nothing!

Turning on the TV with the desperate hope of finding inspiration, I hear some impeccably dressed newscaster intone the words, "And this, just in. A usually reliable Pentagon source, who declined to be identified, has vigorously denied suggesting that published speculation, admittedly based on fragmentary and unconfirmed reports not available to the press, regarding allied troop movements in or near unspecified areas of Indochina and purportedly involving undisclosed numbers of South Vietnamese, Cambodian, Laotian, and perhaps American armed personnel is false, although he cautioned that such published speculation could be dangerously misleading and potentially divisive." The mind is boggled! And the sad truth being that a boggled mind with no experience with the subject might as well abandon all hope of an English paper.

If you are like this student, you have had considerable experience with words, but you cannot always bring this knowledge to conscious awareness. Therefore, you might need a more systematic approach to word choice and vocabulary study.

Much of the traditional advice offered for enlarging your vocabulary is sound:

1. Buy a good dictionary and use it frequently.
2. Obtain a good thesaurus.
3. Try to bring new words into your writing and conversation.
4. Read widely in literature of all kinds.
5. Read aloud passages of unusual force and beauty.

Exercises

1. Write an essay, similar to the student essay on dialect, in which you transcribe as accurately as you can the speech of friends, relatives, acquaintances, radio or television newscasters, and the like, and place these transcriptions into a coherent narrative.

2. Bring to class five new words in the context of a short passage from a magazine ad, newspaper, or book, and discuss their meanings, their effectiveness in context, and their possible origins.

In addition to these more traditional ways of developing your vocabulary, another way of enlarging your vocabulary and increasing your sensitivity to language is by formal study, and it is with the formal study of words that we will be primarily concerned in this chapter.

Denotation and Connotation

Choose words for their literal as well as for their suggested meanings. The **denotation** of a word is *its literal or dictionary meaning.* The **connotation** of a word is the sum total of *its suggested or associative meanings.* Denotations are emotionally or morally neutral, while connotations convey an attitude toward their referents. Words have meanings beyond those in the dictionary. For example, if you look up the word *house* in the dictionary, you will find that the word refers to "a building or shelter that serves as living quarters for people." Then if you look up the related word *home,* you will notice that one of its primary meanings is "a family's place of residence." The **dictionary meaning** of these words is called their *denotative* meaning. In addition to their literal meanings, these words also evoke feelings and emotions and various associations. The word *house* seems to be the more neutral of the two words. You seldom hear or read about someone defending a house, but books and movies are filled with stories about people defending their homes. So the word *home* seems to carry with it stronger connotations than the word *house.* In fact, each of the following synonyms for the words *house* and *home* has slightly different meanings and different connotations from the others:

habitation	residence	retreat
abode	homestead	haunt
dwelling	hearth	nest
lodging	fatherland	quarters
domicile	country	hiding place

The first step in using a word in your writing, then, is to be sure that you understand its basic or referential meaning. If you do not, look it up in the dictionary. The second step is to consider its context, since the context of a word is also an important determinant of its meaning. Notice, for example, the difference in meaning in the words *house* and *home* in the following contexts:

People make houses.
People construct houses.
People make homes.
People construct homes.
People build houses, families make homes.

A third step is to consider the associated meanings of the word you are using. Would a reader be offended by the word, indifferent to it, aroused by it, or persuaded by it? Consider, for example, the differences in connotation of the following sentences, achieved by the substitution of a single word:

It's not much, but it's my *home.*
It's not much, but it's my *habitation.*
It's not much, but it's my *dwelling.*
It's not much, but it's my *residence.*
It's not much, but it's my *domicile.*
It's not much, but it's my *lodging.*
It's not much, but it's my *quarters.*
It's not much, but it's my *hiding place.*

Many connotations are individual and personal and depend on the writer's past experiences with the word and with the idea or thing to which the word refers. For example, for some people the word *snake* has unpleasant associations. For others, the words *country, patriotism, communism, fascism, totalitarianism, socialism, left wing, right wing, radical, liberal, conservative, Republican,* and *Democrat* have emotional overtones. In addition to any personal meanings and associations that words might have for us, there are some meanings and associations that are shared with people as a group. Because you were brought up in a certain country and lived in a particular state, or city, or neighborhood, you hold in common with the people there certain attitudes, beliefs, and feelings about words and about the things to which they refer. But more often than not, the connotation of a word is less fixed than its denotation.

Exercises

1. Explain the differences in denotation and connotation of the following sets of words:

   a. exist, be, subsist, live, vegetate, prevail, pass the time

   b. confusion, disarray, jumble, mess, turmoil, ferment, disturbance, up-roar, rumpus, fracas, disorder

   c. crowd, gathering, throng, multitude, rabble, mob, horde

   d. child, brat, kid, urchin, youngster, tot, youth

   e. spit, sputter, splutter, drool, drivel, slaver, slabber, slobber

   f. meal, repast, spread, banquet, feast, feed

   g. hard, rigid, stubborn, stiff, firm, starchy, unbending, unyielding, inflexible

   h. sea, ocean, main, briny deep, waters, deep, high seas

   i. woman, skirt, lady, broad, female, the fair sex, chick, dame

   j. fat, corpulent, plump, stout, portly, burly, well-fed, fleshy, pudgy, paunchy, chubby

2. Make up sentences illustrating as accurately as possible one of the following sets of words. Use your dictionary if necessary.

   a. rash, incautious, imprudent, heedless, careless, reckless, wild, foolhardy

   b. loathe, dislike, resent, detest, hate, abhor, disgust, scorn

   c. vain, conceited, self-assured, self-satisfied, pretentious

   d. friend, acquaintance, intimate, associate, buddy, bosom pal, comrade, chum, sidekick

   e. fondness, love, affection, tenderness, attachment, passion, rapture, adoration, enchantment

3. Discuss the differences in connotation of the following proper names:

   a. Lulu, Lucile, Matilda, Agatha, Maggie, Percy, Elmer, Hugh, Jud, Edgar, Francis, Henry

   b. Gloria, Ruby, Christy, Stella, Laura, Sylvia, Robin, Scarlet

   c. Josephine/Josie, Marian/Mary, Robert/Bob, William/Will, Susan/Sue, Stephen/Steve, Katherine/Cathy, Thomas/Tom

   d. Jennifer, Elizabeth, Roberta, Florence, Alicia, Madeline, Melanie, Emily

   e. Achilles, Atlas, Hercules, Alfred, Atilla, Merlin, Casanova, Richard, Leonardo, Hero, Aristotle

4. Write an essay in which you discuss the denotative and connotative meanings of words in a letter to the editor or in a magazine advertisement.

5. Discuss the differences in connotation of the following brand names:

   a. Tide, Duz, Lux, All, Rinso, Cheer, Oxydol, Cold Power

   b. Winston, Camels, Lucky Strike, True, Kent, Salem, Viceroy, L&M, Virginia Slims, Marlboro

   c. Duster, Dart, Cheyenne, Pinto, Mustang, Charger, Continental, Imperial, Monarch, Jaguar, Rabbit, Bug

   d. Colgate, Aim, Pepsodent, Crest, Close-up, Pearl Drops, McCleans, Strike, Gleem

   e. Ivory, Palmolive, Dove, Joy, Downy, Borax, Clorox, Purex

6. Write five sentences in which you use the same word in each sentence, each time changing the connotation slightly.

Some categories of words seem to have the power to produce an immediate reaction in people. One category is words pertaining to everyday living such as *mother, father, home, marriage, bride, groom, divorce, widow,* and *God.* Another category is abstract words, such as *honor, virtue, pride, patriotism, truth, love, justice, valor, respect, duty, piety, freedom,* and *liberty.* A third category consists of proper names, especially the names of people who are in the public eye and who stir up emotional reactions: for example, Ayatollah Khomeini, Fidel Castro, and Yassir Arafat. A final category is taboo words. Taboo words, especially profane and obscene words, shock and offend many people. They may be used to create attention, to discredit someone, to provoke confrontations, and to provide a kind of catharsis for the user.

Exercises

1. Give ten examples of emotion-laden words with which you are familiar and discuss their effects on you and the reasons for their effects.

2. What obscene words do you find offensive? Why do you find them offensive?

3. What makes a word obscene or taboo? Are people's attitudes toward taboo words changing? Is there a context in which obscenity might be justified?

4. Discuss the use of euphemisms that people employ to avoid mentioning the blunter taboo words.

Concrete and Abstract Words

Use concrete words to present a vivid picture to the reader's mind. **Concrete words** refer to *actual, specific things in experience.* More than any other words, concrete words bring us closest to immediate sensation. They appeal to the reader's sense of touch, taste, smell, sight, or hearing. They can be especially effective in narrative and descriptive writing, as the following student sentences illustrate:

> The teakettle sat on the stove boiling, the water rumbling against the metal sides, the steam rising in puffs through the top, disappearing into the air only moments after its escape, blowing a shrill whistle as I ran to lift it from the fire.

> About noon, Mom sliced up thick, uneven chunks of homemade bread, covering them with slabs of pink ham and wedges of creamy cheese; then she set out tumblers of foamy milk and clinking glasses of cola.

Not all writing is concrete, nor does it have to be. But even in expository writing, you can be concrete in your choice of supporting details, in your examples, and in your illustrations.

Abstract words *are words that refer to qualities (hot, cold, good, bad), relationships (existence, quantity, order, number) and ideas (curiosity, inquiry, judgments, credulity).* They are likely to be Latinate words and are usually longer and more complex than Anglo-Saxon words.

Abstract words are frequently used to express complex ideas. They can give fine distinctions to thought, and they are often used to convey technical or specialized ideas. They are often learned words, words found more in written than in spoken English. If you engage in any serious discussion of ideas from law, science, medicine, psychology, philosophy, or politics, you will make some use of abstract words. You must use abstract words with care. Otherwise, your writing can become vague, obscure, and inaccurate, as in the following passage taken from a student theme:

> Loneliness is an appalling ordeal, encasing its victim in a desolate world. If he is to survive, the individual must learn to cope with his dilemma. To dispossess this perplexity requires the careful observance of the sufferer's habitat, recreation, and thoughts.
>
> The victim of loneliness must use the eyes of Argus when choosing his environmental habitat. He should try to find a location in the midst of a mass of extroverts. Their gregarious characteristics might draw the victim into their circle, curing him of his problem. If this desired location cannot be found, his abode should be in the approximate area of a center of communal entertainment. This will, in all likelihood, give him a temporary reprieve from the torment of his plight. Under no circumstances should the individual choose a secluded dwelling. Seclusion only adds to the pain, driving him deeper into the depths of his despair.

Phrases such as "appalling ordeal," "dispossess this perplexity," "the sufferer's habitat," "environmental habitat," and the like obscure rather than advance this writer's thought. Not only does the misuse of the abstract words obscure the writer's full meaning, but these words also make the writing seem stuffy and affected. Do not indulge in a fondness for abstract words for their own sake. When you do use them, try to use them with some clarity and precision. Your main task as a writer is actually to combine the abstract with the concrete. If you have been operating at a very high level of abstraction in your writing, you will want to narrow down occasionally and give some concrete illustrations.

General and Specific Words

Choose general words to express general ideas. Use specific words to supply exact details.

A **general word** is *one that applies to many things, to a collectiv-*

ity, to the whole. Any word that takes in a *group* of particulars, in which these particulars are thought of as parts of a whole, is a general word. If, however, a word refers to only a few of these particulars, to the parts, the word is specific. A **specific word** is *one that applies to particular, unique, and distinctive things.* A specific word calls forth a distinct mental image. Thus, the word *clothing* is general, but the term *yellow striped pants* evokes a specific image.

Do not confuse general and specific words with abstract and concrete words. A general word is not necessarily an abstract word, nor is a concrete word necessarily specific. For example, the word *dog* is a general word because it can refer to many animals, but it is obviously not abstract. On the other hand, neither is it very specific, although it is concrete. To make the idea to which the word *dog* refers specific, you need to make the word more particular. For instance, the words *cur, mutt,* and *hound* call forth more distinct mental images than does the word *dog.* Usually, when your instructors ask you to make your writing more concrete, they want you to be both concrete and specific.

The terms *general* and *specific* are relative. A word may be specific in relation to one word, yet general in relation to another. Words specify in varying degrees. In writing, the context often indicates whether a word is being used in a general sense or in a particular sense. *Athlete* is more general than *fighter,* but *fighter* is more general than *Muhammad Ali. Fragrance* is more definite than *odor. Bird* is more general than *thrush; thrush* is more general than *robin.* In your writing, you want to be sure that you are aware of the difference. At times you will want to use general terms, but other times you may want to choose a more vivid and precise word to present the mind of your readers with a more definite picture.

Exercises

1. What is the purpose of the abstract words in the following sentences? What happens to the meaning if concrete words are substituted for the abstract words? Why do the writers of these sentences use abstract words instead of concrete words?

   a. Today's L&M is rich, mellow, distinctively smooth.

   b. Volvo gives you luxury, quality, and a sense of elegance that other so-called luxury cars can't match.

c. Winston gives me real taste and real pleasure; in my book, that's the only reason to smoke.

d. Armstrong carpets give you the easy elegance and warmth of rich autumn hues.

e. Through the years, V.O. has stood apart as a whiskey uncompromising in quality, with a tradition of craftsmanship that has made it The First Canadian in smoothness.

2. Discuss in class your attitudes toward abstract words such as *truth, honor, courage, patriotism, virtue, love,* and *loyalty.* Cite specific experiences in the use of these words, avoidance of them, attempts to articulate them, and so forth.

3. Rewrite the following sentences. Substitute specific concrete details for the more abstract and general words (for example: general—*It was a cold morning;* concrete—*It was twenty degrees below zero*).

a. We went shopping to get some food.

b. He walked down the street in an unsteady manner.

c. They tried to get money from him by dishonest means.

d. The dishes fell to the floor with a loud noise.

e. The dog gave a high, excited bark.

f. He looked at her in an angry way.

g. She had a funny expression on her face as she talked.

h. Slowly he departed from the room.

4. Describe a scene, an event, or an experience using abstract words. Then describe the same scene using concrete words.

5. Paraphrase the following proverbs, eliminating the concrete and specific diction, including the figures of speech:

a. A stitch in time saves nine.

b. A rolling stone gathers no moss.

c. A new broom sweeps clean.

d. When the cat's away, the mice will play.

e. Every cloud has a silver lining.

f. A bird in the hand is worth two in the bush.

g. You can't teach an old dog new tricks.

h. Birds of a feather flock together.

i. Barking dogs never bite.

j. Still water runs deep.

Figurative Language

Use figures of speech to increase concreteness and to secure vividness
in your writing. One student began a paper about an experience she had
while working in the library with this vivid figure of speech:

> Maybe I shouldn't write on this particular topic, but at the moment it is
> the only thing on my mind. The experience is too fresh and disturbing. It
> lingers like a great burn from a popcorn popper, stinging and irritating my
> thoughts.

> —Patti

Not only did the grease-burn comparison effectively convey her feelings about her experience in a way that few abstractions could, but also
it was interesting. It captured my attention. It made me want to read
on.

The **figurative meaning** of a word is *based on a comparison of
unlike things.* To illustrate this, let us look at a couple of examples:

The leopard cannot change his spots.
When the wolf comes in the door, love creeps out the window.

In the first sentence, the leopard is obviously not a leopard but a
metaphor for person. The spots of the leopard symbolize the ways of
humans, so the figurative meaning of the statement is that people
cannot change their ways. In the second statement, the wolf is a
metaphor for poverty, and the meaning of the proverb is that if young
people marry before they have enough money to support themselves,
their love will not last very long.

The **literal meaning** of a word is *its dictionary meaning,* its usual
and customary meaning, as opposed to its figurative meaning. The
literal meaning of the word *dog* is "a domesticated carnivorous mam-
mal, having four legs." But you can call an unattractive person "a dog,"
as in the sentence "I went out last night with a real dog," and it is

obvious that the statement is not literally true. Or you can use the word *dog* or the related word *cur* to refer to a miserable, contemptible person, as in the expression "You cur," and it is apparent that you are not speaking literally. When you transfer the reference of a word so that it covers other meanings and includes new associations, you are writing figuratively.

The following are some common figures of speech. You can use them to express ideas for which there is no literal equivalent, to explore ideas and relationships, to evoke emotional responses in your reader, and to highlight language as being beautiful and interesting in itself.

A **metaphor** is *a comparison of two unlike things, without the use of "like" or "as."* It is related to the modes of comparison, contrast, and analogy. Of all the figures, it is one of the most common. You can use metaphors in your writing to make abstract ideas concrete, to explore connections among ideas, to clarify your ideas, and to lend force and beauty of expression to your writing:

> Among insect architects, the termite is *the champion skyscraper builder.*

> For doctors, the human eye is *a kind of window* on the body.

> The atmosphere is not *a calm ocean* of air, but a *tossing, unquiet sea,* riven and distorted by *swift currents, furrowed* by *tremendous waves.*

> The walrus swims tirelessly, *gliding along with the easy majesty of a blimp.*

A **dead** or **frozen metaphor** is one that has been used so often that people no longer perceive it as a metaphor. In some instances, people may accept the meaning of a word that was once metaphorical as its ordinary meaning. Typical examples of dead or frozen metaphors are *the mouth of a river, the arm of a chair, the leg of a table, the foot of a mountain, the eye of a needle, the head of a pin.*

A **simile** is *a comparison of two unlike things made explicit by the use of words such as "like" or "as."* Like metaphor, the simile is related to the modes of comparison, contrast, and analogy:

> A drunk driver is *like a loaded gun,* with you *as the target.*

> Aspen leaves flutter in the breeze, *as if a thousand green butterflies were on the twigs, opening and closing their wings.*

The whale's jet-black dorsal fin rises *like the conning tower of a submarine,* then disappears in a long slicing arc.

A woodpecker is *like a chisel:* it digs into wood by knocking out small chips with its bill.

Both metaphor and simile can easily degenerate into trite or stale expressions from overuse. Here are a few examples of worn or stale similes: *as stiff as a board, as black as night, as good as gold, as strong as an ox, as fresh as a daisy, like water off a duck's back, like a bolt from the blue.*

Personification is *the representation of an inanimate object or an abstract idea as if it were a person.* It is closely related to metaphor and to the mode of comparison. In fact, personification is sometimes called personal metaphor:

Fly the *friendly* skies of United.

> —United Airlines ad

The cold and *naked* wind *runs shivering* over the sands . . .

> —John Gould Fletcher

Which of these highly *intelligent* Minolta SLRs is right for you?

> —Minolta Camera ad

Violence *reared* its *ugly* head.

An **allusion** is *a reference to a familiar person, place, or event in literature, history, or the arts in order to explain or illustrate a point.* It is an indirect comparison related to the mode of comparison:

For a few glorious weeks the desert is the loveliest of *Edens.*

She has *the patience of Job.*

Paul Revere was a horse thief.

Metonymy is *a figure of speech which consists of substituting a word or idea for some closely related word or idea.* To write a sentence using metonymy as a mode of expressing your ideas, you substitute a cause for an effect, an effect for a cause, the container for the thing contained, the sign for the thing signified, and the possessor for the thing possessed:

She writes a beautiful *hand.*
(cause-for-effect)

We build *excitement*.
(effect-for-cause)
            —Pontiac ad

The drunkard loves his *bottle*.
(container-for-thing contained)

The *heart* will find a way.
(sign-for-thing signified)

Where do you find *Shakespeare* in the library?
(possessor-for-thing possessed)

In the first sentence, the cause of the handwriting (her *hand*) is
substituted for the effect. In sentence two, the effect *(excitement)* is
substituted for the cause (the automobile). In the third sentence, the
container *(bottle)* substitutes for the thing contained ("liquor" "beer,"
etc.). And in the last sentence, the word *Shakespeare* is substituted for
"Shakespeare's works."

Synechdoche is *a figure of speech which substitutes a whole for a
part, a part for a whole, a genus for a species, or a species for a genus.* It
is related to the mode of analysis, the process of dividing a whole into
its parts; to classification, the process of grouping similar ideas into
classes; and to definition, the process of putting a word to be defined
into a class *(genus)* and then differentiating it *(species)* from other
members of the class:

The *world* considers her a genius.
(whole-for-part)

Those are fine *threads* you have on.
(part-for-whole)

Beware of the *dog*.
(genus-for-species)

Pass me the *Kleenex*, please.
(species-for-genus)

In the first sentence, the word *world* is substituted for "those who
knew her." In the second sentence, the word *threads* is substituted for
"clothes," of which they are a part. You use the words *wheels* and *brain*
in a similar way when you refer to your car as "wheels" and when you
refer to a friend as a "brain." In sentence three, the word *dog* substitutes
for a "specific kind of dog." And in the last sentence, the word *Kleenex*,
which is a particular name brand, takes on the general meaning of

"paper tissue." There are many trade names which have become generalized to such an extent that they substitute for the generic name. *Frigidaire*, for refrigerator, and *Coke*, for any cola, soda pop, or soft drink, are typical examples.

Irony is *the use of words to express an idea that is the opposite of their literal or intended meaning.* To use irony in your writing, you say one thing, but mean another. Because irony is based on opposition, it is related to the mode of contrast and to antithesis:

> That was a *brilliant remark*.
> (i.e., a stupid thing to say)

> Howard Johnson eats *home cooked meals*.
> (Howard Johnson owns a chain of restaurants)

> Murder is one of the *fine arts*.
>
> —paraphrase of Thomas De Quincey

When you use irony to get a laugh at someone else's expense, you are using *ridicule.* When you use irony in a mocking, contemptuous, and bitter manner, you are being *sarcastic.* When you use irony to expose wrong or foolishness, you are using *satire.*

Hyperbole is *an exaggerated or extravagant statement in excess of the facts.* Like irony, it is not intended to be taken literally, and like this figure, it is based on the mode of contrast:

> I'm so hungry *I could eat a bear*.

> You could have *knocked me over with a feather*.

> *I'll die* if I don't pass this course.

> *I'd give my right arm* for a cold glass of water.

An **understatement** is *a figure of speech that means more than it says.* You can use understatement to give your reader the impression that a thing is less important than it really is, to intensify a statement, and to achieve irony. Understatement is closely related to hyperbole, a figure that says more than it means, and to the mode of contrast:

> *I didn't do too badly* in that exam.
> (She got an A+.)

> This is *no small task*.

Not a few people went to see *Rocky III.*

Mohammed Ali was *not a bad fighter.*

A **pun** is *a play on words* for humorous or serious purposes and for emphasis. To construct a sentence using puns, you can *repeat the same word in two different senses:*

> *Close-up* is for *close-ups.*
> > —Toothpaste ad

If we don't *hang* together, we'll *hang* separately.
> > —Benjamin Franklin

> The car that *holds* your family should also *hold* the road.
> > > —Ford ad

You can *use a single word to suggest several meanings:*

Take *Aim* against cavities.
> —Aim toothpaste ad

Small boy to playmate: "There's my mother at the *scream* door again."

You'll get a *run* for your money.
> —U.S. Olympic Committee ad

Why were the Middle Ages called the dark ages?
Because there were so many *knights.*

You can *repeat words which sound alike, but which are different in spelling and meaning:*

Call me *cousin,* but *cozen* me not.

They were more *sin-seared* than *sincere.*

To get *ahead,* get *a head.*

Alliteration is *the repetition of the same initial sound in two or more words in a sentence.* You can use alliteration in your writing to emphasize an idea and to make it easier to remember:

Anything *c*reepy and *c*rawly is an insect to many people.

Here's a *l*ight and *l*ucious *l*emony piefilling you don't have to cook.

—Borden ad

The *s*weltering *s*ummer *s*un is turning the house into a *s*ticky, *s*teaming *s*weatbox.

*F*rumpy little *f*rocks with *f*labby *f*it and zero style are just not what we think sewing's all about.

—McCall's Patterns ad

Assonance is *the repetition of similar vowel sounds.* You can use assonance in your writing to create a pleasing combination of sounds, to emphasize important ideas, to secure an emotional effect in your readers, and to present your ideas with wit and humour:

Everything's better with Blue B*o*nn*e*t *o*n *i*t.

—Blue Bonnet Margarine

We think that we shall never s*ee* a service station as lovely as a tr*ee*.

—Shell Oil Co.

Better to ask the w*a*y than to go astr*a*y.

Consonance is the repetition of similar consonant sounds at the end of two or more syllables, words, or lines. Consonance is the counterpart of assonance, and you can use it to achieve similar effects in your writing:

Winston tastes goo*d* like a cigarette shoul*d*.

Hate the gra*y*? Wash it awa*y*.

Inspira*tion* is ninety-percent perspira*tion*.

Judge people by their dee*ds*, not by their cree*ds*.

Exercises

1. Pick out the figures of speech in the following sentences. There may be several figures in the same sentence. Can you guess at the writer's intention in using the figure? Is the figure effective? Many of the sentences are taken from magazines and books. In what kind or writing might those sentences have appeared? For what audiences?

   a. On a map, the river is marked by a snaking blue line, somehow suggesting a broad rush of water.

   b. The smart way to make a sensational, scrumptious strawberry shortcake.

   c. The explosion created no little excitement.

   d. Whereas most birds suggest conventional aircraft, hummingbirds operate more like helicopters.

   e. The fuel injected engine came instantly alive.

   f. *Daughter:* "Father . . . This is Marvin! He's asked for my hand."
      Father: "It's the whole package or nothing, Marv."

      —Wizard of Id

   g. She has a good head for figures.

   h. Bare face giveth and Bare face taketh away.

      —Bare Face acne skin medicine ad

   i. Send plain ice cream to Sundae school.

      —Kraft ad

   j. I'd walk a mile for a Camel.

      —Camel ad

   k. The White House vetoed the bill.

   l. Rest assured.

      —Mattress ad

   m. After your fling, watch for the sting.

   n. Lost credit is like a broken mirror.

   o. Again and again, new Olay Beauty Bar cleanses innocence into your skin.

      —Olay ad

p. A pickle by any other name is not a rose.

   —Rose Brand pickle ad

q. Health is better than wealth.

r. Illiterate? Write now for free help.

s. To the naked eye the stars glitter like silver sequins, spangling the black fabric of the sky.

2. Go to the library, get a book of proverbs, and select five proverbs which illustrate a different use of figurative language.

3. Select an article or story from your reader that makes extensive use of figurative language. Discuss the function of the figures in relation to the writer's purpose, subject, and audience.

4. Compose five original sentences, using as many different figures of speech in each sentence as you can.

5. Select a brief prose passage from your reader or from some other source that uses figurative language. Then rewrite the passage using literal language.

6. Discuss the use of figurative language in the following passages. The first is from an essay. The second is from a short story. What kinds of figures can you identify in each passage? What seems to be the writer's intention in using them? Are these figures effective in achieving the writer's intention?

   a. Wit is a lean creature with a sharp inquiring nose, whereas humor has a kindly eye and comfortable girth. Wit, if it be necessary, uses malice to score a point—like a cat it is quick to jump—but humor keeps the peace in an easy chair. Wit is a better voice in a solo, but humor comes into the chorus best. Wit is as sharp as a stroke of lightning, whereas humor is diffuse like sunlight. Wit keeps the season's fashions and is precise in the phrases and judgments of the day, but humor is concerned with homely eternal things. Wit wears silk, but humor in homespun endures the wind.

      —Charles Brooks, "On the Difference Between Wit and Humor"

   b. The high gray-flannel fog of winter closed off the Salinas Valley from the sky and from all the rest of the world. On every side it sat like a lid on the mountains and made of the great valley a closed pot. On the broad, level land floor the gang plows bit deep and left the black earth shining like metal where the shares had cut. On the foothill ranches across the

Salinas River, the yellow stubble fields seemed to be bathed in pale cold sunshine, but there was no sunshine in the valley now in December.

—John Steinbeck, "The Chrysanthemums"

Doublespeak

Doublespeak is *the use of language to obscure the truth*. Increasingly, critics of contemporary culture point out that when politicians, corporate executives, or advertisers deliberately distort language for their own gain, they are also distorting values. Consequently, the general public ought to be aware of the verbal techniques used to "overload our verbal circuits." These techniques include the use of jargon, meaningless abstractions, euphemisms, slogans, clichés, and so forth.

For example, advertisers attach adjectives such as *amazing, sensational, revolutionary, bold,* and *proud* to products as though these words had concrete referents. But what do these words really mean? Can the latest look in clothing, for example, really be called revolutionary?

More alarming, perhaps, than the use of meaningless abstractions is the use of euphemisms to hide the truth. A **euphemism** is *the substitution of a softened or less explicit expression for a more offensive one.* For example, during the Vietnam War, some government officials used euphemisms to hide from the American public the extent of the United States involvement in Vietnam. In the early stages of the war, despite the presence of United States troops in Vietnam, the word *troops* was never used. Instead, the United States was supposedly employing "advisers," and our role there was "indirect" and "political" rather than military. To soften public reaction to the waging of the war, apologists for the war used such words and expressions as "antipersonnel device" for gun, "routine improvement of visibility" for defoliation and crop destruction, "technical errors" for bombing errors in which civilians were killed, and "harassment and interdiction" for artillery fire. Slogans such as "waging the peace," "peace with honor," and "conducting a peace-keeping action" were also used to present the war in Vietnam in a more favorable light.

Both government deception (from the secrecy involving the U-2 affair in 1960 to the Watergate conspiracy and more recent scandals) and corporate deception (lying in advertising, doubletalk used by corporate executives who give bribes and kickbacks to foreign officials) have occasioned a great deal of public distrust and have diminished confidence in the government and in business. The best way to react to doublespeak is to avoid it in your own language by using words with truth, candor, and precision, and to insist upon a similar use of language on the part of government officials, public figures, and advertisers.

Exercises

1. Bring to class examples of gobbledygook from your textbooks or some other source. Discuss the stylistic features that make the writing gobbledygook and then try to rewrite the passage in clearer language.

2. Bring to class some recent advertisements that use jargon, slogans, clichés, or meaningless abstractions to make a point.

3. Examine the language of advertisements and discuss those which actually tell something about the product and those which merely influence us to buy.

4. Some critics argue that euphemisms are sometimes necessary to make events (jobs, death, and so forth) more bearable. Discuss.

Dialects

In its broadest sense, the word **dialects** refers to *varieties of language based on geographical, educational, or social differences, and writing conventions.* Dialects based on geographical differences are called *regional dialects.* Those based on educational or social differences are called *social dialects.* And those based on writing conventions are called *functional dialects.*

All students have a right to whatever language skills and conventions are necessary to enable them to carry on the tasks of the everyday world and to ensure them a moderate degree of success and happiness. But there is disagreement among scholars and speakers of nonstandard dialects about the best possible means to these goals. Must everyone learn to write in the standard dialect?

Whatever may be true of spoken dialects, there is no doubt that written conventions are rigid and codified. The student who insists upon using the less formal conventions of spoken English in writing will find him- or herself under a great handicap if he or she wishes to get a job that demands formal writing skills. Most employers would find the following student sentences unacceptable:

It takes a femail to have children.
Then there were some black who escape the cruelty of the white man.
Whites says that blacks are not human beings.
The police claimed to have heard they reply, "Shoot it out."
That was all that happen no conversation no nothing.
So, White Americans, watch out of what you say or do concerning the Black Race.
He was young and dress in today fashion.
To me seems like the Mexican-American find themselves in an alien environment.
He taken it.
Very slowly the man what up and pickup the red rose as she had just dropped on a mudded of water.

The dialect features in these sentences are characteristic of those found in many nonstandard social dialects: omission of the plural marker on nouns, omission of the possessive marker, omission of tense markers, a different use or the omission of the auxiliary, spelling errors, and so forth. Whereas in certain kinds of writing dialect features would be perfectly acceptable, in more formal writing, such as professional writing or business writing, dialect features could interfere with clarity and effectiveness of expression.

To use dialect features to report spoken conversation or to use them in writing that is personal or expressive (as in diaries, journals, or autobiographies) is perfectly acceptable, and perhaps even desirable, as the following student paper illustrates:

Mama

Well she was born in a log cabin, in the back woods, black woods of Mississippi. She drank moonshine and chewed tobacco. Raised thirteen children all by herself. Never looked much like a lady. You see, she was too busy providing and raising her babies. Spent her evening sitting in her rocking chair. Never had much of nothing, but was always willing to share.

I'm talking about Mama, my mama.

Education she didn't have none. Never had a sick day in her life. She was as good and strong as any man who ever lived. You better believe she was. Now look here. When papa died, she swore on the good book up and down on it that she would not love nobody else. Made sure we were in church every Sunday. Papa would of wanted it that way, that was what she would always say.

Yes, I'm talking about Mama, yea!! I am talking about the lady who raised me.

Every once and a while when Mama would get depressed, she would go to the closet and get Pa's guitar. She would sit herself down in her rocking chair, start humming and strumming. This was Ma's way of letting off steam. In plain old english we could see, that Ma was doing her thing.

Ma is a very emotional woman. She gets very mad if someone ever tries to do us harm in any way. For example: A school teacher gave my little brother a hard time in his school and in a flash she was on the scene to straighten things out.

She always told us to stick together no matter what instances occurred. Because we would need each other one day as we grew older.

We always appreciated the things she done for us. We never gave her a hard time as we were going through our life cycles.

Till this day, Ma is the same as she was before taking care of her children as she has always have done. And I love her deeply because, without her I wouldn't of been here now. Mom thanks!!!!

—Larry

The repetitions, the fragments, the use of punctuation, and other features are characteristic more of the spoken than the written dialect in this student paper. You can almost "hear" the writer intoning the phrases:

I'm talking about Mama, my mama.
Never looked much like a lady.
Raised thirteen children all by herself.
Yes, I'm talking about Mama, yea!!!

To criticize such a highly personal paper as this would be to criticize the writer's self-image. Nor is there a need to, since the language is perfectly suited to the subject and the mode of discourse. But to use these same conventions in more formal writing would be inappropriate. All students, then, should be encouraged to do some kinds of writing in their own dialects, but they should also be given an opportunity to master the conventions of the standard dialect.

Exercises

1. Point out the dialect features in the following student sentences. Do they interfere with communication? Are they expressive? Appropriate? Inappropriate?

   a. The one room school house is no longer use because the childrens are now bused to a town twenty miles away.

   b. My grandfather used to set on his front porch and tell us of the old times.

   c. He stopped and look at the young girl whom dress in all red.

   d. With this kind of things happening, almost every city is a danger spot.

   e. Today only one city has a majority of black.

   f. Many solution are so simple that they are overlook.

   g. The music at this point liven up.

   h. His only recognition come through sports.

   i. Since you are not knowing much about the campus, I will give you a first hand ride through.

   j. When I first saw he, I could hardly believe it.

2. Write a personal narrative using your own regional or social dialect features.

3. Write a narrative in which you try to capture the language use and dialect of someone you know.

Summary Exercises

1. Discuss the word choice in the following ads. What effect is achieved by the word choice? Consider the denotation and connotation of words, abstractions, concreteness, specificity or lack of specificity, jargon, clichés, figurative language, dialect features, and so forth.

   a. Arandas captures a True Sunrise for those who are into the real McCoy, the legit, the right on, coming clean, on the level, straight goods, Simon Pure in the Grove, and all kinds of sweet vibrations.

Taste the Sun! Pour 1½ ounces Arandas Tequila (White or new Oro) and 4 oz. orange juice into a tall ice-filled glass. Stir. Add ¾ oz. grenadine (more or less) and a squeeze of fresh lime; then drop the lime wedge right in. Now you have a True Sunrise . . . and nothing can outshine it.

—Arandes Tequila ad

b. *Cobra bites man.* Both live. And once bitten, there is no known cure except a long, quick drive down a snakelike road where Cobra II can show off its rack-and-pinion steering. Not to mention the slithering four-speed stick shift, and 2.3 litre engine. And with front/rear spoilers, black louvered back lite and quarter windows, hood scoop, sporty tires, wheels (car shown with optional aluminum wheels), and stripes, this is one snake that doesn't have to shed its skin. So if you're looking for some snake-bite remedy, see your local Ford Dealer.

—Ford ad

c. You have to go beyond moisturizing to deter premature aging.

You must have noticed a woman's skin can often look older than it should.

For this kind of needless aging, new Ultra Vera can be a real deterrent.

First, it has an abundance of moisture elements to shelter your skin from the dryness that may cause little lines.

But Ultra Vera goes beyond that.

You see, contrary to what many women believe, just moisturizing isn't enough to keep your skin youthful-looking.

That's why Ultra Vera Facial Lotion is formulated with aloe vera and UV screen.

Consider the legendary aloe vera gel. It's not by chance aloe has been regarded throughout history as nature's gift to skin beauty. Cleopatra herself is said to have relied on it.

As for our UV screen, a PABA derivative, many dermatologists recommend it to help block out ultra-violet rays. Make no mistake, continual exposure to these rays even in ordinary daylight can wither your skin and add years to the way it looks. Ultra Vera lets you guard against that.

So why limit yourself to just moisturizing? Use Ultra Vera every day, alone or under makeup. It's a big step toward attaining that priceless asset. Ageless-looking skin.

—Ultra Vera ad

d. *This Smuggler Coat Does Everything But Stop Bullets.* Like it stops chicks, for instance, dead in their tracks. Only who's got time for chicks when you got a little business to attend to.

Like lining your pockets with maybe 12 boxes of Cuban cigars, 6 gross Swiss watches, one case good Scotch, 2 snow leopard skins, one German P-38 and 2 solid gold bricks.

Which with a little imagination you can do easy with this coat.

Or take that big collar.

Most guys see it as maybe a pain in the neck, what with keeping it down so it don't mess up your hair.

But any guy sees past his nose sees himself in an open boat in a sudden twister up the Florida Keys, with collar up high to protect the back of his head from taking an awful dousing.

Same goes for the icy blast of a Labrador northeaster down from Fundy.

Or the cold hard stare of a U.S. agent at customs.

There's just about nothing this coat won't do for you when the going gets rough.

Find yourself caught in a tight squeeze on the back of a truck in between a shipment of Picassos and a bunch of Greek vases and you can sleep through the whole night's events and shake off the wrinkles in the AM because the coat's 100% texturized Dacron polyester.

—Smuggler coat ad

e. *Kama baba, kama mwana.* Through his father, a son's eyes are opened to the world. He learns about pride at his father's side. The pride of being black, of being a man.

He learns, too, about pride in his culture and that this beautiful natural is the outward expression of that pride.

And nothing grooms and conditions a proud natural better than Afro Sheen. Afro Sheen makes the difference you can see in your hair. Your natural takes on new body, lustrous and alive. Afro Sheen, the complete product for father . . . for son . . . and for you . . . naturally.

—Afro Sheen ad

CHAPTER 13

Imitation and Style

Important artists and writers down through the years have attested to the value of imitation as *one* way of achieving an original style. "The imitation of other artists," contends Lewis Mumford, "is one of the means by which a person enriches and finally establishes his own individuality, and on the whole such imitation is more promising than an icing of originality that hardens too quickly." "The originals are not original," wrote Ralph Waldo Emerson. "There is imitation, model and suggestion to the very archangels, if we knew their history." Vincent van Gogh, the painter, complained that "we painters are always asked to compose of ourselves. . . . Heaps of people do not copy; heaps of others do—I started it by chance and I find that it teaches me things."

Some writers are very specific as to the manner in which they began to use imitation. "I began to compose by imitating other authors I admired," stated William Dean Howells, "and I worked hard to get a smooth, a rich, classic style." Robert Louis Stevenson confessed that "whenever I read a book or passage that particularly pleased me . . . in which there was either some conspicuous force or some happy distinction in the style, I must set myself to ape that quality. . . . That, like it or not, is the way to learn to write." Somerset Maugham is very explicit about his methodology in his autobiography, *The Summing Up:*

> I studied Jeremy Taylor's *Holy Dying.* In order to assimilate his style, I copied out passages and then tried to write them down from memory.
>
> Later the prose of Swift enchanted me. I made up my mind that this was the perfect way to write and I started to work on him in the same way as I had done with Jeremy Taylor. . . . As I had done before, I copied passages and then tried to write them out from memory. I tried altering words or the order in which they were set. . . .
>
> The work I did was certainly very good for me. I began to write better.

Style can be improved by creative imitation. This approach to style assumes that in assimilating the best features of a writer's style, you will produce writing that in time will come to rival the model itself. You can best do this by following a sequence of steps that might be described as follows:

1. *Select a short passage from a writer's work that has excellencies of style and is relatively complete in itself.*
2. *Read the model carefully, preferably aloud at first to get the full impact, in order to get an overview of the dominant impression.*
3. *Analyze the model carefully, noting the sentence length, the sentence types, and the word choice.*
4. *Do either a close or loose imitation of the model by selecting a subject that differs from the model's but is suitable for treatment in the model's style.*

Ideally, you will follow these steps exactly as outlined. In practice, however, the steps may overlap considerably.

Model Analysis 1

In order to exemplify one method of using models for imitation, I will analyze a few short selections so as to present at least one workable approach to improving style.

The model I have chosen for analysis is the introductory paragraph of the short story. "The Eighty Yard Run," by Irwin Shaw. The passage describes an eighty yard run made in a scrimmage by Darling, the main character in the story. Ironically, this run is the climax in Darling's football career as well as in his life. The rest of the story follows his declining fortunes as his wife gradually takes over the dominant position in the marriage. Because the story is told by means of a flashback, which begins with the second paragraph, the opening paragraph is relatively complete in itself, and thus it makes a suitable model for imitation.

> The pass was high and wide and he jumped for it, feeling it slap flatly against his hands, as he shook his hips to throw off the halfback who was diving at him. The center floated by, his hands desperately brushing Darling's knee as Darling picked his feet up high and delicately ran over a blocker and an opposing linesman in a jumble on the ground near the

scrimmage line. He had ten yards in the clear and picked up speed, breathing easily, feeling his thigh pads rising and falling against his legs, listening to the sound of cleats behind him, pulling away from them, watching the other backs heading him off toward the sidelines, the whole picture, the men closing in on him, the blockers fighting for position, the ground he had to cross, all suddenly clear in his head, for the first time in his life not a meaningless confusion of men, sounds, speed. He smiled a little to himself as he ran, holding the ball lightly in front of him with his two hands, his knees pumping high, his hips twisting in the almost girlish run of a back in a broken field. The first halfback came at him and he fed him his leg, then swung at the last moment, took the shock of the man's shoulder without breaking stride, ran right through him, his cleats biting securely into the turf. There was only the safety man now, coming warily at him, his arms crooked, hands spread. Darling tucked the ball in, spurted at him, driving hard, hurling himself along, his legs pounding, knees high, all two hundred pounds bunched into controlled attack. He was sure he was going to get past the safety man. Without thought, his arms and legs working beautifully together, he headed right for the safety man, stiff-armed him, feeling blood spurt instantaneously from the man's nose onto his hand, seeing his face go awry, head turned, mouth pulled to one side. He pivoted away, keeping the arm locked, dropping the safety man as he ran easily toward the goal line, with the drumming of cleats diminishing behind him.

The passage describes the climactic moment in a scrimmage, just as the halfback is breaking away for a long, broken-field run. As you read, you are caught up in the intense excitement of the action. The narrative movement is vivid, conveying a sense of rapid motion and dynamic action. The descriptive details are sharp and intense.

The paragraph consists of ten sentences. Sentence 1 contains thirty-three words; sentence 2 has thirty-seven words; sentence 3, eighty-six words; 4, forty words; 5, thirty-nine words; 6, sixteen words; 7, twenty-six words; 8, twelve words; 9, forty-one words; 10, twenty-seven words. The shortest sentence is 8, with twelve words; the longest sentence is 3, with eighty-six words. The total number of words in the paragraph is 357. The average number of words per sentence is 35.7. Most of the sentences are relatively long. Sentence length contributes to the overall effectiveness of the passage in two ways: first, it gives variety to the sentences, and second, it lends rhythmic movement to the prose. Notice the difference in effect that is achieved by breaking up sentence number 3, the longest sentence in the paragraph, into shorter sentences:

He had ten yards in the clear. He picked up speed. He breathed easily. He felt his thigh pads rising and falling against his legs. He listened to the sound of cleats behind him. He pulled away from them. He watched the other backs heading him off toward the sidelines. The whole picture was suddenly clear in his head. It was not a meaningless confusion of men, sounds, speed. The men were closing in on him. The blockers were fighting for position. He had to cross the ground.

Not only is the sense of vivid and intense action lost in this version, but this rendering also completely distorts the writer's purpose, which is to show that all these activities are taking place simultaneously. The rewritten version destroys the simultaneity and gives the impression of a sequence of separate actions.

In a preliminary reading of the selection, you will perceive the dynamic action and the descriptive details as being sharp and intense. To support this intuition, you naturally will look closely at what the verbs and verbals are doing. Yet when you make a word count, you find that of the twenty-six main verbs in the passage, only eleven are concrete and specific *(jumped, smiled, shook, headed, diving, tucked, stiff-armed, floated, swung, spurted, pivoted)*. And of the twenty-eight present participles, approximately half are concrete and particular *(brushing, twisting, hurling, breathing, rising, pounding, biting, pumping,* and so forth). On the basis of the evidence, you are forced to conclude either that your earlier intuitions were inaccurate or that Shaw is using other strategies to achieve his purpose. To offset the less specific verbs and verbals, Shaw uses a large number of adverbs describing manner to depict action and to add concreteness to the description:

Adverbs

feeling it slap *flatly* against his hands

his hands *desperately* brushing Darling's knee

picked his feet up *high*

delicately ran over a blocker and an opposing lineman

breathing *easily*

all *suddenly* clear in his head

his knees pumping *high*

holding the ball *lightly* in front of him

his cleats biting *securely* into the turf

coming *warily* at him

his arms and legs working *beautifully* together

feeling blood spurt *instantaneously* from the man's nose

seeing his face go *awry*
ran *easily* toward the goal line

In addition, although some of the participles are general, because they are present participles, they increase the sense of rapid motion felt by the reader. The *-ing* ending helps to create this vivid sense of movement. And finally, the movement of the verbs is strengthened by the fact that there are few auxiliaries to slow the action. The burden of the action is carried directly by the main verbs: *stiff-armed, floated, spurted, pivoted,* and so forth.

With the exception of sentence 8, the predominant sentence type is the *cumulative sentence:*

1

1 The pass was high and wide and
1 he jumped for it,
   2 feeling it slap flatly against his hands, (VP)
      3 as he shook his hips to throw off the halfback who was diving at him. (SC)

2

1 The center floated by,
   2 his hands desperately brushing Darling's knee as Darling picked his feet up high and delicately ran over a blocker and an opposing lineman in a jumble on the ground near the scrimmage line. (Abs)

3

1 He had ten yards in the clear and picked up speed,
   2 breathing easily, (VP)
   2 feeling his thigh pads rising and falling against his legs, (VP)
   2 listening to the sound of cleats behind him, (VP)
   2 pulling away from them, (VP)
   2 watching the other backs heading him off toward the sidelines, (VP)
      3 the whole picture, /, all suddenly clear in his head, for the first time in his life not a meaningless confusion of men, sounds, speed. (Abs)
         4 the men closing in on him, (Abs)
         4 the blockers fighting for position, (Abs)
         4 the ground he had to cross. (Abs)

4

1 He smiled a little to himself as he ran,
   2 holding the ball lightly in front of him with his two hands, (VP)
   2 his knees pumping high, (Abs)
   2 his hips twisting in the almost girlish run of a back in a broken field. (Abs)

5

1 The first halfback came at him and
1 he fed him his leg, then swung at the last moment, took the shock of
  the man's shoulder without breaking stride, ran right through him,
    2 his cleats biting securely into the turf. (Abs)

6

1 There was only the safety man now,
    2 coming warily at him, (VP)
        3 his arms crooked, (Abs)
        3 hands spread. (Abs)

7

1 Darling tucked the ball in, spurted at him,
    2 driving hard, (VP)
    2 hurling himself along, (VP)
        3 his legs pounding, (Abs)
        3 knees high, (Abs)
            4 all two hundred pounds bunched into controlled attack. (Abs)

8

1 He was sure he was going to get past the safety man.

9

    2 Without thought, (PP)
    2 his arms and legs working beautifully together, (Abs)
1 he headed right for the safety man, stiff-armed him,
    2 feeling blood spurt instantaneously from the man's nose onto his
      hand, (VP)
    2 seeing his face go awry, (VP)
        3 head turned, (Abs)
        3 mouth pulled to one side. (Abs)

10

1. He pivoted away,
    2. keeping the arm locked, (VP)
    2. dropping the safety man as he ran easily toward the goal line, (VP)
        3. with the drumming of cleats diminishing behind him. (Abs)

The cumulative sentences lend a sense of rapid motion to the prose and advance the action.

    Another interesting stylistic feature used to convey rapid movement is the deliberate omission of conjunctions between the main verbs. This is one technique that may be used to speed up the action in a narrative.

The first halfback *came* at him and he *fed* him his leg, then *swung* at the last moment, *took* the shock of the man's shoulder without breaking stride, *ran* right through him, his cleats biting securely into the turf.

Darling *tucked* the ball in, *spurted* at him, driving hard, hurling himself along . . .

. . . he *headed* straight for the safety man, *stiff-armed* him, feeling blood spurt instantaneously from the man's nose . . .

Imitation Exercises

Once you go through this kind of analysis with a model, you can then do imitation exercises based on the principles discovered in the model chosen for study. One kind of exercise consists of writing sentences of varying levels, beginning with two-level narrative or descriptive sentences and then adding more complex levels. Within each sentence, the use of participial phrases and absolute constructions would be stressed. So also would the use of active verbs, manner adverbs (those that relate *how* an action is completed), and present participles. The omission of conjunctions between verbs could be emphasized in a few sentences, as could variety in sentence length. Finally, the choice of vivid and precise words appealing to the senses would also be suitable for imitation.

More importantly, the sentences chosen for imitation should be part of a larger unit so that you can see the effect that a stylistic technique has in a particular context. The most useful approach is to begin with a close imitation of the model, putting your own ideas and experiences into the structure of the whole. Then, as you are attending to the stylistic principles within the individual sentences as well as within the paragraph, you can also attend to the manner in which content interacts with form to produce a mature style.

The following student paper is a good example of a close imitation based on the Shaw model:

Close Imitation

(Situation: A grease monkey has only four cars left to lube before he can leave the gas station. He hopes to finish before the other shop workers.)

The Cadillac was long and wide and he jumped for its underside, feeling the suspension with his hands, as he shook his feet to throw off the piece of bubble gum sticking to him. The manager floated by, his finger desperately shaking at Ernie's face as Ernie picked his feet up high and delicately ran over a hydraulic lift and a spare tire in a jumble on the floor near the storage rack. He had three cars in the clear and picked up speed, sighing despondently, feeling his greasy overalls rising and falling against his legs, listening to the sound of tune-ups behind him, pulling away from them, watching the alignment boys heading him off toward closing time, the whole picture, the men trying to finish before him, the other lube specialists fighting for the grease gun, the cars he had to finish, all suddenly clear in his head, for the first time in his job not a meaningless confusion of grease monkeys, machines, speed. He smirked a little to himself as he worked, holding the grease gun tightly in front of him with his two grubby paws, his legs stretching high, his hips twisting in the almost clumsy style of a bull in a china shop. The first car came to him and he filled it with grease, then swung at the last moment, took the shock of several more drops of grease on his face without breaking stride, walked right over some more, his tennis shoes slipping wildly on the slick concrete floor. There was only the Volkswagen left now. Ernie approached it warily, his arms crooked, legs spread. Ernie shoved the grease gun out, spurted at the "bug," driving hard, hurling himself along, his heart pounding, arms high, all one hundred twenty pounds stretched into an awkward attack. He was sure he was going to finish before the tune-up man. Without thought, his arms and legs working somewhat together, he headed right for the oil pan, knocked the plug off, feeling hot oil spurt instantaneously from the spout onto his head, seeing the manager's face go awry, head turned, mouth pulled to one side in an obscenity. Ernie pivoted away, keeping the arms forward, dropping the grease gun as he ran for his own car, with the thunder of boots diminishing behind him.

—Bruce

Contrary to what you might think, this kind of imitation is not mere copying, nor is it slavish imitation. This kind of assignment demands a sensitivity to style and structure, a feeling for the nuances of language, and a knowledge of what type of content goes best with what type of structure.

Here is another student imitation that uses the same style but a different subject matter:

Close Imitation

The toy was pink and cuddly and he clutched it, feeling it squash within his chubby hands, as he wobbled to free himself from his mother's confining grasp. His brother scurried by, his arm jarringly knocking Jamie's shoulder as Jamie swerved to his left and desperately avoided a hard plastic horse and an imposing red wagon in a heap on the living room floor. He had five feet in the clear and became a bit steadier, gurgling loudly, feeling his terry-cloth pajamas stretch around his fat tummy, listening to the encouraging cheers behind him, venturing away from them, unconscious of the restraining relatives heading him into the center of the room, the entire picture, the thrust of the starting push, the relatives reaching with unneeded hands, the soft carpet he had to cross, all new and amazing in his mind, for the first time in his life not a distorted view of people and things from a crawling position. He grinned a little as he stepped, clinging to the toy frantically with his fat little palms, his head wobbling up and down, his pink bottom wiggling in the humorous fashion of a bouncing baby. The first aunt came at him and he shoved her with his bent elbow, then stumbled at the last moment, crashed to the floor, struggled to regain his footing by raising his bottom first, his determination exhibited in his serious little face. There was only an uncle now, squatting in the center of the floor, his arms cocked, his eyes busily watching. Jamie still clung to the toy, toddled toward his uncle, giggling repeatedly, hurling himself along, his legs pumping, free arm flopping for balance, all 19 pounds wobbling forward across the living room. Without thought, his arms and legs working awkwardly, he headed straight toward his uncle, arm flying, knocking his uncle off balance with the slightest brush, his uncle's startled eyes gawking at the tiny child. He waddled past, arm still swinging, then reaching for a huge hand, the safety of his daddy, with excited cheers from the gallery behind him.

—Jeanne

A second kind of exercise is based on a looser imitation of the model. In this type of exercise, you are asked to model your sentences on those of the original, but in any order and in varying lengths. The following is a student imitation which uses a looser form of imitation:

Loose Imitation

The lively notes of the piano began and so did her action, as the three criticizing judges watched, their pencils poised, ready to deduct points. She executed a step-kick-lunge with great ease, her hands and arms reaching upward in perfect time to the smooth music filling the room. Now halfway through the first run of the pattern, she felt her black leotard stretch over her arched body, listening for the cue to continue with a quick front roll, breaking into a high leap, cartwheel, and back roll. She landed lightly on her knees and pointed toes, thinking of what was to come next. The second run, her easiest, was performed with grace and speed. She smiled as she rose to her toes, ran three short steps, did a high hitch kick, toes pointed, a cat leap, then going right into a step-hop, right toe pointed straight back. Next came four leaping steps and a pose, her right hand ending its movement high above her head, her eyes following its path. Abruptly she raised both hands, held a handstand and somersaulted into a flat position on the mat, her arms above her head, then quickly rolled a complete turn and sat up, her back arched, her knees bent. Straightening her right knee, then her left, she stood and turned. Without thought, her arms and legs keeping perfect time to the music, she executed her final run, sliding her right leg to her left, hopping left, sliding her left leg to right, then pivoting abruptly, her hands at the small of her back. Three swift turning steps followed, then two perfect cartwheels, her knees straight, her legs directly over her head, her exhibition ending exactly with the music in a lunge, her back arched, her head proudly held high, her heart pounding with success.

—Linda

Exercises

1. Using the Irwin Shaw model, do either a loose or a close imitation in which you depict a subject in motion (for example, a skier, a swimmer, a basketball player, a skater, an animal, a robot). Use cumulative sentences, with many free modifiers. Use active participles, manner adverbs, and active verbs. Choose words that appeal to the senses.

2. The *periodic sentence* is one kind of cumulative sentence. The *loose sentence* is another. The following passage uses both kinds of sentences. Analyze and discuss in class the sentence structure, the use of repetition and restatement, the images, the sound devices, and the rhythm of the prose in this passage, and then write an imitation.

Some Things Will Never Change

"Some things will never change. Some things will always be the same. Lean down your ear upon the earth, and listen.

"The voice of forest water in the night, a woman's laughter in the dark, the clean, hard rattle of raked gravel, the cricketing stitch of midday in hot meadows, the delicate web of children's voices in bright air—these things will never change.

"The glitter of sunlight on roughened water, the glory of the stars, the innocence of morning, the smell of the sea in harbors, the feathery blur and smoky buddings of young boughs, and something there that comes and goes and never can be captured, the thorn of spring, the sharp and tongueless cry—these things will always be the same.

"All things belonging to the earth will never change—the leaf, the blade, the flower, the wind that cries and sleeps and wakes again, the trees whose stiff arms clash and tremble in the dark, and the dust of lovers long since buried in the earth—all things proceeding from the earth to seasons, all things that lapse and change and come again upon the earth—these things will always be the same, for they come up from the earth that never changes, they go back into the earth that lasts forever. Only the earth endures, but it endures forever.

"The tarantula, the adder, and the asp will also never change. Pain and death will always be the same. But under the pavement trembling like a pulse, under the buildings trembling like a cry, under the waste of time, under the hoof of the beast above the broken bones of cities, there will be something growing like a flower, something bursting from the earth again, forever deathless, faithful, coming into life again like April."

—Thomas Wolfe, *You Can't Go Home Again*

Model Analysis 2

The second model chosen for analysis is taken from a novel by Virginia Woolf titled *To the Lighthouse*. Like the Irwin Shaw passage, it is relatively complete in itself, and it also is an interesting model for imitation. Its style and structure contrast nicely with that of the Irwin Shaw passage.

> The house was left; the house was deserted. It was left like a shell on a sandhill to fill with dry salt grains now that life had left it. The long night seemed to have set in; the trifling airs, nibbling, the clammy breaths, fumbling, seemed to have triumphed. The saucepan had rusted and the mat decayed. Toads had nosed their way in. Idly, aimlessly, the swaying shawl swung to and fro. A thistle thrust itself between the tiles in the larder. The swallows nested in the drawing room; the floor was strewn with straw; the plaster fell in shovelfuls; rafters were laid bare; rats carried off this and that to gnaw behind the wainscots. Tortoise-shell butterflies burst from the chrysalis and patterned their life out on the windowpane. Poppies sowed themselves among the dahlias; the lawn waved with long grass; giant artichokes towered among the roses; a fringed carnation flowered among the cabbages; while the gentle tapping of a weed at the window had become, on winter's nights, a drumming from sturdy trees and thorned briars which made the whole room green in summer.

This model describes the desolation of an abandoned house. Unlike the intense excitement conveyed by the movement of the prose in the Shaw passage, however, the prose in this passage seems static. The tone is somber.

This paragraph consists of ten sentences. Sentence 1 has eight words; sentence 2 contains twenty-one words; sentence 3, twenty words; 4, eight words; 5, six words; 6, nine words; 7, ten words; 8, thirty-three words; 9, fourteen words; 10, fifty-six words. The shortest sentence is 5, with six words. The longest sentence is 10, with fifty-six words. The total number of words in the paragraph is 185. The average number of words per sentence is 18.5, in marked contrast to the 35.7 words per sentence of the Shaw passage. The sentences, therefore, have good variety in length.

In reading this passage, you may perceive the action and the descriptive details as static. To support this intuition, you naturally look at how the verbs are used. A careful analysis reveals that of the twenty-four main verbs in the passage, four are static verbs *(was, was, seemed, seemed)*; three are in the passive voice *(was deserted, was strewn, were laid bare)*; five are in the past perfect tense *(had left, had rusted, had decayed, had nosed, had become)*; and twelve are in the past tense, active voice *(swung, thrust, nested, fell, carried, burst, patterned, sowed, saved, towered, flowered, made)*.

The static nature of the description can be accounted for in part by the static verbs, but the verbs in the passive voice and the verbs in the past perfect tense work more or less in the same fashion as the static verbs. The static verbs (the verb *to be* and the verbs of appearance) are followed by predicate adjectives or some kind of complement that moves back toward the subject and comments on it. The past participle forms of the verb following the auxiliary *was (were)* work in the same manner, as adjectivals moving back toward the subject. Similarly, the main verbs after the auxiliary *had* (in the past perfect tense verbs) act as adjective complements and refer to the subject. The result is that the forward motion of the prose is slowed and the effect is static. The following scheme illustrates this point:

Static verbs

the *house* was *left*

it was *left* like a shell on a sandhill

the long *night* seemed *to have set in*

the trifling *airs* seemed *to have triumphed*

Passive voice verbs

the *house* was *deserted*

the *floor* was *strewn* with straw

rafters were *laid bare*

Past perfect tense verbs

life had *left* it

the *saucepan* had *rusted*

the *mat* [had] *decayed*

toads had *nosed* their way in

the gentle *tapping* of a weed . . . had become . . . a *drumming*

In addition, a large number of verbs, adjectives, and adverbials give the sense of desolation and aimlessness through their meaning:

Verbs

the swallows *nested* in the drawing room

the plaster *fell* in shovelfuls

tortoise-shell butterflies . . . *patterned* their life out on the windowpane

Adjectives

the *long* night

the *trifling* airs

the *clammy* breaths

Adverbials

idly

aimlessly

to and fro

Besides these words, the use of reflexive pronouns referring back to the subject adds to the static nature of the description:

Reflexives

a *thistle* thrust *itself*

poppies sowed *themselves* among the dahlias

Some movement is carried by the active verbs (*swung, thrust, nested, carried, burst, patterned*, among others), but these stand in stark contrast to the static verbs and reinforce the somber tone. The word choice in general conveys this sense of desolation and futility. The plants and flowers, which at first seem to impart life to their surroundings and add color, are growing wild. Everything is overgrown, random, and the plants are prickly or thistly:

long grass
poppies . . . among the dahlias
a fringed carnation among the cabbages
giant artichokes among the roses

In sharp contrast to the cumulative sentences that convey action in the Shaw passage, most of the sentences in this model are balanced sentences, or sentences that give the sense of being balanced;

1

1 The house was left;
1 the house was deserted.

2

1 It was left like a shell on a sandhill to fill with dry salt grains now that life had left it.

3

1 The long night seemed to have set in;
1 the trifling airs,
  2 nibbling, (VP)
1 the clammy breaths,
  2 fumbling, (VP)
    3 seemed to have triumphed.

4

1 the saucepan had rusted and
1 the mat [had] decayed.

5

1 Toads had nosed their way in.

6

  2 Idly, (Adv)
  2 aimlessly, (Adv)
1 the swaying shawl swung to and fro.

7

1 A thistle thrust itself between the tiles in the larder.

8

1 The swallows nested in the drawing room;
1 the floor was strewn with straw;
1 the plaster fell in shovelfuls;
1 rafters were laid bare;
1 rats carried off this and that to gnaw behind the wainscots.

9

1 Tortoise-shell butterflies burst from the chrysalis and patterned their life
 out on the windowpane.

10

1 Poppies sowed themselves among the dahlias,
1 the lawn waved with long grass;
1 giant artichokes towered among the roses;
1 a fringed carnation flowered among the cabbages;
 2 while the gentle tapping of a weed at the window had become, / , a
  drumming from sturdy trees and thorned briars which made the
  whole room green in summer. (SC)
 3 on winter's nights, (PP)

The coordinate and balanced structures combine with the static verb
structures to convey a desolate picture of the abandoned house. The
cumulative sentences in the Shaw passage move the action forward.
The balanced sentences in this passage slow the action and force the
movement backwards, as base clause piles up upon base clause, reinforcing the sense of stillness, decay, and decline in the house.

One final stylistic feature in the Virginia Woolf passage is the use
of sound devices to give a sense of parallelism and balance. Its effect is
similar to that of the syntactic parallelism:

Sound Parallelism
the *s*waying *sh*awl *s*wung to and fro
a *th*istle *th*rust i*t*self be*t*ween the *t*iles in the larder
the floor was *str*ewn with *str*aw
the *l*awn waves with *l*ong grass
a *f*ringed carnation *f*lowered among the cabbages

The net result of all these stylistic devices is to convey a strong
sense of desolation and futility. The somber tone is conveyed strongly
as a single impression.

Imitation Exercises

As with the analysis of the Shaw model, once you go through analyzing
this passage you can do an imitation using balanced sentences, static
verbs, verbs in the passive voice, and words that convey a desolate tone.

The following student imitation, based on the Woolf passage, is a good illustration of how one student handled the assignment:

Close Imitation

The ship was abandoned; the ship was forsaken. She was left like a wreck in a junkyard now that her usefulness had ended. The long day seemed to have its effect on her; the hot sun, burning, the humid air, corroding, seeming to have conquered. Her hull had rotted and her bow caved in. Fish had ambled their way in. Idly, purposelessly, the tattered flag flapped to and fro. Seaweed made its way between the boards in the hull. Some doves made nests in the ballroom; the floor was covered with debris; part of the ceiling had fallen in; the rafters were now exposed; rats had long ago deserted the corroding shell. Gray-colored seagulls tiptoed noiselessly among musty life jackets and then flapped aimlessly about the upper deck. Coral had attached itself to her bottom; crustaceans implanted themselves among the coral; a gray shape glided past in silence; while the gentle movement of a wave at the hull had become, on a still summer's day, a pounding which echoed from the bow to the stern.

—Jackie

The student imitation reprinted below is a looser imitation of the Woolf passage:

The church was empty; the church was abandoned. It resembled an old deserted ship, alone and forsaken. The pages of the hymn books in the pews had corroded and their covers rotted. Mice transported bits and pieces of the pages to nibble between the walls. Dark brown moths implanted themselves in the tattered cloth chairs near the altar, never to escape. Doves nested in the corners of the church, piling dried sagebrush together for a haven. The gloomy fall day appeared to be a sign of winter approaching, the damp brisk air rattling, the gray sky emerging through the broken stained-glass windows. The organ was enveloped in a network of mildew and moss, collecting slowly, spreading like a cancer over the keyboard. Cacti were springing up here and there on the earth visible through cracks in the floorboards. An ocotillo growing near the doorway fastened itself to a piece of dead wood; while the soft thumping of a bottlebrush tree, dwarfed against the giant church door, carried, on these fall afternoons, a pleasing scent to counteract the foul air inside the church. Loudly, continuously, a large, rusty bell above the doorway of the church repeated its mournful sound.

—Scott

Exercises

1. Write an imitation of the Virginia Woolf passage in which you describe a deserted mine, a ghost town, a cemetery at night, an antique shop, a junk shop, an abandoned house, or some other, similar subject. Try to achieve a dominant impression of desolation. Use balanced sentences, with a sequence of coordinate clauses. Intersperse these with short sentences of single clauses that, when combined with the coordinate sequences, give the impression of being coordinate with them. Use static verbs, verbs in the passive voice, or verbs that give the sense of being static. Choose words whose meaning conveys desolation, futility, or some other tone you want to achieve. If you like, use sound devices such as alliteration that will give a sense of parallelism and balance.

2. At the end of the chapter on the sentence, there is an excellent selection that uses balance and parallelism effectively: Kennedy's inaugural address. Analyze this passage in class, and then do an imitation, using the style of the original

3. Choose a short passage using parallel structure, by a writer you admire. Then do an imitation of that passage.

Model Analysis 3

The final model chosen for analysis is taken from Mark Twain's *Autobiography.*

The Farm

As I have said, I spent some part of every year at the farm until I was twelve or thirteen years old. The life which I led there with my cousins was full of charm and so is the memory of it yet. I can call back the solemn twilight and mystery of the deep woods, the earthy smells, the faint odors of the wild flowers, the sheen of rainwashed foliage, the rattling clatter of drops when the wind shook the trees, the far-off hammering of woodpeckers and the muffled drumming of wood-pheasants in the remoteness of the forest, the glimpses of disturbed wild creatures scurrying through the grass—I can call it all back and make it as real as it ever was, and as blessed. I can call back the prairie, and its loneliness and peace, and a vast hawk hanging motionless in the sky with his wings spread wide and the blue of the vault showing through the fringe of their end-feathers. I can see the woods in their autumn dress, the oaks purple, the hickories washed with gold, the maples and the sumachs luminous with crimson fires, and I can hear the rustle made by the fallen leaves as we plowed through them. I can see the blue clusters of wild grapes hanging amongst the foliage of the saplings, and I remember the taste of them and the smell. I know how the wild blackberries looked and how they tasted; and the same with the pawpaws, the hazelnuts, and the persimmons; and I can feel the thumping rain upon my head of hickory-nuts and walnuts when we were out in the frosty dawn to scramble for them with the pigs, and the gusts of wind loosed them and sent them down. I know the stain of blackberries and how pretty it is, and I know the stain of walnut hulls and how little it minds soap and water, also what grudged experience it had of either of them. I know the taste of maple sap and when to gather it and how to arrange the troughs and the delivery tubes, and how to boil down the juice, and how to hook the sugar after it is made; also how much better hooked sugar tastes than any that is honestly come by, let bigots say what they will.

—*Mark Twain's Autobiography*

This passage is written in the form of a reminiscence. Twain uses the order of memory to organize the descriptive details. The first two sentences announce the subject, the memories of a man who lived on a Missouri farm when he was twelve or thirteen years old:

As I have said, I spent some part of every year at the farm until I was twelve or thirteen years old. The life which I led there with my cousins was full of charm and so is the memory of it yet.

The subsequent sentences add concrete and sensory images, detailing the memories of the farm.

The predominant sentence type is the *parallel series*. The structure of the sentences is relatively simple, each one beginning with a similar kind of base ("I can call back," "I can see," "I can hear," "I can feel"). Then to the base is added a *catalog* of sights, sounds, smells, and tastes of things found on a Missouri farm. The following are examples of the sentence structure, presented in graphic form.

1 I can call back
    2 the solemn twilight and mystery of the deep woods,
    2 the earthy smells,
    2 the faint odors of the wild flowers,
    2 the sheen of rainwashed foliage,

  2 the rattling clatter of drops when the wind shook the trees, the far-off hammering of woodpeckers and the muffled drumming of wood-pheasants in the remoteness of the forest,

  2 the snapshot glimpses of disturbed wild creatures scurrying through the grass—

1 I can call it all back and make it as real as it ever was, and as blessed.

1 I can call back

  2 the prairie, and

    3 its loneliness and peace, and

  2 a vast hawk hanging motionless in the sky with his wings spread and

    3 the blue of the vault showing through the fringe of their end-feathers.

1 I can see

  2 the woods in their autumn dress,

    3 the oaks purple,

    3 the hickories washed with gold,

    3 the maples and the sumachs luminous with crimson fires, and

1 I can hear

  2 the rustle made by the fallen leaves as we plowed through them.

1 I can see

  2 the blue clusters of wild grapes hanging amongst the foliage of the saplings, and

1 I remember

  2 the taste of them and the smell.

1 I know

  2 how the wild blackberries looked and

  2 how they tasted; and

  2 the same with

    3 the pawpaws,

    3 the hazelnuts, and

    3 the persimmons; and

1 I can feel

  2 the thumping rain upon my head of

    3 hickory-nuts and

    3 walnuts

      4 when we were out in the frosty dawn to scramble for them with the pigs, and

      4 [when] the gusts of wind

        5 loosed them and

        5 sent them down.

1 I know
   2 the stain of blackberries and
   2 how pretty it is, and
1 I know
   2 the stain of walnut hulls and
   2 how little it minds soap and water,
   2 also what grudged experience it had of either of them.

1 I know
   2 the taste of maple sap and
   2 when to gather it, and
   2 how to arrange
      3 the troughs and
      3 the delivery tubes, and
   2 how to boil down the juice, and
   2 how to hook the sugar after it is made;
   2 also how much better hooked sugar tastes than any that is honestly
      come by, let bigots say what they will.

In a passage that uses a cataloging technique to convey a sequence of sensory experiences, you would expect the sentences to be fairly long, and your expectations are fulfilled. The shortest sentence contains twenty-one words. The longest sentence is eighty-five words. The average sentence length is 43.5 words. So the *sentence length* is effective in achieving Twain's purpose. The following scheme illustrates the variety in sentence length:

Sentence 1	22 words
Sentence 2	21 words
Sentence 3	85 words
Sentence 4	38 words
Sentence 5	42 words
Sentence 6	26 words
Sentence 7	62 words
Sentence 8	37 words
Sentence 9	59 words

The word choice is predominantly concrete and specific, with some use of imagery and figurative language. The vocabulary is too extensive to permit an exhaustive sampling, but the following examples are representative:

Images of Sight

the snapshot glimpses of disturbed *wild creatures scurrying* through the *grass*

a vast *hawk hanging motionless* in the *sky* with his *wings spread wide*

the *blue* of the *vault* showing through the *fringe* of their *end-feathers*

the *oaks purple*

the *hickories* washed with *gold*

the *maples* and the *sumachs luminous* with *crimson fires*

the *blue clusters* of wild *grapes* hanging amongst the *foliage* of the *saplings*

Images of Sound

the *rattling clatter* of drops when the wind shook the trees

the *far-off hammering* of woodpeckers

the *muffled drumming* of wood-pheasants in the remoteness of the forest

the *rustle* made by the fallen leaves as we plowed through them

Images of Smell

the *earthy smells*

the *faint odors* of the *wild flowers*

the smell . . . of *wild grapes*

Images of Taste

the *taste* of *maple sap*

[taste] of hooked *sugar*

[taste] of *wild blackberries*

Tactile Images (Images of Touch)

the *thumping rain* upon my head of *hickory nuts* and *walnuts*

the *frosty dawn*

the *gusts* of *wind*

Figures of Speech

the far-off *hammering* of woodpeckers

the muffled *drumming* of wood-pheasants

the *snapshot* glimpses of disturbed wild creatures

the blue of the *vault*

the woods in their autumn *dress*
the hickories *washed* with gold
the maples and the sumachs *luminous* with *crimson fires*
the thumping *rain* upon my head of hickory-nuts and walnuts

The effect of the concrete and specific images and the figures of speech is to allow the reader to share the sensations and vivid experiences of a Missouri farm experienced by the writer.

Imitation Exercises

The Mark Twain passage lends itself well to imitation. Using this model, you would write a short reminiscence of your own, using parallel sentences with series of words and phrases in balanced constructions. The word choice should be concrete and specific, using images that appeal to the senses and figures of speech that present a vivid picture to the reader's mind.

The following student imitation follows fairly closely Mark Twain's model.

The Farm

Until I was thirteen or fourteen, I spent at least a week or more on the farm each year. The life there with my cousins was delightful and I still have memories of it yet. I can call back the brilliant sunlight and the expanse of the open farmland, the earthy smells, the pleasant aroma of cut alfalfa, the glistening of dew-drenched foliage, the crinkle and flap of corn leaves in the wind, the far-off roar of a tractor in the field and the sound of a single truck raking and grinding the gravel as it passed, and the split-second glimpses of prairie dogs scurrying across the pasture into their underground shelters—I can call it all back and see it as real as the day I was there. I can call back the farmland, and its apparent loneliness and peace, and a hen pheasant safely leading her brood of chicks through the tall brush in search of food. I can see the farmland in its summer dress, the corn green, the pastures brown from the scorching heat, the wheat golden ripe and ready for harvest, and I can hear the rustle of the tall grass and weeds as we plowed through them. I can see the pink clusters of wild plums hanging amongst the foliage of the brush down in the bottoms, and I can remember the sweet taste of the jelly we made from them. I know how the wild mulberries looked and how they tasted; and the same with the strawberries, the raspberries, and the cherries; and I can feel the thud of over-ripe peaches hitting my shoulder as we passed under the trees, as

the wind loosened them and caused them to fall. I know the stains of raspberries and strawberries and how red they are, and I know only too well
how they resist soap and water. I know how to irrigate, and when this job
should be done, and how to arrange the plastic dams and siphon tubes, and
when enough water has been applied, and how long it will be before water
is to be added again; also how much better it is to irrigate than to farm dry
land, let bigots say what they will.

—Jim

Here is another student paper that uses the same model, with an
unusual choice of subject matter:

The Morgue

I seldom mention it, but while I was in the Army I spent two years in
Japan working in a mortuary. The life in death which I led with my
sergeants, the embalmers, Japanese morgue attendants, and physical
anthropologists was full of charm and so is the memory of it yet. I can call
back the ominous midnights and the mystery of the deep dark preparation
room, the smell of embalming fluid, mingling with the faint odor of perk-
ing coffee from the front office, the rattling clatter of the doors and windows when the wind shook them, the far-off sound of a refrigerator motor
starting up, the sound of a plane flying over which sounded exactly like
the back door sliding open, the snapshot glimpses of disturbing shadows I
swore were scurrying across the floor as I looked up. I can call it all back
and make it as real as it ever was, and as frightfully blessed. I can call back
the identification room with its tables of bones and their loneliness and
peace, and a vast skeleton hanging motionless in a cabinet with its arms
dangling and the green of the cabinet showing through its yellowish white
ribs. I can see the Japanese morgue attendants in their work uniforms,
white jackets with white trousers stiff with starch, their hands in red plastic gloves, their heads in white dome caps, making them look incon-
gruously like Santa's elves working around a gigantic doll, and I can still
hear their laughter as they scrubbed, stuffed, and stitched. I can see the
sponge with different sized needles hanging on the wall, and I remember
the purpose of each needle and its feel. I know how the viewing chapel
looked and how it smelled, and the same with the casket room, the
carpenter shop, and the embalming room, and I can feel the dull slap on
my buttocks caused by the motion of the corpse's hand as I worked nervously trying to lift the legs in order to take the body off the draining
braces at two in the morning, and I can feel the gust of wind I made as I
ran like hell down the long dark hall. I know the stain of blood and how
undistinguished it looks, and I know the stain of embalming fluid and how

little it minds soap and water, also how hard it is to scrub to get rid of either of them. I know the look of a dead body and how to embalm it, and how to arrange the hoses and tubes, and how to start the fluid, and how to stop the flow when it is complete, also how much better cremated remains are than those that aren't, let the Pope say what he will.

—Dale

In writing an imitation, you need not use the same subject as in the original model. In fact, part of the challenge is to put your own ideas into different kinds of styles and structures, as both the previous student papers and this one illustrate.

The Dorm

As many others can say, I spent nine months one year in a dorm when I was 17 or 18 years old. The existence which I led there with the other dormies was fascinating and so are the memories of it yet. I can call back the noisy nights and the scariness of the dark halls, the perfume smells, the faint odors of popcorn, the piles of freshly washed clothes in the laundry room, the scrambling clatter of feet when the alarm clocks pierced the air, the nearby hammering on doors and the muffled roar of stereos in the adjoining rooms, the snapshots of funny friends clowning in the halls—I can call it all back and make it as real as it ever was, and as pleasing. I can call back the lounge, and its furniture and terrible acoustics, and a small TV hanging immobile on the wall with its antennas spread wide and the orange of the wall showing through the maze of its wires and cords. I can see the coeds in their fall wardrobes, the coats bright, the brunettes striking in golds, the blondes and the redheads glowing in greens, and I can hear the whistles from the freshman guys as we walked past them. I can see the long lines of hungry students waiting on the stairs of the cafeteria, and I remember the taste of the food and the smell. I know how the desserts looked and how they tasted; and the same with the salads; the meats, and the vegetables; and I can feel the clunking upon my tray of knives and forks when we went over in the early morning to grab for them among the early risers, and the press of classes rushed us and sent us on. I know the drape of fishnet and how pretty it is, and I know the problems of thumbtack holes and how hard they are to cover, also what frustrating experiences I had with them. I know the taste of rum in coke and when it is safe to drink it, and how to conceal it and get it to the room, and how to hide the bottles, and how to keep it a secret after it is hidden; also how much better drinks in your room taste than in any legal place, let the regents say what they will.

—Christy

Exercises

1. From your experience, write a reminiscence similar to Twain's, using the rhetoric of the series. Use concrete imagery, sensory details, and figures of speech.

2. The use of light is interesting in the following description by James Baldwin. Pick out the images, such as "pale end-of-winter sunlight," and discuss them. What other images does Baldwin use to create a certain impression of the kitchen? Discuss Baldwin's use of word repetition, parallelism, and the series to reinforce the description. What effect does the grammatical structure have? Then write a description of a room using the Baldwin passage as a model. Focus on one or two details: the smell (floral, musty, damp), the colors, the clutter or order of the objects in the room, and so forth.

The Kitchen

Their mother, her head tied up in an old rag, sipped black coffee and watched Roy. The pale end-of-winter sunlight filled the room and yellowed all their faces; and John, drugged and morbid and wondering how it was that he had slept again and had been allowed to sleep so long, saw them for a moment like figures on a screen, an effect that the yellow light intensified. The room was narrow and dirty; nothing could alter its dimensions, no labor could ever make it clean. Dirt was in the walls and the floorboards, and triumphed beneath the sink where roaches spawned; was in the fine ridges of the pots and pans, scoured daily, burnt black on the bottom, hanging above the stove; was in the wall against which they hung, and revealed itself where the paint had cracked and leaned outward in stiff squares and fragments, the paper-thin underside webbed with black. Dirt was in every corner, angle, crevice of the monstrous stove, and lived behind it in delirious communion with the corrupted wall. Dirt was in the baseboard that John scrubbed every Saturday, and roughened the cupboard shelves that held the cracked and gleaming dishes. Under this dark weight the walls leaned, under it the ceiling, with a great crack like lightning in its center, sagged. The windows gleamed like beaten gold or silver, but now John saw, in the yellow light, how fine dust veiled their doubtful glory. Dirt crawled in the gray mop hung out of the windows to dry.

—James Baldwin, *Go Tell It on the Mountain*

The kind of imitation I am advocating is not "mere copying" or slavish imitation, but *imitation based on a thorough understanding and assimilation of the principles* of a writer's style. There are formal principles in all writing that recur from one writer to another, and it is valuable to learn something about these principles. Imitation may not make you a James Joyce, a Mark Twain, or a Virginia Woolf. Only natural ability will. But it can help you to achieve an effective and pleasing style.

Summary Exercises

1. Analyze in class the following selection from *The Yearling*, by Marjorie Kinnan Rawlings. Discuss the sentence structure, word choice, imagery, and figures of speech. Then, do an imitation in which you depict some subject in motion:

Two Bears

Two male bears were moving slowly ahead down the road, a hundred yards distant. They were on their hind legs, walking like men, shoulder to shoulder. Their walk seemed almost a dance, as when couples in the square dance move side by side to do a figure. Suddenly they jostled each other, like wrestlers, and lifted their forepaws, and turned, snarling, each trying for the other's throat. One raked his claws across the other's head and the snarls grew to a roar. The fighting was violent for a few moments, then the pair walked on, boxing, jostling, harrying. The wind was in Jody's favor. They could never smell him. He crept down the road after them, keeping his distance. He could not bear to lose sight of them. He hoped they would fight to a finish, yet he should be terrorized if one should end the fight and turn his way. He decided that they had been fighting for a long time and were exhausted. There was blood in the sand. Each attack seemed less violent than the others. Each shoulder-to-shoulder walking was slower paced. As he stared, a female walked out of the bushes ahead with three males following her. They turned silently into the road and walked on in single file. The fighting pair swung their heads a moment, then fell in behind. Jody stood until the procession passed from sight, solemn and ludicrous and exciting.

—Marjorie Kinnan Rawlings, *The Yearling*

2. The following selection from "The Lagoon" by Joseph Conrad has some interesting characteristics of style: the tone (somber, brooding, heavy, still), the position of the conjoined adjectives after the noun, the use of alliteration and other sound devices, and the use of negatives. After reading and analyzing this passage, do the following exercises:

a. Do a statistical count in which you give the total number of words in the passage, the number of words in each sentence, and the average sentence length.

b. Isolate those sentences with sound devices and underline the sounds that are repeated.

c. Discuss the use of the conjoined adjectives in this passage. What is the effect of their position after the noun?

d. Discuss those characteristics of style that support the tone in this passage.

e. Make a list of all the adjectives in the passage. Do they fall into meaning clusters? Discuss their use in the passage. Make similar lists for the adverbs, verbs, and nouns. What characteristics do these words have?

f. Discuss the use of imagery and figures of speech in this passage.

g. Do an imitation of this model, choosing a subject that lends itself to a somber tone.

The Lagoon

The Malay only grunted, and went on looking fixedly at the river. The white man rested his chin on his crossed arms and gazed at the wake of the boat. At the end of the straight avenue of forests cut by the intense glitter of the river, the sun appeared unclouded and dazzling, poised low over the water that shone smoothly like a band of metal. The forests, sombre and dull, stood motionless and silent on each side of the broad stream. At the foot of big, towering trees, trunkless nipa palms rose from the mud of the bank, in bunches of leaves enormous and heavy that hung unstirring over the brown swirl of eddies. In the stillness of the air every tree, every leaf, every bough, every tendril of creeper and every petal of minute blossoms seemed to have been bewitched into an immobility perfect and final. Nothing moved on the river but the eight paddles that rose flashing regularly, dipped together with a single splash; while the steersman swept right and left with a periodic and sudden flourish of his blade describing a glinting semicircle above his head. The churned-up water frothed alongside with a confused murmur. And the white man's canoe, advancing upstream in the short-lived disturbances of its own making seemed to enter the portals of a land from which the very memory of motion had forever departed.

—Joseph Conrad, "The Lagoon"

CHAPTER 14

Revising and Editing

Thomas Huxley maintained that he wrote essays a half-dozen times before he could "get them into proper shape." Robert Louis Stevenson vehemently declared: "When I say writing, O, believe me, it is rewriting that I have chiefly in mind." Yet many writers believe that the main task of writing is getting words down on paper.

Revision is *the process of matching what you have written against the intentions you form before you write, as you are writing, and after you have put the last word down on paper and of making modifications and changes.* The word *revision* means "to see again." **Editing** is *the process of making surface changes in a text,* such as changes in spelling, punctuation, format, and so forth. These are relative, rather than absolute distinctions, of course, since the movement of a single comma could signal a change in the writer's intention.

Before you put a single word down on paper, you go over ideas in your head, making choices, discarding some of those choices, substituting others. In other words, you revise in your head. After you construct your paradigm, you check the sentences to make certain that each is properly constructed and that each accurately conveys your intended meaning, the needs of your reader, your attitude toward your subject, your ethical and emotional stance, and your reasoning. As you are writing your paper, you continue to revise, matching your text against your original intention and against any new intentions that you might form as you are writing. Finally, after you finish your first draft, you revise by adding, deleting, substituting, rearranging, and reorganizing ideas and even entire paragraphs.

Whether you characteristically revise in your head as you are writing or stop to revise after you have finished a sentence or two or revise after you have finished your first draft, you can ask yourself certain questions that can be useful in helping you to make your revisions. The following checklist is intended to help you in this important task:

Revision Checklist

Revise so that what you have written fits your **intention:**

1. Does what I have written convey my intended meaning?
2. Does it fulfill the needs of my intended readers?
3. Does it accurately convey my attitude toward my subject?
4. Does it accurately reflect my ethical and emotional stance?

Revise so that what you have written fits into **the paper as a whole:**

1. Do I have a suitable introduction? Is it interesting and appropriate? Will it make my readers want to read on?

2. Do I have a clearly-defined thesis? Does it accurately convey my intended meaning? If I do not have a thesis sentence, is my intention implicit in the paper as a whole?

3. Does my paper clearly indicate a plan of development?

4. Are the successive steps easy to follow? Are there transitions from one part to another?

5. Do I use supporting details so that they strengthen the general statements in the paper?

6. Is my evidence appropriate? Is my reasoning sound? Have I considered possible objections?

7. Does my conclusion follow logically from all that has gone before? Is it effective? Does it leave my readers satisfied?

8. Is my paper as a whole clear? Have I included as many details as are necessary? Have I remembered that my audience may know little or nothing about my subject and that it is my responsibility to fill in the gaps?

9. Have I maintained a consistent point of view, or have I shifted unaccountably from one viewpoint to another, from one person to another?

10. Do I have an appropriate title? Does it reveal a close relationship to my central idea?

Revise so that your **paragraphs** accurately convey your intended meaning and fit into your overall plan:

1. Is each paragraph logically developed?

2. What is its function in the paper as a whole?

3. Does it function paradigmatically?

4. Is it used to support a general idea?

5. Is it used as a means of going from one part of the essay to another?

6. Do the sentences in each paragraph relate to each other and to the paragraph as a whole?

7. Are the sentences grammatical and effective?

8. Is the paragraph punctuated properly?

Revise so that your **sentences** accurately convey your intended meaning and fit appropriately into your paragraphs and into the plan of your entire essay:

1. Are my sentences varied in form?

2. Are my sentences varied in length?

3. Is each sentence clear and complete in itself?

4. Are the modifiers close to the words they modify?

5. Is there agreement between the subjects and the verbs?

6. Are subordinate ideas properly subordinated?

7. Are coordinate ideas properly coordinated?

8. Is each sentence properly punctuated?

9. Can any of the sentences be written more concisely?

10. Does each sentence relate logically and stylistically to the sentences around it?

Revise so that your **word choice** accurately conveys your intended meaning within the context of each sentence and in the paper as a whole:

1. Is my wording clear and accurate?

2. Is it appropriate in context?

3. Is it free from jargon and trite or stale expressions?

4. Is it formal when it should be formal, idiomatic when it should be, conversational when it is appropriate that it be so?

5. Is it free from vagueness or from unwarranted generalities?

6. Can I find a better word or phrase than the one I am currently using?

Finally, revise so that you match what you have written against **accepted rules** of spelling, punctuation, and other conventions:

1. Have I checked all doubtful spellings? Words I habitually misspell? Capital letters? Hyphens? Apostrophes?

2. Does my punctuation convey my intended meaning? Is it correct? Are commas used correctly? Dashes? Semicolons? Colons? Periods?

3. Are quotations properly credited and enclosed in quotation marks? Are ellipses and interpolations properly marked?

4. Is my manuscript neat and clean? No blotted or crossed-out lines?

5. Does this paper honestly represent my best effort?

A revision checklist can be helpful in assisting you to read and revise your writing. In addition to using a checklist, you might want to keep a notebook in which you record the kinds of problems you characteristically encounter in your writing.

The following are typical problems that recur in student writing.

Wordiness

Improve sentences and paragraphs that are needlessly wordy. Notice that this kind of advice is not necessarily the same as that which encourages you to write simply and directly. There are times when complex ideas should be expressed in complex grammatical structures. Nor is the injunction to avoid wordiness merely a matter of asking you to cut down on the length of a statement or a passage.

One type of wordiness to avoid in your writing is **tautology,** *the needless repetition of the same meaning in different words.* For example, in the following student sentence, the words *carelessly discarded* are not necessary to make out the sense of the sentence:

> Among the increasing tons of *carelessly discarded* litter befouling the country's beautiful scenery are hundreds of thousands of beer cans.

Since the word *litter* means "trash that has been carelessly discarded," the phrase *carelessly discarded* is a tautology that should be eliminated.

Similarly, in the following student sentence, there is no need to use the word *necessary* before the word *prerequisites.* The word *prerequisites* contains the meaning of "necessary."

> I don't think I have the *necessary* prerequisites for graduation.

Another type of wordiness to avoid is **redundancy,** that is, *using more words than are absolutely necessary.* Quite often, redundancy is the result of padding or of an inability to see how words work. In revising, therefore, you will want to cut out the padding.

For example, in the following student sentence, the word *today* can be substituted for the phrase "in this day and age" since both mean the same thing. The substitution immeasurably improves the sentence.

> *In this day and age,* a bachelor's degree is becoming commonplace.

> *Today,* a bachelor's degree is becoming commonplace.

Some kinds of wordiness are so obvious that they should be easy for you to spot:

> Dates with persons of the opposite sex, *be they male or female,* can be classified in many ways.

You can improve this sentence merely by deleting the phrase "be they male or female," since this information is already contained in the words *persons of the opposite sex.*

Other kinds of wordiness may not be as obvious, but with a little practice you will be able to spot these as well. The following student sentence is grammatically correct, but the revised version, which is less wordy, is much more effective:

> As long as *there are pressures from parents to force students to try and obtain* a college degree, *there will be the problem of the overcrowding of disinterested students* in the universities.

> As long as parents pressure students to get a college degree, uninterested students will crowd the universities.

In revising your paper to eliminate wordiness, you may want to combine several sentences within a paragraph, as in the following student example:

> Have you ever had the misfortune to own a misconceived piece of junk better known as a late-model car? Well, if you have or do own one of these lifelong lemons and want to sell or unload it, please listen close. If you follow the following steps, you can be successful.

The rewritten version is not only more concise, but it is also more effective:

> If you own a late-model car which is a lemon and if you want to unload it, follow these simple steps and you will be successful.

Jargon

Improve sentences that contain jargon. Jargon is characterized by the following faults.

1. *Using several words when one word will do:*

exhibits a tendency	tends
in an efficient manner	efficiently
make inquiry regarding	inquire
a not inconsiderable number	many

resembling in nature	like
reach a decision	decide
render operative	fix
causative factor	cause

2. *A preference for abstract nouns ending in -tion, -ity, -ment, -ness, -ance, -ative, -ate, -ous, -cy, -ist, and the like:*

utilization	dentition
nullity	pertinacity
apportionment	exigency
credulousness	diplomatist
discountenance	parsimonious

3. *Excessive use of words with Latin or Greek prefixes:*

abnegation	debriefing
circumspect	upgrade
contravene	antitechnology
nonpreferential	bioelemetric
intrazonal	dishabituate

4. *The use of stock phrases:*

in the final analysis
other things being equal
from the point of view of
within the framework of
in the event that

5. *The substitution of euphemisms for less explicit or offensive terms:*

terminal living	dying
mortician	undertaker
defensive maneuver	retreat
mild irregularity	constipation
bathroom tissue	toilet paper
loan expert	pawnbroker
senior citizens	old people
underprivileged	delinquent
criminally assaulted	raped
liquidation	assassination

6. *The overabundant use of clichés:*

lock, stock, and barrel	one and all
as thick as thieves	a grievous error
all to the good	null and void
blank amazement	safe and sound
pick and choose	fair and square

7. *The extensive use of the passive voice rather than the use of the more direct active voice:*

Job opportunities may be increased by higher education.
Higher education may increase job opportunities.

Competitive activities should be avoided.
Avoid competitive activities.

The report has been solicited by the committee.
The committee has solicited the report.

Almost all of these characteristics of jargon, of course, need qualifying. Occasionally, a long phrase such as *along the lines of* might be more appropriate for your purpose than *like.* You can't always avoid abstract nouns, especially if you need to refer to the special vocabulary of a particular discipline or profession. Latin and Greek prefixes often add flexibility to the language. Stock phrases such as "with reference to" sometimes enable your thoughts to flow more smoothly than do single words, and aid the rhythm of your sentence. It might be necessary occasionally to use euphemisms to avoid offending your audience, especially if you are dealing with death or bodily functions. Sometimes clichés add intensity to the language. Finally, there are times when you can't avoid the passive voice, especially when you don't know the agent of the action in your sentences.

Here are some guidelines that you may want to keep in mind in revising your sentences to avoid jargon.

Substitute short words for long words.
Avoid an excessive use of abstractions.
Substitute Anglo-Saxon words wherever possible for those of Latin or Greek origin.
Eliminate clichés and stock phrases.
Take out the euphemisms.
Change the passive voice to the active voice, unless you have a particular reason for using the passive voice.

Clearly, you must modify these guidelines in relation to your purpose, your audience, and the occasion. But much of the writing that you do will be of the kind that emphasizes economy of language for a general audience.

Shift in Point of View

Improve passages in your writing that contain unnecessary or illogical shifts in point of view. Illogical shifts in point of view may be the result of moving from one person or number to another, from one subject to another, or from one voice or tense to another.

Avoid illogical shifts in person and number. Notice how, in the following student theme, the writer shifts confusingly from *pilot* to *he* to *you* to *one*. I have included the pronoun *you* in places where it is understood.

A Preflight Inspection of Aircraft

A preflight inspection of an aircraft is a must before every flight. If the *pilot* does not make a preflight inspection, *he* will not know if the aircraft is fit for flight. *He* will be endangering the passengers' lives as well as his own. There are several checkpoints *one* must inspect in making a preflight check.

The first checkpoint is the cockpit. In the cockpit, *you* should first turn the main switch on and check the fuel gauges and the generator light, then turn the main switch off. Also, *you* should make sure the ignition switch is off and the fuel valve is on.

The second checkpoint is the rudder. *One* should check the rudder for proper movement and do the same for the elevator. Then *you* should disconnect the tail tie-down.

At checkpoint three, [*you* should] look for lumps or cracks in the wing. Also, [*you* should] check the flaps and ailerons for proper movement.

Checkpoint four is in the front of the wings. There *you* should check the main wheels for proper inflation. *One* should also make sure that the airspeed static source is not clogged.

Checkpoint five is the cowling. At this checkpoint, *you* should check the oil level and fill if necessary. Next [*you* should] make sure the propellor is free of nicks and cracks and that it is attached securely. Then [*you* should] check the carburetor for cleanliness and the fuel supply for quantity and contamination. In addition, [*you* should] make certain the tire is properly inflated.

Checkpoint six is at the end of the left wing. At this checkpoint, *one* should remove the pilot tube covering and check the pilot tube for stoppage. [*You* should] check also the stall warning vent for interference.

A *pilot* should make this preflight inspection before every flight so it becomes a habit. If *he* does not, *he* may get off the ground, but *he* might never come down.

You can improve this paper by rewriting it, keeping consistently to the same person and number, as in the following revision:

A preflight inspection of an aircraft is a must before every flight. If you do not make a preflight inspection, you will not know if the aircraft is fit for flight. You will be endangering the passengers' lives as well as your own. There are several checkpoints you must inspect in making a preflight check.

The first checkpoint is the cockpit. In the cockpit, you should first turn the main switch on and check the fuel gauges and the generator light, then turn the main switch off. Also, you should make sure the ignition is off the the fuel valve is on.

The second checkpoint is the rudder. You should check the rudder for proper movement and you should do the same for the elevator. Then you should disconnect the tail tie-down.

At checkpoint three, you should look for lumps or cracks in the wing. Also, you should check the flaps and ailerons for proper movement.

Checkpoint four is in the front of the wings. There you should check the main wheels for proper inflation. You should also make sure that the airspeed static source is not clogged.

Checkpoint five is the cowling. At this checkpoint, you should check the oil level and fill if necessary. Next you should make sure that the propellor is free of nicks and cracks and that it is attached securely. Then you should check the carburetor for cleanliness and the fuel supply for quantity and contamination. In addition, you should make certain the tire is properly inflated.

Checkpoint six is at the end of the left wing. At this checkpoint, you should remove the pilot tube covering and check the pilot tube for stoppage. You should check also the stall warning vent for interference.

You should make this preflight inspection before every flight so it becomes a habit. If you do not, you may get off the ground, but you might never come down.

There are other problems in this student paper, of course, but keeping consistently to the same person and number improves the paper considerably.

Avoid illogical or confusing shifts in subject, as in the following example:

The new cars are not very comfortable, but you can drive in relative safety.

In this sentence, there is a shift from talking about the comfort of new cars to talking about *your* driving them in relative safety. You can correct this by keeping to the same point of view.

The new cars are not very comfortable, but they are relatively safe.

Avoid confusing shifts in voice (from active to passive or from passive to active). The following student paragraph shifts awkwardly from the active to the passive voice:

Still another ad shows an endless amount of sand, sunlight, and heat. Then the camera is zoomed in and is focused on a can of underarm deodorant. The announcer's voice then explains that X deodorant will keep you dry.

You can rewrite this paragraph and make it more effective by changing the passive-voice verbs to the active voice:

Still another ad shows an endless amount of sand, sunlight, and heat. Then the camera zooms in and focuses on a can of underarm deodorant. The announcer's voice then explains that X deodorant will keep you dry.

Avoid awkward shifts in tense where such shifts are not clearly warranted, as in these student sentences:

The pitcher *came* up quickly and *tries* to strike out the batter.

Laura *asks* the doctor about her brother's condition but *received* an evasive answer.

She *goes* her way silently and no one *took* notice of her.

By getting back to town late, they *missed* the sale and thus *lose* the opportunity to buy the TV.

You can make these sentences clearer and more effective by sticking to one tense within a given sentence:

The pitcher *came* (comes) up quickly and *tried* (tries) to strike out the batter.

Laura *asked* (asks) the doctor about her brother's condition but *received* (receives) an evasive answer.

She *went* (goes) her way silently and no one *took* (takes) notice of her.

By getting back to town late, they *missed* (miss) the sale and thus *lost* (lose) the opportunity to buy the TV.

Revising the Whole Theme

In addition to revising your paper along the lines suggested, you may need to make more extensive changes in your paper, in keeping with your original intention, your organizational plan, and your audience. Some of the questions in the revision checklist that pertain to the paper as a whole would be appropriate here. Remember that to revise is not merely to make superficial changes in your paper or simply to recopy it. It is rather to see your work again with a new vision, to improve it over your first effort.

The following student revision goes beyond making a few mechanical changes. The paper is an analysis of a Lindsay olive ad that appeared in *Sunset* magazine. The picture depicts a young boy dressed like a poor character from a Charles Dickens novel. He gazes longingly at a huge sandwich which is in the foreground of the picture. The sandwich has layers of ham, salami, and cheese, with olives generously sprinkled about. The text reads as follows:

The Oliver Twist from Lindsay!

(It beats the Dickens out of ordinary sandwiches.)

Great Expectations! Feed a family of four with fun and frivolity. It's easy! Just slice, hollow and butter a loaf of round bread. Then pile on slices of ham, salami, cheese and anything else your family loves in a sandwich. Add pimento pieces, lettuce and fresh onion rings. Now sprinkle a generous handful of Lindsay Ripe Pitted Black Olives between the layers. They add a special nutlike mellow flavor—plus added color and excitement. That's the Oliver.

Now the Twist: Press your sandwich to blend the ingredients together. Slice, serve and enjoy! That's the Oliver Twist from Lindsay—a Dickens of a great sandwich!

An olive is just an olive . . . unless it's a Lindsay.

Here is the student paper, which was written in response to an assignment to analyze an ad and evaluate its effectiveness in relation to its intended audience:

With Oliver Twist (or possibly his literary first cousin, David Copperfield) gazing longingly in the background at a huge sandwich called "The Oliver Twist," Lindsay foods presents a clever ad in the December 1978 edition of *Sunset* magazine. By using heavy literary allusions, a little alliteration, and sophisticated manipulation of puns, the ad is successful in presenting and marketing Lindsay olives.

The ad is rich in literary allusions, both visually and textually. The sanwich itself, made of round bread suggests a bygone era to the world of 24-slice one-pound loaves, as well as forming the triangle base that eventually leads the eye to the waif in the background, heavily reminiscent of Oliver Twist asking for "some more."

The literary allusions are continued in the text. The headline mentions Oliver Twist, the secondary headline recalls the author, Dickens, and *Great Expectations* (another Dickens work) leads off the body copy. These references appeal to the more learned audience as they would be unintelligible to anyone not familiar with Dickens, they also form the base for the sophisticated use of puns.

By far the most successful stylistic device is the use of puns. The primary headline develops the frame of mind needed for the two major plays on words. The Oliver Twist, we are told, "beats the Dickens out of ordinary sandwiches." The use of literary allusions, but especially the puns, causes the audience to keep reading. *Great Expectations* is another play on words as it parallels the reader's anticipation as well as continues the literary theme. After detailing the process of making the sandwich (appropriately called the Oliver), the audience is told there's a "Twist"— completing the second major point. The pun cycle is completed with Dickens again being used in a different wordplay.

The simple expository sentences, heavy in parallelism, are momentarily suspended with a strong alliterative "f" causing a sense of frivolity. This sense of frivolity causes the reader to continue.

By appealing to a literary audience, developing a general sense of frivolity, and by using sophisticated puns, the Lindsay ad causes the reader to finish the ad and envision himself using the product. These are features of a successful ad.

This paper is good in parts, but it certainly needs more than the correction of mechanical and grammatical errors. These consist primarily of a lapse in spelling or editing (sanwich), a run-on-sentence ("These references appeal to the more learned audience as they would be unintelligible to anyone not familiar with Dickens, they also form the base for the sophisticated use of puns"), and a dangling modifier ("After detailing the process of making the sandwich, appropriately called the Oliver, the audience is told there's a "Twist"—completing the second major point").

What this student has failed to do is to develop and explain his ideas fully, especially in the fourth and fifth paragraphs. He needs to give more examples, explain them, and quote from the text. Finally, he needs to rewrite some sentences that are awkward or in which the meaning is not clear.

The following is a revised version of this paper.

> With Oliver Twist gazing longingly in the background at a huge sandwich called "The Oliver Twist," Lindsay foods presents a clever ad in the December 1978 edition of *Sunset* magazine, the magazine of western living. The ad uses literary allusions, puns, alliteration, and parallel structure to sell Lindsay olives.
>
> The ad is rich in literary allusions. The waif in the background of the illustration is heavily reminiscent of Oliver Twist, a character in the Dickens novel of the same name. The sandwich itself is made of a round bread that could have been made in the nineteenth century. The sandwich is cut into two pieces and arranged in the shape of a triangular wedge that leads the reader's eye to the young boy who is looking hungrily at the sandwich.
>
> The literary allusions are continued in the text. The headline, which reads "The Oliver Twist from Lindsay," is a reference not only to the sandwich, but also to the character Oliver Twist, in the Dickens novel. The next line ("It beats the Dickens out of ordinary sandwiches") is a play on the word *dickens* and an allusion to Charles Dickens. The opening line of the copy ("Great Expectations!") refers literally to what the reader could expect from a can of Lindsay olives and is an allusion to the title of another of Dicken's novels. The ad concludes with two more allusions: to Oliver Twist ("That's the Oliver Twist from Lindsay") and to Charles Dickens ("a Dickens of a great sandwich!").
>
> By far the most successful stylistic device is the use of puns. "The Oliver Twist," we are told, "beats the Dickens out of ordinary sandwiches." The puns on the words *Oliver Twist* and *Dickens* can be understood in at least two senses. Oliver Twist is the name of the sandwich and the name of the young boy in the Dickens novel. The word *dickens* refers to Charles Dickens, and it is also a mild oath. Other puns similar to these can be found in the lines "That's the Oliver," "Now the Twist," "That's the Oliver Twist," and "a Dickens of a great sandwich."
>
> Alliteration is used effectively in the line "Feed a family of four with fun and frivolity." The alliteration (the "f" sounds) seems to reinforce the playful tone of the ad.
>
> Finally, the parallel structure combines with the word choice to convey a concrete, descriptive picture of the "makings" that go into the sandwich: "Just slice, hollow, and butter a loaf of round bread"; "Then pile on

slices of ham, salami, cheese and anything else your family loves on a sandwich"; "Add pimento pieces, lettuce, and fresh onion rings."

The reader of *Sunset* magazine is probably a person who has some education and money for leisure living, since the contents of the magazine have to do with food, outdoor living and travel. Such a reader would be delighted by the allusions to Charles Dickens, by the playful language, and by the alliteration and parallelism. These stylistic devices, combined with the illustration, make for a very effective selling appeal.

Exercises

1. Before turning in your next composition, bring it to class. Then read it aloud to the class. The other members of the class should criticize it, using the revision checklist and offering constructive suggestions for revision.

2. As an in-class project, exchange papers with one of your classmates and make suggestions on the paper for revision.

3. Ask your instructor to put one of your themes on an overhead projector or an opaque projector and then have the class analyze it and offer constructive criticism.

4. Discuss in class the problems in the following student essays, and suggest ways of improving these essays.

Doodles

People who doodle during passive periods often reveal more about themselves than they do about their artistic ability. Although doodling is merely a means of relieving nervous tensions, it often times is a graphic manifestation of an individual's unconscious mind. Therefore, doodles in fact, can be insights to an individual's personality, thoughts, and even sexual attitudes.

Generally speaking, a person's personality is determined by the way in which the individual acts and reacts. People who do not outwardly express themselves through actions and verbal communication may do so through doodling. People with different personalities will doodle in a different manner. For example, a person who is meek and timid might doodle with thin lines and unattached figures. The thin line indicates that the person is very frail and afraid to bear down when faced with perplexing problems. Also, meekness can be equated with an inferior feeling about themselves.

Thus, an inability to assert a solid position in a particular situation or circumstance. The unconnected configuration is also a sign of meekness. This type of figure illustrated an inability to cope with any task which is too hard to complete. Rather than attack the problem at its base the timid person would rather let it drop with the excuse of being too difficult. Other doodles that might indicate meek personalities are: unshaded squares and geometric figures; indicating emptiness and loneliness, and circles; which relates to a continuous fear of inferiority.

On the other hand, in a strong, dominating personality the doodles change radically in the opposite direction. A person with this type of personality is most often very sure of intended actions and will usually see a problem through to the very end. Their doodles are usually bold, precise, and definite in shape and size. Such doodles are objects, and depending upon artistic ability, closely resemble the object as it appears in real life. The objects might include human caricatures; indicating a positive relationship with others, animals, and a three-dimensional-objects; indicating solidity of thought and firmness of mind.

A person's thoughts can also be interpreted by analyzing their casual scribblings. By looking at their doodles it is possible to determine what mood or state of mind the person was in at that particular time. For example, if the doodles are made up of cross-hatched lines or a series of broken-line designs this could show an existant state of confusion in the mind of the individual. Moods of happiness, sadness, and loneliness can also be seen in the doodles of the individual. Doodles which might indicate happiness are quick, curly, and generally take the form of flower-like sketches. A person might unknowingly draw this type of doodle while speaking to someone whom they haven't seen in a long period of time. Sadness can also be a factor in determining the type of doodle which is produced at that particular instant. For example, a mood of sadness can be linked with small circular-like objects; denoting emptiness and a sense small and unimportant. Other doodles which also seem to indicate sadness are first names of an actual person. Such a case might involve the departure or breakup of friends or lovers. The sad individual might write the other person's name over and over, thus showing an actual mood of sadness because the other person has left. In most cases, loneliness is a factor of sadness and, therefore, the doodles are similar to those of sadness.

In most cases, doodles can reveal the sexual attitude or tendency of an individual. A person who is pre-occupied with the thought of sex will doodle in a very distinct manner. All the doodles will indicate sexual body parts and sexual ideas. Those doodles which might be equated with sexual thoughts are short straight lines, rounded objects, circular objects with depth, and the intersection of circles and lines. Logically, the circular and rounded objects indicate the female body, and the straight-line object represent the male body. All of these types of doodles might indicate the desire to take part in sexual relationships. Although this is not a positive means of determining sexual attitudes it does, in fact, give a good indication of it.

In conclusion, by analyzing the doodles of an individual it is possible to determine certain aspects of that individual's character at a particular time. Doodles often leave a picture of the mood a person was in while drawing them. Doodles can determine a person's personality, thoughts, and sexual attitudes.

How to Survive Loneliness

Loneliness is an appalling ordeal, encasing its victim in a desolate world. If he is to survive, the individual must learn to cope with his dilemma. To dispossess this perplexity requires the careful observance of the sufferers habitat, recreation, and thoughts.

The victim of loneliness must use the eyes of Argus when choosing his environmental habitat. He should try to find a location in midst a mass of extroverts. Their gregarious characteristics might draw the victim into their circle, curing him of his problem. If this desired location can not be found, his abode should be in the approximate area of a center of communal entertainment. This will, in all likelihood, give him a temporary reprieve from the torment of his plight. Under no circumstances should the individual choose a secluded dwelling. Seclusion only adds to the pain, driving him deeper into the depths of his despair.

When the pangs of loneliness strike, the victim must find some way to salve his feelings. People are the only balm which can truly help this attack. If no people can be reached, a movie or play could prove helpful. He should show discretion in picking his subject, making sure not to choose one that would bring an old memory to surface. This memory would only be likely to increase his pain. To become a Bacchanalian is another route. It is not as desirous as the others because of an unwanted self-reproach which accompanies such indulgences. This self-reproach can cause a more serious problem than the symptom it was to have cured. It occurs the individual should abandon this means immediately.

The person afflicted with loneliness will find, in the long run, only he can find his own cure. No lasting results can be achieved unless the individual convinces himself that loneliness is just a state of mind. He should start telling himself that he is equal to the next man. This has a tendency to lower the barriers separating him from others. It is only when those barriers of the difference are lowered can loneliness be uprooted and expelled. The suffering individual should not, at any time, feel sorry for himself. If he should start feeling this way, it will increase his feeling of isolation, causing him to slide further into desolation.

If an individual is to defeat his loneliness, he must meet it head on. There are an infinite number of ways a person may vie with this feeling. I have shown you the three that have helped me the greatest in my struggle with this adversary. It is through these eternal battles that I found that a careful regulation of habitat, recreation, and thoughts prove effective as a nemesis of loneliness.

Don't Be Fooled by Advertisements

Don't be fooled into thinking advertisements are innocent. They will stoop to any means to manipulate your mind. The diabolical weapons of the advertiser include slanted language, inferences, sly use of connotation, generalization with no supporting fact and claims that certain things will happen after buying their product. Our best defense against these diabolical weapons is objective analysis.

"It could well be the world's most wanted car," is the opening statement of an advertisement for 1972 Cadillac. Look at how extremely general and shallow the statement is. General, in the sense that it could be applied to any car. Shallow, in the sense that it doesn't say anything specific. A classic example of generalization without factual foundation. Working upon the assumption that the reader has accepted this primary statement we proceed. "Some want it for the way it looks . . . its beauty of line and form." Line and form are used for their connotative meanings. These words are used in description of art like great paintings and sculpture. An example of the sly use of connotation is seen here. It is ridiculous to equate a mass produced car with a sculpture of Michelangelo. A parallel statement appears later in the advertisement. "The finest of the automaker's art." The word "art" is used to deceive reader into thinking each car is tediously worked upon like a sculpture of Michelangelo. The word "achievement" is important to look at as well. It has a connotation of something that has been accomplished successfully, especially by means of exertion, skill, practice or perseverance. It reinforces the art connotation very well. "Some for what it says about them to others." This phrase exhibits a terrible lack of specifics. What does it say to others? Instead of answering the question in words, the advertiser cleverly uses a picture. Above the picture of the car, appears a group of affluent people at an expensive restaurant. A faint image of a flower appears over the scene. The importance of the restaurant scene is it shows what image you will, supposedly, produce if you own a Cadillac. The importance of the flower is it has a connotation of beauty and elegance. Owning a Cadillac is no indication of how elegant and affluent you are. If a person has 8,000 dollars he or she can own a Cadillac. This is regardless of how beautiful or affluent they may be. An illustration of how things will happen if you buy our product is seen here. "Some for its resale value, traditionally highest of any car in the land." Strange, recently, on television, I heard Skylark had the highest resale value. Factual information seems to be lacking in this claim. "Some for what it represents in driving peace of mind." Peace of mind has the connotation of inner contentment, calm and serenity. Driving a Cadillac doesn't remove the fears and dangers of driving. These factors exist no matter what type of car you're driving. Peace of mind is a phrase people love to hear because of what it implies. Mrs. Merritt, a well-known figure, once said, "If you put things into nice language, you can make anything sound nice." Cadillacs don't produce peace of mind in driving but by using the nice phrase "peace of mind" they are tricked into accepting it. "It could well be everything you've ever wanted in an automobile." Does the form look familiar? It should, they are using the same ambiguity they used to begin the advertisement to end it. The statement infers Cadillac is everything you've ever wanted in a car. However, by using the word "could" the company has completely detached itself from all liability. Meaning, that if their car isn't what you wanted you can't hold it against them because they said "it could be everything you've ever wanted," not it *is* everything you've ever wanted. Appearing at the bottom of the page is an article about how GM is progressively reducing exhaust emissions was because of government action. Don't believe they care more about the consumer than their profits. If they did care they would have taken more action earlier and on a much larger scale.

Now for an overall look at the advertisement. The language is sophisticated to express the prestige of the car and appeal to the class of people who buy it. The word "some" is used over and over again. There are two reasons behind it. The first reason is because it has a connotation of individualism. Knowing the society stresses rugged individualism, the advertiser wants to make you feel like one. This advertisement used language usage integrated with visual suggestion fantastically. Advertisements are extremely subversive. I urge the reader to really consider the points I have made. The next time you see an advertisement don't automatically swallow it hook, line and sinker, use objective analyzation!!!!

CHAPTER 15

The Research Paper

Classifying Research

Popular Research

You may not realize it, but you read research every day. Newspaper reporters who call in their stories to the copywriters have "researched" their assignments. The magazines you read, whether they are news magazines or magazines dedicated to your favorite sport or hobby, are full of carefully researched articles. Usually a magazine maintains a staff who, jointly or individually, receive assignments from the editor on specified subjects, just as you do in the classroom. On the other hand, many articles are written by freelancers, people who are not attached to one magazine, but who sell their skills to several magazine editors and publishers.

Freelancers are faced with much the same dilemma as you may be if you're writing a research paper for your composition class or for any other class in which a research paper might be required. They must come up with a topic interesting to a general audience, then submit it for approval. (They request this approval in a query letter to an editor, who must "buy" the idea—just as your instructor may want to pass judgment on your topic before you begin writing.) Next, article writers immerse themselves in their topic, live with it, talk about it to their friends, research it in and out of libraries, write their article, submit it in the manuscript form required by the magazine—and wait. The only difference between you as a student and the professional article writers is this: the professional waits for a check; you wait for a grade. But you are both writers, and you both have the satisfaction of having become a mini-expert on a topic that shortly before, you knew nothing about. Most popular magazines are geared to a general audience, which has needs somewhat different from those of the scholarly audience we will look at later.

Think, for a minute, of the reasons that lead you to pick up a magazine, and about the kinds of titles that attract you. Most of us like to find out about other people, especially celebrities. The cover of *Tennis* offers us "What Top Pros Tell Themselves on Court" (Dec. 1983). We also like reassurance that others have the same problems we do. *Working Woman* offers its readers "The Child Care Conundrum" (Sept. 1983). We like to learn how to make things, where to travel, how to save money. *Yankee Magazine's Travel Guide to New England* (Summer/Fall 1983) features on the cover "Fun-Filled Day Trips," "Shopping Finds," and " 'New England Favorites' Including Hikes, Clambakes, Muffins, Foliage Tours, Bike Rides, Ice Cream and Much More." Finally, we read simply to satisfy our curiosity. The cover of *Food and Wine* tempts us with "The Seductive Flavors of Hong Kong" (March 1983). *Newsweek* tells us what it's like to be "Homeless in America" (Jan. 2, 1984). Why look at this inventory of titles? Because they help us to classify the ways in which research on popular topics is presented to the general audience. They clarify for the writer what formats a reader has come to expect: the process pattern, outlined for you in Chapter 7, the analysis pattern (Chapter 4), and a pattern used frequently by popular magazines, the informative pattern. You will find more on the informative pattern in the section "Patterns for Presenting Research."

For now, let us move away from research intended for the general audience, which we will call "popular research," and into a discussion of academic research.

We may read an article in a magazine out of sheer curiosity, and then never think of it again, or think of it just fleetingly. Unless the article is persuasive, the author has succeeded, simply by having us read the article. But scholars who write journal articles would not be pleased if readers merely read their work. Scholars write to share, test, and apply knowledge, and the product of their research appears in journals.

Academic Research

Like popular research, academic research is written in part to satisfy curiosity. Popular research, however, is written to sell magazines or newspapers—it is designed to have broad, popular appeal. The primary purpose of academic research is to share, test, and apply knowledge; it is read primarily by the scholarly community. In fact, the audience for this type of research narrows still more; each discipline has its own journals, and even within disciplines, there are specialties that in turn create more journals. Figure 1 represents some of the journals and target audiences aimed at English departments. The journals are arranged from general to most specific audiences.

Figure 1 illustrates for you the range of audiences in one field, and we didn't even touch upon linguistics and style, another area subject found in English departments. Remember this range in your own research writing, and have a target audience in mind when you design the format for your work.

We might have illustrated a similar hierarchy of general-to-specific audiences for popular magazines. Many general magazines, for example, contain sections on recipes and cooking techniques. But some magazines like *Bon Appétit, Gourmet,* and *Food and Wine* are devoted exclusively to culinary interests. Even more specifically, some food magazines are directed to cooking with one piece of equipment. *The Pleasures of Cooking,* for example, is aimed at those who own food processors.

But we have assumed that you probably have hobbies or special interests and already read magazines geared to those interests. You are familiar then with the way in which information is presented in such publications. In fact, if asked, you could probably write an article on

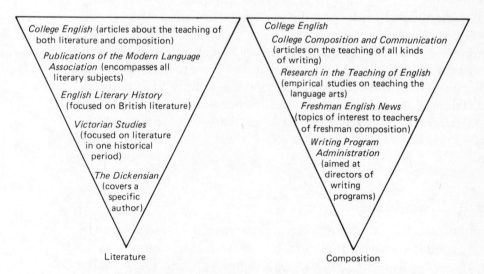

Figure 1   **Some journals and target audiences available for English Departments**

your hobby or interest and do a fair imitation of the style in your favorite magazine.

But understandably, you may not be familiar with the style of scholarly writers. One reason beginning scholars have some difficulty with their first research assignment is that they are not accustomed to journal articles; students like yourself, they are unfamiliar with the expectations of an academic audience. Until you have assimilated the formats of patterns in which academic research occurs, you cannot reproduce them as you could, perhaps, a "how-to" article geared to a popular magazine. You may have gathered excellent material, but the organization of that material will not meet your scholarly reader's expectations, whether in biology, psychology, art, communications, or any of the academic fields.

We have seen some of the major journals in English studies, and later in the chapter, under "Looking for Material," you will learn how to find the major journals in your field or subject of interest. But what are these mysterious patterns of scholarly research? Two scholars, Robert A. Schwegler and Linda K. Shamoon, have helped us become more aware of the precise shape these patterns take. Their article appears in *College English* and is titled "The Aims and Process of the Research Paper."[1] Here is a summary of what these authors have discovered about academic research. The academic research paper (or "article," as it is called when published) has four basic patterns, like those you have studied in this text in that they provide an organization for the article.

1. Review of research (sharing knowledge). The review-of-research paper may be your first long paper assignment in your chosen field, coming as early as your freshman year if you are enrolled in one of the professional schools or in a program such as nursing, pharmacy, dental hygiene, or engineering. Because you are just beginning, you probably don't know enough about your subject to test a hypothesis or perform an experiment, or even to apply someone else's theory to a new area. But you can find out what has already been accomplished in your field, and sometimes more important, what has not—that is, subjects requiring research. When you do a review of the literature, it must be more than a strung-together list of what everyone has written about or experimented upon. You, as author, are re-

---

[1] Robert A. Schwegler and Linda K. Shamoon, "The Aims and Process of the Research Paper," *College English* 47, no. 8 (December 1982): 817–24.

sponsible for identifying areas of agreement among scholars, areas of conflict, and areas that remain to be researched. In short, you must synthesize and analyze the material you find. Carrie Rae's paper on seabed mining, at the end of this chapter, is a review-of-research paper.

2. Applying or implementing a theory (applying knowledge). When you apply a theory, it doesn't always have to be your own. In using this pattern of research, the writer applies a generally accepted theory to a new situation or subject. The writer is not required to prove the theory, but need only show that the theory is useful in explaining a new phenomenon. You may even have encountered this pattern in an essay exam question, in a form something like this:

> Apply X's theory of media exploitation as a partial explanation of the phenomenal rise in home computer sales. Cite specific advertisements.

The excerpt from the student paper below illustrates this pattern. The student applies training in clinical pharmacy (theory) to the hospital setting to demonstrate how hospitals that adopt a clinical pharmacy program can save patients' lives (phenomenon). Though her explanation is practical, the clinical pharmacy program itself is based on a theory of doctor-pharmacist-patient interaction.

> An elderly woman was admitted to the hospital for chest pain. Her heart doctor prescribed a drug to regulate her heartbeat and relieve the pain. At the same time, her family physician prescribed medication for blood pressure, which altered the function of her kidneys. Her kidneys could no longer eliminate the heart medication from her system at the same rate, causing toxic levels of the drug to rise in her body. Three days later, the patient died from overdose.
>
> Incidents similar to those, although maybe not as severe, happen quite often in the hospital setting. The demand for pharmacists with the ability to analyze therapeutic problems and work with physicians to construct optimal drug therapy for specific patients gave rise to the development of clinical pharmacy.
>
> Such pharmacists practice on the wards, obtain drug histories from patients, and advise the prescriber at the time and place that drug use decisions are made. These clinically oriented pharmacists are also involved in monitoring drug therapy, detecting and treating adverse drug reactions, and counseling patients on appropriate drug use upon discharge.

Pioneering such a program may be costly to the hospital; the program, however, will pay for itself by saving time, lawsuits, unnecessary pain for the patient, and most important, human life, which is *priceless.*

The hospital hires the clinical pharmacists and their staff. The program is incorporated into the general routine of the hospital and is recognized by both physician and nursing faculty.

The pharmacists review a patient's drug regimen and then may consult with the prescriber, give advice, or question the drug dispensed. The physician must give a reason for the drug prescribed that is acceptable to the clinical pharmacists. If the reason is unacceptable, the drug is discontinued. If the physician refuses to discontinue the drug, he may be dismissed from the care of his patient or not allowed to practice in the hospital.

The program is invaluable because human life is involved. The unlimited number of drug interactions guarantees a bright future for clinical pharmacy and proves that this is truly a program for the patient.

—Marita Sherbo

3. Refute, refine, or replicate prior research (testing knowledge). Again, this pattern is one that may be familiar to you from essay exams. You have probably seen a question like this:

> Marshall McLuhan states that "The medium is the message." Agree or disagree.

In a fifty-minute class period, you are not usually expected to provide documentation for your answer, unless you have been studying work by several scholars on one issue, and your instructor has indicated that you should be prepared to support your opinions with scholarship. In a lengthy research assignment, however, you may choose to replicate another's experiment. In performing the same experiment, you may decide to change the methodology, by adding another step or refining steps already used; to try a different data base; or even to duplicate a prior experiment exactly, but to disagree with the researcher's conclusions. You may find that the methods used previously were unworkable or unreliable; you may then reject the prior research entirely. Of course, this pattern includes refuting or refining theories in the humanities as well as modifying or corroborating experiments as they are performed in the sciences and social sciences.

The essay exam question suggested above is an example of a

theory that might be debated. Below is an example of experimentation in the sciences that the author believes needed refinement. Michael wrote the following passage as an abstract of his research paper "The Blue Mussel as an Indicator of Stressed Environments":

Prior research

Refinement of prior research

Environmental research has indicated that the blue mussel (*Mytilus edilus*) is a valuable organism in marine research. These organisms concentrate pollutants in their tissues, have a large geographic range, filter debris from seawater, supply food for a variety of animals including man, and occur in abundant numbers along shorelines. Thus, the organism plays a key role when determining biological effects of the pollutants on marine ecosystems. Variations in morphology occur because of climate, geographic location, and season. Scientists must consider these variations during analysis of data. Histopathology, the study of tissues at the cellular level, had not been noticed as a potential asset to marine research until recently. Histopathology was included in a marine project and has proven itself. Results showed adverse effects in animals to PCBs, petroleum, DDT, and nuclear waste, but showed no effects in animals exposed to high concentrations of metals.

—Michael Casey

4. Testing a hypothesis (testing knowledge). You learned about testing hypotheses back in elementary school when you studied the steps in the scientific method. We test hypotheses all the time in our daily lives:

My new car has been stalling. It has an electronic fuel injection system and so it shouldn't stall. Let me check my owner's manual. Maybe I'm starting it wrong. I'll try not turning the key all the way until I hear the beep that means the fuel is finished pumping into the tank.

*   *   *

My car hasn't stalled for a month, ever since I've been careful starting it. It's been just as cold and wet out as it was before, and so it couldn't be the weather. I must have been starting it wrong.

But even though you are probably most familiar with this pattern of research, some experimenters consider it the most challenging form because of the close observation of phenomena and the original thinking it requires. This method of research also frequently includes patterns one and three above: reviewing research (called "review of the literature") and refuting prior research for faulty methodolgies, inaccurate premises, inadequate or unsubstantial conclusions, and so on.

When You Are Assigned a Research Paper

So much of successful research depends on attitude that it's a good place to start when considering the procedures to follow in your research. When you hear that your course will include a research paper, view the task as a challenge, not a chore. To be immediately practical, realize that a research project usually carries much weight in the final grade. Isn't it reassuring to know that you are in control over that grade, that you have several weeks to put into displaying your talents and knowledge rather than one or two periods of in-class exams? Research papers take a long time to grade and consume large blocks of an instructor's time. Therefore, instructors who assign them are providing you with a chance to succeed by what you can give, and not just what the instructor can give you.

But aside from grades, there are other advantages to writing a research paper. You can become a mini-expert on a subject that many people will know little about. Researching provides you with fresh material for conversation and with new knowledge you may find helpful in other courses or in your future career.

If you become truly engrossed in a subject that has popular appeal, you might look into marketing your article to a magazine, enriching your bank account as well as your mind. "Me?" you ask. Certainly. Several of my students, even at the freshman level, have successfully sold their articles to Sunday supplements or to other magazines. But the result depends on your initial attitude. You must think of yourself as a writer and a researcher, not as a student mechanically completing an assignment.

If there are so many advantages to writing a research paper, why are so many students numb with terror when they hear a lengthy paper is part of the course? It is because of that one word—lengthy. Inexperienced researchers think they will never be able to fill up ten pages. The blank space stretches frighteningly before them.

Experienced researchers, on the other hand, know that their hardest job will be selecting from a pile of material, and cutting their work to fit the appropriate space. If you can lose your fear of blank pages, and look forward instead to the excitement of finding material on your topic, you'll be ready to carry out successful research.

Choosing a Topic

Talk About Your Assignment

In some courses, a topic will be assigned. At the end of this chapter you'll read a paper by Arlene Nardiello, who was assigned the broad topic "American Politics" in her communications skills class. She was free to choose anything encompassed by that topic, and she chose small-town campaigning. Her reason was a good one. When Arlene told her father about her assignment, he offered to help her arrange interviews with politicians in her hometown. Arlene thought about her assignment a bit more, and realized that one of her professors at URI was campaigning and might be willing to grant her an interview. Arlene quickly realized that her opportunities to interview politicians would not extend to the national level, and so she limited her topic to "Small-Town Politics." Later, when her material began to suggest a pattern, Arlene further narrowed her subject to campaigning for election in a small town. She had not yet been to the library, but was able to arrive at her focused topic by talking about her assignment to many people.

When Arlene did eventually use the library for background material, she met several frustrated fellow students trying to "find a topic in the card catalog." Professional researchers and writers agree that the library is frequently the last stop for them, not the first.

Live with your assignment, talk about it to your family and friends, think about it when you're driving to and from work or school (instead of turning on the stereo), even talk out loud to yourself about it. Undoubtedly, you will not only find a topic, you will experience it through other people's eyes, and you will collect information and ideas. When you go to the library, you will be in control of your topic; you won't be waiting for it to leap out at you from a card-catalog drawer. Carrie Rae, author of the second research paper you'll read, was not able to collect quite as much information as Arlene before using the library. But Carrie did talk about her assignment with an engineer (she is a civil engineering major). She knew she wanted to do something related to her major. Her engineer friend suggested that very few people knew anything about ocean dredging, the gathering of minerals from the ocean floor. Intrigued, Carrie decided to find out more. The system she used begins in the section "Looking for Material."

Deciding on Audience

We have looked at the range of audiences for both popular and scholarly materials. Your first decision will be at which audience you are aiming your article. If you are assigned a research paper for your freshman composition class, it is quite acceptable to imagine a general, popular audience as your target unless your instructor specifies otherwise. If the assignment is in your major field, you will want to check with your instructor about the intended audience. The instructor may suggest you model your article after a specific journal in the field and may recommend one; if not, inquire about one.

Arlene's paper "On the Road to Success" is aimed at the general audience, readers of *Newsweek* or *Time*, perhaps. She wrote it for a freshman writing and speaking course. Carrie's audience is a bit more specialized, though not as technical as a journal article. She imagined her audience as readers of a magazine like *Science*, a general audience with a specific interest. Her paper was written for a course in scientific and technical writing, and illustrates a "review of research" pattern.

Looking for Material

Why Start Early?

So often, when students are admonished to "Start early!" they shrug and reply "But I work better under pressure." Ah, yes! But you can't work if you don't have the material to work with. The library is not the only source of information. You may decide your topic requires personal interviews, or you may want to write to government agencies for information. (Interviewing and contracting sources are covered in later sections of this chapter.) Arranging interviews within schedules besides your own, and waiting for material to arrive in the mail can take several weeks.

Although Carrie Rae decided on her topic early in the semester, she began her research only three weeks before the project was due. As she began finding material, she realized there were people she could talk to and sources she could write to about seabed mining. If only she had more time! I interviewed Carrie after her paper had been turned in, graded, and selected as a model for this chapter. Her biggest regret was that she didn't start earlier because she couldn't think of an approach to her topic. As she became excited about what she found in the library, she realized "It would have been fun to get more material in the mail. I would like to have seen myself take more initiative." She also realized that if she'd begun early, interviewing local experts, her problem of an approach would probably have been solved in conversation. Arlene Nardiello, on the other hand, began her project early in the semester and found her experience much richer because she had the time to schedule interviews during Thanksgiving break, when she was home in New Jersey. She also had time to wait for materials to arrive in the mail.

On top of interviewing and sending away for material, tracking down leads in the library can take you hours or even days longer than you expect if you are unfamiliar with the library. A sketch of a morning I spent in the library will begin to introduce you to research in the library. Notice two themes in this example: (1) the time it takes to do research, and (2) the system of thinking to follow in looking for material.

Using the Library: A Narrative Tour

Recently, I set out to learn a little about children whose parents decide to educate them at home. It was one of those things I wanted to read up on. I didn't have a paper due; it wasn't an urgent quest.

After a morning meeting in the library one day, I began by checking the Library of Congress Subject Headings. A thick book usually lying on tables near the card catalog, it tells how the headings are arranged in the card catalog so that you'll waste no time looking under headings that don't exist. Neither Carrie nor Arlene knew about the subject headings, and both expressed to me their frustration with the card catalog. Carrie looked in the catalog under "ocean dredging," "dredging," and many other headings. Finally, she hit on "mining" and found "seabed mining." But she lost time that the Library of Congress headings would have saved her. Here is my tour.

I open the book to "Education," the broadest possible category for my topic. I don't find one heading that strikes me as exactly what I want, and so I approach the nine drawers of catalog cards on education, still without a clue as to what to look under.

Because the phase of the phenomenon I want to investigate is fairly recent, I decide to check under "Education—Periodicals," for periodicals carry more up-to-date information than books. There I find some possibilities, among them *The Journal of Experimental Education.* Maybe that will tell me something about education at home, a type of experiment. Then I find, on a card marked "MFORM," *The Massachusetts Teacher: A Journal of School and Home Education.* I know that this journal is downstairs in the microform room and that I'll have to spend time reading it at one of the machines if I decide it's useful. The card also tells me the magazine was printed from 1848 to 1874—it may have value as a historical precedent for home education. I also learn that in January 1875 this journal was united with several others to form the *New England Journal of Education.*

I decide to check Education—History in the card catalog, but find nothing useful there. Next, I try an index, a list, by subject, of articles in various publications. Indexes range from guides to popular literature (*Readers Guide to Periodical Literature*) to very specific scholarly material (*Music Index*). A list of indexes that might be useful to you appears in the next section.

For my purpose, I choose to look in the Public Affairs Information Services Bulletin (PAIS), because education is most often a public affair. I always start with the most recent volume of an index unless I want a particular date, and so I open volume 69 of PAIS, covering October 1982 till September 1983. Under "Education" is a note to see also "Politics and Education" and "Literacy." The articles on education are listed by state. I keep reading down the list, and under "California" I find an entry that might be useful.

> Everhart, Robt B., ed. The Public School Monopoly: a critical analysis of education and the state in American society. '82

The PAIS tells me under what headings the contents are grouped in the Everhart book, and I see one that looks right: "Alternatives to Monopoly Schooling." Thinking I might use this publication, I take down the full citation, noticing that the collection is published for the Pacific Institute for Public Policy Research in San Francisco. I may have to check still another index to find the address of this publisher in case I decide to write for a copy of the book.

Reading down the list, still under "California," I spot an article that suits my needs exactly.

> King, Gerald M. Home schooling: up from underground; parents who want to teach their kids at home are increasingly winning court battles and organizing self-help networks. *Reason* 14:21–9 Ap. '83

I'm excited. I read through the other states and find nothing immediately relevant, although I find many articles on the quality of education that might pertain to my topic. But I take down no more citations for now. *Reason* is not a magazine I'm familiar with, I'm fairly certain a university library won't have it, and so I consult *The International Directory of Little Magazines and Small Presses*. I'm in luck! I find this entry: *Reason*, Robert Poole, Jr. P.O. Box 40105, Santa Barbara, CA 93103 (805)963-5993. 1968. Now I know I can write to the publisher of that magazine and ask for the copy I need. Because the entry provides a phone number, I could even call the publisher if I were in a hurry. My detective work has paid off so far.

Next, I consult the *Statistical Abstract of the United States*, a publication of the federal government, Bureau of the Census. The *Statistical Abstract* has statistics on everything, and under education I find tables like "School Days Lost Associated with Acute Ailments" and "Mode of Transportation, Distance and Time Travelled to School: 1978." But I find nothing about home schooling. I have time for one more index. I look in Katz and Katz's *Magazines for Libraries*.

Suddenly I hit upon it. Under education I find a whole magazine devoted to my topic. It's called *Growing Without Schooling*. The citation tells me I can get a sample copy of the magazine by writing to the publisher. I read on to the magazine's description:

> A magazine for people who have taken—or want to take—their children out of school and have them learn at home. This 24 page publication contains short articles, legal information, listings of learning resources, and a state-by-state directory of families whose children are learning at home. All kinds of practical information on home schooling is included. Certainly not a basic title, but it contains a goldmine of material for people interested in the growing trend toward "unschooling." (Katz & Katz, 1982, p. 334)

I feel elated that I have discovered something that exactly suits my topic. Fortunately, I'm not in a hurry for my information, because I will have to send away for two publications and one is in California. But what if I were in a hurry? I'd be out of luck. Feeling successful, I decide to go have lunch. I look at my watch. What! I've been researching my topic for two and a half hours. I had fun and I don't have a paper due. But now you know the answer to "Why start early?"

Finding Reference Tools

If you are truly a novice in research, the first reference guide you will want to use is your college English handbook. If your freshman composition course does not require a handbook you can easily pick one up at the college bookstore. Many fine handbooks are available, and many paperback textbooks are devoted exclusively to the research paper. Your handbook or research-paper guide lists basic reference tools, such as general and specialized encyclopedias and dictionaries, almanacs, bibliographies, and indexes. They also have extensive sections on styles of documentation.

In the following sections we will concentrate primarily on indexes as in-the-library reference tools, and suggest other, out-of-library sources of information.

Using and Evaluating Indexes

Experienced researchers rarely begin with the library card catalog if they have some idea of their topic and want up-to-date information. Two to three years elapse between the time an author begins writing a book and the time the book appears in print. Books are excellent, however, for general background on a topic, and for finding the original sources of ideas. If you are unfamiliar with your topic, you will probably want to thumb through several books to familiarize yourself with the vocabulary associated with your topic, and to find lists of related reference works. You may want to include in your paper a history of your topic, and citations of books are acceptable for your background section. In fact, Carrie Rae used several books for her review of research on seabed mining.

But if you choose a topic or an issue that has reached public notice only within the last few years, your most likely sources for information, in the library at least, are periodicals and journals. "Periodicals" generally are popular publications, and "journals" are for scholarly writings. You would not want to have to page through journals or magazines to find articles on your topic; this step has been done for you by professional indexers. You have encountered several indexes in our narrative library tour; we will review those and look at several others. The reference librarian in your college library probably posts a list of all the indexes your library holds. Before deciding to use any of these mentioned here, check to make sure your library has them.

General Indexes

Reader's Guide to Periodical Literature. Do start with the *Reader's Guide* if you have chosen a popular, contemporary topic, but don't end with it. The *Reader's Guide* indexes more than a hundred popular magazines, and is a valuable first exposure to indexes. But remember that popular magazines like *Newsweek, Redbook, Psychology Today,* and so on get their material from another source, called a "primary source." The purpose of magazines like those is to research specialized material, and to present it in a popular style. Therefore, when you use only magazines listed in the *Reader's Guide,* you run the risk of quoting your material solely from what we call "secondary sources." To your reader, your resorting to these shows that you have not taken the trouble to find any original material, but have relied upon magazine writers to do your research for you. Of course, you do not always have the access to celebrities and experts that the staff of a national magazine does, and if you are looking for colorful quotations to round out your material, nothing is wrong with quoting an interview in, say, *Rolling Stone.* Just be aware of the difference between primary and secondary research methods.

If, during your research, you should find a citation to a magazine not listed in the *Reader's Guide,* you may want to try the *Popular Periodicals Index,* published only since 1973, and containing periodicals not listed in the *Reader's Guide.* Also, don't forget *The International Directory of Little Magazines and Small Presses* that I used in my search for material on home education. It's very helpful for finding publishers' addresses for magazines not carried by many libraries, magazines that may have exactly the article you need.

Newspaper Indexes

The New York Times Index. This index can help you identify public reaction to national and international events. It can also help you identify the specific date on which an event occurred if you want to check your local newspaper for the views of your own community. Other indexed newspapers include: *The London Times, The Wall Street Journal, The Washington Post,* and *The National Observer.*

Special Indexes

Here is a partial list of special indexes, selected to indicate the range of specification available to you:

Public Affairs Information Service Bulletin. (PAIS) An interdisciplinary index in the social sciences, PAIS is the one I used in my own search because my topic, education, is considered a social science. It indexes all articles that have to do with the making and evaluation of public policy—in all, it indexes more than 600 periodicals in the social sciences, political science, economics, sociology, international law, public administration, education, business, social work, and medicine. It includes books and government documents related to the social sciences. Therefore, PAIS should be one of the first places you look for material on current events; it is a basic reference tool and yet few college students are aware of it.

The *Humanities Index* and the *Social Sciences Index* have been published separately since 1974. From 1963 to 1974, these indexes were combined in the *Social Sciences and Humanities Index.* Before 1965, the combined volume was called the *International Index.*

Of the many other indexes in the humanities and social sciences, these are just a few: *Art Index, Music Index, Education Resources Information Center* (ERIC), *History Abstracts, Language and Language Behavior Abstracts, Child Development Abstracts and Bibliography, Urban Studies Abstracts,* and *Womens' Studies Abstracts.*

The sciences also have indexes ranging from broad to specific. There's the *General Science Index,* first appearing in 1978 and indexing more than 90 major journals in the natural sciences. The *Science Citation Index* also includes all the natural sciences. Just as in the humanities and social sciences, each discipline has its own index, including these: *Environment Abstracts Index, Aquatic Sciences and Fisheries Abstracts, Biological Abstracts, Bioscience Index, Engineering Index, Index Medicus, International Nursing Index, Energy Research Abstracts* (and the less technical version, *Energy*), *Abstracts for Policy Analysis, Mathematical Reviews, Physics Abstracts, Zoological Record.* And that is only a partial listing. In addition to indexes in the specific fields of study, there are indexes of statistics, or statistical abstracts, of which you have been introduced to one, *The Statistical Abstract of the United States.* Going into more depth, but a little more complicated to use, is the *American Statistics Index,* which indexes between 800 and 900 federal reports, then gives abstracts, brief summaries, on most of the material indexed. Federal reports are in the "Government Documents" section of your library, and if you keep in mind that the United States government is the largest publisher in the country, you'll realize the wealth of material available to you there.

A counterpart to the *American Statistics Index* is the *Statistical Reference Index,* which covers all nongovernment periodicals, reports, and so on. In short, it indexes any article or piece that has anything to do with statistics and doesn't appear in ASI. It seems that all knowledge has been indexed. There's even an index to the indexes!

Katz and Katz's *Magazines for Libraries.* This section is called using and evaluating indexes. Suppose you want to decide whether an index, or even a specific journal, will be either too general or too technical for your purposes. You can look up both indexes and periodicals in *Magazines for Libraries* by Bill Katz and Linda Sternberg Katz. This invaluable guide will tell you whether a magazine is published on the topic you are interested in, the level of the magazine, and where the magazine is indexed. In fact, many researchers begin with the Katz guide precisely to find out if there is a periodical they don't know about on their topic, and whether that magazine is likely to be in their library, or whether they will need to allow time to send away for it. Katz, a guide for libraries as well as for general users, advises libraries on the usefulness to them of the various periodicals it lists.

Saving Time in the Stacks

These are practical hints acquired over the years. Saving time begins with going to the library fully prepared and equipped for the task ahead of you. Here is what you need to bring:

1. A list of any book titles, periodicals, or authors you may have encountered while talking about your topic to others. Any little piece of information is better to start with than no information at all.

2. Several inexpensive pens. You can count on losing many pens in the library over your college years and thereafter — sometimes two or three in an afternoon if you're inclined to be absent-minded; always take a few pens along to spare yourself frustrating minutes.

3. Index cards, a tablet, or a notebook to be used solely for your research project. Many textbooks recommend 3-by-5-inch cards to be used as bibliography cards and 5-by-8-inch cards for taking notes. Carrying around two sets of different-sized cards is cumbersome, and so I use 5-by-8-inch cards for bibliography

entries as well as for note-taking. The larger card allows me to assess the usefulness of the source as well. The advantage to using cards rather than long sheets of paper with other than bibliographical information on them is this: When it's time to document your research paper, simply arrange the bibliography cards in alphabetical order and type from them (assuming that you have the entry in correct form—see number 4). If you prefer a hardbacked tablet or notebook for taking notes, use it. Research should be comfortable, not cumbersome. If you decide to use cards, remember to buy a big clip for keeping them all together. Otherwise, they're too easy to lose.

4. Your freshman handbook or the style manual suggested by your instructor. You will gradually become familiar with basic documentation style, and refer to manuals only for unusual questions. But as a beginner, you will find it easiest if you refer to your manual and document your sources in the correct form right in the library, as you look them up. Write down the call number of any source you think you might use, so that you won't have to make repeat trips to the card catalog. Remember that for full documentation, you need not only author and title, but place of publication, publisher, date of publication, and page references. For magazines, you will need the name of the article you use, author's name (if there is one), title of the magazine, week or month and year in which it was published, as well as the page numbers of the article. For journals, you will also need to cite the volume used, and the number of the issue within the volume. Newspapers, films, plays, musical performances, works of art, personal interviews—all these have their own specific form of documentation. The section on documentation in this chapter explains why using the correct form is important, and refers you to the appropriate sources for finding that form.

5. A roll of the appropriate coins for your college library's copying machine. You will not have time to read and take notes from all the material you find in the library. Because periodicals and material on microform cannot be removed from the library, you will eventually find material that you will want to copy so that you can work with it at home. You can copy from both microfilm and microfiche as well as from printed pages. A word of caution: When you copy, be sure to write out the complete documentation form right on the copied material. Often, page

numbers, month and year of the source, even title, are not legible after copying, and you return home with only the title of the article if you do not take this precaution.

This completes the list of equipment necessary for your trip to the library. Let's look at some other ways to save time.

Computer Search

If your topic is very specific, and you are clever at choosing key words, you may want to ask your reference librarian about a computer search. Costs vary, depending on the source you want researched, but computer time for a general source, like ERIC (Educational Resources Information Center) is about a dollar a minute today.

That may sound expensive, but if you have chosen the right key words, you can get quite a lot of information in five minutes. At our library, a five-minute search would be $3.50, because the balance of the amount is subsidized by a special fund for research. Your library may have a similar subsidy; look into it. A five-minute computer search can give you a list of articles on your topic that it could take you hours to track down on your own.

Union List of Serials

Every library has a list of its periodical and journal holdings, contained in a book with the title "Union List." Usually several copies are available. Find a copy and keep it with you when you use the indexes. You would not want to end up with a list of seemingly important articles, none of which is available in your library, unless you had months before your due date. You are encouraged to send for some periodicals not held by your library, but it is wise to track down some immediately available sources. After using the list of serials a few times, you will become familiar with the material the library holds, at least in your field. If a library is weak in that subject, you may want to visit other nearby university libraries until you find one that meets your needs.

Contacting Other Sources

The University Community

Amazingly, many students forget that a tremendous source of live information—primary sources—sits all around them: the faculty and staff of their college or university. Most researchers are only too glad for an opportunity to talk about their work, and most departments list the interests of their faculty, sometimes held by the department secretary. If no such publication is available, the department chairs are aware of the special interests among their faculty.

You would simply call the department, ask to make an appointment with the chair, and identify yourself and your needs. By interviewing a faculty member or staff person familiar with your topic, you can cut the time you would ordinarily spend looking for sources. Faculty members write articles and present conference papers regularly, and so they will have bibliographies to share with you. Staff people who work with students frequently keep detailed statistical records of what's happening at your own and other universities. If you attend a state university, it probably has a public-relations director whose job is to issue press releases about the university, and who is also responsible for knowing what is going on in your own and surrounding states. Students are told time and again, "This is your college, your university," but they sometimes fail to take advantage of their university's most valuable resource—its people.

The Telephone Directory

The telephone directory is another untapped source of information for research projects. At the back of the phone book is a section called "The Blue Pages of Government Listings." Here are listed hundreds of government agencies you can call or write to for information. Even if you live in a small town, you'll be surprised at the number of federal and state agencies with offices in your community. Government agencies are very cooperative about granting interviews and mailing out information to students because they want the public to be informed of the service they have to offer.

A phone call to the right office can save you hours in the library. Even if you should contact the wrong office, chances are if you explain your needs articulately, you'll be referred to the appropriate office, and provided with a phone number and the name of a contact person. The government is so frequently the victim of bad press that its representatives in local agencies go out of their way to be friendly and helpful to the public when they can.

Let me give you an example of how the blue pages helped me. It was a rainy summer afternoon, very dark, and I didn't particularly want to go out of the house. But I had a report due the next day and in running through the draft, I noticed a chunk of information was missing. I was supposed to find out how many programs in English as a second language (ESL) were available, free of charge, around the state. I sat and muttered a while about how I didn't want to go out. Then, inspired, I picked up the phone book. Government agencies are listed alphabetically by subject first (listings like "Senior Citizens Services" and "Consumer Complaints"), then alphabetically by city and town. I tried "Educational Programs" first and found a number for "State of Rhode Island Information and Referral." I figured I could try this general number, but decided to see if I could find something more specific. Because Providence is our major city, I looked under PROVIDENCE, CITY OF   SCHOOL DEPT.   Administrative Office. There I was rewarded. I found an office I didn't know existed: "Language Administrator's Office." I called this office and was given the exact information I needed, complete with the names of ten ESL programs around the state, phone numbers, and contact persons. My research had taken me about half an hour and I didn't have to leave the house. Even if you don't have an assignment due, you might browse through the blue pages of your telephone directory just to see what is available in your immediate area.

Courtesies of Interviewing

We have suggested that you use interviewing, and observing a few simple courtesies of interviewing is bound to yield you the best results:

1. Call ahead. Faculty, staff, administrators, government officials, celebrities—all working people, in fact, have calendars filled up in advance. Call your source at least one or two weeks ahead of when you would like the information. Students who say, "Oh, but I need the information tomorrow because my paper's due this Friday" are likely to receive cool responses. If you do hear about a source only a few days away from a due date, apologize politely but briefly for your sudden demand on your

source's time and specify how much of their time you would need.

2. Plan for telephone interviews. If you cannot meet with a source personally because of distance or demands on the source's time, you might want to arrange for a telephone interview. It's not fair to expect that when you call someone out of the blue, they will have fifteen minutes or more available right then and there. Instead, it's best to identify yourself and then say something like, "I was wondering if I might ask you a few questions about X over the telephone at a time that's convenient to you. When could I call back?"

3. Prepare your questions. Some sources will require very little prompting other than knowing the topic you are interested in. Others will wait for you to ask specific questions and may become annoyed if you give the impression of not having prepared for the interview.

When Arlene Nardiello lined up her interviews, she realized she was inexperienced and asked for guidance in preparing her questions. She visited the journalism department and asked for help. A journalism major gave her some conventional interviewing formats, and then talked with her about interviewing with results. You might consult your journalism department for tips on preparing questions, or pick up a book intended for beginning writers of magazine articles, which will provide you with plentiful information on interviewing.

4. Thank your sources. Remember to thank the source for their time, and always offer to provide them with a copy of the finished product. If an issue is particularly controversial, your source may ask to see how you have used the information given you before you write the final product. That is your source's privilege; accommodate graciously.

Taking Notes

Even if you have copied material or returned home with a taped interview, you must read or listen thoroughly, decide what's important, and take notes. Simply reading with highlighter in hand is not enough. Your note-taking can cost time or save time, depending on your system.

Notes to Yourself: Commenting on Source Material

When you begin to take notes, you may still not know the exact approach you want for your topic. Don't panic. The reading and note taking will help you decide on that approach. But whether you are uncertain of your approach or not, the first rule is to resist copying long quotes verbatim on your note cards. You may feel that the author's words are better chosen than yours will be, but unless you try to comprehend the material; fit it into the other material available; decide whether the source concurs with others you have read, disagrees with them, or presents entirely new information; you will wind up with a stack of note cards and still no idea of how to approach your topic. The most important notes you take during research are those in your own words on how the source material strikes you—your reaction to the source. Here is a list of questions you might ask yourself as you read, listen to interviews, and write:

1. Organization. Where might this material fit in a paper? Is it so startlingly significant that it would make a good opening? Is it background material that readers will need before they can understand or evaluate the rest of the information? Does it help me understand other material? Is it a kind of summary of what my other sources have said? Would it fit at the end of my paper?

Deciding roughly where material might fit, whether at the beginning, middle, or end, is the first step in figuring out the specific pattern or patterns you will want to use for the research paper. This initial decision helps shape your material. Think of how you do a jigsaw puzzle. Most people put the border together first, because the pieces with straight edges are easiest to identify. Then they begin to look for other patterns: different colors, shades of one color, and finally, the shapes of individual pieces. The thinking that underlies these two tasks—putting together a complicated puzzle and writing a complex report—is the same, except that one uses your visual facility, the other your facility with words. Find the big patterns first and little ones will fall into place with some nudging and hair-pulling.

2. Synthesis and Analysis. Have I read this theory or fact before? Do all or most of my courses cite it? Is it a "given" in the field? Or does the source point out disagreements with other researchers? Does the source have an alternative theory? New evidence? Does the source fail to mention anyone else in the field? Is any of the material here and nowhere else?

Of course, you will learn to ask yourself many other questions as you become an experienced researcher, but this list will get you started. Here is one of Carrie Rae's note cards with source material and her own comments:

> Shusterich, pp. 64-65
> Dr. John Mero- 1st to recognize nodules as potential resources while grad students at Univ. of CA (1957). Studied worldwide distribution and metal contents of nodules. Wrote *Mineral Resources of the Sea*.
> (Significant--use early in history section)

There are occasions when you will want to quote directly from a source, especially from a primary source whom you may have interviewed. When are direct quotations useful?

1. Facts and statistics not widely available to the public should be quoted directly. On one note card, Carrie wrote this:

> Britton, p. 66
> Potato-sized, lie at depths of 12,000-20,000 ft., some places barely distributed others, thick. "as much as 100 billion tons of nodules may litter the floor of the world's oceans."

2. Opinions that are controversial are best directly quoted. If I tell a reporter, "Many colleges and universities need to make remedial courses available for students," that interviewer can probably find a multitude of sources to agree with me. On the other hand, if I say, "All institutions of higher learning should supply remediation work," the statement would evoke wide disagreement. Watch for the catchwords "all," "always," "never," "none," and other qualifiers that indicate absolutes. If your source has used one of these qualifiers, chances are the state-

ment could spark controversy. Controversy makes a research project interesting, but be sure to quote directly—and accurately.

3. Interesting, unusual analogies. Good writers of specialized material are aware of the need to provide a lay audience with vivid images that use familiar objects or events to explain unfamiliar, complicated phenomena. Carrie marked such a quote on one of her note cards:

> Britton – Use!
> Getting minerals to surface like "sucking grains of sand up a straw from a bed of mud to the top of a skyscraper — at night, in a high wind."

4. Particularly eloquent quotations that can open or close the paper. Sometimes someone else does say it better—and when you find a particularly memorable quotation, don't be afraid to use it. Mark it for special use in an introduction or conclusion, with a note to yourself.

Patterns for Presenting Research

The emphasis in this text has been on using our natural thought patterns as a means of shaping written discourse. You are familiar with such patterns as narration, process, analysis, comparison, analogy, and so on. You will find that although all these patterns may be useful in presenting some part of your research (narration, for example, can be an interesting opening), only a few of them are suitable as the dominant pattern for an extended research paper. Probably the most suitable are analysis, cause and effect, and process. If, as you sort through your note cards, you find your material fits one of these patterns, by all means use it.

In fact, Arlene Nardiello's paper illustrates an extended use of the process pattern. But there is another pattern you should be aware of.

Carrie Rae has a long process section in her paper, but her predominant pattern is one you have not seen illustrated in this text. It is the informative pattern, introduced in the textbook *Communication: Writing and Speaking* by Richard Katula, Celest Martin, and Robert Schwegler. This is a useful pattern for an extended research paper because it is based on an audience's expectations. In other words, it provides a guide for writers so that they do not omit the answers to questions readers may have about a topic. The questions are general and may be applied to any topic. The informative pattern looks like this:

> Significance: What is the topic and why is it useful to learn about it?
> Background: What is the history of the topic? What terms need to be defined?
> Features: What are its special characteristics, capabilities. What is its appearance?
> Procedures: How does it work? Where can it be gotten? How can it be done?
> Applications: What is the present and future importance of the topic? How will it affect people? What should they do?[2]

You may use this pattern in the order outlined above, or you may find another order that better suits your material. Of course, you will want to begin your paper by explaining the significance of your topic, but significance can recur in other sections of the paper as well. Also, you may find that one or two of the questions in the informative pattern dominate your paper, and other questions require only a paragraph or two of explanation. Turning to Carrie Rae's paper at the end of this chapter, you will find marginal notations indicating the questions of the informative pattern as they occur in her paper. You will see that "Features," "Good/Bad," "Applications," and "Significance" recur throughout the paper. You will also notice that for her topic, the "Procedures" section required most explanation.

Choosing a Pattern

No one can tell you what pattern to choose for your paper. Just as your intended audience shapes the purpose of your paper, the purpose and

[2]Richard Katula, Celest Martin, and Robert Schwegler, *Communication: Writing and Speaking* (Boston: Little, Brown, 1983), 233–34.

the kind of material you have gathered in your research must shape your pattern.

If as you are taking notes on your material, you find that expert opinion divides itself into two distinct camps, you could decide to do a pro and con (issue-analysis) paper. On the other hand, if you find yourself siding strongly with one side over the other, and you want to win converts to your side, you will want to use persuasion.

If, like Arlene Nardiello, you learn how to do something during your research, you may decide to direct your knowledge to a specific, interested audience and write a process paper. Finally, if your topic would be unfamiliar to a general audience, and you decide you just want them to be informed about it, the informative pattern is the one to use. There is one thing to remember, though. By the time you choose a pattern, you must be in control of your material, and not feel overwhelmed or controlled by it. If you have used a wide range of sources and taken thoughtful notes, your choice will present no difficulty.

Working with an Outline

Outlines are of all shapes and sizes and all levels of formality. I have never used a highly formal outline, but some writers prefer them. The real purpose of an outline should be to help you, not to hinder you. If you use an outline and then feel so tightly bound by it that you can't shift your focus a bit, you're defeating the purpose.

In the first place, an initial outline can be too ambitious. As you begin to write, one section of the outline may turn out to be a topic in itself. If you become engrossed in that section, you may want to revise your initial outline into an outline covering just one of its sections. On the other hand, you may decide that a topic in the outline is too involved and will detract from the true purpose of your paper. You might refer to the topic briefly, direct the reader to other sources of information on the topic, and then drop it. Outlines should be flexible tools that can change with your perception of your audience's needs, move within the framework of the pattern you have chosen, and work within any limitations of length imposed by your instructor or by a publication for which you are writing.

A good reason to use some kind of outline is so that you don't forget what you want to say. When I outlined this chapter, for example, I knew I wouldn't forget to distinguish between popular and academic research, because that's a big distinction. But I almost forgot that I wanted to include a section on saving time in the library. And if I hadn't listed for myself key words like "pens," "change for copier," and "Union List of Serials," I might easily have forgotten one of the tips.

Also, although your final organization may change, an outline also helps you sort out the logic of your organization in black and white. I initially had "courtesies of interviewing" before "contacting other sources." Reading over the outline, I realized it would make no sense to tell you how to interview before mentioning that you should consider interviewing as a source of information.

Finally, as Carrie Rae pointed out when I interviewed her, an outline can serve as a reward system. She had written her paper in sections, but not always in the sequence in which she planned to present those sections. As she finished writing each section, though, she checked it off on her outline with satisfaction. Her outline is presented below as a sample. No attempt has been made to fit it to a precise numbering or lettering system. Please notice that Part III, which has four sections, is itself outlined in great detail. As Carrie assembled her notes, she realized that her "Procedures" section was by far the longest, and that for the procedures to be understood by a general audience, she had better outline that section separately. She wanted to be sure she left nothing out. (Carrie's paper has been cut for this chapter; her original manuscript has an additional five pages of detail— mostly on procedures.)

I. manganese nodules exist —define
　　　　　　　　　　　　　　—origin
　　　　　　　　　　　　　　—history
II. constituents of nodules —demand
　　　　　　　　　　　　　　—supply from present reserves
　　　　　　　　　　　　　　—source from nodules
　　　　　　　　　　　　　　—surge of mining in past few years
　　A. compare—ocean mining to land-based mining
　　B. political problems—politics and law
III. process of ocean mining operation
　　A. locate site, keep track of it
　　B. choose extraction technique
　　C. transportation
　　D. extracting process

IV. outline variables affecting costs and operation of system
  V. environmental considerations
     1. saltwater disposal (suction dredgers)

Kildow (227)
ditto 1   2. storing tailings and slag, sludges, hydrous slime
Pearson   3. effect of discharging deep water on surface (suction dredgers)
(133–134)
Compare to
natural
processes   4. removing and redistributing sediment and organisms
Pearson (143)   5. at-sea processing of waste

III. parts of a system
   A. locate site
     1. establish navigational system
      —choice includes Loran
               Omega
     2. coordination with government to be sure which site is free
Herbich   3. general surveys, also used by offshore oil industry
         a. seismic
Pearson (167)   b. side-scan sonar
         c. magnetometer
Shusterich (66)   d. gravity meter
         e. bottom characteristics and obstruction
           → topo map
Pearson   4. other general considerations
(147–148)   a. commercial value of located nodules
(171)   —grade
          —concentration
          —etc.
         b. proximity of site to prospective market
     5. specific surveys
Herbich   a. sediment samples—corers—gravity
                  —core petrometer
        sediment samples—grab samplers
Pearson (167)   b. soil strength for prospective construction—vane testing
     6. evaluate and assay deposit—character
                 (accessibility)
                 —composition
                 —value
     7. assay sea conditions
         a. ocean currents—current meters

b. wave characteristics—wave spectra
—US Weather Serv.

Herbich
—Coastal Eng.
—Research Cknt.

c. storm forecasting—frequency

d. corrosion—salinity—salinometer
—temperature—salinometer } profiles

e. depth pressures

B. relocating—keeping track
    1. navigation satellites to direct vessel
    2. onboard computer system

C. choosing technique for extraction—today's technology narrows it down to three choices:
    1. continuous line bucket (CLB)
       —describe system—3 components

Pearson
(44–47, 168)
       —cost
       —adv. vs. disadv.

Herbich
    2. hydraulic dredging   3 components   —air-lift
       —describe system—attached dredger-suction
                             —self-propelled dredger

       —cost—
              —
       —adv. vs. disadv.—attached vs. self-prop.
                          —hydraulic vs. mech.
                          —air-lift vs. suction

Herbich
dittos
Shusterich
(66)
    3. shuttle ships, submarine tractors
       —describe system—three components
       —cost
       —adv. vs. disadv.

D. transporting material to shore
    1. mining vessel—loses time

Pearson (147)
                —smallest capital (additional)
    2. ore carriers

Shusterich (66)
    3. oceangoing tugs pulling barges

E. extracting and processing

Pearson (174)
Shusterich (254)
ditto (1)
    1. pyrometallurgical—describe (hydrometallurgical)
    2. acid leaching—describe

Ready to Write: An Inventory of Openings

After spending weeks preparing your material, you won't want to alienate your audience by opening the paper with a flat, boring introduction—no matter how technical or abstract your subject may be. If you haven't found a significant opening quote that has eloquence and style, you may want to try a little creative writing. A good way to begin is to encourage audience participation. You can place your audience directly in the scene, have them observe it, or ask them a question. Here are some sample openings from student papers.

Indicates persuasion   "Meet me at ten in the Ram's Den; we'll have a cup of coffee and discuss it." That quote is used more at the University of Rhode Island than this rare one: "I can't, I'm going to the Library." However, this type of conversation is not limited to the college community. Americans consume 35 million pounds of caffeine each year. Should you or I be concerned about our caffeine intake? I feel the answer is no. Listen to what I have to say, then make your own decision.

—Greg Glovach, "Caffeine—It's Your Decision"

Indicates issue analysis   Americans take more than twenty billion aspirin tablets a year—one hundred for every man, woman, and child in the country. Advertising has successfully conditioned most of the population to reach for the aspirin bottle when bothered with anything from a hangover to arthritis. There have been widely publicized reports that daily doses of aspirin may prevent blood clotting, strokes, and heart attacks. Is aspirin overused or is it a wonder drug?

—Marita Sherbo, "Aspirin"

States significance and applications of specialized topic   What are liquid crystals and why should we learn about them? A liquid crystal is an intermediate state of matter—neither a solid nor a liquid but something between. The molecules in a liquid crystal line up in certain well-defined arrangements, as opposed to the random arrangement of molecules in a liquid, which give it some optical and other properties that solids have but liquids do not. Liquid-crystal applications range from digital watches to the structure of biological membranes.

—Elizabeth Page, "Lyotropic Liquid Crystals"

Creates scene   "Whoa Nelly, we've struck it rich!" That phrase conjures up images of miner forty-niners; those old sourdoughs who, back in the late 1800s and early 1900s panned for gold in creeks, streams, and rivers, all over this continent. One would expect that gold panning died out with the miners *Indicates process paper* and their mules, but it isn't so. Many people today still pan for gold. Some do it just for fun and others do it for a living. A few people even have "gold fever" and can't help themselves. With gold selling at around $400 an ounce, the rewards can be very rich indeed. Just what does it take to go panning for gold? If you ever want to go gold panning, you will need only two things: a gold pan and a stream to use it in.

—Bob Mathis, "Go Pan For Gold!"

Attention-grabbing

The twentieth century has brought many changes to our unsuspecting society. Not only can we put a man on the moon, but we can microwave our frozen vegetables and watch a Soviet press conference on cable television. With all this new knowledge being collected, more and more Americans are exposed to many diverse and varied life-styles. We have softened in our judgments and learned to accept, if not live with, situations that would once have seemed totally against the norm. Every morning we turn on our television sets to Phil Donahue and confront prostitutes, heroin addicts, homosexuals, transsexuals, and alcoholics. And they all seem perfectly nice.

Does not yet reveal real topic

—Carolyn Liberman, "Child Pornography"

The forest ground is thickly covered with a light brown carpet of sand and dried pine needles. Pine cones and tall brown grass cover the few areas open to sunlight. Streams filled with trout and bass meander thoughtlessly through these woods, dividing the forest floor. In some places, pines are so thick that daylight never passes through the branches. Many a swamp, marsh, and cranberry bog is to be found in this vast forest.

These woods cover seventeen hundred square miles of southeastern New Jersey. This forest is none other than the Pine Barrens. A person can travel miles at a time and never come upon any sort of civilization. Not that there ever was any civilization. In colonial days, many a person attempted to live off this harsh land. Because of its sandy soil, however, most failed and moved elsewhere. Iron ore was once dug and furnaced here for the Revolutionary War, as well as for the War of 1812.

Soon, however, better ore was found in the West and the forest was once again abandoned. Only a few remained selling what they could, such as moss or pine cones. They made their homes of lean-to's or tents. These people became known as "Pineys." It is from the beginning of these peoples' lives, some 240 years ago, that a legend was born, a legend that still exists today, and still keeps some people inside after dark. Then again, who said it was a legend? Perhaps the Jersey Devil is not fiction at all. Perhaps his existence is real.

Arouses curiosity

—Bart Hellwig, "The Jersey Devil"

Setting up Readers' Expectations

An opening should go a step further than exciting your readers; it should also tell them what to expect, by indicating the pattern you have chosen for presenting your information. The openings we have looked at do that. The first paper, on caffeine, indicates its form with the sentence, "I feel the answer is no." The writer clearly intends to persuade the reader to accept his point of view.

The opening paragraph below also indicates persuasion, suggesting a specific proposal. But the writer also feels his audience should have some background on the topic so that they can make an intelligent decision about his proposal. The last sentence indicates, therefore, that the author will begin his paper with the definition pattern, then follow it with cause and effect. After that, the reader can expect the substance of the argument:

> Acid rain: it is a problem far more serious than we had thought. Scientists have proven that this phenomenon is causing all sorts of trouble for humanity and wreaking havoc on our environment. Plants in our fields and our forests are subjected to showers of sulfuric and nitric acid. The deadly rain has substantially lowered the PH levels of thousands of freshwater lakes and streams all over the world. The result? Not merely dead fish, but complex ecosystems totally disrupted. Our present government is very concerned, but no real action has yet been taken to correct the problem. I'd like to propose that we pressure our elected officials so that they may see to the righting of this situation, and see to it now. First, though, I'd like to explain three things: what acid rain is; what harm acid rain is doing; where acid rain comes from.

> —Bob Mathis, "What We Can Do about Acid Rain"

Most long papers are skillful combinations of patterns, as Bob's is. The writer controls their use by preparing the audience whenever a switch in pattern is necessary. The paper on liquid crystals is an account of the experimenter's own work with liquid crystals, following a process pattern.

Because process is an easy pattern to recognize, she didn't worry about setting up her pattern immediately, but concentrated on getting the reader's interest on a subject that she realized could be dry. Thus, Elizabeth used a significance opening.

"Go Pan for Gold!" is a process paper, and Bob strives to create an opening scene that will make the reader want to try the process he is writing about. The opening paragraph of "Child Pornography" arouses the reader's curiosity precisely because it does not yet get to the point. But Carolyn's second paragraph leaves no doubt as to what pattern the reader can expect:

> Learning to live with people and their different life-styles is all well and good—but we cannot accept deviant behavior that is harmful to others. A prime example of our society compromising its morality is the current multi-million-dollar child pornography industry. The situation created by this industry is a desperate one, and it is our responsibility not to close our eyes to the abuse inflicted on its innocent victims.

We are going to hear an argument, and a good one.

The final opening, from "The Jersey Devil," was chosen for the spooky atmosphere it creates, appropriate to its topic. You probably recognized part of the "Background" question from the informative pattern. This is a purely informative paper, written to pique curiosity about the topic. Despite the facetious last sentence of the opening, it is by no means an argument for the Jersey Devil's existence. It merely presents a series of events and lets readers judge for themselves.

Creating your own opening can be done in your head as you go through the experience of living with your topic. Let your mind work on the topic while you're performing some mechanical task, and you'll be surprised at the interesting openings that surface.

Having an opening—or several—in mind when you sit down to write up your material gives you an initial boost, because you don't have to stare at the blank page for long.

Writing and Revising: Pacing Yourself

Everyone has a different method for composing. Some writers do one draft, revising it as they go along. Some write several drafts, and rarely interrupt their flow of ideas with revision. I usually write one draft, revising as I go. When I am writing an extended piece, I use revision as a way of getting started each day. I read over the previous days' work, changing phrases and looking for places where I have leaped from one section of the work to another without enough explanation or transitional material between. I know from experience that my greatest weakness is leaving too much unexplained. I rarely have to cut my drafts, but I almost always have to add pages marked "insert." Some writers have the opposite problem. They overexplain in first drafts, and write subsequent drafts cutting chunks of unnecessary material.

But the most important thing I know about my composing—and the thing you should learn about yours—is pace. I know that my maximum writing time is about five hours a day. In those five hours I can expect to produce about ten typed pages if I'm writing on something I'm very familiar with—the material in this chapter, for example. On the other hand, if I am writing up recent experiments or new research, my output will probably be less, maybe only six to eight pages.

I know that after about two and a half hours, I need a break, some physical movement before I can continue, and so I have to allow five and a half to six hours for the time set aside for writing. After four or five days in a row of writing, I need a break. If I'm really pressed for time on a project, I may then start typing up the manuscript.

Many writers now compose directly on word processors, saving themselves the tedium of typing from longhand. If you have a word processor to use, do try composing on it. If you're a multiple-draft writer, the word processor can save you hours, even days.

Ideally, after four or five days, I like to just walk away from a project for a day, and then come back to it. You must study your own composing needs, because if time doesn't permit you the luxury of a break, and you need one, your product will suffer.

Carrie Rae discovered that she had not paced herself well, and ended up with continuous blocks of writing time with no break periods. She later remarked, "It would have been nice to have some leeway, just to know I could walk away from it for a little while." Over and over she repeated, "I could have enjoyed this project so much more if it weren't for the time thing. And I had a whole semester; I did it to myself." The pressure so many students claim they need results in both mental and physical fatigue.

Be honest with yourself and be comfortable with your composing pace. I know people who can put in twelve hours a day writing, and I know people who can put in only two. But writing isn't an endurance contest. What matters is that these people know their time limits and their capacity for production and pace themselves accordingly. If you take yourself seriously as a writer and researcher, you must do the same.

Documentation: Form Is Important

Anyone who works with computers knows the significance of a misplaced comma. It can invalidate your whole program run. In the scholarly world, precision is equally important. Incorrect form signals to your audience that you are a careless researcher. Your audience reasons that if you have gone to all the trouble of researching a topic, surely you would not skip the basic research of putting your sources into the appropriate scholarly form. Therefore, if there are mistakes in your documentation, your research itself is suspect.

Each discipline has its own preferred style of documentation. The humanities, the social sciences, and the sciences all use different formats for documentation. In fact, just now the field of humanities uses two forms: languages and literature have switched to the Modern Language Association (MLA) style, but history, philosophy, religion, and theology still require a footnote or endnote system. We have provided examples of both the MLA system and the APA system; they are explained in the *MLA Handbook for Writers of Research Papers*, Second Edition, and the *Publication Manual of the American Psychological Association*, Third Edition.

Works Cited: MLA

Your bibliographic items are arranged in alphabetical order, author's last name first. The first line of a bibliographic entry is aligned with the left margin; succeeding lines are indented five spaces. Double-space bibliographic entries, and double-space between entries. Center the words "Works Cited" one inch down from the top of the page and double-space between this title and your first entry. Listed here are sample entries:

Book with one author

> Bassey, E. Joan. <u>Exercise: The Facts</u>. New York: Oxford UP, 1981.

Two books with the same author

> Shephard, Roy J.   <u>Alive Man! The Physiology of Physical Activity</u>.
>   Springfield: Thomas, 1972.
>
> ---.   <u>Endurance Fitness</u>.   2nd ed.   Toronto: U of Toronto P,
>   1977.

Book with two or three authors

> Morehouse, Lawrence E., and Augustus T. Miller.   <u>Physiology of</u>
>   <u>Exercise</u>.   4th ed.   St. Louis: Mosley, 1963.

Book with more than three authors

> Robertson, Leon S., et al.   <u>Changing the Medical Care System: A</u>
>   <u>Controlled Experiment in Comprehensive Care</u>.   Praeger
>   Special Studies in U.S. Economic, Social, and Political
>   Issues.   New York: Praeger, 1974.

Book with corporate authorship

> Institute of Medicine.   <u>Assessing Quality in Health Care: An</u>
>   <u>Evaluation: Report of a Study</u>.   Washington: National
>   Academy of Sciences, 1976.

Book with an editor (also, notice form for book in series)

> Ghista, Dhanjoo N., ed.   <u>Human Body Dynamics</u>.   Oxford Medical
>   Engineering Series.   Oxford: Clarendon, 1982.

Book with an author and an editor

> Licht, Sidney Herman. Therapeutic Exercise. Ed. Ernest W.
>   Johnson. 2nd ed. New Haven: E. Licht, 1965.

A translation

> Nadeau, Maurice. The Greatness of Flaubert. Trans. Barbara
>   Bray. New York: Library, 1972.

Selection from an anthology

> Auden, W. H. "The Poet and the City." Modern Poetics. Ed. James
>   Scully. New York: McGraw, 1965. 167–82.

Work in more than one volume (volume unspecified)

> Beck, Simone, Louisette Bertholle, and Julia Child. Mastering
>   the Art of French Cooking. 2 vols. New York: Knopf, 1970.

Work in more than one volume (volume number of book specified)

> Beck, Simone, Louisette Bertholle, and Julia Child. "Veal
>   Stews." Mastering the Art of French Cooking. 2 vols. New
>   York: Knopf, 1970. 2: 209–13.

Periodicals: Journals, Magazines, and Newspapers

Journal article—continuous pagination

> Carton, Evan. "On Going Home: Selfhood in Composition."
>
> College English 45 (1983): 340–47

(Notice that "45" denotes volume 45, and that "pp." is not used to indicate "pages." Page numbers given indicate the length of the article, not just the pages cited.)

Journal article—separate pagination

> Breland, Hunter, and Robert J. Jones. "Perceptions of Writing
>
> Skills." Written Communication 1.1 (1984): 101–19.

(Notice that "1.1" denotes volume 1, number 1. The issue number must be included because page numbers will not locate an article in a journal in which every issue is paged separately.)

Signed monthly magazine article

> Kinnucan, Paul. "Superfighters." High Technology Apr. 1984:
>
> 36–48.

Signed weekly magazine article

> Quinn, Jane Bryant. "A New War on Health Costs." Newsweek
>
> 9 Apr. 1984: 87.

Unsigned magazine article

> "Canning Campbell's Can." Newsweek 9 Apr. 1984: 84.

Signed newspaper article

> Rosenblum, Mort. "A Parched Trail of Misery." <u>Providence</u>
>
> <u>Sunday Journal</u> 8 Apr. 1984: B1.

Bulletins, pamphlets, and public documents

> United States. Cong. Senate. <u>Social Security Amendments of</u>
>
> <u>1965: Report</u>. 89th Cong., 1st sess. S. Rept. 404.
>
> Washington: GPO, 1965.
>
> Rhode Island Dept. of Health. <u>Health Services—Handbook</u>.
>
> Providence, 1978.

Committee report

> <u>Health Economics: Report on a WHO Interregional Seminar</u>.
>
> Geneva: World Health Organization, 1975.

Other Sources

Unpublished dissertation

> Martin, Celest A. "Syntax and Success: A Comparison of Stylistic
>
> Features with Holistic Ratings in Freshman Essays." Diss.
>
> U of Southern California, 1979.

Performances

> And a Nightingale Sang. By C. P. Taylor. Dirs. Wayne Adams,
> Sherwin Goldman, and Martin Markinson. With Joan Allen.
> Newhouse Theatre, New York. 1 Apr. 1984.

Records

> Joel, Billy. An Innocent Man. Columbia, 7464-38837-1.

Films and television programs

> Benjamin, Richard, dir. Racing with the Moon. With Sean Penn,
> Elizabeth McGovern, and Nicolas Cage. Paramount Pictures,
> 1984.
>
> George Washington. Writ. Richard Fielder. With Barry Bostwick,
> Jaclyn Smith, and Patty Duke Astin. WCBS, New York. 8
> Apr. 1984.

Personal interview

> Katula, Richard A. Personal interview. 14 June 1983.

References: APA

So that you may see the differences between the two styles, we have
used the same titles, where possible, for APA style as we did for MLA
style. Notice the following differences:

1. APA uses the word "References" instead of "Works Cited."
2. APA uses only the initial of an author's first name (and middle
   initial, if included); APA inverts names of all authors.
     MLA: Kamholtz, Jonathan Z. and Robin A. Sheets
     APA: Kamholtz, J. Z. & Sheets, R. A.
(Notice also that APA uses the ampersand in place of "and.")

3. APA places the date of a work in parentheses immediately following the author's name, rather than at the end of a reference. APA indents the second and succeeding lines of each entry three spaces.

> MLA: Holtzman, Michael. "Teaching Is Remembering." College English 46 (1984): 229–38.
>
> APA: Holtzman, M. (1984). Teaching is remembering. College English, 46, 229–238.

4. APA capitalizes only the first word in the title of a book or article, and does not use quotation marks for article titles. Journal titles, however, are capitalized.

> MLA: Holtzman, Michael. "Teaching Is Remembering."
>
> APA: Holtzman, M. (1984). Teaching is remembering.

5. APA underlines the volume number of a journal.

> MLA: Holtzman, Michael. "Teaching Is Remembering." College English 46 (1984): 229–38
>
> APA: Holtzman, M. (1984). Teaching is remembering. College English, 46, 229–238.

Note: Both styles include the issue number for journals paged separately by issue. The APA includes the issue number in parentheses following the volume number, like this:

> APA 46(3)
>
> MLA 46.3

MLA places a period between the volume number and the issue number, as above. See also that MLA uses a colon between the year of publication and the page numbers of an article; APA simply uses a comma following the volume number. Finally, APA uses the "pp." abbreviation for magazines and newspapers, but no abbreviation for page numbers of journals.

Book with one author

> Bassey, E. J. (1981). Exercise: The facts. New York: Oxford
> University Press.

(Note: Give surnames and initials for *all* authors, regardless of the number of authors. See "In-Text Citations" for listing multiple authorship in text.)

Book with three authors

> Katula, R. A., Martin, C. A., & Schwegler, R. A. (1983).
>
> Communication: Writing and speaking. Boston: Little,
>
> Brown.

Book with corporate authorship

> Institute of Medicine. (1976). Assessing quality in health care:
>
> An evaluation: Report of a study. Washington, DC: National
>
> Academy of Sciences.

(Note: Sometimes in a corporate work, the author and publisher are the same. Then, use the word *Author* as the name of the publisher.)

Book with an editor

> Ghista, D. N. (Ed.). (1982). Human body dynamics. Oxford Medical
>
> Engineering Series. Oxford: Clarendon Press.

A translation

> Nadeau, M. (1972). The greatness of Flaubert (B. Bray, Trans.).
>
> New York: Library Press. (Original work published 1969.)

(Note: APA requires date of original work; MLA does not).

Multivolume work

> Beck, S., Bertholle, L., and Child, J. (1961–1970). Mastering the
>
> art of French cooking (Vols. 1–2). New York: Knopf.

Periodicals: Journals, Magazines, and Newspapers

Journal article—continuous pagination

> Carton, E. (1983). On going home: Selfhood in composition. College English, 45, 340–347.

Journal article—paginated by issue (two authors)

> Breland, H., & Jones, R. J. (1984). Perceptions of writing skills. Written Communication, 1(1), 101–119.

Signed monthly magazine article

> Kinnucan, P. (1984, April). Superfighters. High Technology, pp. 36–48.

Signed weekly magazine article

> Quinn, J. B. (1984, April 9). A new war on health costs. Newsweek, p. 87.

Unsigned magazine article

> Canning Campbell's can. (1984, April 9). Newsweek, p. 84.

Newspaper article

> Rosenblum, M. (1984, April 8). A parched trail of misery. Providence Journal, p. B1.

Bulletins, pamphlets, and public documents

> U.S. Congress. Senate. (1965). <u>Social Security amendments of
> 1965: Report</u> (89th Cong., 1st sess. Report No. 404).
> Washington, DC: U.S. Government Printing Office.

Committee report

> <u>Health economics: Report on a WHO interregional seminar</u>. (1975).
> Geneva: World Health Organization.

Other Sources

Dissertation

> Martin, Celest A. (1980). Syntax and success: A comparison of
> stylistic features with holistic ratings in freshmen essays
> (Doctoral dissertation, University of Southern California,
> 1979). <u>Dissertation Abstracts International</u>, <u>40</u>, 4010A.

Published interview

> Britton, P. (1981, July). [Interview with Marne Dubs]. <u>Popular
> Science</u>, pp. 64–67.

Film

> Benjamin, R. (Director). (1984). <u>Racing with the moon</u> [Film].
> Hollywood, CA: Paramount Pictures.

Personal Communications
Cite personal interviews, letters, memoranda, telephone conversations, and the like in the text only. The APA does not include personal communications in the reference list because they do not provide recoverable data. The in-text citation looks like this:
(R. A. Katula, personal interview, June 14, 1983)

In-Text Citation: MLA and APA

Most disciplines now use a form of documentation giving credit to the source right in the body of the paper, instead of in notes at the bottom of the page (footnotes) or notes at the end of the paper (endnotes). So that you may see how in-text citations work in practice, the two student research papers at the end of this chapter exemplify both styles. "On the Road to Success" represents MLA style; "Deep-Sea Mining" illustrates APA style. Neither style is difficult. In fact, only one essential difference distinguishes the two. The APA citations emphasize the date; the MLA cares about page numbers. Both styles emphasize brevity of citation, and encourage authors to introduce their source in the body of the paper as Arlene Nardiello does here:

> According to Mr. Edward Schwartzman, author of *Campaign Craftsmanship*, the new candidate should first name an experienced finance chairman who has extensive contacts in the business community and among civic groups (40).

The citation above gives only the page number in parentheses because the author's name is already mentioned in the sentence. In-text parenthetical citations include only author's name and page number (MLA) or date (APA) when a work is authored. If the work has no author, the title of the article or book is cited, along with the page number or year.

> Because writing courses are not lecture courses, but courses in which all participate in discussion and constructive criticism, attendance is crucial. (*Writing at URI* 7) (MLA) or (*Writing at URI*, 1983) (APA).

Multiple Authors

MLA: If a work has more than three authors, cite only the surname of the first author, followed by "et al." When a work has three authors, cite all three names in the first reference, but use only the first name and "et al." in subsequent references.

APA: Cite all names up to six authors in a first reference. Use surname and "et al." in later references. If a work has six or more authors, cite only the surname of the first author, followed by "et al." in all references.

Both styles: If a work has two authors, cite both names in all references.

Because MLA cites page numbers, it is not necessary to worry about whether you are paraphrasing or quoting directly. The APA, however, cites only author and date *unless you are quoting directly*. In that case, you must include the page number:

> "Although this line of reasoning is only suggestive, oral writing may bear a particularly close relationship to decoding" (Cioffi, 1984, p. 186).

(Notice that APA uses the abbreviation "p." for "page" and "pp." for "pages" in an in-text citation. The MLA uses no abbreviation for page numbers in the text.)

Setting off Quotations

When you are quoting directly from a source, incorporate your quotation directly into the text if it is of four lines or fewer.

> Before losing the primary, Mrs. Davis remarked, "I don't think you can buy your way into office" (Pepper 2).

If you are quoting five or more lines, however, indent your quotation five spaces (APA) or ten spaces (MLA). Do not use quotation marks.

Finally, you will want to become familiar with the documentation style used in your discipline, and so you will eventually want to purchase the *MLA Handbook* if you are in the humanities, or the *Publication Manual of the American Psychological Association* if you are in the social or physical sciences. Check with your instructor about the preferred style of documentation. The physical sciences sometimes use a number system quite different from the name-and-date styles.

The Finished Product

And so it is over. The act of creation has produced a thick manuscript where none existed before and you are ready to present your work. Don't relax yet! Many students apologize for typing done the night before and into the wee hours, but this is a poor excuse for typographic errors. The appearance of a paper adds to or detracts from its credibility, and after all the hours you've put in, you and your research product deserve the maximum of respect and credibility. Here's how to get it.

Assuming that you are using a typewriter and not a word processor, follow these suggestions:

1. Select a medium-weight bond paper—nothing erasable, because that smears dreadfully.
2. Be sure to have a clean, fresh ribbon in your typewriter. Gray print is hard on the eyes.
3. If you are the typist, type your references first, while you are fresh. Straight typing is easier than typing in a form that requires a lot of underlining. Also, you will need to refer to your reference list so that you may do your in-text citations properly.
4. If you are fortunate enough to have a self-correcting typewriter, proofread each page before you pull it out of the typewriter so you won't make a mess reinserting it later.
5. Do proofread. If you don't do it page by page as suggested above, make certain you are alert when reading over the entire manuscript. Make corrections neatly with a black ballpoint pen.
6. Fasten your manuscript in the way your instructor has requested, and only in that way. Do not add fancy covers if they are not called for.
7. *Make sure you have the required information on the title page.* (See title pages of sample research papers.) Don't forget your Table of Contents, if one is required.

Congratulations! You're finished. You can be proud of your research project and consider yourself on the way to being a writer.

Exercises

1. Go through current magazines and newspapers until you find a topic that piques your curiosity. Then live with it. Talk about your topic and see how much information you can gather without going to a library.

2. Browse through the current copy of *The Writer's Market* in your library and see how many topics, hobbies, and interests are represented by specific magazines.

3. Go to the library and list five journals in your field of interest or major. Then look them up in Katz & Katz's *Magazines for Libraries* to determine their level and usefulness to you.

4. Take the topic you have lived with from exercise 1 above, and look it up in PAIS. Try using at least two other indexes as well.

5. Using the same topic as you arrived at above, try contacting someone on campus who is an expert in that area. Set up an interview and plan questions ahead of time.

6. Use the blue pages of the telephone directory as a follow-up to your campus interview. Are any government agencies listed that might provide you with information? Call or write to them.

7. Browse through several magazines and scholarly journals. Try to pick out the patterns of academic research exemplified for you early in the chapter. See how many magazine articles use the informative pattern, and identify its sections within the article.

8. If you were going to write up the information you have gathered, what pattern would you choose? Why?

9. Make up several outlines for your topic. Which one appeals to you most, as writer? Which has the most audience appeal?

10. Try writing a creative, scene-setting opening for your topic. Try a straightforward opening. Which seems more appropriate?

On the Road to Success

By

Arlene Nardiello

College Communication Skills

C. Martin

December 1, 1982

1

On the Road to Success

Narrative,
scene-setter
opening

Strolling down the deserted street, I noticed
remnants of our last town election. Big bright posters
with eye—catching slogans were hanging on every other
telephone pole. Discarded flyers and other election
novelties lay crumpled in the gutter. Obviously, a lot
of time and money had been spent by the candidates
during their campaign. But where did all this time and
money come from? How did the candidates collect enough
money to successfully run their campaign?

Because of poor party discipline, candidates are
forced to seek revenues outside the main political

Method; indicates
pattern reader can
expect—process

party. In this paper I plan to show how candidates
gather money needed to run a campaign. Because the
techniques used to raise money for a presidential

Limits phenomenon
being studied

campaign are quite involved, I will limit this paper to
raising funds for small—town campaigns. In other
words, I will construct a framework that will help
small—town candidates successfully raise enough money
to run their campaign.

A candidate who devotes some time and thought

2

Statement of
thesis—reiterates
what audience
should learn from
paper

beforehand can usually conduct an effective campaign
without excessive expense. Money does indeed count,
but it certainly does not ensure victory. Even
overspending is no guarantee of success. A prime
example of excess occurred during a Kansas City
primary. Mrs. Roberta Davis spent $12.44 per vote
during the primary--and lost. Before losing the
primary, Mrs. Davis had remarked, "I don't think you can
buy your way into office" (Pepper B9). Obviously, you
can't!

Step 1 of process

It is especially difficult for a new candidate to
raise money. According to Mr. Edward Schwartzman,
author of Campaign Craftsmanship, the new candidate
should first name an experienced finance (or
fundraising) director who has extensive contacts in the
business community and among civic groups (40). By
doing so, the "unknown" candidate will borrow some
recognition from the better-known director. The
candidate will also be able to make use of the
director's experience in fundraising to get the
campaign under way.

Step 2 of process

To start the campaign funding, the candidate

3

should apply as much effort as possible to getting

donations from friends and relatives. It may sound

like begging (and essentially it is), but personal

contributions form a great part of the candidate's

account. During an interview Mrs. Agnes Doody Jeffrey,

who recently ran for Rhode Island State Representative

of the 47th District, told me that the first people she

went to for contributions were her friends and

relatives:

Direct quote from
primary source

> I politely put the bite on friends and
> relatives. Personal letters were sent to my
> friends with a cute slogan added on asking
> for contributions. I also sent invitations
> to the Faculty Club, which consists of URI
> [University of Rhode Island] faculty, and
> also asked for their money. This effort on
> my part raised almost $2,000 for my $3,200
> campaign.

The candidate may feel uncomfortable at first

asking relatives for money, but the outcome is worth the

discomfort. Besides, close relatives might find the

idea of a family member running for office exciting, and

4

along with contributing money, they might even
volunteer their services--or interest their friends and
colleagues in helping out (Schwartzman 42). The same
idea may even apply to friends. Still others might take
a stand on issues and contribute to the campaign because
of the candidate's proposed platform.

A second method a candidate should use to gain
contributions is setting up a small party, such as a
cocktail party, a tea, or a coffee hour. With this
method, the candidate can accomplish three goals rather
than one. The candidate can add to the campaign fund
while using the comfortable atmosphere to gain
recognition and to present the platform.

In his book, Mr. Schwartzman makes these
suggestions:

> Sometimes the candidate's friends,
> neighbors, or relatives may be willing to
> sponsor small gatherings consisting of 20 to
> 25 people, with each person contributing
> perhaps $10 to the campaign fund. Each such
> party might raise only one hundred dollars,
> but one may gain additional workers and

Section marker

5

contributions from those voters whom the

candidate is able to impress with his views.

(42)

   Mrs. Agnes Doody used the coffee hour for the

second reason—to gain recognition.   Because she was a

relative "unknown," her objective was for her guests to

"meet the candidate."   In the interview, Mrs. Jeffrey

said that these coffee hours "were held in the evening

after 7:30 and consisted of eight to twenty—five

people.   They were effective because I was able to

discuss my views on almost a one—to—one basis."

Section marker

   The third method a candidate can use to obtain

donations is the controversial direct—mail system.

That system has the same effectiveness as the small

cocktail party.   It raises money while giving the

candidate the opportunity to express views in the

Indicates area of
debate

campaign literature.   I call this method controversial

because although it may gain some contributors, it

depletes the funds available, because sending out these

letters costs money.   Also, because a few finance

committees use the scare tactic to frighten the public

into giving money to the "right" party, some may feel

6

Defines and
explains term
introduced above

this tactic isn't morally right.

Although the scare tactic usually doesn't apply to small-town campaigns, I offer an explanation of how it works. Campaign workers send out thousands of attention-getting letters to frighten the public into giving money. Evidently, large-scale campaigns can devote the necessary time and effort to this method.

According to Mr. Roger Craver, head of the Democratic Direct Mail Fund Raising Committee, "one must have controversial aides on the opponent's side to write about in the letters" (Farmey 1). One example is the Social Security letter that was sent to senior citizens. Arriving in a Social Security envelope, this letter contains details about the proposed Social Security benefits by the Republicans. It then elicits support for the Democrats, ending with the statement: "A mere $15 will do the trick" (Farmey 1).

Mr. Schwartzman proposes a way of applying direct-mail systems to smaller campaigns:

> The principle of large-scale
> direct-mail solicitations is to establish
> lists and send campaign literature to

7

possible contributors. In smaller
campaigns, this method is not economical; but
the principle of establishing lists of
possible contributors who are likely to be
receptive to your candidacy and then
appealing to them for funds is a good one.
Potential contributors—-both businesses and
individuals—-might be identified by going
through local newspapers to see which local
groups have taken positions on which issues,
or by having a member of one's staff check
through the city's commercial directory,
chamber of commerce, and professional
association membership lists. (45--46)

In my opinion, to be truly effective the
direct—mail system should be applied to a large—scale
campaign rather than to a small—town one. The
objective of the methods I am discussing is to obtain
money. With the cost of printing and sending direct
mail, I think the small—town candidate might lose money
rather than gain it.

The fourth method a candidate can use to raise

Reminds audience
of purpose of
paper

Section marker

8

money is the testimonial dinner, given in honor of the
candidate. Both big businesses and individuals sell
tickets in an effort to raise money and also to get
people interested in the candidate. Although the
average price per plate is $25, ticket prices may vary
with the average individual's financial status.

In an interview with Mr. Vincent Jennings,
Chairman of the Democratic Executive Committee for
Middletown Township (New Jersey), I was given an
explanation of how the tickets are sold for a
testimonial dinner:

Direct quote from
primary source

> We start with a base price of
> twenty-five dollars per plate, which is used
> to cover expenses. These tickets are sent in
> twos to people interested in the candidate
> with an accompanying letter asking for a
> twenty-five dollar donation for dinner.
> About two weeks after they have received the
> letter, a staff member calls to confirm their
> place. If they are unable to make it, we ask
> them to please send the tickets back and, if
> possible, to make a donation.

9

For people who are able to afford more
than twenty-five dollars per plate (lawyers,
doctors, owners of big businesses), we
ask for a higher price--say, one hundred
dollars per plate. By taking twenty-five
dollars out of the hundred to cover dinner
expenses, we have a seventy-five dollar
profit per plate. This is how we are able to
make money on these affairs.

As Election Day draws closer, the candidate
focuses on getting the people's vote. This change in
emphasis leaves the task of organizing testimonial
dinners and other big fundraisers to the finance
committees. Mr. Schwartzman mentions the special
attention that should be given to detail:

Many political functions literally
leave a bad taste in people's mouths--the food
is served cold or the wine may be bitter. The
prices normally charged for tickets to these
affairs should justify a choice of quality
entrées, and, since some people don't eat
meat, fish should be available. The

10

       temperature of the room should be comfortable
and the seating uncrowded.   The microphones
should be tested beforehand for the speakers
and the band.   The seating list should be
sensitive to who is not speaking to whom, and
care should be given in general to a sensible
placement of guests at the table.   (44)

An important aspect of testimonial dinners that
shouldn't be overlooked is the main speaker.   According
to Jennings, a prominent politician is usually asked to
give a speech; however, another popular speaker who may
be asked is one who discusses a recent controversial issue
(Jennings).   The committee in charge of the dinner should
call the potential speaker months in advance to see if
this person is available for that night.   I feel that an
interesting speaker or speech will definitely lead to an
increase in ticket sales.   It is so much more pleasant to
hear a fascinating speech than a dull, boring one.

    Testimonial dinners seem to be very important
sources of funds for the candidate's election.
Although a lot of preparation must go into these

11

dinners, the funds gained can be substantial. While
researching preelection expenses and contributions, I
found that by holding just one testimonial dinner
during the 1980—81 election period, Richard Kelly, who
ran for Middletown Township Committeeman, was able to
raise more than $8,600 for his campaign (Jennings).

Section marker

The main political party usually provides a
limited amount of funds to the candidate. This source
is the fifth that the candidate has for money. The
party organizes events to gain money and afterward
allots a specific amount to each candidate. Some
typical events are clambakes, "Monday Night Football"
parties, Chinese auctions, and Middletown Township's "A
Day at the Races." So far, these affairs have proved
very successful--a look at the recent expense figures
will clearly back up this statement.

The final campaign spending reports for
the Monmouth County Board of Freeholders
position came to approximately $150,000, the
combined amount used by the two opposing
candidates. Republican Frank A. Campione
spent $89,909 on his unsuccessful campaign,

12

and the new freeholder, Ray Kramer, spent
approximately $61,085 on his campaign.   The
Republican Organization raised and
contributed more than $10,600 to Mr.
Campione's campaign, and the Democratic
Organization raised $27,436 to contribute to
Mr. Kramer's campaign.   (Siegel 12)

Twice a year the Middletown Township Democratic
Club organizes a fundraising event entitled, "A Day at
the Races." During an interview with Mr. Vincent
Jennings, I was given an explanation of this affair
along with its significance:

Throughout the year, the Middletown
Township Democratic Club attempts to raise
money which will eventually go to the
campaign funds of upcoming Democratic
candidates. We organize different affairs
along with "A Day at the Races," which is held
twice a year at the Freehold Racetrack in
Freehold, New Jersey.

"A Day at the Races" is a buffet luncheon
with cocktails that is held in the Jockey

13

Clubhouse overlooking the racetrack.   The
Clubhouse can hold between 80 to 100 people,
and so far, we've been successful in selling
out all our tickets every year.   The cost is
$100 per ticket, but the price can be lowered
for staff members of the Democratic Club.   We
try not to do that because it eludes the
purpose of the whole affair—we mostly sell
the tickets to professionals who are able to
donate to the party.

The significance of "A Day at the Races"
is to obtain money for our candidates—but we
also have fun doing it.   Our total profit
from the racetrack events was a combined
$11,500 for this year.   (1982)

For the most part, I have obtained positive
information regarding the contributions given by the
head party to each separate candidate.   Mrs. Agnes
Doody Jeffrey remarked that "the head party was pretty
good in giving each candidate some money which was
raised from events such as clambakes."   I did, however,
obtain some negative information on this method.   In

14

his book, Mr. Schwartzman says that the head political
organization may provide some funds, but it generally
uses the funds raised to pay off debts from previous
campaigns (44). In other words, Mr. Schwartzman thinks
that candidates should not count on receiving funds
from the party but rely on their own financial
resources.

The sixth method differs from the first five in
that although it involves raising funds, these funds
are not obtained from contributions. I refer to loans
from banks. This method is not used much by small-town
candidates. When worst comes to worst, however, and
there's no other place to turn to for money, even
small-town candidates find that a bank loan is better
than nothing.

According to Mr. Harry Weinstein, a writer for the
Los Angeles Times, bank loans have become prevalent in
politics:

> Bank loans are currently used in
> political campaigns. They are perfectly
> legal under certain conditions--basically
> that the loans are made in the normal course

15

of business and don't involve favorable terms
that an ordinary borrower couldn't get.
[This implies that some banks give "favors"
to the candidate by lowering the interest
rates.]

For a campaign loan by a nationally
chartered bank to be legal, the recipient
must disclose the loan's guarantors because
the guarantors, according to federal
election laws, in essence have made a
campaign contribution until the loan is
repaid. (3)

Illustrates why
phenomenon is a
subject of debate

Many candidates avoid bank loans, because they
fear going into debt and being unable to pay back the
loans. Sometimes, though, the situation is reversed.
Some candidates are so sure they are going to win the
election that they take out loans confident they will be
able to pay them back. But what happens if the
candidate takes out several loans and loses?

Writer Henry Weinstein provides a good example of
overborrowing in his article "Bank Loans Assuming a Key
Role in Political Campaigns":

16

In Los Angeles during the 1981 election, Ira Reiner ran for city attorney. Because not enough people contributed to his campaign, Reiner's campaign manager borrowed money from three Los Angeles banks feeling confident that Reiner would win. Unfortunately, Reiner lost the election. Almost 77 percent of the money Reiner raised for his campaign was borrowed, leaving him $540,000 in debt. (3)

This incident is a good example of how using bank loans for campaign funding has gotten out of hand. When I talked to Mr. Vincent Jennings, I asked if his committee had ever had to take out a bank loan to help defray campaign expenses. His answer was plain and simple: "We never had to, and, pray to God, we never will."

Section marker

The final method is using services as contributions. Even though this method provides no actual funds, it saves the candidate a lot of money, which can then be put toward getting out the people's vote for the upcoming election.

17

This method involves using various sources for contributions in services rather than in cash. The candidates or their staff take it upon themselves to go out and ask for contributions in services. By that I mean people volunteering to do activities such as answering phones, licking envelopes containing campaign literature, or operating sound trucks to get the candidate recognized.

The candidate must remember to thank the volunteers for their work. A polite way to do so is sending a personal letter. This simple gesture does more than just thank the workers—while expressing appreciation, it shows that the candidate cares enough to put aside some time to write a thank-you note. This caring touch might, in turn, bring out more votes.

Because I have had firsthand experience as a campaign volunteer, I know how helpful services as a form of contribution can be to the candidate. My job was to apply address stickers to what seemed to be a million envelopes. It was a long and tedious job that took a lot of time to complete, but afterward, I felt quite good about myself for having done it. I knew that

Example of phenomenon

Section marker

Primary source—own research

18

if people like me hadn't volunteered their services, the candidate would have had to pay someone to do these jobs, thus depleting the campaign funds.

Conclusion—restatement of thesis. Use of summary quotation. Practical applications of information for audience.

As one very knowledgeable politician put it, "Money is the mother's milk of politics" (Herzberg and Peltson 28). To run a campaign, a candidate needs money. By explaining various methods currently used in politics, I hope I have helped the candidates and their committees understand how to raise enough funds for their campaign. Even readers who are not running for office can apply these methods to raise funds for various organizations.

19

Works Cited

Farmey, Dennis. "'GOP Devils' Help Democrats Increase
    Direct Mail Giving." <u>Wall Street Journal</u> 1 Feb.
    1982: 1+.

Herzberg, Donald G., and J. W. Peltson. <u>A Student Guide
    to Campaign Politics</u>. New York: McGraw, 1970.

Jeffrey, Agnes Doody. Personal Interview. 18 Nov.
    1982.

Jennings, Vincent. Personal Interview. 27 Nov.
    1982.

Pepper, Miriam. "When Campaign Funds Talk, Voters
    Don't Always Listen." <u>Kansas City Star</u> 30 Aug.
    1981: B9.

Schwartzman, Edward. <u>Campaign Craftsmanship</u>. New
    York: Universe, 1973.

Siegel, Joel. "Spending War Won, But Election Lost."
    <u>The Daily Register</u> 22 Nov. 1982: 12.

Weinstein, Harry. "Bank Loans Assuming a Key Role in
    Political Campaigns." <u>Los Angeles Times</u> 1 June
    1982: 3.

Deep—Sea Mining

1

Deep—Sea Mining for Manganese Nodules:

A Technical Perspective on a New Frontier

Carrie Rae

Writing 333

Dr. Martin

December 9, 1983

Deep—Sea Mining

2

Contents

Deep—Sea Mining

3

Note: This is Carrie's original table of contents.   We reprinted it exactly to give you some notion of the detailed way in which she planned her paper.   We did, though, cut some sections of her paper for inclusion here, and so some of the sections listed here may appear brief as you read the paper.

Deep—Sea Mining

4

Abstract

Phenomenon
studied

This presentation is written to familiarize the reader with the technology of seabed mining for manganese nodules. Recently discovered to have commercial value, manganese nodules contain worthwhile amounts of nickel, copper, cobalt, and manganese. Scientists are not sure where they came from, but we do know that they exist in abundance. Several national and international consortia are already spending millions of dollars on research for this new industry.

Significance of
topic

Because of dwindling worldwide reserves of these metals and unreliable governments that supply most of them, it is highly desirable to tap the store of manganese nodules on the ocean bottom.

Indicates process
reader will learn
about

Seafloor mining operations are still expensive and call for further research. Entire systems should be detailed and studied so that engineers can create economically feasible alternatives to land—based mining. A mining operation includes four general steps: locating a site that will be productive for mining, designing a technique for extracting nodules from the seafloor, transporting the material, and processing the nodules. These four steps break down into more detailed stages of the operation.

Directions for future research; cites current debate

After a planner details a cost analysis of the operation and accounts for effects of the system on the environment, the technology is complete. Before industry will invest the millions that it will take to exploit these seabed minerals, however, some legal questions have to be answered. Industrial countries and the Third World are competing for rights to this resource. The only thing that holds back the delivery of these much—needed minerals is not technological weakness, but unformed and untested legalities.

Deep—Sea Mining for Manganese

Nodules: A Technical Perspective

on a New Frontier

Describes significance of topic in language suited to lay audience

Seven—tenths of the earth's surface lies underwater, an area popularly believed to be less charted than the surface of the moon. Due to recent exploration, however, ambitious prospectors have discovered an abundance of rich mineral deposits in the ocean. The 330 million cubic miles of ocean water are probably the world's largest continuous source of ores. About 50 quadrillion tons of solids are dissolved in seawater, including, for instance, 10 billion tons of gold. Large amounts of minerals are also deposited on the ocean floor. There is excellent potential for such valuable commodities as titanium and zircon, as well as tin, iron ore, and coal.

The real targets for prospecting the seafloor are manganese nodules––fist—sized chunks, rich in manganese, copper, cobalt, and nickel, which litter the ocean floor. They are the highest grade of ore found anywhere on earth and they're found in almost every

Deep-Sea Mining

7

ocean and sea on the planet.

During the first great oceanographic expedition

from 1872 to 1876, the HMS Challenger made a landmark

discovery (Shusterich, 1982). The three-masted

explorer used trawl lines to dredge up debris from the

ocean bottom that would later be analyzed for its

significance to the oceanic environment. Among the

sediment, researchers discovered brown-to-black lumps,

thought to be meteorite fragments. The curiosities

were displayed in the British Museum for visiting

scientists to see. Later expeditions found even more

nuggets. It wasn't until the late 1950s, however, that

scientists really analyzed these nodules for their

mineral content. At this time, underwater cameras

discovered that they existed in abundance--peppering

some ocean bottoms like "words on a page" (James, 1982).

In 1957, Dr. John Mero, a graduate student at the

University of California, became interested in the

nodules. Studying the metal content of these nuggets,

he recognized that the higher-grade nodules had

commercial potential. Observing their worldwide

Background history—opening sentences tell us we are learning about origins of phenomenon, and can expect chronological order

distribution and value, Mero wrote a book on the
subject, entitled <u>Mineral Resources of the Sea.</u> He
went on to investigate feasible techniques for
recovering and processing the nodules. For instance,
Mero's enthusiasm prompted him to design and patent a
hydraulic-lift system--a dredging operation that
represents the state of the art in the ocean-floor
mining industry today (Shusterich, 1982).

    For all Dr. Mero's studies, as well as subsequent
research, we still lack knowledge of how the nodules
came about. Named for their copious supply of
manganese, these nodules pose a scientific mystery.
Generally potato-sized, lying at depths of 12,000 feet
or so, the nuggets are oxide materials and contain no
sulphur. They vary in thickness from a film to a
thickness of 5 cm, coating a solid nucleus. They vary
in size from small grains to one of 1770 pounds found
east of the Philippine Islands (Pearson, 1975). The
composition of the nuggets has been estimated from
samples found in waters southeast of Hawaii: 25-30
percent manganese, 2 percent iron, 1.5 percent nickel,

Focuses
phenomenon being
studied

Features

Deep—Sea Mining

9

1.4 percent copper, and .25 percent cobalt by weight.

Several theories explain the origin of manganese nodules. One theory proposes that the nodules are formed from the minerals contained in fallout from seafloor volcanic eruptions. Researchers propose that seawater minerals precipitate around the fallout minerals to form the chunks (Britton, 1981). The distribution pattern of the known nodules, however, is wrong for that theory. Other theorists suggest that the minerals precipitate around sand grains and other impurities (James, 1982). For example, some fully formed nodules were discovered with World War II spark plugs and shrapnel at their centers. This theory opposes those of others who believe biological interaction at the sea surface controls the nodules' distribution. These researchers propose that metals are extracted from the water by microscopic plants. The process should take time, but the discovery of young nuclei at the center of the nuggets conflicts with this idea.

The real stumper is that, theoretically, the

(margin notes) Summarizes other research

Debate area

Debate area

nuggets should be yards below the seafloor surface.
Sediment forms on the sea bottom much more rapidly than
the nodules grow. Some say that this rate could vary
because the biology of the seafloor means that sediment
falling from above is circulated underneath heavier
objects. Some scientists believe that small,
bottom—dwelling organisms constantly nudge them upward
(Britton, 1981). No one knows for sure—-manganese
nodules still present a mystery.

Science is aware that as much as 100 billion
nodules may be found on the floors of the world's oceans
(Britton, 1981). Discovering such amounts in the scant
3 percent of the ocean floor that has been surveyed,
geologists estimate that roughly 20 percent of the
seafloor contains nodules. This prevalence could mean
that at least 15 percent of our earth's surface is
littered with the metal nuggets. More than 300 prime
nodule—mining sites are known (Pearson, 1975), and
explorers are still searching for more. Certain places
have sparsely distributed nodules, others display thick
coatings of the nuggets—-the concentration of seafloor

Significance

Deep—Sea Mining

11

manganese nodules is widely varied. The area that has

the richest supply to date is in the eastern Pacific,

north of the Equator in the Clarion—Clipperton

fracture. A band that measures 200 kilometers by 1,500

kilometers houses a copious supply of high—grade

nodules. The nodules found in the Pacific have a higher

mineral value than those found in the Atlantic or Indian

Oceans (Pearson, 1975).

Manganese nodules are significant for four

valuable minerals: manganese, nickel, copper, and

cobalt. These minerals are all essential to the world

today: steel can't be made without manganese, nickel is

used in making stainless steel, cobalt is significant

to cancer treatment and manufacture of high—temperature

alloys for jet engines, and copper is critical for

generating and conducting electricity (Britton, 1981).

There is a worldwide demand for these minerals—some

experts predict the world demand will increase 174

percent by the year 2000, and 257 percent by 2020

(Pearson, 1975). And the land supplies are either

unpredictable or just plain running out.

Significance of
research
underscored

        Metal deposits in the oceans can make a major

contribution to the world's needs. Marne Dubs,

director of ocean resources for one ocean mining

interest, the Kennecott Group, states the facts simply:

"The nodules are the most significant untapped source

of raw materials in the world" (Britton, 1981, p. 66).

        One strong argument in favor of ocean mining is

Advantages   this: In many ways, marine mining is better and cheaper

than conventional (land—based) mining. Engineers have

compared the two sources and produced several

advantages in seafloor systems (Pearson, 1975).

> — There is no need to uncover material to be mined
>   from the seafloor. Trenches would be
>   nonexistent or at least much smaller than those
>   needed on land.
>
> — For most ocean systems, there is no need to build
>   dumps and places for residue.
>
> — Preparatory work within the outlined marine
>   deposits would be minimal.

— Land—based mining enterprises involve high
capital investment for many phases of an
operation. Ocean mining systems require one
capital investment and a shorter time to mine
the minerals.

— Ocean mining for manganese nodules produces a
higher yield. For instance, 24 pounds of copper
per ton of nodules mined is much more than the 8
pounds of copper produced from a ton of ore mined
on land.

— It often takes ten or more years to find a new
mineral deposit on land (Kildow, 1980). Three
hundred possible ocean mining sites are known
today, and more are yet to be discovered.

Disadvantages

The operation in seafloor mining is complicated,
however. A lot of research is necessary before
engineers can perfect mining systems to make them
economically feasible. Even the best methods used
today are still costly and inefficient. In—depth

Deep—Sea Mining

14

models of the whole mining procedure will expose
details that can be individually analyzed and improved
upon to produce more nearly adequate systems.   In the
next section of this report, I will outline and detail
such a system.

A system for mining manganese nodules from the
seabed can be divided into four parts: locating and
evaluating a site, choosing an extraction technique for
mining the materials, transporting the material ashore,
and finally, processing the nodules for their valuable
content.   Engineers can model a complete system
according to these five areas.

A mining site is worth investment only if it has
sufficient potential for profit.   Because assays of
metal vary from one location to another, certain sites
are more favorable than others.   When looking for
nodule sites, several factors will determine the
economic value of a deposit.   The most important
considerations are these: grade of nodules,
concentration of nodules per unit area of ocean floor,
size distribution of the nodules, physical

Procedures
section—reidenti-
fies phenomenon
being studied;
indicates treatment
of research material
and pattern of
discussion

Process with 4
parts

Part 1

Deep—Sea Mining

15

characteristics of the associated sediments, depth of
water, distance to a port or processing facility,
topography of the ocean floor, and weather (Pearson,
1975). The most important factor of these is the grade
of the nodules.

Along with these considerations, one must
coordinate with governmental bodies to be sure which
areas are free for mining. Political instability and
indecision on the subject of seafloor mining make this
precaution a necessity. Governmental agencies,
unfortunately, use the marine environment for such
purposes as submarine warfare training and as a dumping
ground for chemical and radioactive material or
explosives (Herbich, 1975).

Detailed determination of bottom characteristics,
once a potential area has been located, depends on
sampling systems. Many such systems are available as a
result of other seafloor technologies; the Deep Sea
Drilling Project out of Scripps Institute in
California, for instance, is an extensive program that
uses sophisticated sampling and soil testing devices.

Sediment samples are classified in two categories, disturbed and undisturbed samples.

Features

Undisturbed samples are best for determining the characteristics of sediment in its natural (in situ) state. A laboratory technician can test this sediment for strength, permeability, and water content to determine the characteristics of the foundation at a site. This information is necessary if a structure or vehicle is to put pressure on the sediment. Corers, which recover a vertical column of sediment, are used to obtain samples in their natural state. The Core Penetrometer is the best and most widely used coring system. Shaped like a bullet, it is dropped from an airplane or ship. The bullet, accelerated by gravity, penetrates the bottom soil and a technician measures its deceleration. The magnitude of deceleration is proportional to the type of soil penetrated. The Core Penetrometer is both quick and economical. Soil strength is measured by vane testing, with a device that measures the force with which the soil resists a turning propeller.

Grab samplers and dredges take disturbed samples of surface material by scooping up buckets of sediment that contain the nodules themselves. After a satisfactory sample has been procured, standard evaluating techniques determine the character, composition, and value of the deposit.

Prospectors can now make a good estimate of the proposed site: Are the potential mineral returns worth the costs involved in a mining operation?

The final phase in locating and evaluating a site is to assay the sea conditions in the area. As a July 1982 special feature of Mechanix Illustrated put it, the "worthwhile ore is found where pressures mount to over 6000 pounds per square inch, where undersea currents flow at various depths in opposite directions like atmospheric winds" (James, 1982, p. 88). An ocean environment has five basic characteristics: storm frequency, depth pressure, corrosion potential, wind and wave characteristics, and currents.

A wave spectrum represents a composite wave system that details wave height, wave period (or wave length),

Signals end of part 1 of process

New subsection

and direction of wave travel.   Such information on
waves is available for most parts of the world through
the United States Weather Service Command.   The Coastal
Engineering Research Center has also accumulated a
great deal of data on wave characteristics along the
Pacific, Atlantic, and Gulf coasts of the United States
(Shusterich, 1982).   Windspeed spectra are also
available through these agencies.

Ocean currents produce forces on offshore
structures and vehicles.   These currents, when strong,
have been likened to strong winds, running both
vertically and horizontally.   Currents are measured by
current meters over a year or more to detect seasonal
changes in the magnitude and direction of the current.
Current meters must be able to operate in salt— and
silt—laden water.

By observing the history of storms on record for an
area, a researcher can forecast future storm activity.
The researcher conducts an analysis of the frequency of
storms to determine the interval between storms on
record.   In this way, storms can be predicted and

Deep—Sea Mining

19

provided for.

Large pressures accompanying the extensive water depths where mining is to occur can be predicted. Data from pressure meters can be put in the form of a profile that indicates the changes in pressure with increasing depth. It is very important to study these forces so that a designer can create mining equipment.

Introduces part 2 of process

After establishing a good site for prospecting, great care will be needed in choosing a technique for extracting the minerals. Locating and keeping track of the minerals is one thing; getting them to the surface in commercial quantities is quite another. One expert likens this task to "sucking grains of sand up a straw from a bed of mud to the top of a skyscraper—at night, in a high wind" (Britton, 1981, p. 66). Several operations have been devised to do this job, all of them forms of dredging.

Marks subsection with 3 parts

Three basic methods of dredge excavation are deemed feasible today: hydraulic suction, continuous—line bucket, and submersible vehicles. All exhibit different capabilities according to the

circumstances surrounding a particular mining
operation.

Subsection 1

Hydraulic systems consist of three operational
phases: First, a suction pipe is suspended from a
floating platform or vessel. A gathering head collects
minerals from surface sediments and feeds them to the
bottom of the pipeline, rejecting oversized materials.
Last is some means of causing water and materials inside
the pipeline to flow upward with enough velocity to suck
nodules into the system and to the surface.

Hydraulically operating dredges can be classified
in three types——the Dustpan Dredge, the Self—Propelled
Hopper Dredge, and the Hydraulic Pipeline Cutterhead
Dredge (Herbich, 1975). Only the cutterhead is
considered applicable to seabed mining, but the others
warrant mention. The Dustpan Dredge is so named
because its suction head resembles a large vacuum
cleaner or dustpan. Due to its lack of a cutterhead,
which would loosen up hard, compact materials, the
Dustpan Dredge is suited mainly for high volume,
soft—material dredging.

Deep—Sea Mining

21

Disadvantages

The capital investment for hydraulically operated systems is costly due to the complication of the systems. It costs $30—60 million for a system that can recover one million tons of nodules per year at depths of up to 18,000 feet (Pearson, 1975). The system requires $10—20 in operating costs to raise one ton of nodules to the water surface. These systems also require large amounts of energy, have structural problems, and have problems with fluid flow.

Advantages

An advantage of the hydraulic dredges is that they serve as transporting devices in addition to digging and elevating. They are also capable of yielding considerable amounts of material.

Subsection 2

Another method under serious investigation is the continuous—line bucket (CLB) system, which is being developed by French and Japanese groups (Britton, 1981). These dredgers consist of 40—50,000—foot cables that carry buckets at 25—50 meter intervals. The looped cable is suspended from two ships and circles slowly as the ships move forward. The buckets skim over the bottom, filling with nodules, and return to the vessel to empty their loads.

Advantages

Capital costs——$2.5 million for a system,
excluding the cost of the vessels——are not high.
Operating costs are on the order of 50 cents per ton of
recovered nodules (Pearson, 1975). These costs are low
because of the simplicity of the system.

Disadvantages

The system is easily modified to operate in any
depth of water and all parts can be easily reached for
inspection and repair. But the system is awkward,
slow, and apt to get stuck in the mud. Rope strength and
speed in hauling the buckets aboard ship could limit
production.

Subsection 3

Researchers have been studying submersible
dredging methods as an alternative to transferring
material over great ocean depths. A consortium with
major French interests, Afernod, is developing
satellite beetle—undersea shuttle ships that travel to
the seabed, scoop up material, and return to a mother
ship to unload (Britton, 1981). In one version of this
design, the mother ship is a semisubmersible. Eight
remote—controlled shuttles spend less than eight hours

on a round trip. The shuttles contain several tons of ore, and dock 130 feet below the surface in the submerged portion of a platform. Researchers estimate a daily production rate of 6,000 tons and include a nodule—processing station at sea.

Advantages and disadvantages

This "robot system" avoids the use of pipelines or buckets, and can bring in large payloads with several shuttle "miners." The system could be a very effective mining method, although it is not cost—effective in its present stage of development.

Even though a lot of research is needed to perfect the systems that exist today, we have come a long way from mechanical dredges that work only in coastal areas.

Introduces part 3 of process

Subsection 1

To transport the mined material ashore to be processed, there are three methods to choose from. Some dredging operations include an oceangoing mining vessel, which could transport material to shore after aiding in the extraction process. The relatively small capital cost is a result of not purchasing additional vessels to transport material. The disadvantage of

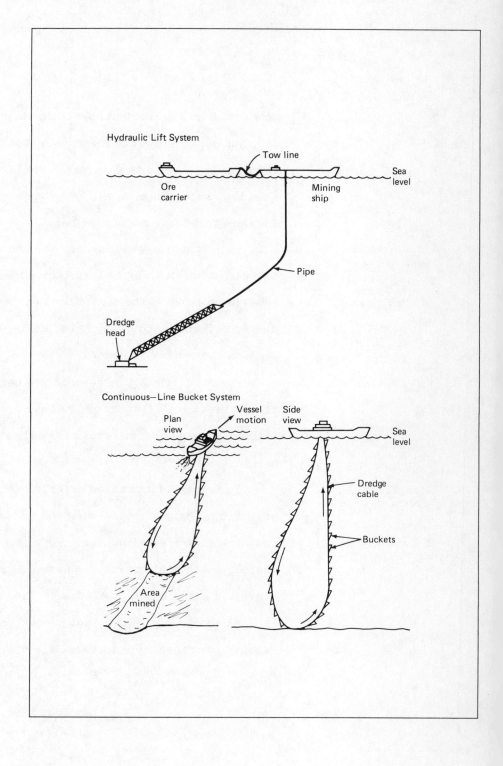

Hydraulic Lift System

Tow line

Sea level

Ore carrier

Mining ship

Pipe

Dredge head

Continuous—Line Bucket System

Plan view

Vessel motion

Side view

Sea level

Dredge cable

Buckets

Area mined

Deep—Sea Mining

24

this method of transport is that it makes the entire mining process quite time—consuming. Operators would have to disconnect the rig from cables or ladders, wait for the vessel to return, and reconnect before resuming mining operations.

Subsection 2

There are two other methods for getting the prospects ashore. Nodules could be transferred at sea from hoppers in mining ships to ore carriers, which could even conduct partial processing to separate some waste from the nodules (Shusterich, 1982).

Subsection 3

A final alternative is to dump mined material onto barges that are pulled by oceangoing tugs.

Advantage

Sea transportation is cheaper than land—based transport of mining materials, enhancing the sea—mining operation. Transportation is not a major problem; ocean mining is quite amenable to seagoing vessels.

The fourth and final step in an ocean—mining operation is to process the manganese nodules. This leg of the operation is still undeveloped on a commercial basis, though several pilot plants have been started. Deepsea Ventures, for example, has a pilot

plant that can process up to one ton of nodules per day.
They plan to enlarge the plant to a capacity of more than
5,000 tons per day (Pearson, 1975). Some experts
believe that processing will account for more than half
of the operation's cost (Britton, 1981). This is
because an entirely new chemistry is needed. Experts
say that no ores on earth are like manganese nodules.
The elements of interest are locked in a complex
ferromanganese compound that has to be chemically
processed to break up its constituents (Britton, 1981).

Several environmental effects of ocean mining
warrant consideration. Before a system can be
implemented, engineers must account for these problems.

Basically, two problems arise when prospectors use
the ocean environment for their mines. First, deep
water is brought up and discharged at the surface in
hydraulic dredging operations. This transport could
affect the natural order of nutrients in the ocean area
to be mined: the concentration of nutrients changes
along a vertical column of water. The order effects the
organisms that live at various depths in the column.

Introduces pattern
of analysis;
emphasis on cause
and effect

Disruption of the natural order could cause changes in the organic food chain. Scientists are still studying the extent of this effect.

The second major effect of seabed mining is on the sediment and organisms that lie on the seafloor. Studies of the long—term effects on organisms that form the base of the food chain (those which live at or near the seafloor) are still under way.

Directions for future research

These are the main aims of the Deep Ocean Mining Environmental Study that the National Oceanic and Atmospheric Administration (NOAA) began in 1975 (Britton, 1981). The study is also examining the environmental aspects of processing the nodules. Refining on shore will leave wastes of solids, sludges, slag, and tailings. Engineers have to design methods to treat the wastes at the plant. As well as onshore processing, some refining of mined manganese nodules will be done at sea. The waste must be handled aboard ship rather than dumped overboard. This treatment could present problems with storage.

The facts and comparisons are now obvious. The

technology exists to make seafloor mining a feasible

alternative to the world supply of important mineral

Future research
needed

resources.   Yet the whole thing is still in second gear.

In order to set up a commercial—scale mining operation,

financial groups must invest millions of dollars in the

industry.   The role of private consortia in the

worldwide seafloor mining industry, however, is

unclear.   Many political and legal decisions must be

made that will determine exactly who has rights to what.

Until government legislation dissipates these

uncertainties, private interests are reluctant to take

the big plunge by investing millions.   Marne Dubs of the

Use of summary
quote for
conclusion

Kennecott Group summarizes the problem nicely: "We've

done all the simple things.   The next major step is to

build a prototype mining ship and operate it for several

months.   Eventually, deepsea mining will be an

important source of metals.   The only thing that could

stop it is not technology or the marketplace, but a

screw—up by governments" (Britton, 1981, p. 67).

After the political ambiguity has been reduced,

domestic licensing is put in full swing, and we reach an

Deep—Sea Mining

28

Applications

Conclusion

international arrangement that satisfies the
industry's need for access to seabed minerals, we could
apply our technology to commercial ocean mining by the
mid—1990s. Ocean mining industries have agreed upon
this date as a feasible takeoff time. At that time,
complete mining systems will be designed and ready for
action.

Deep—Sea Mining

29

References

Britton, P. (1981, July). The challenge of ocean
    treasure: Deep—sea mining. Popular Science, pp.
    64—67.

Herbich, J. B. (1975). Coastal and deep ocean dredging.
    Houston, TX: Gulf Publishing Company.

James, R. (1982, July). Billion—dollar treasures at the
    bottom of the sea. Mechanix Illustrated, pp. 62—64,
    88—89.

Kildow, T. T. (Ed.). (1980). Deep—sea mining.
    Cambridge, MA: MIT Press.

Mero, J. (1965). The mineral resources of the sea.
    Amsterdam, NY: Elsevier Publishing Co.

Pearson, J. (1975). Ocean floor mining. Park Ridge, NJ:
    Noyes Data Corporation.

Shusterich, K. (1982). Resource management and the
    oceans: The political economy of deep seabed mining.
    Boulder, CO: Westview Press Inc.

A REFERENCE
HANDBOOK

CHAPTER 16

Grammar Review

Although the emphasis in composition is primarily on connected stretches of writing, because these larger units are composed of sentences, you should have a basic knowledge of the grammar of the sentence. The principles of grammar of importance are those that concern words and those that concern word relationships.

Parts of Speech

The traditional grammarians list and define eight parts of speech. The structuralists classify fifteen or more. The transformationalists do not concern themselves with classifying words. Yet for compositional purposes, it is useful to know some of the basic terms of grammar.

My own preference is for transformational grammar, but since the transformationalists do not deal with many of the topics that are of interest to the composition student, I will here attempt to pick and choose from the various grammars.

The Noun

Nouns name things. They name persons, animals, places, objects, and abstract ideas. It is true that the other parts of speech can name things, too, but we usually associate the naming function with nouns. Here are some examples of nouns:

Cheryl	stone	honesty
woman	cactus	love
girl	desert	infinity
armadillo	sand	pride
scorpion	stream	courage

You learn to recognize nouns because they appear in certain positions in English sentences:

> *Sunflowers* bloom in the *spring.*
> *Hurricanes* form at *sea.*
> The *Babylonians* and the *Hittites* built *temples* to *eagles.*

They pattern with articles, demonstrative pronouns, and possessive pronouns (what the structuralists call **determiners**):

an *alcoholic*	this *fact*	your *telephone*
a *Buick*	these *cars*	my *troubles*
the *world*	that *threat*	her *eyes*

Nouns take characteristic inflectional endings to form plurals and possessives:

SINGULAR	PLURAL	POSSESSIVE
bell	bells	bell's
cargo	cargoes	cargo's
city	cities	city's
fiesta	fiestas	fiesta's
knife	knives	knife's

They also have characteristic derivational endings:

white + ness	whiteness
natural + ist	naturalist
play + er	player
music + ian	musician

There are two main kinds of nouns: common nouns and proper nouns. **Common nouns** name members of a class of things:

> *Insects* thrive in warm weather.
> Botany is the study of *plants.*

Proper nouns name particular members of a class of things. They always begin with capital letters:

> The *Milky Way* has a graceful, pinwheellike form.
> *Switzerland* owes much to its glaciers.

The Pronoun

Pronouns take the place of nouns or noun phrases. **Personal pronouns** indicate the speaker *(I, my, mine, me, we, our, ours, us)*, the person spoken to *(you, your, yours)*, and the person spoken about *(he, his, him, she, her, hers, it, its, they, their, theirs, them)*.

Pronouns have four forms, as indicated below:

NOMINATIVE	OBJECTIVE	POSSESSIVE	POSSESSIVE
I	me	my	mine
we	us	our	ours
you	you	your	yours
he	him	his	his
she	her	her	hers
it	it	its	its
they	them	their	theirs

These pronouns appear in the following positions in sentences:

I dislike smoking. *(nominative)*
Tell *me* the truth. *(objective)*
Did you receive *my* letter? *(possessive)*
That book is *mine (possessive)*

Reflexive pronouns are personal pronouns that combine with the nouns *self* and *selves* to form compounds:

The forest *itself* is a shelter.
I'd rather do it *myself.*

Relative pronouns introduce relative clauses and refer to some antecedent in the sentence. The relative pronouns are *who, whose, whom, which,* and *that.*

Shakespeare is the writer *who* wrote *Romeo and Juliet.*
I remember the day *that* the earth stood still.
The sound of bells is a sound *which* I like to hear.

Interrogative pronouns ask questions. The interrogative pronouns are *who, whose, whom, which,* and *what.*

Whose car has a new paint job?
What are we having for supper?

Indefinite pronouns are pronouns that do not specify or identify their antecedents. These are some of the most common indefinite pronouns:

some	any	everybody	one
someone	anyone	everyone	another
somebody	anybody	everything	each
something	anything	either	both
nobody	nothing	neither	many

The Adjective

Adjectives describe, limit, qualify, or specify the nouns that they modify:

> The roadrunner walks with a *clownish* gait.
> Lightning is a *violent, fearsome* thing.

You learn to recognize adjectives because of their positions before nouns, as in the sentences above, and because they can often be distinguished by various suffixes: *-able, -ous, -full, -less, -ic, -er, -est.*

> The bells in the *historic* town of Taxco have been ringing for more than two hundred years.

> Your family will love the *delicious* taste of orange juice.

Most adjectives have different inflectional forms: *positive* (plain form), *comparative*, and *superlative*. Here are a few examples:

POSITIVE	COMPARATIVE	SUPERLATIVE
brave	braver	bravest
lively	livelier	liveliest
simple	simpler	simplest
good	better	best
many	more	most

Many adjectives attain their comparative and superlative meanings by using *more* or *most:*

POSITIVE	COMPARATIVE	SUPERLATIVE
hopeful	more hopeful	most hopeful
hesitant	more hesitant	most hesitant
squalid	more squalid	most squalid
terrible	more terrible	most terrible

The Adverb

Like adjectives, **adverbs** can qualify, limit, or add details to words. But the words they modify are verbs, adjectives, or other adverbs:

> Some fish can swim *backward.*
> The trip was *unexpectedly* short.
> The Yankees played *unusually* well.

Some adverbs modify complete clauses or sentences:

> Rivers carry silt into the sea *constantly.*
> *Certainly* I would prefer to read.

Adverbs are usually classified according to meaning; there are adverbs of *time, place, manner, degree* or *extent,* and *negation:*

> The plane will arrive *soon. (time)*
> Put the package *there. (place)*
> Alpine flowers grow very *slowly. (manner)*
> San Francisco was *almost* destroyed by an earthquake in 1960. *(extent)*
> I am *not* sick, but I am very tired. *(negation)*

Adverbs seldom can be identified by derivational endings. The only suffix of note is the *-ly* of manner adverbs:

generously	wildly
gracefully	carefully
suddenly	entirely

Although they do not have as many derivational forms as adjectives, adverbs also have three degrees of comparison: *positive, comparative,* and *superlative.* But most adverbs form their comparative and superlative degrees by using *more* or *most:*

POSITIVE	COMPARATIVE	SUPERLATIVE
slowly	more slowly	most slowly
loudly	more loudly	most loudly
wildly	more wildly	most wildly

A few adverbs, however, form their comparatives and superlatives by adding *-er* and *-est:*

POSITIVE	COMPARATIVE	SUPERLATIVE
soon	sooner	soonest
early	earlier	earliest
late	later	latest

Qualifiers

Qualifiers are words that pattern in sentences with adjectives and adverbs. Traditional grammarians classify these words as adverbs, but they don't always function in English sentences in the way that adverbs do.

Some typical examples of qualifiers are words such as the following:

very	rather	really
quite	real	more
too	pretty	somewhat

These qualifiers pattern in sentences in similar ways:

The Arizona sun can be *very* hot.
The Arizona sun can be *quite* hot.
The Arizona sun can be *pretty* hot.

The Verb

Verbs express action, occurrence, condition, or existence. Other parts of speech can show action, too; for example, the noun *reaction* shows action of some kind. Other parts of speech can show existence; for instance, the adjective *happy* depicts a state of being or existence. Nevertheless, these are the characteristics usually associated with verbs.

Spiny lizards *scuttle* over the rocks.
To all appearances, our earth *hangs* solidly in the heavens.
She *is* our family doctor.
Does life *exist* on other planets?

Besides identifying verbs by characteristics of meaning, you can identify verbs by their *inflectional endings.* Verbs have an unmarked form and four marked forms, with the endings -s, -ed, -ed or -en, and ing;

PLAIN	THIRD PERSON SINGULAR	PAST TENSE
turn	turns	turned
mend	mends	mended
drive	drives	drove
know	knows	knew

PAST PARTICIPLE	PRESENT PARTICIPLE
turned	turning
mended	mending
driven	driving
known	knowing

These forms provide the basis for *conjugating* verbs.

To conjugate a verb, you list the various forms and put them into a paradigm:

PRESENT TENSE

Singular	*Plural*
I walk	we walk
you walk	you walk
he, she, it walks	they walk

PAST TENSE

Singular	*Plural*
I walked	we walked
you walked	you walked
he, she, it walked	they walked

FUTURE TENSE

Singular	*Plural*
I shall walk	we shall walk
you will walk	you will walk
he, she, it will walk	they will walk

PRESENT PERFECT

Singular	*Plural*
I have walked	we have walked
you have walked	you have walked
he, she, it has walked	they have walked

PAST PERFECT

Singular	*Plural*
I had walked	we had walked
you had walked	you had walked
he, she, it had walked	they had walked

FUTURE PERFECT

Singular	*Plural*
I shall have walked	we shall have walked
you will have walked	you will have walked
he, she, it will have walked	they will have walked

Besides these forms of the verb, there are *progressive forms* that emphasize the idea of ongoing action. The progressive tenses of verbs are formed with the verb *be* and the present participle:

PRESENT TENSE

Singular	*Plural*
I am walking	we are walking
you are walking	you are walking
he, she, it is walking	they are walking

PAST TENSE

Singular	*Plural*
I was walking	we were walking
you were walking	you were walking
he, she, it was walking	they were walking

FUTURE TENSE

Singular	*Plural*
I shall be walking	we shall be walking
you will be walking	you will be walking
he, she, it will be walking	they will be walking

PRESENT PERFECT

Singular	*Plural*
I have been walking	we have been walking
you have been walking	you have been walking
he, she, it has been walking	they have been walking

PAST PERFECT

Singular	*Plural*
I had been walking	we had been walking
you had been walking	you had been walking
he, she, it had been walking	they had been walking

FUTURE PERFECT

Singular	*Plural*
I shall have been walking	we shall have been walking
you will have been walking	you will have been walking
he, she, it will have been walking	they will have been walking

Tense

The *present tense* indicates action going on in the present time *(I run)*. The *past tense* indicates action in the past *(I ran)*. The future tense indicates action that will take place in the future *(I shall run)*. The *present perfect tense* indicates completed action at the time of the assertion *(I have run)*. The *past perfect tense* indicates completed action in the past *(I had run)*. The *future perfect tense* indicates that the action will have been completed before some future time *(I shall have run)*.

Voice

Verbs can be in the *active* or the *passive* voice. If the subject performs the action of the verb, the verb is active. If the subject receives the action of the verb, the verb is passive.

> The cook *baked* the fish. *(active)*
> The fish *was baked* by the cook. *(passive)*

The *passive voice* is formed by using the appropriate form of the auxiliary *be* with the past participle of the verb. The following paradigm gives only the third person singular of each tense:

Present	he *is* asked
Past	he *was* asked
Future	he *will be* asked
Present perfect	he *has been* asked
Past perfect	he *had been* asked
Future perfect	he *will have been* asked
Present progressive	he *is being* asked
Past progressive	he *was being* asked

Mood

There are three moods: the *indicative*, the *subjunctive*, and the *imperative*. The first expresses a statement of fact. The second expresses a contingency, wish, doubt, or uncertainty. The third expresses a command or entreaty.

> Some people *dream* of money. *(indicative)*
> If my car *were* here, I could leave early. *(subjunctive)*
> Please *visit* me soon. *(imperative)*

The subjunctive is seldom used by modern writers. When it is used, it often takes the form of the verb *were* and the conditional word *if* to express a hypothetical action.

Two-Part Verbs

A *two-part verb* is a verb followed by a particle. The particle looks like a preposition, but unlike the preposition, it can be freely moved about in a sentence, and it doesn't take an object:

> The student *looked up* the reference.
> The student *looked* the reference *up*.

The Auxiliary

In traditional grammar, the *auxiliary* is classified with the verbs as a "helping verb." The structuralists classify it as a functional word that patterns with verbs, as in the expression *can go.*

There are several kinds of auxiliaries: the *modal auxiliaries (may, might, can, could, shall, should, do, did, will, would,* and *must),* the *perfect aspect auxiliaries (have, had),* and the *progressive aspect auxiliaries* (forms of the verb *be*).

> Sharks *will* swallow anything. *(modal)*
> The sea *can* build as well as destroy. *(modal)*
> The best snake charmers *have* always lived in the East. *(perfect aspect)*
> I *am* losing patience. *(progressive aspect)*

Aspect

Aspect is a category of the verb indicating primarily the nature of the action performed in regard to the passage of time. There are two aspect categories: progressive and perfect.

The *progressive aspect* is that form which is used to convey the idea of ongoing action. It is formed with the connecting verb *be* and the present participle, which ends in *-ing:*

> She *is* leav*ing*. *(present progressive)*
> She *was* leav*ing*. *(past progressive)*

The *perfect aspect* is that form which is used to convey the idea of completed action. It is formed with the word *have* (and its variants *has* and *had*) and the past participle, which ends in *-ed* or *-en:*

> I *have* eat*en*. *(present perfect)*
> He *has* eat*en*. *(present perfect)*
> He *had* eat*en*. *(past perfect)*

The progressive and perfect aspects can be combined to form various tenses, as in these examples:

> She *has been* leav*ing*. *(present perfect progressive)*
> She *had been* leav*ing*. *(past perfect progressive)*

Both the progressive and the perfect aspects can combine with the modal auxiliaries to form tenses:

> I *will* be eat*ing*. *(future progressive)*
> He *will have been* eat*ing*. *(future perfect progressive)*

The Preposition

Prepositions show spatial, temporal, and logical relationships between the nouns or pronouns that follow them and some other word in the sentence:

> *In* the desert, water is life itself.
> The concert will begin *at* eight o'clock.
> Birds can escape *by* air.

These are some commonly used prepositions:

above	below	for	since
across	beneath	from	through
after	beside	in	to
against	between	into	under
along	beyond	like	until
among	by	of	up
around	concerning	off	upon
at	down	on	with
before	during	over	within
behind	except	past	without

Some prepositions are groups of words which have the force of a single word:

by means of	with respect to
in spite of	on account of
instead of	in reference to
out of	according to

A *prepositional phrase* is a group of words in which a preposition is followed by a noun or noun substitute. The word following the preposition is called the object of the preposition:

> The turtle looks *like a lump of mud.*
> *In a total eclipse,* the entire sun is obscured.

There are two prepositional phrases in the first example above: "like a lump" and "of mud." The objects of the respective prepositions are *lump* and *mud.* In the second sentence, the noun *eclipse* is the object of the preposition *in.*

Do not confuse prepositions with particles or adverbs, words that often have identical forms. Prepositions always take objects:

Look *up! (adverb of direction)*
Look the reference *up. (particle)*
Look *up* the reference. *(particle)*
Look *up* the street. *(preposition)*

The Conjunction

Conjunctions join words, phrases, and clauses. Like prepositions, they show spatial, temporal, and logical relationships.

There are three kinds of conjunctions: *coordinating, correlative,* and *subordinating:*

Diamonds *and* gold are the earth's most dazzling prizes. *(coordinating)*

Either moist, juicy pineapple *or* ripe, red strawberries will make your mouth water. *(correlative)*

When you give, you also receive. *(subordinating)*

The coordinating conjunctions are *and, but, or,* and *nor.* The correlative conjunctions are *either . . . or, neither . . . nor, both . . . and, not only . . . but also, whether . . . or.* The following is a list of some frequently used subordinating conjunctions:

after	because	so that	when
although	before	than	whenever
as	if	though	where
as if	in order that	unless	wherever
as long as	since	until	while

Coordinating conjunctions join items of equal grammatical rank and importance:

Few substances look less alike than *coal* and *diamonds.*

Subordinating conjunctions join items of unequal grammatical rank and importance:

If too many climb aboard, the boat will sink.

The Sentence Connector

Sentence connectors, like conjunctions, can join independent clauses. Traditional grammarians call them *conjunctive adverbs.* Here is a partial list:

accordingly	however	similarly
also	indeed	still
besides	likewise	then
consequently	moreover	therefore
furthermore	nevertheless	thus

In current usage, sentence connectors are preceded by a semicolon when they join two independent clauses:

> I prefer to stay home tonight; *besides,* I have a cold.
> Streams run; *however,* glaciers merely crawl.

The Article

Articles limit the words they modify. *A* and *an* are indefinite articles, having the general meaning of *any:*

> Bring me *a* chair to stand on.
> Give me *an* envelope.

The is a definite article:

> Bring me *the* the chair in the corner.

The article *a* is used before words beginning with a consonant. The article *an* is used before words that begin with a vowel:

a masterpiece	an idea
a seagull	an only child
a leaf	an eagle

Some grammarians group articles, demonstrative pronouns, and possessive pronouns in a single class called *determiners:*

ARTICLES	DEMONSTRATIVES	POSSESSIVES
a	this	my, your
an	that	his, her
the	these	its, our
	those	their

Their reasoning is that all of these words can pattern with nouns and noun phrases in similar ways:

an iguana	a fishing fleet
this iguana	that fishing fleet
these iguanas	those fishing fleets
your iguana	his fishing fleet
our iguana	her fishing fleet

Exercises

1. List the parts of speech in the following sentences. Use a separate column for each category.

   a. Swarms of insects filled the air.

   b. The world's energy is running out.

   c. Erosion builds, but it also destroys.

   d. Gold is very beautiful.

   e. Kick up your heels.

   f. Ensenada is the home of Mexico's largest fishing fleet.

   g. His car collided with an oil truck.

   h. You're reading this through a glass.

   i. Visit this unspoiled Pacific island.

   j. Who called for me?

2. Give the plural and possessive forms of the following nouns: *book, piece, bus, sheep, city, monkey, studio, tomato, loaf, tooth, antenna.*

3. Write the comparative and superlative forms of the following adjectives and adverbs: *good, bad, perfectly, slow, easy, often, brave, lucky, little, cool.*

4. Give the principal parts of the following irregular verbs: *break, do, buy, go, lie* (recline), *raise, rise* (ascend), *sit* (rest), *set* (place), *hit, meet, slide, win.*

5. Give the principal parts of the following regular verbs: *work, play, believe, drop, submit.*

The Sentence

A **sentence** is a structured string of words containing a subject and a predicate. The subject and predicate can be single words or several words:

> Maps/speak.
> The Mayan civilization/flourished for nearly 2000 years.

Sentences are classified by purpose and by structure. According to purpose, sentences may be categorized as declarative, interrogative, imperative, and exclamatory.

A **declarative sentence** makes a statement:

> The basic fare is forty cents.

An **interrogative sentence** asks a question:

> Do galaxies evolve?

An **imperative sentence** expresses a command, a request, or an entreaty:

> Take time out to stretch on the soft white sands of Micronesia.

An **exclamatory sentence** expresses strong feeling or emotion:

> It's a shark! Let's get out of here!

According to structure, sentences are traditionally classified as simple, compound, complex, or compound-complex.

A **simple sentence** is one that has a subject and a verb.

> The old explains the new.

A **compound sentence** contains two or more subjects and verbs, and it coordinates two or more simple sentences:

> You touch a bowl of jelly, and the whole thing will jiggle.

A **complex sentence** contains at least two clauses, one of which is subordinate:

> Lobsters shed their shells as they grow.

A **compound-complex sentence** contains at least two independent clauses and one or more dependent clauses:

> Our excitement grew in the ninth inning, and everyone stood up when Reggie Jackson hit a home run.

Exercise

Classify each of the following sentences according to purpose and structure.

    a. In her dream, her son was calling for her.

    b. Do we live more than once?

    c. Help me!

    d. Americans across the country are buying cable T.V.

    e. Japanese T.V. sets telecast in stereo sound, but most Americans sets do not.

    f. Germany turns out the best Super 8 cameras.

    g. Solar energy won't come of age until it's competitive in price.

    h. Let us fly you to Acapulco.

    i. Are the rich happy?

    j. Cave diving is risky recreation.

Basic Sentence Patterns

Every sentence consists of at least two parts, a **subject** and a **predicate.** These are the essential parts of all sentences:

> It works.
> Time flies.

Some sentences have a third part, called a complement. A *complement* completes the meaning of the subject or the object.

There are five kinds of complements: *the direct object*, the *indirect object*, the *objective complement*, the *predicate nominative*, and the *predicate adjective:*

> Clothes screen *heat. (direct object)*
> The computer saved *us* hours of work. *(indirect object)*
> Her boss considered her an *asset. (objective complement)*
> Love is the *answer. (predicate nominative)*
> The sea is *old. (predicate adjective)*

There are six basic sentence patterns, five of which correspond to the five kinds of complements listed above:

> *Subject-Verb*
>
> Most snakes can swim.
> Times change.
>
> *Subject-Verb-Object*
>
> Money begets money.
> Silence gives consent.
>
> *Subject-Verb-Indirect Object-Object*
>
> His friend gave him the answers.
> The salesperson showed me two suits.
>
> *Subject-Verb-Object-Objective Complement*
>
> She called him a phony.
> The police labeled the crime a felony.
>
> *Subject-Linking Verb-Predicate Noun*
>
> Corn is the only American grain.
> Poverty is no sin.
>
> *Subject-Linking Verb-Predicate Adjective*
>
> Art seems timeless.
> The weather is awful.

Exercises

1. Pick out the complements in the following sentences and tell what kind each is.

   a. The symbol of dowsing is a forked branch.

b. Nature wastes nothing.

c. Beggars can't be choosers.

d. Knowledge is power.

e. The bones of most birds are hollow.

f. You can't teach an old dog new tricks.

g. Still waters run deep.

h. My cousin bought me a dictionary.

i. Her boyfriend thought her a kook.

j. No answer is also an answer.

2. Write six sentences to illustrate each of the basic sentence patterns.

Noun Phrases and Verb Phrases

The simplest kind of noun phrase that can combine with a verb to form a simple sentence is the noun by itself, such as the word *leaves* in the sentence "Leaves decay." Usually the noun has an article (or determiner) paired with it to form a simple noun phrase: *the wind, this day, my stereo*. Besides the article, the most common noun modifiers are adjectives: *golden apples, purple sky, azure water.* Prepositional phrases also combine with nouns to form noun phrases: *cheese on rye, the king of Siam, pheasant under glass.*

There are other ways of expanding noun phrases which we will consider later. These are a few of the most basic ways:

> this summer
> crushed velvet
> the right spot
> an island for two
> the greatest show on earth

Just as the noun phrase is an expansion of a single noun (or pronoun), the verb phrase is an expansion of a single verb. The verb itself can take an auxiliary or several auxiliaries: *did* imagine, *are* thinking, *have* contemplated, *must have been* dreaming. To the main verb, you can add a single adverb: *never fear*, drive *carefully, frequently* drive. Prepositional phrases can also combine with the verb to form verb phrases: arise *in the morning*, sleep *until noon*, think *about you.*

And as you have already seen, verbs can take complements: painted the table *brown*, considered the woman *a saint*, is a *good lawyer*. These complements are considered part of the verb phrase.

There are other ways of expanding the verb phrase, but these are some of the most basic:

> can be delightful
> kick up your heels
> treat you royally
> getting yourself in hot water
> can go camping in style
> always cooking up something new

Exercises

1. List the noun phrases and the verb phrases in the following sentences. Make a separate column for each.

   a. You can appreciate the difference.

   b. Some people set their sights very high.

   c. In the jungles, the fighting continues.

   d. Are we, as individuals, helpless in the face of inflation?

   e. With hunger in his eye, an abstract painter goes realist.

2. Write five sentences. Then underline the noun phrases in each. Write five more sentences and underline the verb phrases in each.

Expanding Sentences by Coordination

Compound sentences are formed by combining two or more sentences. The process of combining two or more sentences into one sentence is called the **conjunction transformation:**

The earth may be cooling off. It may be getting hotter.	The earth may be cooling off, *or* it may be getting hotter.

When sentences are conjoined, they may be punctuated with a semicolon or with a comma and a conjunction:

Moths spin cocoons.   }   Moths spin cocoons;
Butterflies do not.   }   butterflies do not.

The ideas are old.   }   The ideas are old, *but* the
The technology is new.   }   technology is new.

If two or more sentences have parts in common, the common elements that appear in each sentence can be deleted:

The fish grabbed the sea   }
gull.   }   The fish grabbed the sea
                             }   gull, pulled it beneath
The fish pulled it beneath   }   the water, and drowned it.
the water.   }
                             }
The fish drowned it.   }

The result of deleting the identical noun phrases that appear later in the sentence is a series of parallel verbs.

Conjoined sentences with identical grammatical structures can be reduced to simple sentences with compound subjects or compound predicates:

Robin *failed the driving*   }
test.   }   Both *Robin* and *her brother*
                             }   failed the driving test.
Her brother *failed the*   }
driving test.   }

Most drivers obey traffic }   Most drivers *obey traffic*
laws.   }   *laws* and *stop at stop*
                             }   *signs.*
Most drivers stop at stop }
signs.   }

Not all compound subjects and predicates, however, can be formed by deleting identical grammatical structures. Some are formed by joining the subjects or predicates directly.

Two and *two* are four.
Sarah, Mary, and *Alice* met in New York.

Exercise

Combine the following sentences into compound sentences or sentences with compound subjects or predicates:

   a. The player limped off the field.
      He collapsed on the sidelines.

   b. The waiter took my order.
      He handed me a bill.

   c. I took your advice.
      I studied harder.

   d. You like horror films.
      I like horror films.

   e. We hated the movie.
      You liked it.

Expanding Sentences by Subordination

Adverbial clauses are formed by joining two or more sentences so that one sentence becomes a subordinate clause with the addition of a subordinate conjunction:

> The horned lizard squirts
> blood from its eyes.
>
> The horned lizard is
> disturbed.

> The horned lizard squirts
> blood from its eyes *when
> it is disturbed.*

     There is a close connection between sentences that contain adverbial clauses and compound sentences:

> *If Carl said that,* then he is wrong.
> Carl said that; *then* he is wrong.

> *Because it is raining,* I will stay home.
> It is raining; *therefore,* I will stay home.

> *Although I would rather stay home,* I must go.
> I would rather stay home, *but* I must go.

> *Unless you go,* I will be mad.
> You go, *or* I will be mad.

This connection can be partially explained by assuming that sentences that contain adverbial clauses and their compound-sentence counterparts both come from underlying sentences:

Carl said that. He is wrong.	} If Carl said that, he is wrong.
Carl said that. He is wrong.	} Carl said that; then he is wrong.

Exercise

Combine the following sentences. Make one into an adverbial clause (for example: You are near a fire. Be careful. *When you are near a fire,* be careful).

a. The Raiders lost.
   Three players were hurt.

b. I am not an expert.
   I do like good food.

c. Your legs hurt.
   Then stop jogging.

d. You come at once.
   I shall be mad.

e. You were out.
   Someone called for you.

Expanding Sentences by Relativization

Relative clauses, and adjectival modifiers such as adjectives, participles, and prepositional phrases, are formed by combining two sentences. The *relative-clause transformation* makes one sentence into a relative clause:

All rocks contain some minerals. The minerals dissolve in water.	} All rocks contain some minerals *which dissolve in water.*

Notice that in order for a sentence to be relativized, there must be identical noun phrases in both sentences. One of the noun phrases is then replaced by a relative pronoun:

The magazine has been thrown away. You asked for *the magazine*.	The magazine *that you asked for* has been thrown away.
He is a singer. *He* entertains his audience.	He is a singer *who entertains* his audience.

There is a close relationship between adjectives and relative clauses. **Adjectives** come from relative clauses, which in turn come from complete sentences:

Mint has an odor. The odor is strong.	Mint has an odor *which is strong.*
Mint has an odor. The odor is strong.	Mint has a *strong* odor.

In traditional grammar, the **participle** is defined as a verbal adjective. It is a form of the verb used as an adjective to modify nouns. The participle can be a single word or a participial phrase:

The *running* girl tripped over the skates.
The child, *filled* with alarm, began to cry.

Like adjectives, participles are closely related to relative clauses. Both come from two or more complete sentences:

Rain carries salt. The salt is dissolved from the rocks.	Rain carries salt *that is dissolved from the rocks.*
Rain carries salt. The salt is dissolved from the rocks.	Rain carries salt *dissolved from the rocks.*

Participles take the following forms in English sentences:

PRESENT   PAST

asking   having asked
being asked   asked
            having been asked

These in turn can combine with other words to form participial phrases:

I saw an old man *asking for food.*
Having asked for food, the old man departed.
Being asked for food by the old man, the woman said yes.
Asked for food, the woman said yes.
Having been asked for food, the woman could hardly refuse.

Since the *prepositional phrase,* when it modifies a noun or a pronoun, is adjectival (the whole phrase acts as a single adjective), it too is related to the relative clause:

The flower withered.   } The flower *which is in the*
The flower is in the vase. } *vase* withered.

The flower withered.   } The flower *in the vase*
The flower is in the vase. } withered.

Not all prepositional phrases are related to relative clauses. But when the prepositional phrase modifies a noun (unless it shows possession), a relative clause can always be substituted for it.

Appositives are nouns or noun substitutes, but like adjectives, they limit, describe, and explain other nouns:

We spent the night in Flagstaff, *a city in northern Arizona.*

Charlemagne, *a foreigner,* was never popular in Italy.

Although appositives are not considered to be verbals, nevertheless there is a close connection between appositives and relative clauses:

The thumb is a master-
piece of nature.

The thumb is an anatomical
work of art.

}

The thumb, *which is an anatomical work of art*, is a masterpiece of nature.

The thumb is a master-
piece of nature.

The thumb is an anatomical
work of art.

}

The thumb, *an anatomical work of art*, is a master-piece of nature.

What all of these grammatical structures have in common is that they modify nouns and are related to relative clauses.

TV shows *that depict violence* irritate censors. *(relative clause)*
Violent TV shows irritate censors. *(adjective modifier)*

The child *who is sleeping* should not be disturbed. *(relative clause)*
The *sleeping* child should not be disturbed. *(participle)*

That book *which is on the desk* is torn. *(relative clause)*
That book *on the desk* is torn. *(prepositional phrase)*

Richard, *who is my friend*, married my girl. *(relative clause)*
Richard, *my friend*, married my girl. *(appositive)*

Exercise

In combining these sentences to form single sentences, make some sentences into relative clauses, some into adjectival, participial, or prepositional phrase modifiers, and some into appositives.

a. Dandelions form a setting.
   The setting is golden.

b. They ate its fruit.
   It has a red pulp.

c. A volcano sends out streams of rock.
   The streams are like molasses.

d. Tell Clara you want the dress.
   I returned it.

e. I dropped the jar.
   The jar was filled with honey.

f. He received the invitation.
   The invitation was from someone he didn't know.

g. The flood paralyzed the city.
   It caused the governor to seek emergency funds.

h. My friend was driving recklessly.
   He passed me like a bat out of hell.

i. Carol enrolled in Psychology 101.
   Psychology 101 is an interesting course.

j. Her home has an excellent view of the ocean.
   Her home is near San Francisco.

Expanding Sentences with Noun-Phrase Complements

Noun-phrase complements are noun substitutes. They are words or groups of words that can be used in nominative positions in English sentences. Three important noun-phrase complements are the noun clause, the infinitive, and the gerund or gerundive.

In traditional grammar, a **noun clause** is one that can serve as the subject of a verb, the object of a verb, the object of a preposition, or a complement:

> *That he will appear* is certain. *(subject)*
> They said *that he will appear*. *(object)*
> I am not happy about *what you told me*. *(object of preposition)*
> Sand storms are *what we expect in the West*. *(complement)*

In traditional grammar, an **infinitive** is called a verbal, a form of the verb with the word *to* in front of it. Here are some typical examples of the infinitive forms:

PRESENT	PAST
to ask	to have asked
to be asked	to have been asked

Like the noun clause, the infinitive can be used as a noun substitute:

> *To err* is human. *(subject)*
> She likes *to dance*. *(object)*
> *To eat* is *to live*. *(subject and complement)*

The **gerund** in traditional grammar is defined as a verbal noun. It has the following forms:

PRESENT	PAST
asking	having asked
being asked	having been asked

Notice that some of its forms resemble those of the participle. But the participle is an adjectival modifier. The gerund is a noun substitute. As a noun substitute, it functions in sentences the way nouns do:

> *Jogging* is not much fun. *(subject)*
> *Seeing* is *believing*. *(subject and complement)*
> I do like *walking*, however. *(object)*
> We were captivated by her *singing*. *(object of preposition)*

In transformational grammar, the noun clause, the infinitive, and the gerund are called **noun-phrase complements.** They come from complete sentences:

> I know something.   I know *that you like movies.*
> You like movies.

> My mother told me   My mother told me *to eat*
> something.   *my dinner.*
>
> I should eat my dinner.

> She likes something.   She likes *climbing*
> She climbs mountains.   *mountains.*

In these examples, the second sentence of each pair is embedded in the first as a clause, an infinitive phrase, or a gerundive phrase. This is done partially by means of **complementizers.**

There are three kinds of complementizers: the clause complementizer *that*, the infinitive complementizer *for . . . to*, and the gerundive complementizer *'s . . . ing*. Here are some examples of sentences that use these complementizers:

> *That* Bob smokes worries me.
> It worries me *that* Bob smokes.
> *For* Bob *to* smoke worries me.
> Bob*'s* smok*ing* worries me.

Notice the close relationship that exists among these sentences. This relationship suggests what I have already pointed out—that complements come from two or more sentences. Their differences can be accounted for by the different complementizers. Complementizers enter sentences by means of transformations:

It worries me. Bob smokes.	*That* Bob smokes worries me.
It worries me. Bob smokes.	It worries me *that* Bob smokes.
It worries me. Bob smokes.	*For* Bob *to* smoke worries me.
It worries me. Bob smokes.	Bob*'s* smok*ing* worries me.

What the traditional grammarians classify as noun clauses, infinitives, and gerunds are all related. They come from sentences, and then they are changed into clauses, infinitives, or gerunds by the appropriate complementizer:

It is astonishing. Fossils exist at all.	It is astonishing *that fossils exist at all.*
Robins arrive X. Robins greet worms.	Robins arrive *to greet worms.*
The leaves began X. The leaves fade.	The leaves began *fading.*

Exercise

Combine the following sentences to form single sentences. Make some sentences into noun clauses, some into infinitives, and some into gerunds.

    a. It seemed obvious to me.
       He was safe at home.

    b. We stopped.
       We get gas.

    c. We shop at several stores.
       In this way we get the best deal.

    d. Jan has an irritating habit.
       She smokes cigarettes.

    e. I lost my driver's license.
       This was a great inconvenience.

    f. He pretended.
       He never saw me before.

    g. The fact sickens me.
       He has bad breath.

    h. Don't leave the lights on.
       It wastes electricity.

    i. Something is dangerous.
       Someone drives in heavy traffic.

CHAPTER 17

Problems in Grammar

It is almost impossible to understand the compositional principles that govern the writing of sentences without some understanding of grammatical principles. The following are a few problems in grammar that continue to be troublesome for many writers.

Subject/Verb Agreement

Make the verb agree with the subject in person and number.

> Disaster *movies are* my favorites.
> This *movie is* especially good.

If a phrase comes between the subject and the verb, do not make the verb agree with the noun in the phrase. Make the verb agree with the subject:

> UNACCEPTABLE   The paint *on these houses* are expensive.

Notice that the prepositional phrase comes between the subject and the verb. The verb *are* has incorrectly been made to agree with the noun *houses*. The sentence should read:

> ACCEPTABLE   The *paint* on these houses *is* expensive.

Do not allow phrases such as *in addition to, including, as well as,* and *accompanied by,* which come between the subject and the verb, to affect the subject/verb agreement:

UNACCEPTABLE   My arm, *as well as my leg,* were injured in the accident.

ACCEPTABLE   My *arm,* as well as my leg, *was* injured in the accident.

In general, use a singular verb after words such as *each, every, everyone, anyone, someone, somebody, one, no one, everybody, either,* and *neither*:

Each of them *is* anxious to leave.
Everyone was irritated by the gasoline shortage.

Use a plural verb after a compound subject connected by *and:*

A shirt *and* a tie *are* needed to get in.
July *and* August *are* hot months.

Use a singular verb after singular subjects joined by *or nor, either . . . or,* and *neither . . . nor:*

Neither Ben *nor* Jane *has* the answer to the energy crisis.
Lori *or* her friend *is* willing to help.

When you join two subjects, one of which is singular and the other plural, by *or* or *nor,* make the verb agree with the closer subject:

Neither my truck nor my two *cars get* good gas mileage.
Neither my two cars nor my *truck gets* good gas mileage.

Make the verb agree with the subject, even when the subject comes after the verb, especially in sentences beginning with *here, there,* and *where:*

UNACCEPTABLE   There *was* five *people* in line before me.

ACCEPTABLE   There *were* five *people* in line before me.

When a complement comes after the verb, make the verb agree with the subject, not with the complement:

> *Books are* my favorite recreation.
> My favorite *recreation is* books.

Use a singular verb after a collective noun that stands for a unit. Use a plural verb after a collective noun that stands for individuals:

UNIT	The *team is* convinced it will win.
INDIVIDUALS	A *majority are* opposed to gas rationing.

Use a singular verb after words denoting weights, measurements, amounts of money, and periods of time:

> *Thirty dollars is* a high price to pay for shoes.
> *Fifty minutes was* not enough time for the test.

Use a singular verb after nouns that are plural in form but singular in meaning:

> *Measles is* no longer a serious disease in many parts of the world.
> *Physics was* my most difficult subject in high school.

Use singular verbs after the nouns *kind* and *sort* and plural verbs after their plural forms:

> That *sort* of answer *bothers* me.
> These *kinds* of shoes are expensive.

Exercises

1. Pick out the correct form of the verb in parentheses:

   a. There (is, are) times when you'd like to get away from it all.

   b. It (is, are) television, not movies, that (distract, distracts) me.

   c. There (is, are) two groups of tourists who want to see the Grand Canyon.

d. The president, accompanied by his aides, (is, are) going to China.

e. Coffee and doughnuts (is, are) my weakness.

f. Neither of the candidates (has, have) any appeal.

g. The food in this chain of restaurants (is, are) awful.

h. Everybody (was, were) concerned about the energy shortage.

i. Neither Joan nor Jane (have, has) a job they really like.

j. Twenty pounds (is, are) the correct weight.

2. Correct the errors in the following sentences:

a. Each of your papers need revision.

b. The sofa, as well as the chair, are in need of repair.

c. The rest of these clothes goes to the Salvation Army.

d. Neither she nor I were willing to apologize.

e. Where's the papers that were due for today?

f. Dan and his fiancée is coming over tonight.

g. Odd jobs is his only source of extra money.

h. A TV set or a stereo are given to the winners.

i. Here is my plans for the new house.

j. Ten minutes aren't enough time.

k. Those kind of flowers don't grow well here.

l. The jury was not in their seats when the judge came in.

Noun/Pronoun Agreement

Make pronouns agree with the words to which they refer in person, number, and gender.

PERSON	The *leopard* cannot change *its* spots.	*(third person)*
NUMBER	*People* are known by the company *they* keep.	*(plural number)*
GENDER	*Nature* meant woman to be *her* masterpiece.	*(feminine gender)*

The first-person pronouns are *I, my, me, we, our,* and *us.* The second-person pronouns are *you* and *your.* The third-person pronouns are *he, him, she, her, it, they, their,* and *them.* All nouns are in the third person.

Use a plural pronoun to refer to two or more words joined by *and:*

> Jan *and* Ellen will use *their* cars.
> Books *and* stamps keep *their* value for many years.

Use a singular pronoun to refer to two or more words joined by *or* or *nor:*

> Neither Jan *nor* Ellen will use *her* car.
> Either Mike *or* Ted lost *his* notebook.

Use a singular pronoun to refer to words such as *each, either,* or *neither* when the gender is known:

> *Each* of the applicants believed *she* would get the job.
> *Neither* of the boys apologized for *his* actions.
> *Either* of those girls will lend you *her* copy.

To avoid sexism in language, use two pronouns of different genders or a plural pronoun to refer to indefinite pronouns such as *nobody, anybody, somebody, everybody, no one, anyone, everyone,* and *any:*

> ACCEPTABLE   *Everybody* thinks *their* children are bright.
>
> ACCEPTABLE   *Anyone* who wants a class picture should bring *his* or *her* money tomorrow.

Their is acceptable in the first sentence above when a plural subject is meant. Otherwise, use *his* or *her.*

If the noun to which the pronoun refers could be either masculine or feminine, use either a plural noun or two pronouns of different genders:

> SEXIST   The good *student* never worries about *his* grades.
>
> ACCEPTABLE   Good *students* never worry about *their* grades.
>
> ACCEPTABLE   The good *student* never worries about *his* or *her* grades.

Use a singular pronoun to refer to a collective noun such as *team, class, band, squad,* or *committee* if the noun refers to the group as a whole. If the noun refers to the individuals of a group, use a plural pronoun:

> The *band* is playing *its* own compositions now.
> The *class* took turns reading *their* papers aloud.

Use *who* to refer to people, *which* to refer to animals or things, and *that* to refer to persons, animals, or things:

> Masseurs are *people who* knead people.
> The marriage ceremony is a *knot which* is tied by your teeth.
> Today is the *tomorrow that* you worried about yesterday.

When there are two possible antecedents (words to which they refer) for a pronoun, rewrite the sentence to make the antecedent clear and definite:

> UNCLEAR   Mary told Kay that *she* should vote in the next election.
>
> CLEAR   *You* should vote in the next election, Mary told Kay.

Rewrite sentences in which the antecedent of a pronoun is not expressed or in which the pronoun refers to an entire clause rather than to a single word:

> UNCLEAR   You did not return my call *which* makes me very angry.
>
> CLEAR   You did not return my call. Your *thoughtlessness* makes me very angry.

Rewrite sentences in which pronouns such as *you, they,* or *it* do not refer to a clear antecedent:

> UNCLEAR   *They* don't allow smoking in this building.
>
> CLEAR   Smoking is not allowed in this building.
>
> UNCLEAR   *It* says on the ten o'clock news that there will be rain tomorrow.
>
> CLEAR   The announcer on the ten o'clock news says that there will be rain tomorrow.

Exercises

1. Underline the antecedent and cross out the incorrect pronoun in the following sentences:

   a. Both Ray and Carl did (his, their) best.

   b. This is the boy (who, which) volunteered.

   c. Neither Ann nor Patricia would lend me (their, her) book.

   d. The committee was divided in (its, their) decision.

   e. Each of his sisters gave him (her, their) favorite recipe.

   f. Sue has a dog (who, that) loves to howl at midnight.

   g. If any girls are interested in swimming (you, she, they) should see the coach.

   h. If you find a pen and a notebook, take (it, them) to the front office.

   i. A cat or a dog will always defend (their, its) young.

   j. The jury has made (their, its) decision.

2. Supply the appropriate pronouns in the following sentences:

   a. Whenever a person is sick, _____ should go to a doctor.

   b. Everybody has a right to _____ opinion.

   c. Ask anyone where the Statue of Liberty is and _____ can tell you.

   d. If you drop a plate or a bowl, you'll have to pay for _____.

   e. Allan and his brother didn't eat _____ oatmeal.

   f. No one in _____ right mind would eat TV dinners.

   g. The class was ready to take _____ test.

   h. The entire faculty made _____ decision.

   i. As you enter the hotel, the first thing _____ see is the check-in desk.

   j. After a customer rents a car, _____ must return it.

3. Rewrite the following sentences to avoid vague pronoun references or to avoid sexism in language:

   a. The bus driver backed into my car, which irritated me very much.

b. A good doctor always respects his patients.

c. They say that gasoline will go up to two dollars a gallon.

d. If nuclear energy is banned, they will have to develop new sources of energy.

e. A criminal always gets what he deserves.

Dangling Modifiers

Avoid dangling modifiers. A dangling modifier is so called because it does not refer to some specific word in the sentence.

In the student sentence below, the dangling modifier confuses the reader. Who is entering the car? Is it "the condition of the interior"? One way to correct sentences that contain dangling modifiers is to supply a word to which the modifier can refer. The simple inclusion of the word *I* in the following sentence makes the meaning clear:

> UNCLEAR   *Upon entering the car*, the condition of the interior was impressive.
>
> CLEAR   Upon entering the car, *I* was impressed by the condition of the interior.

If you think of modifiers as reductions of complete sentences, you may gain a greater understanding of dangling modifiers. Take, for example, the following sentence:

> *Working for his father*, Ned learned much about cars. *(participial phrase)*

This sentence is derived from two underlying sentences:

> [Ned was] working for his father.
> Ned learned much about cars.

In the first sentence, if the words *Ned* and *was* are deleted, what remains is the participial phrase "working for his father." This phrase can then be positioned as a modifier in the second sentence to produce the sentence "Working for his father, Ned learned much about cars." There is no danger of confusion in this sentence because the modifier has a clear reference in the word *Ned*. This is an appropriate word for the participle to modify since the deleted subject of this phrase is also the word *Ned*.

But what is the relationship between the modifier and the main clause in this sentence?

> *Driving behind a truck*, a car hit me from behind.

If you reconstruct the two sentences from which this sentence is derived, you get

> [*I* was] driving behind a truck.
> A car hit me from behind.

The problem here is that the participle *driving* must go with the word *I*. But the word *I* has been deleted, and when the participial phrase combines with the main clause of the second sentence, the phrase is incorrectly made to modify the noun *car*.

To correct the dangling modifier, you have to include the word *I* somewhere in the new sentence. You can do this by making the dangling modifier into a dependent clause or by rewriting the main clause with *I* as the subject:

> As *I* was driving behind a truck, a car hit me from behind.
> Driving behind a truck, *I* was hit from behind by a car.

Dangling modifiers can be participles, gerunds, infinitives, or elliptical clauses:

> *Sitting behind the goalpost*, the football hit him in the head. *(dangling participle)*
>
> *By coming in early*, the work was completed before closing time. *(dangling gerund)*
>
> *To succeed in your new career*, three things are necessary. *(dangling infinitive)*
>
> *If adopted*, we hope the new energy plan will solve our problems. *(elliptical clause)*

We have already discussed the participle as a modifier, but notice that in the last three sentences the problems are very similar to those discussed previously. A noun or pronoun subject has been deleted from each of the sentences from which the modifiers were derived. Without the deleted word, the modifier dangles. How might you correct these dangling modifiers? By putting in the deleted words:

> As *he was* sitting behind the goalpost, the football hit him in the head.
> By *your* coming in early, the work was completed before closing time.
> *For you* to succeed in your new career, three things are necessary.
> If *it is* adopted, the new energy plan will solve our problems.

Let's take a closer look at the gerundive, infinitive, and elliptical modifiers. Each of these modifiers is a reduction of a complete sentence.

The gerundive phrase "by coming in early" begins as a sentence:

> You were coming in early.

The sentence is then transformed into a gerundive phrase:

> Your com*ing* in early

If the writer had inserted this phrase after the preposition *by*, there would have been no problem. But he erroneously deleted the word *your*, and this deletion causes the confusion. To put it briefly, anytime there is a dangling gerundive phrase, a possessive noun or pronoun must have been deleted. To correct the phrase, supply the missing word.

The sign of the gerund is a possessive form of a noun or pronoun and the suffix *-ing:*

> the girl's sing*ing*   her sing*ing*
> the band's march*ing*   its march*ing*
> Ned's play*ing*   his play*ing*

The infinitive phrase "to succeed in your new career" also begins as a sentence:

> You succeed in your new career.

This sentence is then transformed into an infinitive phrase:

> *for* you *to* succeed in your new career

As in the previous instance, here the writer erroneously deletes a part of the infinitive complementizer *(for)* and the noun subject *you*. Without the word *you* to relate to, the infinitive dangles. Infinitive complements always have the structure "for ... to ..." with the ellipsis (three dots) standing for the subject and verb:

> *for* Jack *to* go   *for* the boys *to* camp
> *for* you *to* gossip   *for* him *to* work

To correct dangling infinitives, add the word *for* and an appropriate noun before the infinitive.

In the last example, the elliptical clause "if adopted" goes through this series of changes:

> It is adopted
> if it is adopted
> if . . . adopted

To correct elliptical clauses, put in the words deleted from the original sentence.

Exercise

1. The following sentences contain dangling modifiers. Rewrite the sentences to correct them.

   a. After seeing the film, strange images began to haunt my sleep.

   b. If admitted, his tuition will cost him five hundred dollars a semester.

   c. To sell this automobile, it must be advertised in the want ads.

   d. While at the beach, sand got into my clothes.

   e. Sitting on the steps, the speeding cars looked dangerous.

   f. After talking with the dentist, my tooth continued to ache.

   g. A boat suddenly appeared walking along the river.

   h. By voting "no," the bill was defeated.

   i. Since coming home, the town doesn't seem the same.

   j. Being shy, going to a new school was terrifying.

Misplaced Modifiers

Place modifiers as closely as possible to the words they modify.

My aunt gave a chest to my sister *over fifty years old.*

Placing the modifier "over fifty years old" at the end of the sentence results in momentary confusion for the reader. Who or what is "over fifty years old"? The sister? The chest? This sentence can be corrected in two ways, both of which require moving the prepositional phrase close to the noun *chest:*

My aunt gave a chest *over fifty years old* to my sister.
My aunt gave my sister a chest *over fifty years old.*

Place single-word adverbs such as *only, nearly, almost,* and *just* close to the words they modify. Notice the difference in meaning suggested by the placement of a single word:

She *only* tasted the cheese.
(However, she didn't eat it.)

She tasted *only* the cheese.
(She didn't taste the other food.)

Do not place a modifier where it could refer confusingly to the words before it or to the words that follow it. Such a modifier is called a *squinting modifier.*

UNACCEPTABLE   Because we finished our work *in one hour* we could go home.

The reader is not certain if the work was finished in one hour or if the workers could go home in one hour. One way to correct the problem is by punctuation. Another is by repositioning the modifier:

ACCEPTABLE   Because we finished our work *in one hour,* we could go home.
UNACCEPTABLE   Because we finished our work, we could go home *in one hour.*

Here is another example:

Anyone who goes downtown *occasionally* will notice the new streetlights.

In this situation, punctuation would be of little use. The sentence would still be ambiguous. The adverb must be moved to its proper place in the sentence:

> Anyone who *occasionally* goes downtown will notice the new streetlights.
> Anyone who goes downtown will *occasionally* notice the new streetlights.

Exercise

Correct the misplaced modifiers in the following sentences:

a. We only saw the end of the film.

b. Did you put the meat in the trashcan that was spoiled?

c. Jack discussed the accident he had in the bus.

d. She finished her talk on fishing in Canada.

e. As we looked around now and then we saw a deer.

f. Would you like to read this book on how to digest your food after dinner?

g. People who smoke constantly irritate others.

h. I got on a plane that was going to Chicago by mistake.

i. I turn on the television whenever I eat for entertainment.

j. You can see Bob cutting the lawn from the kitchen window.

Faulty Parallelism

Express parallel ideas in parallel structure.

> There's an energy crisis and
>   a food crisis and
>   any number of other crises.

> Many try, but
> few succeed.

> Swim,
> surf, and
> sail in the warm clear ocean.

In all of these sentences, the parallel ideas are expressed in similar grammatical constructions.

You cannot shift from one kind of grammatical construction to another in expressing parallel ideas. You must keep nouns with nouns, verbs with verbs, prepositional phrases with prepositional phrases, and so forth. In the sentence below, the comparison is faulty because a gerund is paired with a noun:

> *Opening* crabs is a harder job than *oysters.*

The comparison should not be between *opening* and *oysters,* but between *opening crabs* and *opening oysters.*

You can correct faulty parallelism in one of two ways. You can grammatically subordinate one of the parallel elements, if one of the ideas is subordinate:

> Fred is a figure of perfection and closely resembles a Greek god.
> Fred is a figure of perfection *who closely* resembles a Greek god.

Or you can rewrite coordinate elements that are supposed to be coordinate in form. In the following sentence, the words *television* and *walks* are incorrectly coordinated with the phrase "sitting on the porch."

> Some summer nights, people relax by *television, walks,* or *sitting on the porch.*

Television and *walks* are nouns. "Sitting on the porch" is a gerundive phrase. You can correct the faulty parallelism by putting the words *television* and *walks* in phrases:

> Some summer nights, people relax by *watching television, taking walks, or sitting on the porch.*

In the following student sentence, two adjectives are incorrectly coordinated with a verb phrase:

> The movie is *funny, heartwarming,* and *appeals to almost everyone.*

You can revise this sentence in two ways: by changing the verb phrase to an adjectival one, or by adding a subject to the second verb phrase and making this phrase into a coordinate clause.

> The movie is *funny, heartwarming,* and *appealing.*
> The movie is funny and heartwarming, and *it* appeals to almost everyone.

Exercise

Rewrite the following sentences to correct faulty parallelism:

a. Good writers must know punctuation and how to spell.

b. My friend is considerate, friendly, and she gives help.

c. She thought that her dress was better than the other girls.

d. Hiking in the desert is different from anywhere else.

e. Jane was more interested in the movie than her date.

f. The car runs smoothly and quiet.

g. She likes hiking and to go jogging.

h. My boss caught me taking a smoke and on the telephone.

i. He was broke, disgusted, and had no job.

j. Carl prefers tennis to playing golf.

Run-on Sentence

Do not join sentences together with a comma or with no punctuation mark between them.

UNACCEPTABLE	We will take Flight 217 to New York, it is the quickest flight.
ACCEPTABLE	We will take Flight 217 to New York. It is the quickest flight.
UNACCEPTABLE	It was late in the fourth quarter the score was six to nothing.
ACCEPTABLE	It was late in the fourth quarter. The score was six to nothing.

The first kind of error indicated here, in which a comma is used between two sentences instead of a period, a semicolon, or a conjunction, is called a *comma splice* or *comma fault.* The second kind of error, in which no mark of punctuation is used between two sentences, is called a *period fault.* This latter sentence type is sometimes referred to as the *fused sentence.* However, I shall use the expression **run-on sentence** to cover both kinds of errors.

You can correct run-on sentences in a number of ways. You can use a period to separate the sentences:

UNACCEPTABLE	Lori has never been interested in "girlish" games, give her a ball, a bat, or a tennis racket and she is perfectly happy.
ACCEPTABLE	Lori has never been interested in "girlish" games. Give her a ball, a bat, or a tennis racket and she is perfectly happy.

You can use a semicolon in place of a comma, if the sentences are close in thought:

UNACCEPTABLE	The process isn't really very hard, it just takes patience.
ACCEPTABLE	The process isn't really very hard; it just takes patience.

You can insert a coordinate conjunction, usually with a comma, between the two sentences:

UNACCEPTABLE	The bus stops just long enough for tourists to get one photograph then it takes them someplace else.
ACCEPTABLE	The bus stops just long enough for tourists to get one photograph, and then it takes them someplace else.

Or you can make one sentence into a subordinate clause and embed it in the other sentence:

UNACCEPTABLE	Sharon did not take that part-time job, she needed time for her studies.
ACCEPTABLE	Sharon did not take that part-time job because she needed time for her studies.

Many run-on sentences are caused by using adverbs such as *then, therefore, however, consequently, nevertheless,* and *furthermore* which the writer mistakes for conjunctions. When these words are used between independent clauses, they should come after a semicolon, or they should be capitalized to start a new sentence.

UNACCEPTABLE	It rained for most of the day, then it began to sleet.
ACCEPTABLE	It rained for most of the day; then it began to sleet.
ACCEPTABLE	It rained for most of the day. Then it began to sleet.

Exercise

Rewrite the following run-on sentences, separating the main clauses by a period, a semicolon, a coordinating conjunction, or a subordinating conjunction.

a. We were an hour late, the concert had not started.

b. The old man sat down under a tree, then he began to fish.

c. Dan ate a whole box of candy no wonder he wasn't hungry.

d. The story was boring, the acting was awful.

e. The letter was unintelligible, none of us could understand it.

f. At first I said I would go later I changed my mind.

g. The store didn't have celery, however, it had plenty of lettuce.

h. The road was slick we almost slid off the road.

i. Yesterday I was ready to quit, today I will probably do so.

j. The dress was one size too small, nevertheless, she tried it on.

Many handbooks advise the writer never to use commas between independent clauses, yet many professional writers deliberately violate this advice if the clauses are short, if they are parallel in structure, if they are antithetical, or if there is no chance that they will be misunderstood.

The following run-on sentences were taken from a variety of sources, including magazine advertising and articles in *Time, Harper's, Psychology Today, Esquire,* and the *Saturday Review:*

> Some can easily afford it, some cannot. *(antithetical)*
>
> They don't just wipe up, they clean up. *(antithetical)*
>
> Tire inflation pressures are important, so are lubricants. *(additive)*
>
> Most doctors agree, the best treatment for a patient with severe and permanent kidney failure is the surgical transplant of a healthy kidney from a donor. *(breaks the rule of short clauses)*
>
> Abuse is not something we think about, it's something we do. *(antithetical)*
>
> Hit the beaches, beat the sandy traps. *(series)*

Proverbs make extensive use of the run-on sentence. Perhaps the ideas in them are so familiar and the expressions are so succinct that there is little danger of their being misunderstood. Proverbs use very short phrases and balanced clauses:

> Man proposes, God disposes.
> The more you have, the more you want.

They use phrases and clauses in a series:

> Hear no evil, see no evil, speak no evil.
> Be civil to all, sociable to many, familiar to few.

And they make extensive use of antithesis:

> Do as I say, not as I do.
> United we stand, divided we fall.

Graffiti make frequent use of the comma fault:

> Be nice to someone, kick a masochist.
> I came, I saw, I flunked.

Advertising slogans use it almost as frequently:

> Fly now, pay later.
> Tide's in, dirt's out.

Run-on sentences, then, are not always inappropriate, even though they may be grammatically incorrect. Purists may condemn them, but I would suggest that you learn how to use them effectively, according to the guidelines given here. Then you'll have to determine when it is best to use them. Naturally, you will have to consider your audience, your purpose, and the occasion. Some readers may accept them; some may not. Know your readers and write accordingly. For example, there is no harm in using them in personal letters, but they may be inappropriate in business letters.

Sentence Fragment

Do not write a part of a sentence as if it were a complete sentence unless you have a good reason to do so. Sentence fragments do appear in the work of professional writers. They appear extensively in magazine advertising. But in the writing of students, they are almost always due to carelessness. To many teachers and editors, sentence fragments suggest ignorance.

Let's look at the concept of fragments, first from a traditional point of view and then from a nontraditional point of view. Some sentence fragments are groups of words lacking a subject or a predicate. Others are modifiers that have been cut off from an independent clause:

> They look strong. Last long. *(subject omitted)*
>
> There are some things you never want to change. Like the feeling you get when you reel in that big one. *(modifier cut off)*

If the sentence fragment takes the form of a dependent clause, attach it to a previous clause or rewrite the clause as a complete sentence:

> UNACCEPTABLE   Johnny Carson usually has several guests. While Dick Cavett often devotes his entire show to one guest.
>
> ACCEPTABLE   Johnny Carson usually has several guests, while Dick Cavett often devotes his entire show to one guest. *(clause attached)*
>
> ACCEPTABLE   Johnny Carson usually has several guests. Dick Cavett often devotes his entire show to one guest. *(clause rewritten as sentence)*

If the sentence fragment lacks a subject or a verb, supply the subject or verb, or tie the fragment to some previous or subsequent sentence:

> UNACCEPTABLE   Drag racing is dangerous. Especially on city streets.
>
> ACCEPTABLE   Drag racing is dangerous. It is especially dangerous on city streets. *(added subject and verb)*
>
> ACCEPTABLE   Drag racing is dangerous, especially on city streets. *(modifier attached to main clause)*

For the past three years, I have been collecting examples of sentence fragments from both informal and formal writing, and I have found these kinds to be the most common:

The answer to a question

How did we do it? With an unusual engineering development.

Why do boxers like Ken Norton jump rope? To stay in good condition.

Predicate adjective

Each is a masterpiece. Realistic, yet delicate.

It's creamy. Positively luscious.

Appositive

I guess that's what makes a classic a classic. The ability to look completely different depending on how it's used.

We're all accustomed to high-impact, hard-hitting visual information. The kind only television can deliver.

Prepositional phrases

They're shaped for kids' feet. With lots of room in the front.

People are taking it everywhere. On any kind of road, in any kind of weather, on every kind of trip.

Participial phrase

Imagine golden yellow peaches. Bathing in a fresh stream of lightly sweetened real fruit juices.

We are waiting. Waiting for "someone else" to solve our energy problems.

Adverbial clause

In the Polynesian Pacific, the wind can be a devil. Because the breezes seem to blow from all directions.

Years ago, everything was created one of a kind. Because everything was created by hand.

Subject omitted

I like the way I look. Love the way I feel.

Never needs ironing.

Most of these sentences can be corrected simply by attaching the fragment to the main clause:

UNACCEPTABLE   It's creamy, Positively luscious.

ACCEPTABLE   It's creamy, positively luscious.

Exercise

In the sentences below, attach each sentence fragment to the main clause of the other sentence or rewrite it as a complete sentence.

a. Are there any hotels left in the world that still practice the fine art of attention to detail? Precious few.

b. Mustang is sporty and sleek. Inside and out.

c. Corn Bran is crispy. Even in milk.

d. It tastes the way lemonade was meant to taste. Delicious. Refreshing. Thirst quenching.

e. The colors are very special. Delicate shadings that look like they were created from nature's own sensitive palette.

f. The Spanish have a saying, *"Quidese con la uva."* Stick to the grape.

g. Chevy Monza is a thrill to drive. To take out on the open road and enjoy. To take into a corner and come out impressed.

h. Return to Los Angeles if you like. If you can bear the thought of coming back at all.

i. You scrub. Wax. Do a hard day's work every day.

j. Everything is compatible. Simpatico.

It must be admitted that in most of the sentence fragments we have looked at so far, there is little danger that the reader will misunderstand the writer's intention. Each fragment is placed so close to the sentence to which it is obviously related that the meaning is clear and evident.

Advertisers use fragments frequently and deliberately for easy reading and swift-moving copy:

> How does Webster's New Collegiate accomplish such a feat? With over 3,000 quotations from poets, comics, critics, and presidents. With over 24,000 phrases showing you how a word is used in context. And with scores of illustrations, charts, and tables.

> When you plan your visit to Colorado, make sure your trail takes you throughout the state. Up. Down. And all around.

Professional writers use them for emphasis or for special effects. In the following paragraph, taken from an article in *Time* (March 12, 1979), fragments are used in the opening paragraph to give the reader a sense of disorder and anarchy, of things coming apart:

Revolution in Iran. A souring of the important U.S. special relationship with Saudi Arabia. A looming economic crisis, and soon, caused by oil shortages and runaway price boosts. A danger that much of the region might change its tilt away from the U.S. and toward the Soviet Union. A Middle East peace seemingly more elusive than ever. These are the troubles and threats that America faces in the so-called crescent of crisis—that great swath of countries running from the Horn of Africa through Egypt and across the Middle East to Afghanistan and Pakistan. Here, more than in any other area of the world, the U.S. has vital interests that are threatened by forces it has not been able to control, and all too often seems unable to influence.

In the first paragraph of an article titled "Interferon: Medicine for Cancer and the Common Cold?" in *Saturday Review* (November 25, 1978), the fragments are used to define and to emphasize:

Interferon. A chemical that interferes. A mystery molecule made by the body itself to thwart the subversive intentions of invaders.

Because the American Cancer Society (ACS) has announced the launching of a $2 million program to test it clinically, interferon is already being referred to as a "cancer drug"—which it may well prove to be. But those who have been studying interferon for its multiple other potential uses fear that, should it perform disappointingly in its cancer trials—if it is only marginally useful, for instance, as has been the case with so many other promising anticancer agents—then, as one scientist puts it "interferon may become a dirty word, because 'It was tried and didn't work.' "

And in this paragraph, also taken from *Saturday Review* (April 14, 1979), the fragments are used to freeze images in the reader's mind, images that are almost too frightening to contemplate:

The first step into a children's cancer ward seems like a step into unreality. Images swim before you. A sign in boldface lettering, "Remove Prosthesis Before Being Weighed." Mothers weary, waiting. A teenager with no more hair than the fuzz of a newborn, a tiny girl with ribbons tied to the two or three strands that are left. They look like small-sized veterans of some long-ago war, wraiths returned in a bad dream. Your eyes register them but your mind refuses them; for they are children, you think, who are waiting for death. The first step into a children's cancer ward brings with it a queasy feeling of hopelessness, and there seems to be only one way of coping with it: leaving.

Fragments, then, can be very effective in both formal and informal writing. The advice I would give to the novice writer is to learn first the difference between a sentence and a fragment. Then learn how to use the fragment to achieve various effects. Finally, in using fragments, always consider your audience, your purpose, and the occasion. Will your reader object to your using fragments? Can you achieve your purpose better by using fragments in this *particular* piece of writing, for this *particular* occasion, than you can by using complete sentences?

CHAPTER 18

Punctuation

Punctuation is *the use of standardized marks to separate words into phrases, clauses, and sentences.* Punctuation should be audience-centered. As you write, keep your readers in mind and try to determine where they will need the help of punctuation marks to follow your meaning or your emphasis. If you use too many punctuation marks, you may confuse your readers. If you use too few, you may make it difficult for them to see at a glance the words that go together and those that should be kept apart. A badly punctuated sentence or an unpunctuated sentence can mislead or confuse your readers.

The Period

Use a period at the end of a declarative sentence or one that is mildly imperative. A declarative sentence makes a statement:

> Good fences make good neighbors.
> Truth is stranger than fiction.

An imperative sentence expresses a *command, request,* or *entreaty:*

> Do not wear out your welcome.
> Never judge by appearances.

Put a period after abbreviations of titles, names, degrees, months, countries, states, and so forth:

TITLES	Dr., Mr., Ms., Mrs., Rev.
NAMES	H. G. Wells, Chas. Smith
DEGREES	Ph.D., M.A., B.S., M.D., D.D.S.
MONTHS	Sept., Oct., Nov., Dec.
STATES	Mass., Ill., Ariz., Ga., La.
CITIES	N.Y., N.O., L.A.
MISCELLANEOUS	A.M., P.M., St., Ave.

The Question Mark

Put a question mark at the end of a direct question. There are two kinds of questions: the *yes/no* question and the *wh* question. The *yes/no* question is one that takes a simple yes or no for an answer:

> Did Shakespeare write *Romeo* and *Juliet?*
> Are you coming over tonight?

The *wh* question is one that cannot be answered by a simple yes or no. It is called a *wh* question because the questioning word usually begins with *wh* (*who, which, what, when, why;* but *how* is an exception):

> Who painted *The Starry Night?*
> What did she say to you?

Put a question mark in parentheses to express doubt.

> Plato's *Phaedrus* was written around 370(?) B.C.

Use a single question mark after a double question. The following sentence asks a question, and within that question is a quoted question:

> Who was the wise guy who cracked, "Did Adam and Eve have belly buttons?"

The Exclamation Point

Use an exclamation point after expressions that show strong feeling or emotion:

> No! No! No! You shouldn't do that!
> Come here immediately!

Frequently, the words in your sentences will carry their own emphasis. Do not, therefore, use the exclamation point unless your expressions require unusual emphasis.

The Semicolon

Put a semicolon between independent clauses that are closely related.

> Drive with care; life has no spare.
> Keep Chicago clean; eat a pigeon a day.

Use a semicolon between independent clauses to show balance or contrast.

> Art is long; life is short.
> Walk on the grass; don't smoke it.
> People make mistakes; computers don't.

Put a semicolon between independent clauses joined by a sentence connector (also called a *conjunctive adverb* or *transitional expression*). A sentence connector is a word such as *therefore, however, nevertheless, accordingly, moreover, furthermore, consequently, then, thus,* and *still:*

> You may be right; nevertheless, I'd like another opinion.
> We get along fine; however, we don't always agree.

Use a semicolon to show the main divisions in a series that is set off by commas.

Among those receiving sports awards were Magic Johnson, of the Los Angeles Lakers; Larry Bird, of the Boston Celtics; Julius Irving, of the Philadelphia Seventy-Sixers; and Kareem Abdul Jabbar of the Los Angeles Lakers.

Do not use a semicolon in place of a colon.

WRONG The following are the most popular movies of the past year; *Indiana Jones and the Temple of Doom, Gremlins, Romancing the Stone, Terms of Endearment,* and *Footloose.*

RIGHT The following are the most popular movies of the past year: *Indiana Jones and the Temple of Doom, Gremlins, Romancing the Stone, Terms of Endearment,* and *Footloose.*

Do not use a semicolon in place of a comma. The exception is to show the main divisions in a series:

WRONG For many years; we believed that chimps were smart enough to learn a language.

RIGHT For many years, we believed that chimps were smart enough to learn a language.

WRONG Ask a friend to balance a wooden pencil on the index finger of each hand; one hand at a time.

RIGHT Ask a friend to balance a wooden pencil on the index finger of each hand, one hand at a time.

Exercises

1. Put in the appropriate end punctuation in the following sentences:

   a. Two heads are better than one

   b. What are we going to do tomorrow

   c. What a lousy day

   d. You never know what you can do until you try

e. Who found the coin

f. Liars should have good memories

g. Never call me after midnight again

h. Lend your money and lose your friend

i. You didn't leave the water running, did you

j. Stop in the name of the law

2. Supply semicolons where necessary in the following sentences:

a. Old mailmen never die they just lose their zip.

b. First build your house then think of your furniture.

c. He who loses money loses much he who loses a friend loses more he who loses his nerve loses all.

d. It is raining therefore, I will stay home.

e. Get high on helium it's a gas.

f. Our instruction in writing was excellent nevertheless, we had some trouble with our first assignment in college.

g. Attending the meeting of the city council were Sam Sloane a salesman Charles Channing a lawyer Paula Perkins a clinical psychologist and Harriet Haynes a decorator.

h. Petty crimes are punished great ones are rewarded.

i. Rome wasn't built in a day the pizza parlors alone took several weeks.

j. If a man deceives me once, shame on him if he deceives me twice, shame on me.

The Comma

Put a comma in front of a conjunction (and, or, nor, but, for) **that connects the two main clauses of a compound sentence.**

> A lawyer's advice may be expensive, but it will cost you more if you consult yourself.
>
> Experience keeps a dear school, yet fools will learn in no other.
>
> Sing before breakfast, and you'll cry before night.

Put a comma between introductory words, phrases, or clauses and the main clause.

> If life gives you lemons, make lemonade.
> When in doubt, don't.
> Overhead, the leaves rustled in the breeze.

Some writers suggest that if the introductory element is short, there is no need for commas. But if you get into the habit of punctuating introductory elements, you can increase ease of reading for your audience and prevent a misreading, as in the following sentence:

> CONFUSING   In addition to the socks she had mended two sweaters.
>
> BETTER   In addition to the socks, she had mended two sweaters.

Use a comma to separate words, phrases, and clauses in a series.

> Eggs, sausage, bacon, and ham are foods you love to eat.
>
> A dozen roses, a dozen golf balls, or cash—they're all tried and true gifts.
>
> You cross the equator, pass the international date line, and steam through the Panama Canal.
>
> The shopping is superb, the cuisine is gourmet, and the weather is sublime.

Some writers prefer to omit the final comma in a series (the comma before the conjunction). This is acceptable practice, provided that you are consistent. However, omitting the final comma can sometimes lead to ambiguity:

> Sausage, ham, bacon and eggs are foods you love to eat.

Are bacon and eggs to be considered a single unit, or is each a separate item in the series?

Do not separate pairs of words, phrases, and clauses.

> WRONG   Books, and friends should be few but good.
>
> RIGHT   Books and friends should be few but good.
>
> WRONG   By the bag, or by the box . . . your best candy buy is Brach's.
>
> RIGHT   By the bag or by the box . . . your best candy buy is Brach's.

Set off nonrestrictive relative clauses with commas.

The novel is by William Faulkner, who wrote *The Sound and the Fury*.

The dislike of the Oakland Raiders by other teams, who consider them unnecessarily rough, is great.

The nonrestrictive clause acts as a kind of parenthetical element, containing information that is not crucial to the meaning of the main clause. The idea in the nonrestrictive clause is often a kind of afterthought or an interruption in the main flow of ideas. Paraphrasing the nonrestrictive clause is a good way to show these relationships.

ORIGINAL	My cousin, who lives in New York, is an actress.
PARAPHRASE	My cousin, and she happens to live in New York, is an actress.
PARAPHRASE	My cousin is an actress, and she lives in New York.

Do not enclose restrictive clauses with commas.

He that cannot obey cannot command.
A family who smokes together chokes together.
Blessed is he who expects nothing, for he shall never be disappointed.

In all of these sentences, the relative clause identifies, describes, or expands on the meaning of the noun it modifies. These sentences would make little sense and would have little relationship to the intended meaning of the original if you deleted the restrictive relative clause:

He . . . cannot command.
A family . . . chokes together.
Blessed is he . . ., for he shall never be disappointed.

Use commas to set off appositives, nouns of address, and conjunctive adverbs.

Welcome to Hawaii, a place as unique and varied as its flowers. *(appositive)*
Julie, my best friend, called from New Orleans. *(appositive)*
Laura, please don't get upset. *(noun of address)*
Come in, Uncle Albert, and sit down. *(noun of address)*
Nevertheless, I understand your position. *(conjunctive adverb)*
I believe, moreover, that you lied to me. *(conjunctive adverb)*

Use commas to separate items in dates, addresses, and place names:

> July 4, 1776
> 125 Apache Boulevard, Phoenix, Arizona
> We travel occasionally to Juarez, Mexico.

Do not put commas between the subject and the predicate or between closely related parts of a sentence.

WRONG	That last ball, should have been a strike.
WRONG	She indicated, that she would arrive Wednesday.
WRONG	The swing on the front porch, is broken.

Do not put a comma in place of a period between two sentences.

WRONG	It takes all kinds of people to make a world, some are open-minded and some are bigoted.
RIGHT	It takes all kinds of people to make a world. Some are open-minded and some are bigoted.
WRONG	She walked very slowly, as I approached her, she picked up speed.
RIGHT	She walked very slowly. As I approached her, she picked up speed.

Do not use an excessive number of commas in a sentence.

EXCESSIVE	Saturday, at ten o'clock, on Central Avenue, an old, battered truck struck a bright, red van and injured two, young children.
BETTER	Saturday at ten o'clock, on Central Avenue, an old battered truck struck a bright red van and injured two young children.

Exercises

1. Insert commas where necessary in the following sentences:

   a. If there were no clouds we would not enjoy the sun.

b. Everybody complains about pollution but nobody wants to empty the wastebasket.

c. For more than sixty centuries people have relentlessly scratched tunneled panned stripped dredged and blasted for gold.

d. Swim surf and sail in the warm clear ocean.

e. When the wolf comes in the door love creeps out the window.

f. The house lonely and forlorn stood on the hill.

g. He who hesitates is lost.

h. Borrowed wives like borrowed books are rarely returned.

i. Ann please call when your plane arrives.

j. We left Phoenix on April 6 1972.

k. Thomas Gray a professor at Cambridge wrote *Elegy in a Country Churchyard.*

l. We thank you Susan for the lovely gift.

m. Saturday August 21 1970 was an important day in my life.

n. He felt moreover that she was right.

o. Do as I say not as I do.

2. Supply commas for the nonrestrictive modifiers, but not for the restrictive modifiers:

a. Golf which is a sport I really don't care for is her favorite sport.

b. The story was written by Asimov who also happens to be a scientist.

c. He travels the fastest who travels alone.

d. A family that prays together stays together.

e. I tried to get at the oranges that hung down into my neighbor's yard.

f. I ate the last piece of cake while you were at the store.

g. Tom who is my neighbor works in the library.

h. There were the keys dangling from the dashboard.

i. The car abandoned in an alley no longer had wheels.

j. That silver tray which almost everybody admires has been stolen.

The Colon

Use a colon to indicate that a series will follow.

Rum comes in three shades: white, gold, and dark.

We all know what a team needs to get somewhere: strong pitching, good hitting, a savvy manager, and plenty of speed and hustle.

Use a colon to introduce a formal statement or explanation.

There was no doubt about the outcome: He would be a ruined man forever.

Use a colon to introduce a quotation.

Pindar once wrote: "Hopes are but the dreams of those who are awake."

Use a colon to separate the hour from the minute in telling time.

My plane leaves at 9:00 P.M.

Use a colon after a formal salutation of a letter.

Gentlemen:
Dear Ms. Harris:

The Dash

Use a dash to indicate a sudden or abrupt break in thought.

He tried—and who could do more—to spare my feelings.
The desert—although not everyone will agree—is a place of beauty.

Use a dash after a summarizing series.

Deviled ham, chunky chicken, hearty roast beef—they all deliver that good, wholesome change of pace a great sandwich needs.

A basket of fruit, a fine natural cheddar—this is our pick for a really fresh dessert.

Use a dash to emphasize an important idea or to achieve suspense, climax, or irony.

> For that rundown feeling—jaywalk.
> The only way to stop smoking is to stop—no ifs, ands, or butts.
> People are like beer cans—they crush when you step on them.

Use a dash in place of a comma to set off an appositive, if greater emphasis is needed.

> No football player ever became great without practice—long, hard hours of practice.

> Three things—imagination, patience, and fortitude—are necessary for success.

Use a dash instead of the more formal colon.

> High schools used to recommend certain books for outside reading—*The Scarlet Letter, Moby-Dick, The Grapes of Wrath,* and A Tale of Two Cities.

> There are two objections to business monopolies—they eliminate competition and they fix prices.

The Ellipsis

Use elipsis points (three periods separated by single spaces) to indicate that something has been omitted from quoted material.

ORIGINAL	For some people, the largest group, loneliness feels like desperation.
ELLIPTICAL	For some people . . . loneliness feels like desperation.
ORIGINAL	History, according to the accepted definition, began with writing, with recorded languages written on clay, stone, and papyrus, languages we have learned to decipher and to read, if not to speak.
ELLIPTICAL	History . . . began with writing, with recorded languages written on clay, stone, and papyrus. . . .

Notice that in the second example the ellipsis comes at the end of the quoted sentence. When the material to be omitted comes at the end of a sentence, consists of a whole sentence or paragraph or more, and is grammatically complete without it, add the ellipsis, but keep the period that ends the sentence. In other words, use four periods at the end of the sentence:

ORIGINAL   The Romans greeted everyone with a kiss—not just friends and relatives, but their cobblers, bakers, blacksmiths, and even tax collectors.

ELLIPTICAL   The Romans greeted everyone with a kiss. . . .

Use ellipsis points to indicate that a series of numbers or a statement is incomplete or interrupted.

The odd numbers are 1, 3, 5, 7, 9, ...
The speaker's voice droned on and on and . . .

Parentheses and Brackets

Use parentheses to enclose ideas that explain, amplify, qualify, exemplify, or interpret.

The news that gets reported seems for the most part to be either bad (if something is really bad, it is good enough to report) or trivial.

The findings are that Americans (children and adults) watch between twenty-five and thirty hours of television a week.

Excessively wet kisses are unpopular (as the Danes say, "He is nice to kiss—when one is thirsty"); but a dry, tight kiss is usually regarded as either immature or inhibited.

Use parentheses to enclose cross-references.

(See page 762.)
(See Appendix C.)
The suicides and mental breakdowns of gifted people (see A. Alvarez's *The Savage God: A Study of Suicide*) are well known.

Use brackets to supply editorial explanations, comments, corrections, and omissions.

On the drawing, Michelangelo wrote: "Master Tommaso, if you don't like this sketch tell Urbino [Michelangelo's servant] in time for me to make another by tomorrow evening."

I was appalled to see the picture in your magazine of Dave Armstrong driving while holding his two-month-old baby in his lap ["Falling in Love with Four-Wheel-Drive," June 5].

"Unwarranted rises in oil prices mean more worldwide inflation and less [economic] growth. That will lead to more unemployment, more balance of payments difficulty, and [will] endanger stability. We deplore the [OPEC] decision."

Exercise

Insert dashes, colons, ellipses, parentheses, or brackets where needed in the following sentences:

a. Jones I think it was Jones called to say he would be late.

b. The legislature met in February actually in March.

c. You get a lot to like with a Marlboro filter, flavor, flip-top box.

d. New York is a city that moves to many rhythms the early morning jogger along the river, the ancient carriage clop-clopping through the park, and the jets crisscrossing the sky above.

e. Benjamin Franklin wrote "Fish and visitors stink after three days."

f. Gentlemen Please don't leave until 530 pm when the meeting is over.

g. Sign in reducing salon We Recycle Waists.

h. Patience long, long hours of patience is necessary to catch fish.

i. I can't remember all of the even numbers but to the best of my ability they are as follows 2, 4, 6, 8.

j. See Neumann's *Art and the Creative Unconscious*.

k. The article titled "The High Cost of Living" December 1973 contains many inaccuracies.

Quotation Marks

Use quotation marks to enclose the words of a speaker.

Again the answer was "Not guilty."

"Actually," says Dr. Marsh, "I doubt if you could drug a chicken. Their metabolic rate is too high."

Mother: "What's that?"
Child: "Fishy."
Mother: "Yes, and see him swimming?"

Use quotation marks to enclose quoted material.

As Gene Lyons wrote in *Harper's* magazine, "American students are not learning to write because nobody bothers to teach them how."

Like Heller's other novels, *Good as Gold* "is a book that takes large risks."

Chekhov, who was a doctor as well as a playwright, makes one of his intelligent characters say, "Lawyers merely rob you; doctors rob and kill you too."

Do not enclose indirect quotations in quotation marks.

Sigmund Freud, oddly enough, was among the more recent scholars to have contributed to the ridiculous notion that money can't buy happiness. Happiness, he said, is the adult fulfillment of childhood dreams, and children, he said, do not dream of money. Therefore, money does not buy happiness.

Use quotation marks to call attention to words as concepts.

Suppose a child must learn the category "bird." He or she must pay attention to features common to the class, such as wings, while ignoring color or size.

"Panic" is such a strong word that I was wondering whether to use it.

Some builders anxious to stimulate sales during slow periods will sometimes offer such "free" extras as self-cleaning ovens.

Use quotation marks for the titles of stories, songs, poems, magazine articles, essays, paintings, and so forth. Titles of books, however, should be italicized or underlined.

In Cheever's short story "The Brigadier and the Gold Widow," Charlie Pastern and his wife build a bomb shelter in their garden.

Many of his best tunes, like "Fool's Gold," portray quite another character entirely.

Although Matthew Arnold's poem "Dover Beach" contains but one brief mention of personal affection, the primary theme is the power of love.

Use single quotation marks for quotations within quotations.

Theodore Roosevelt once wrote: "I am not sure that I understand 'Luke Havergal,' but I am entirely sure that I like it."

Sarah answered, "The salesman said to me, 'You will never find another new car at that price.' "

Punctuation and Quotation Marks

Put commas and periods inside quotation marks.

"It is perhaps as difficult to write a good life as to live one," said Lytton Strachey, author of *Eminent Victorians.*

Says Dr. V. I. Sarianich, "We've been trying to figure out the history of these people for years."

Put exclamation marks and question marks inside quotation marks if the quotation is an exclamation or a question; otherwise, put them outside:

"It's a catastrophe!" exclaimed Alfred Kahn, President Carter's chief inflation fighter.

"Save us! Save us!" shouted a refugee as naval vessels towed two boats back out to sea.

"Is this for real?" she cried, and turned to her sister.

Can you imagine her saying, "You never help with the dishes"?

Put semicolons and colons outside quotation marks unless the punctuation mark is actually a part of the quotation:

Laura vowed, "You can be sure I'll meet you at 6:00 P.M."; but at 7:00 P.M. Laura still hadn't arrived.

I have only one reply to your comment "Absence makes the heart grow fonder": "Out of sight, out of mind."

Exercise

Put in the proper punctuation along with quotation marks in the following sentences:

a. Sorry I'm late. I had to attend a seminar on acupuncture and I got stuck.

b. Kiwi is a four-letter word.

c. The politician droned in on the fields of sewage and pollution we can't afford to bury our heads.

d. Robert Frost wrote Stopping by Woods on a Snowy Evening.

e. She looked at him intensely and asked are you seeing someone else.

f. Marc asked the first person he met where is the French Quarter?

g. Small boy to playmate there's my mother at the scream door again.

h. This is a curious play Marian told her friend.

i. I think these new cars are roomy Helen said.

j. Would you go as far as the governor of Oregon who said I'd like to have you visit but please don't come to stay.

k. Senator, the problem of getting rid of the radioactive waste products has not been solved yet, has it the reporter asked.

l. American researchers use the term psychokinesis to describe psychic physical effects on both living and nonliving objects.

m. When my two African friends told me the word for father in their tribal language was *dadi* I replied that the American word was similar.

The Apostrophe

Use an apostrophe followed by <u>s</u> to form the possessive of a singular or plural noun not ending in <u>s</u>.

child's	children's
man's	men's
woman's	women's
ox's	oxen's

Use an apostrophe without s to form the possessive of a plural noun that ends in s.

boys'	girls'
boxes'	ladies'
kings'	babies'

Use an apostrophe with s or use the apostrophe alone to form the possessive of proper nouns ending in s.

James's	James'
Burns's	Burns'
Jones's	Jones'

For singular common nouns ending in *s*, such as *boss*, add *'s*.

Use an apostrophe with s to indicate the possessive case of indefinite pronouns.

anybody's	everybody's
anyone's	someone's
one's	another's

Do not use an apostrophe, however, for possessive pronouns.

his	yours
hers	theirs
its	whose
ours	

Use an apostrophe to indicate that letters or figures have been omitted in contractions.

isn't	doesn't	class of '79
can't	I'll	best film of '60
o'clock	it's	hurricane of '53

Use an apostrophe with s to form the plural of letters, figures, and words that are referred to as words when there is a possibility of confusion. otherwise use an s alone:

Don't forget to dot your i's.
Your 9s look like upside-down 6s.
You use too many *and*'s in your sentences.

Exercises

1. In the following sentences, put apostrophes only where they belong:

   a. Its seven oclock.

   b. I like its sleek lines.

   c. The car is his.

   d. If youre fired, you will receive a months salary.

   e. I'll accept no ifs or maybes for answers.

   f. The Smiths car is always parked in front of our house.

   g. Its not anybodys business.

   h. The doctors diagnosis stunned me.

   i. Do you believe in childrens rights?

   j. James guess is as good as anyones.

   k. The best film of 79 was *A Little Romance.*

   l. Hers are better than ours.

2. For each of the following words, write the possessive singular plural forms (for example: *boy, boy's, boys'*).

   a. mat

   b. man

   c. lawyer

   d. reader

   e. Jones

   f. creditor

   g. enemy

   h. flowers

   i. ambassador

   j. Picasso

CHAPTER 19

Mechanics

Capital Letters

Capitalize the first word of every sentence or group of words written as a sentence.

> Procrastination week has been called off.
> Beauty is in the eye of the beholder.
> Really? I never would have guessed.
> Tough luck. Perhaps you'll do better next time.

Capitalize the first word of each line of poetry. Don't capitalize, however, if the line is from a poem in which the writer deliberately wants to avoid capitals:

> Tyger! Tyger! burning bright
> In the forests of the night, . . .
>
> Because I could not stop for Death,
> He kindly stopped for me; . . .
>
> My thoughts still cling to the mouldering past.

Capitilize the first word of a direct quotation. Do this if the original begins with a capital letter or, if it was spoken, if it's the beginning of a sentence.

> The doctor said gently, "Try to get some sleep."
>
> The newscaster made this announcement: "Skylab will fall into the Indian Ocean."

576

Capitalize proper nouns and proper adjectives.

Cinderella, Oedipus, Laura, Hester
Asia, Europe, Australia, Canada
Middle Ages, Renaissance, Victorian Age
Arizona State University, Museum of Modern Art
United Nations, American Embassy
Democratic party, Republican party
American cars, European clothes

Capitalize all titles that go in front of a proper name or that take the place of a proper name.

President Carter is losing his popularity.
The President is losing his popularity.
Senator Goldwater opposes recognizing Red China.
The Senator opposes recognizing Red China.

Do not capitalize a title if it does not substitute for the proper name:

WRONG   He has been a College Professor for twenty-five years.

RIGHT   He has been a college professor for twenty-five years.

Capitalize all words used to designate the deity.

God, the Messiah, the Supreme Being
Lord, Providence, the Holy Ghost
Savior, the Almighty, He, His, Him

Capitalize abbreviations of degrees, titles, and other capitalized words, including acronyms.

Ph.D., D.D.S., M.D., Jr., Sr.
USMC, UNESCO, NATO, NASA

Capitalize titles of magazines, books, plays, movies, chapter headings, and sections of a book.

Time, Psychology Today, Newsweek
Crime and Punishment, The Immense Journey
The American Dream, Antigone, King Lear
Alien, Picnic at Hanging Rock, Manhattan

Capitalize the names of holidays, the months of the year, and the days of the week.

Fourth of July, Christmas, Easter, Halloween
January, February, March, April, May
Sunday, Monday, Tuesday, Wednesday

Capitalize the names of points of the compass when they refer to geographical parts of the country or the world.

Admiral Byrd discovered the South Pole.
The oil crisis could cause a decline in the civilization of the Western world.
People are leaving the cold climate and settling in the South and in the West.

When these words refer to directions, they are not capitalized:

A cold wind came out of the northeast.
In New York, we lived on the west side of the park.

Exercise

Capitalize the words that should be capitalized in the following sentences:

a. he disliked english, but he liked latin.

b. I have classes on monday, wednesday, and friday because I work on tuesdays and thursdays.

c. professor garcia, my spanish professor, just returned from mexico.

d. one of wordsworth's best-known poems is *tintern abbey.*

e. mrs. adams called out: "please pick me up before dark."

f. sleeping beauty takes nytol.

g. the president will make his state of the union speech tonight.

h. the west is noted for its modern architecture.

i. mario puzo directed *the godfather.*

Italics

Italics are a special type of printing in which letters are slanted to the right to set off words or passages in a text. In typing, you can get a similar effect of emphasis by underlining. In writing, draw a line under each word to be italicized.

Use italics to emphasize key words and expressions. Quotation marks can also be used for this purpose.

> Don't tell me that *she* is coming to the party?
> That is *exactly* what I mean.
> It's not *who* you love but *that* you love.

Use italics to call attention to a word as a word. Quotation marks can be used here, too.

> How do you spell *Mississippi?*
> You begin too many sentences with the word *and.*
> *Neat* is a much-used, general-purpose word.

Use italics for foreign words that have not yet been accepted as everyday english expressions. Consult a dictionary if you are in doubt.

> *au revoir*   *in medias res*
> *in absentia*   *fait accompli*

Use italics for titles of books, plays, magazines, movies, Broadway shows, and so forth.

> *Catch-22, My Antonia, Prose Style*
> *Who's Afraid of Virginia Woolf?, Waiting for Godot*
> *Saturday Review, Atlantic, New Yorker*
> *Chorus Line, The Wiz, On the Twentieth Century*
> *Gremlins, Ghostbusters, Flashdance, Sixteen Candles*

Use italics for the names of trains, ships, planes, and the like.

> *Pioneer 10, Queen Elizabeth, Yankee Clipper*
> *U.S.S. Missouri, Apollo 8*
> *The City of New Orleans* (train)

Exercise

Put italics where necessary in the following sentences:

a. What does the phrase la dolce vita mean?

b. One of his best stories was printed in Harper's.

c. The word creed comes from the Latin word credere, which means to believe.

d. Chorus Line is one of the best Broadway musicals I have seen in years.

e. The Sound and the Fury was made into a movie.

f. Does the Metroliner still carry passengers?

g. Federico Fellini directed Amarcord.

h. Life magazine is back in print again.

Abbreviations

Abbreviations are shortened forms of words and phrases used to represent the complete forms. Abbreviations should follow the conventions set forth in dictionaries. In formal writing, few abbreviations are used. In scientific writing, technical writing, and some kinds of scholarly writing, many abbreviations are used. In ordinary writing, abbreviations are used moderately, in the following ways.

To name the days of the week and the months.

Mon., Tues., Wed., Thurs., Fri.
Aug., Sept., Oct., Nov., Dec.

To name organizations and government agencies.

NFL, AFL, MIT, NBC, CBS, AMA
FBI, IRS, HEW, CIA, NASA, AEC
OPEC, NATO, UNICEF, PLO

To name cities and states.

L.A., N.Y., S.F., N.O., Phil.

Calif., Ill., Mass., Ariz., Kans., Nebr.

To indicate names, titles, and degrees.

Mr., Messrs., Ms., Mrs., Jr., Sr.
Rev., Hon., Dr., St. (Saint), Msgr.
B.S., M.A., Ph.D., LL.D., D.D.S., M.D.

For certain standard terms.

i.e., e.g., etc., et al., vs., viz.
B.C., A.D., A.M., P.M., MPH, mpg
O.K., G.I., TNT, TV, DDT, LSD, R.s.v.p.
anon., esp., intro., Ave., Inc., orig.
lbs., ft., no., amt., qt., vol., wt.

Exercises

1. Look up the following abbreviations in a good dictionary and write down their meaning:

   a. USSR   f. cwt.   k. pseud.

   b. TNT   g. mgr.   l. P.S.

   c. Btu   h. RPM   m. mfr.

   d. anon.   i. HP   n. A.B.

   e. atty.   j. N.B.   o. AWOL

2. Change all of the abbreviations to words in the following sentences:

   a. The French Quarter in N.O. is an interesting place to visit.

   b. In the Olympics, the U.S. finished 1st in the 100-yd dash.

   c. Eng. is my most difficult subject.

   d. There is a Main St. in many small cities in the United States.

   e. Meet me in front of the Federal Bldg. at 6:00 P.M.

3. Put abbreviations in place of the italicized words in the following sentences:

   a. *Doctor* Jones will lecture tomorrow at 6:30 P.M.

b. The new *Chevrolet* Citation gets 24 *miles per gallon* in the city.

c. The best coverage of sports is by the *American Broadcasting Company.*

d. Los Angeles is often referred to as *Los Angeles.*

e. Children watch too much *television.*

Hyphenation

The hyphen is a punctuation mark used to divide a word at the end of a line or to connect the parts of a compound word.

Use a hyphen to divide a word at the end of a line.

at-tic	back-lash	cou-pon
cir-cle	check-book	de-fense
hap-pen	furni-ture	la-ment
in-sult	ginger-bread	ma-jor
jour-nal	king-fish	pa-poose

Divide words between the prefix and the root.

anti-biotic	intro-duce	per-turb
bi-focal	trans-late	circum-scribe
ex-cavate	pan-orama	contra-dict
syn-thesis	auto-matic	un-concerned

Divide words between the root and the suffix.

king-dom	sensa-tion	woman-hood
prank-ster	secre-cy	mag-ic
lov-er	centu-ry	defeat-ist
loyal-ty	ex-pect	happi-ness

Do not divide words of one syllable.

WRONG	ben-ch, flu-sh, gra-sp
WRONG	hin-ge, my-th, pl-ate
WRONG	sai-nt, sei-ze, tr-ail

Divide compound words between the main parts of the compound:

COMPOUND WORD	HYPHENATED COMPOUND
pantyhouse	panty-hose
airplane	air-plane
countdown	count-down
minibike	mini-bike
speedboat	speed-boat

Hyphenate compound numbers from twenty-one to ninety-nine.

twenty-two   thirty-three   forty-four

Hyphenate compound adjectives before a noun:

high-powered car   alien-looking beings
blue-gray eyes   fly-fishing lessons
time-consuming tactics well-informed senator

Exercises

1. Consult a good dictionary. Then rewrite the following words as two separate words or as hyphenated words. If a word is all right as it is, simply recopy it.

   a. inlaws

   b. allinclusive

   c. anticommunist

   d. foulsmelling

   e. oldfashioned

   f. twothirds

   g. ninetynine

   h. reenter

i. allpowerful   o. icecream

j. cityhall   p. hotdog

k. selfmade   q. expresident

l. hairstylist   r. flashbulb

m. hitchhiker   s. sodapop

n. unAmerican   t. drivein

2. Check your dictionary to determine how the following words are divided into syllables:

a. beware   f. reeducate   k. logical

b. mileage   g. coordinate   l. proposition

c. troublesome   h. precedes   m. committee

d. disappear   i. hypocritical   n. curious

e. invalid   j. hitchhiker   o. laser

Numbers

In formal writing, numbers less than one hundred are usually written out. In scientific writing, figures are frequently used. In informal writing, usage is divided. For such writing, the usual advice is to write out numbers that can be expressed in a word or two, but to use figures when the numbers are large.

Use figures to write dates and hours.

from 1936 to 1945   12:00 P.M.
between 1800 and 1900   6:15 A.M.
on January 1, 1980   9:45 P.M.

Use figures to write street numbers, but spell out the name of the street when the streets are numbered.

125 Apache St.   215 Fifth Ave.
2200 East Cairo Dr.   102 Forty-second St.

If, however, a word such as *North, South, East,* or *West* comes between the street number and the street name, and if there is no danger of misreading the address, then use figures instead of the street name:

CONFUSING	1016 16th St.
CORRECT	1016 Sixteenth St.
ACCEPTABLE	210 East 50th St.

Use figures to record sums of money, decimals, and percentages.

The shoes cost me $32.50.
Her grade point average was 3.5.
Living expenses rose by about 11.3 percent since January.

Use figures to record telephone numbers, volume numbers, chapter numbers, and page numbers.

My telephone number is 736–5234.
You will find an accurate description in volume 1, chapter 5, page 17.

Express numbers in words when it is easy to do so; for large numbers, use figures.

one, three, five	first, second, third
32,320 students	2762 feet

If the figures are in round numbers, you may find it easier to write them out:

a thousand dollars	a hundred yards

Write out figures when they appear at the beginning of a sentence.

RIGHT	Fifty-two passengers got off the plane.
WRONG	52 passengers got off the plane.

Don't try to guess in writing Roman numerals. The following list of numbers will help refresh your memory:

1	I	11	XI	30	XXX		
2	II	12	XII	40	XL		
3	III	13	XIII	50	L		
4	IV	14	XIV	60	LX		
5	V	15	XV	70	LXX		
6	VI	16	XVI	80	LXXX		
7	VII	17	XVII	90	XC		
8	VIII	18	XVIII	100	C		
9	IX	19	XIX	500	D		
10	X	20	XX	1000	M		

Exercise

Replace the figures in the following sentences with words:

a. My grade on the last test was 100.

b. 10 dollars is too much to spend on a tie.

c. For 12 months, she lived at 747 5th St.

d. Pick me up at 7:30 P.M.

e. 50,000 Frenchmen can't be wrong.

f. About 1000 new students enrolled in school in the fall.

g. Jody grew 3 inches taller this summer.

h. She is 7 years older than her husband.

i. I have 4 sisters and 2 brothers.

j. Tickets for the concert cost $10.

Spelling

Although it is true that the logical development of ideas is more important in writing than are mechanics, spelling is nevertheless important. Writers who habitually misspell words run the risk of confusing their readers and making their writing incoherent.

Writers who do misspell usually do not misspell a large number of words. (There are exceptions, of course.) Most so-called poor spellers misspell the same words over and over again. What can you do to improve your spelling?

1. *Master a few simple spelling rules.* Do not disdain memorization. Memorization and understanding should go together.
2. *Consult your dictionary frequently.* Notice how the dictionary spells each word and divides it into syllables.
3. *Proofread your writing carefully,* paying special attention to problems in spelling.
4. *Keep a notebook in which you put the words you frequently misspell.* Review these words regularly.

Spelling Rules

The ie or ei rule. Put *i* before *e*, except after *c* or when pronounced like *a*, as in *neighbor* and *weigh:*

I BEFORE *E*	EXCEPT AFTER *C*	EXCEPTIONS
achieve	receive	either
relieve	deceive	neither
grief	conceit	leisure
chief	deceit	seizure
yield	receipt	foreign
wield	ceiling	sovereign

The final e. Retain the final *e* before a suffix that begins with a consonant:

SILENT *E*	WITH SUFFIX	EXCEPTIONS
nine	ninety	truly
rude	rudeness	judgment
arrange	arrangement	argument
care	careful	awful
love	lovely	
move	movement	

Drop the final *e* before a suffix that begins with a vowel:

SILENT *E*	WITH SUFFIX	EXCEPTIONS
dine	dining	noticeable
grieve	grievance	courageous
admire	admiration	dyeing
fame	famous	hoeing
deplore	deplorable	canoeing
imagine	imaginary	mileage

The final y. To form the plural of nouns ending in *y* preceded by a consonant, change the *y* to *i* and add *es:*

FINAL *Y*	*I* PLUS *ES*	PLURAL
lady	ladi + es	ladies
copy	copi + es	copies
story	stori + es	stories
fly	fli + es	flies

If a vowel comes before the final *y*, add *s:*

FINAL *Y*	PLUS *S*	PLURAL
monkey	monkey + s	monkeys
journey	journey + s	journeys
attorney	attorney + s	attorneys
chimney	chimney + s	chimneys

Final consonant. For words of one syllable that end in a consonant preceded by a single vowel, double the consonant before a suffix that begins with a vowel:

hot	hott + est	hottest
plan	plann + ing	planning
drop	dropp + ed	dropped
man	mann + ish	mannish

For words of one syllable that end in a single consonant preceded by two vowels, do *not* double the final consonant before adding a suffix beginning with a vowel:

foam	foam + ed	foamed
reveal	reveal + ing	revealing
cool	cool + est	coolest

For words of one syllable that end in two consonants, do *not* double the final consonant before adding a suffix beginning with a vowel:

talk	talk + ing	talking
grasp	grasp + ed	grasped
strong	strong + est	strongest

For words of two or more syllables ending in a consonant, double the final consonant before a suffix beginning with a vowel *if the last syllable of the word is accented* and *if a single vowel precedes the consonant:*

regret	regrett + able	regrettable
allot	allott + ing	allotting
defer	deferr + ed	deferred

Both of these conditions must be met for this rule to hold true. These words do not meet both of the conditions:

obtain	obtain + ed	obtained
profit	profit + ed	profited
return	return + ing	returning

For words whose accent does not fall on the last syllable, do *not* double the final consonant before a suffix:

travel	travel + ed	traveled
enter	enter + ing	entering
benefit	benefit + ed	benefited

-cede words. Spell words ending with the sound "seed" with *-cede.:*

concede	precede	accede
recede	intercede	secede

There are four exceptions to this rule:

supersede	exceed
proceed	succeed

-ly suffix. To form adverbs from adjectives ending in *l*, keep the *l* and add *-ly:*

final	final + ly	finally
real	real + ly	really
accidental	accidental + ly	accidentally

-ful words. When a word that ends in *ll* is used as a prefix or suffix in another word, drop one *l:*

spite	spite + full	spiteful
fear	fear + full	fearful
fill	full + fill	fulfill

Exercises

1. Rewrite the following words, adding *ie* or *ei* where needed:

ch____f
rec____pt
fr____ght
c____ling
for____gn

p____ce
th____f
pr____st
rec____ve
dec____t

fr____nd
conc____ted
n____ghbor
for____gn
bel____f

2. Combine the following stems and suffixes. Review the rules for the final *e.*

type + ing
care + ful
use + less
lone + ly
excite + ment
come + ing

use + ing
true + ly
write + ing
argue + ment
shine + ing
extreme + ly

improve + ment
excite + ing
smile + ing
entire + ly
hope + ful
sincere + ly

3. Form the plural of the following nouns ending in *y* and the third-person singular of verbs ending in *y* (for instance, *reply, replies*):

worry
party
employ
marry
memory

delay
baby
enjoy
carry
stay

berry
study
journey
alley
turkey

4. Combine the following stems and suffixes. Remember the rules for doubling the final consonant.

propel + ed	wet + est	stir + ed
prefer + ence	plan + ing	prefer + able
happen + ing	refer + ing	steer + ing
excel + ing	reel + ed	develop + ed
benefit + ed	allot + ing	counsel + ing

5. Combine the following stems and suffixes:

total + ly	practical + ly	beauty + full
wonder + full	general + ly	sweet + ly
natural + ly	use + full	master + full

Bases, Prefixes, Suffixes

Familiarity with the elements that go to make up words can help you to avoid many spelling errors.

Base (root or stem). The *base* of a word is the *main part* of a word. It cannot be subdivided into smaller units of meaning. There are two kinds of bases, free bases and bound bases. A *free base* is a stem that is a word by itself:

phone	sharp	green
ship	walk	live

A *bound base* is a stem that cannot stand alone as a complete word. It must be combined with prefixes, suffixes, or other bases:

alter-	nav-	neg-
tele-	vid-	magn-

You can combine bound bases with other word elements to get the following words:

alternative	navigate	negative
telephone	video	magnify

Compounding is the process of joining two or more bases to form a new word:

tele + graph	telegraph
cheese + burger	cheeseburger
over + pass	overpass

Prefix. A *prefix* is a word element *(morpheme)* that goes before the stem:

un-	im-	circum-
pre-	anti-	dis-

Suffix. A *suffix* is a word element that follows the stem:

-ly	-age	-y
-able	-ure	-ize

You can combine prefixes and suffixes with appropriate stems to get the following words:

unable	import	circumvent
prefix	antidote	disgrace
likely	shrinkage	noisy
teachable	failure	realize

Exercises

1. Write down the prefixes embedded in the following words. Then write down the meaning of each (for example: *advise,* prefix *ad,* meaning "to").

excavate	nonsense	convene
introduce	ambiguous	pervade
unconcerned	circumvent	proponent
bifocal	interfere	semifinal
contradict	avert	ultimate

2. Pick out the suffixes in the following words. What is the general meaning of each?

confidence	friendship	fortify
bookish	heritage	rivulet
favorite	assistant	donor
velocity	compentent	dramatic
countless	humorist	realize

3. Write down the base or bases in the following words. Then write down the meaning of each.

audible	spectator	microphone
benefit	aqueduct	manuscript
finite	infidelity	vocation
liberate	transport	magnificent
patron	advent	tenacious

Homonyms

Homonyms are words that sound alike but that are different in meaning and often in spelling. They can cause trouble for the poor speller.

The following pairs of words are frequently confused. Know the differences in meaning and spelling.

We have *already* seen that movie.
They were *all ready* to go at seven.

She is *altogether* too advanced for this class.
My family was *all together* for Christmas.

The *capitol* building of Arizona has a copper dome.
He invested his *capital* in property.

He has *coarse* manners.
I could eat a three-*course* meal.

This week the election of the city *council* will be held.
My adviser gave me good *counsel*.

I get embarrassed by *compliments*.
These shoes *complement* your dress.

The list of words that follows was taken recently from a large sampling of student papers. Learn the differences in the meaning and spelling of these pairs.

accept/except	nob/knob
affect/effect	pain/pane
allusion/illusion	parish/perish
and/an	piece/peace
boarder/border	pitcher/picture
breaks/brakes	pored/poured
by/buy	principal/principle

coarse/course	revue/review
complement/compliment	right/write
creak/creek	see/sea
do/due	seen/scene
fore/for	sense/since
fowl/foul	sights/cites
here/hear	sum/some
latter/later	their/they're
maid/made	there/their
mined/mind	through/threw
no/know	to/too

Exercises

1. Use each word of the following pairs of homonyms in a separate sentence.

bare/bear	dye/die	pedal/peddle
boarder/border	fare/fair	weather/whether
cite/sight	led/lead	wave/waive
dessert/desert	minor/miner	stationery/stationary

2. What is the difference in meaning of the following pairs?

accept/except	quiet/quite	clothes/cloths
affect/effect	passed/past	principal/principle
choose/chose	formerly/formally	your/you're
all ready/already	council/counsel	lose/loose
who's/whose	brake/break	quite/quiet

Confusing Pairs

The following groups of words are responsible for a large number of spelling errors in student writing. Learn to use them correctly.

Than/then. *Than* is a conjunction. *Then* is an adverb.

> Joan sings better *than* Jane.
> *Then* I went to the movies.

Its/it's. *Its* is a possessive pronoun. *It's* is a contraction, meaning *it is.*

> I could tell it was a leopard by *its* spots.
> *It's* safer to wear seat belts.

To/too. *To* is a preposition, or it can be a part of an infinitive. *Too* is an adverb, meaning *also*, or a qualifier that patterns with adjectives.

> I'll send the tickets *to* you.
> If you want *to* swim, come over.
> The day is *too* hot for cutting the grass.

They're/their/there. *They're* is a contraction of *they are*. *Their* is a possessive pronoun. *There* is an adverb or a word used in a *there is, there are* construction.

> *They're* not for sale.
> *Their* nerves are on edge.
> Give me that book over *there.*
> *There* are several reasons for his behavior.

Advise/advice. *Advise* is a verb. *Advice* is a noun.

> I *advise* you to go to the dentist.
> I hope you take my *advice.*

Exercise

Rewrite the correct form of the word in parentheses in the following sentences:

a. (Its, it's) too late to worry now.

b. (There, their, they're) clothes are shabby.

c. The movie was (to, too) long.

d. Did you get a car (to, too)?

e. (Its, it's) later (than, then) you think.

f. (Its, it's) going to be a cold winter.

g. This car gets better mileage (than, then) (its, it's) competitors.

h. Come (to, too) your senses.

i. She is prettier (then, than) ever.

j. (There, their they're) buying this house for an investment.

One Word or Two Words

Over the past few years, more and more students are combining words that should be written as separate words and separating words that should go together. One reason for these errors may be a lack of knowledge about prefixes, suffixes, and bases. If you are having similar problems, check the spelling of such words in your dictionary and review the material on prefixes, suffixes, and bases.

Two words mistakenly written as one

alot/a lot	atleast/at least
alright/all right	socalled/so-called
maybe/may be	inspite/in spite

One word written as two

where as/whereas	up set/upset
over come/overcome	all so/also
when ever/whenever	with out/without
no where/nowhere	my self/myself
any where/anywhere	its self/itself
to gether/together	in to/into
through out/throughout	pass time/pastime

Variant Spellings

Spelling takes effort. Student writers often get impatient with traditional spelling and look for economical ways to get to the point. Occasionally, they are influenced by shortened forms of words that they pick up from the media. There is nothing wrong with shortcuts, but if you decide to spell words in ways not indicated in the dictionary, it might be better to confine these shortened forms to your less formal writing. In formal writing, they are usually unacceptable.

The following spellings keep recurring in student themes:

thru	tonite	tho
nite	lite	fore

These words are either clipped forms or alternate forms used to replace:

through	tonight	though
night	light	before

Look for these shortened forms in your own writing and replace them with conventional spellings.

(Continued from page iv)

The New Columbia Encyclopedia, 1975. © 1975, Columbia University Press. Entries for "pidgin" and "lingua franca." Reprinted by permission of the Columbia University Press.

Joseph Conrad, "A Tropical Landscape," from *The Secret Sharer*. Copyright 1910 by Harper Bros. from the book *Twixt Land and Sea* by Joseph Conrad. Reprinted by permission of Doubleday & Company, Inc.

Consumers Union, "A Guide to Grind-Your-Own Beans" from *Consumer Reports*. Copyright 1983 by Consumers Union of United States, Inc., Mount Vernon, NY 10553. Reprinted by permission from *Consumer Reports*, 1983.

Stephen Crane, excerpt from *The Red Badge of Courage*. From the University of Virginia edition of *The Works of Stephen Crane* 1975, Vol. II. Reprinted by permission of the University of Virginia Press.

Gerald Durrell, excerpt from *The Overloaded Ark*. Copyright 1953, renewed copyright © 1981 by Gerald Durrell. Reprinted by permission of Viking Penguin Inc.

Kenan T. Erim, "Aphrodisias: Awakened City of Ancient Art," in *National Geographic*, June 1972. Reprinted by permission of The National Geographic Society.

Ralph Faulkingham, "Where the Lifeboat Ethic Breaks Down," from *Human Nature*, October 1978. Copyright © 1978 by Human Nature, Inc. Reprinted by permission of the publisher, Harcourt Brace Jovanovich, Inc.

E. M. Forster, excerpt from *Aspects of the Novel*. Copyright 1927 by Harcourt Brace Jovanovich, Inc., renewed 1955 by E. M. Forster. Reprinted by permission of Harcourt Brace Jovanovich, Inc.

W. Nelson Francis, "Three Meanings of Grammar," in *The Quarterly Journal of Speech*, Vol. XL, no. 3 (October 1954). Reprinted by permission of the University of Wisconsin, Madison. Excerpt from *The English Language* reprinted by permission of W. W. Norton & Company, Inc.

Edward T. Hall, "Let's Heat People Instead of Houses," from *Human Nature*, January 1979. Reprinted by permission of the author.

Stephen Hitchcock, "Can We Save Our Salt Marshes?" from *National Geographic*, June 1972. Reprinted by permission of The National Geographic Society.

W. H. Hudson, "The Snake" from *Far Away and Long Ago*. Copyright 1918 by E. P. Dutton, renewed 1946 by The Royal Society for the Protection of Birds. Reprinted by permission of E. P. Dutton, Inc.

James Joyce, excerpt from "The Dead" in *Dubliners*. Copyright 1916 by B. W. Huebsch. Definitive text copyright © 1967 by the Estate of James Joyce. Reprinted by permission of Viking Penguin Inc.

Michael Kernan, "Chair Commands High Spot in Human History," in *The Washington Post*. Reprinted by permission of The Washington Post.

Joseph Wood Krutch, excerpt from *The Desert Year*. Copyright 1951, 1952 by Joseph Wood Krutch. Reprinted by permission of William Morrow & Company.

R. D. Laing, excerpt from *The Politics of Experience*. Copyright © 1976 by R. D. Laing. Reprinted by permission of Viking Penguin, Inc.

Enid Nemy, "Public Sleepers Steal the Show," in *The New York Times*, February 1981. Copyright © 1981 by The New York Times Company. Reprinted by permission.

"Kennedy Likened to Ben Franklin," from *The New York Times*, January 5, 1964. Copyright © 1964 by The New York Times Company. Reprinted by permission.

Marjorie Kinnan Rawlings, excerpted from *The Yearling*. Copyright 1938 Marjorie Kinnan Rawlings: copyright renewed 1966 by Norton Baskin. Reprinted by permission of Charles Scribner's Sons.

Albert Rosenfeld, "Interferon: Medicine for Cancer & the Common Cold," in *Saturday Review*, November 28, 1978. Reprinted by permission of Saturday Review, Inc.

John Ruskin, "The Stones of Venice," from *The Stones of Venice*. Copyright © 1970 by John Ruskin. Reprinted by permission of E. P. Dutton and J. M. Dent & Sons, Ltd., London.

Bertrand Russell, "What I Have Lived For" from *Autobiography of Bertrand Russell*. Reprinted by permission of George Allen & Unwin Ltd. Paragraph

Kitchen Aid advertisement, "Other Disposers Can't Compare to Kitchen Aid," reprinted by permission of the Hobart Corporation.

Lindsay olive advertisement, "The Oliver Twist from Lindsay . . ." reprinted by permission of Lindsay International Inc.

"She Needs Your Love" reprinted by permission of the Christian Children's Fund.

"Shoplifting is a Crime," a public service advertisement for S.T.E.M. of Arizona, Inc. Reprinted by permission of The Arizona Republic.

Snowdrift shortening advertisement, "What Every Good Cook Knows," reprinted by permission of Hunt-Wesson Foods.

Spanish Olive advertisement, "Spanish Olives. How to Tell the Original," reprinted by permission of the Spanish Olive Commission.

Steinway piano advertisement, "The Man Who Thought He Couldn't Own a Steinway," reprinted by permission of Steinway & Sons.

Texaco advertisement, "Texaco is working to get more than oil out of the ground" reprinted courtesy of Texaco, Inc.

Timberland boots advertisement reprinted by permission of Timberland Company.

Whirlpool washer advertisement (text only) reprinted by permission of Whirlpool Corporation.

Index

Revision Checklist

The Writer's Intention

1. Does what I have written convey my intended meaning?
2. Does it fulfill the needs of my intended readers?
3. Does it accurately convey my attitude toward my subject?
4. Does it accurately reflect my ethical and emotional stance?

The Whole Theme

1. Do I have a suitable introduction? Is it interesting and appropriate? Will it make my readers want to read on?
2. Do I have a clearly defined thesis? Does it accurately convey my intended meaning? If I do not have a thesis sentence, is my intention implicit in the paper as a whole?
3. Does my paper clearly indicate a plan of development?
4. Are the successive steps easy to follow? Are there transitions from one part to another?
5. Do I use supporting details in such a way that they strengthen the general statements in the paper?
6. Is my evidence appropriate? Is my reasoning sound? Have I considered possible objections?
7. Does my conclusion follow logically from all that has gone before? Is it effective? Does it leave my readers satisfied?
8. Is my paper as a whole clear? Have I included as many details as are necessary? Have I remembered that my audience may know little or nothing about my subject and that it is my responsibility to fill in the gaps?
9. Have I maintained a consistent point of view, or have I shifted unaccountably from one viewpoint to another, from one person to another?
10. Do I have an appropriate title? Does it reveal a close relationship with my central idea?

The Paragraph

1. Is each paragraph logically developed?
2. What is its function in the paper as a whole?
3. Does it function paradigmatically?
4. Is it used to support a general idea?
5. Is it used as a means of going from one part of the essay to another?